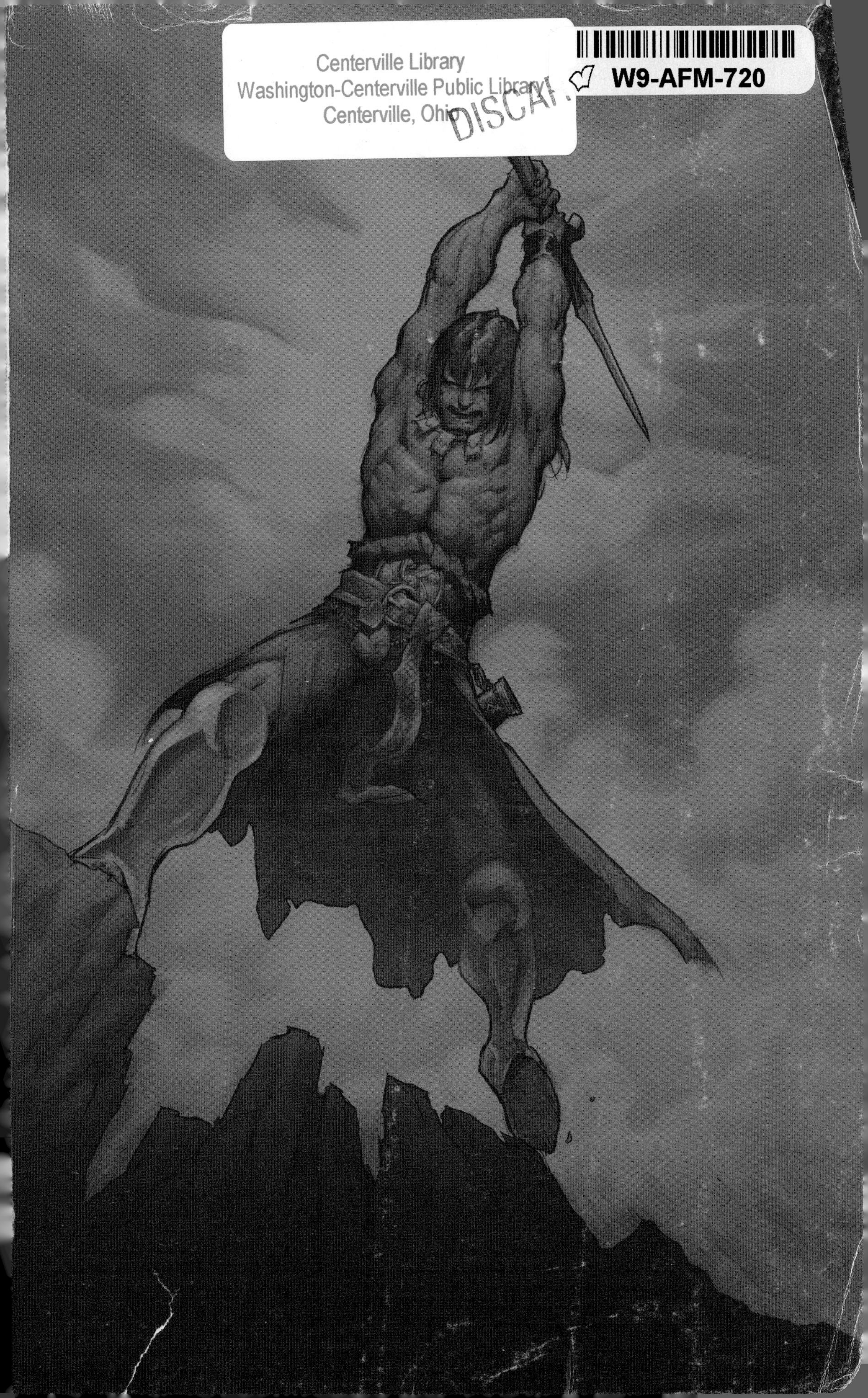

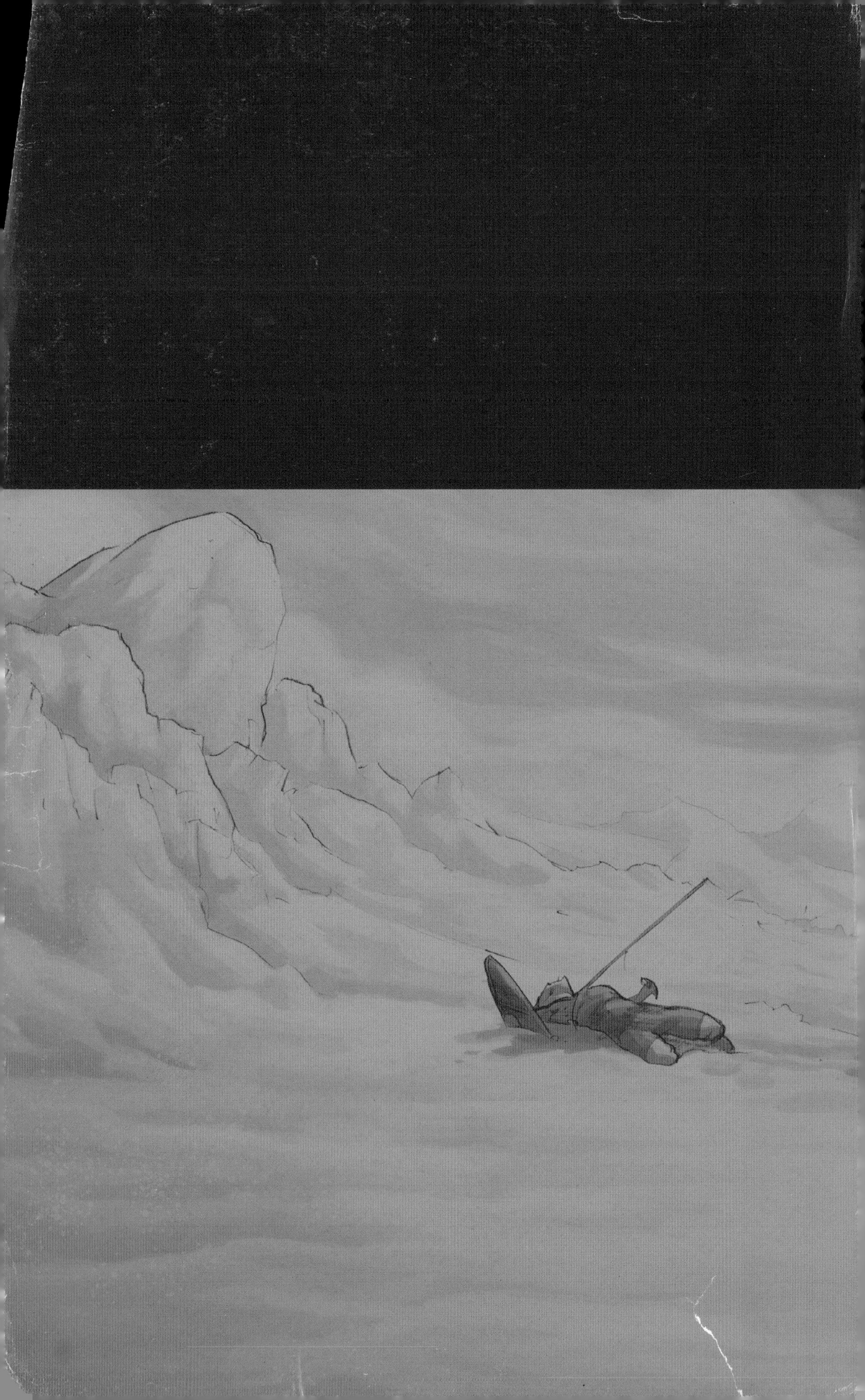

CONAN®

THE FROST-GIANT'S DAUGHTER AND OTHER STORIES

Writer KURT BUSIEK

Artists CARY NORD and THOMAS YEATES

Color Artist DAVE STEWART

Letterer RICHARD STARKINGS and COMICRAFT

Chapter Break Artist JOSEPH MICHAEL LINSNER

Creator of Conan ROBERT E. HOWARD

"Nemedian Chronicles" and "The Frost-Giant's Daughter"
adapted from stories by **Robert E. Howard**

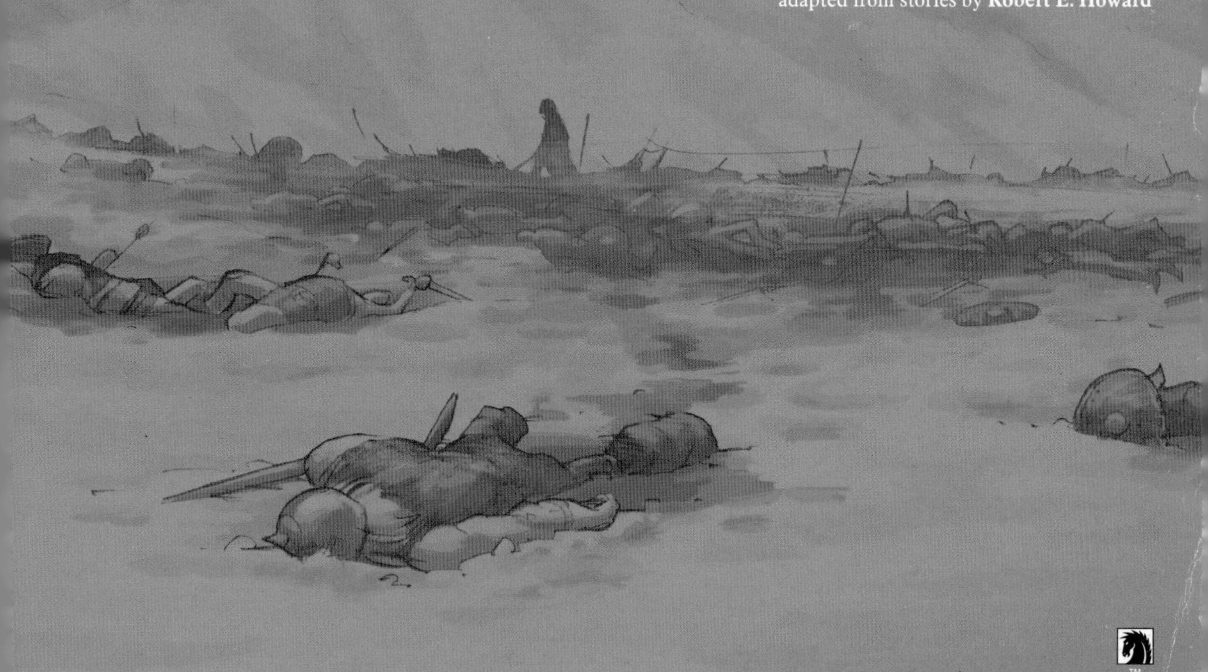

DARK HORSE BOOKS™

Publisher MIKE RICHARDSON Designer DARIN FABRICK
Art Director LIA RIBACCHI Assistant Editor MATT DRYER Editor SCOTT ALLIE

Special Thanks to THEODORE BERGQUIST, JEFF CONNER, and FREDRIK MALMBERG at CONAN PROPERTIES and MARK FINN

Thanks also to JASON HVAM and CHRIS HORN

This volume collects issues zero through six and part of issue seven of the Dark Horse Comics monthly *Conan* series.

Published by Dark Horse Books
A Division of Dark Horse Comics, Inc.
10956 SE Main Street
Milwaukie, OR 97222

www.darkhorse.com

To find a comics shop in your area, call the Comic Shop Locator Service toll-free at 1-888-266-4226

First edition: April 2005
ISBN: 1-59307-301-1

Limited hardcover edition: March 2005
ISBN: 1-59307-324-0

10 9 8 7 6 5 4 3 2 1

Printed in China

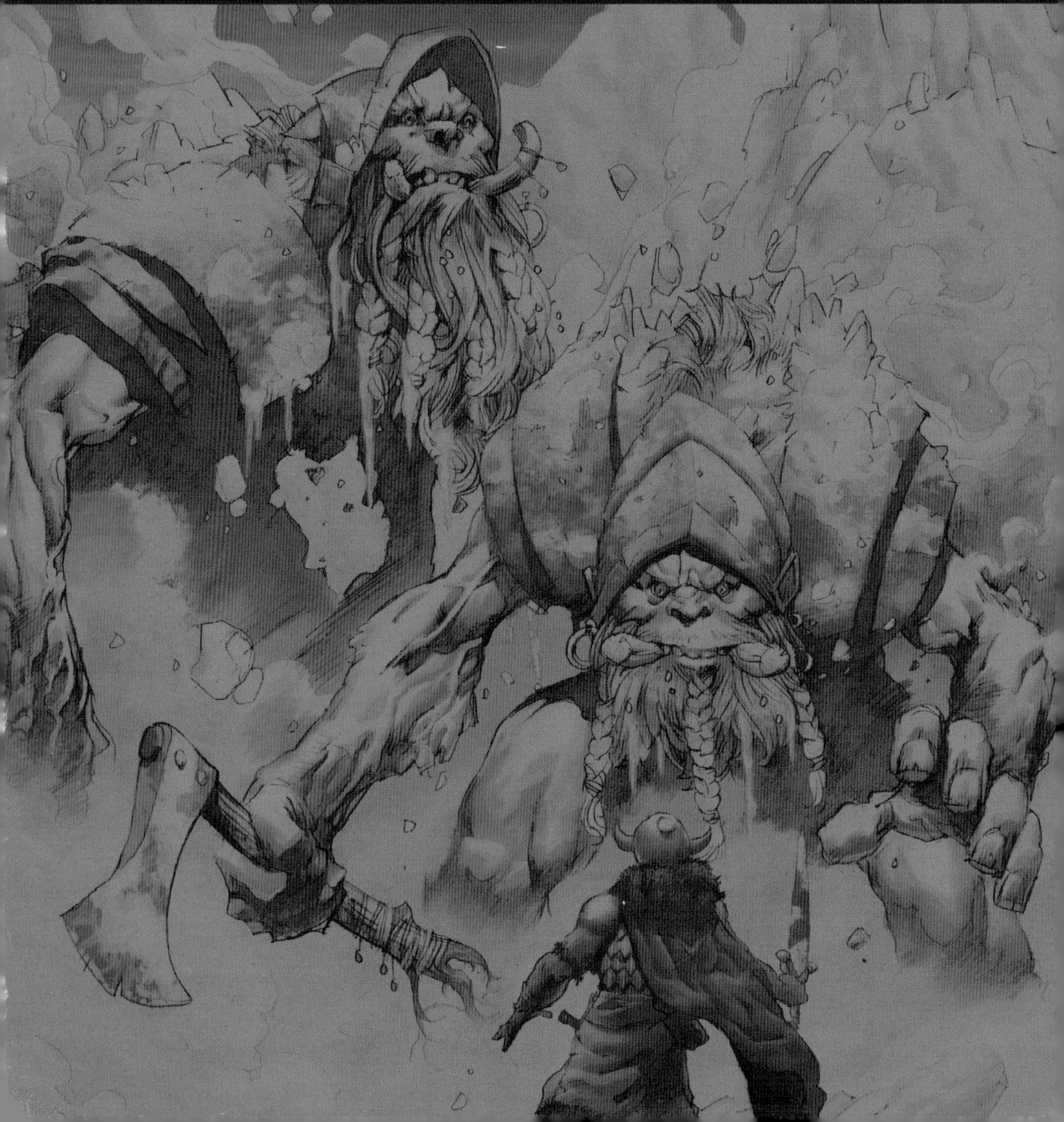

FOREWORD

I came to Conan—and to Robert E. Howard— through the comics.

I hadn't followed the series as it came out from Marvel Comics in the early seventies. I was a superhero loyalist, and didn't see the appeal in a half-naked brawny guy with a sword hacking up other guys with swords. I know, I know. I was young. It wasn't until I was sick in bed for a while, and wanted something to read that I hadn't read before, that I borrowed most of the first hundred issues from a friend and, buzzed on antibiotics, read them through in the space of a few days.

It was a revelation. The power of the storytelling, the energy, the epic scope, the sheer joy of adventure in those stories! And at the heart of them, this one surly, passionate, magnificent, indomitable warrior with a passion for life, for battle, for ale and women, for whatever lies beyond the next horizon. The very fact that he wasn't on a mission, wasn't out to rid the world of evil-doers or anything else but to benefit himself, just made it more fun, and the fact that there was no status quo, that Conan's long, rambling journey through the Hyborian worlds took him through so many changes, so many "careers," as step by step, inch by inch, he grew from an unlettered barbarian to king of the mightiest nation in his world, gave it a sweep and ambition I hadn't experienced before. I was hooked, and hooked hard.

The comics, both *Conan the Barbarian* and *Savage Sword of Conan*, largely by writer Roy Thomas and artists Barry Windsor-Smith, John Buscema and Gil Kane, led me to the original Conan stories by Robert E. Howard, which were a revelation of their own—and Howard's lush, muscular prose and visceral, relentless storytelling hooked me as hard as or harder than the character he'd created.

I came to Conan, and to Robert E. Howard, through the comics. I know many others who've done the same. But for some years, the Conan comics were a shadow of their former self, and in the end, despite an entertaining return from Roy Thomas, they were gone. Now, thanks to Dark Horse Comics, they're back —not only those original comics that hooked me so hard, but a new series, and this time I get to write it, and I get to work with astounding talents such as Cary Nord, Thomas Yeates and Dave Stewart.

And I'm not the guy to judge how well we succeed or fail. But is there somewhere some kid, sick in bed, reading these stories and getting caught up in them, starting on a path that'll lead him to more? To Conan, to Howard, to all the other wonders born out of a battered typewriter in Cross Plains, Texas? Do these stories work for him as well as the ones that worked for me?

I don't know. But I'd very much like to think so.

Conan lives again. You can join him on his travels, if you like ...

— Kurt Busiek
November 2004

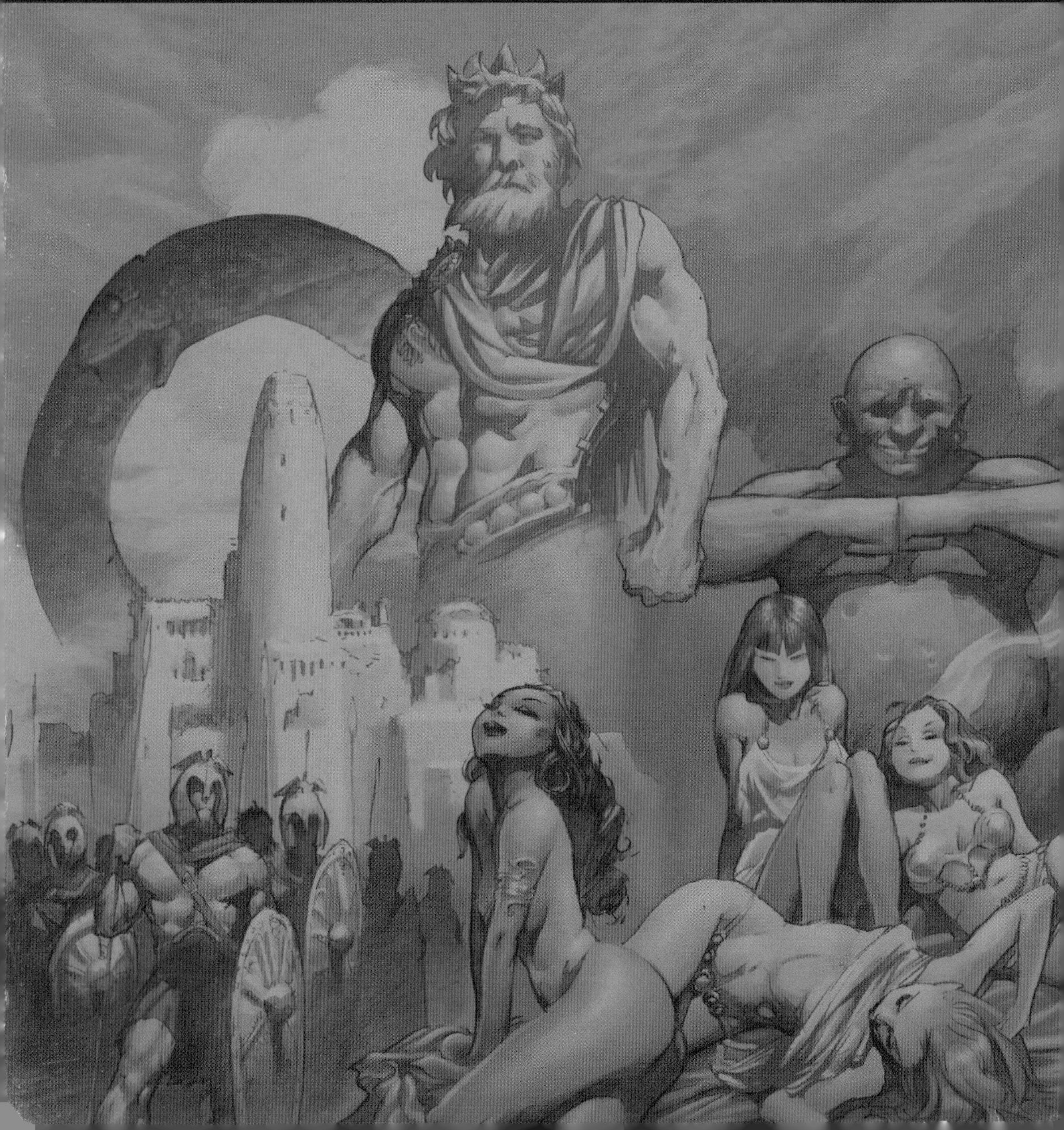

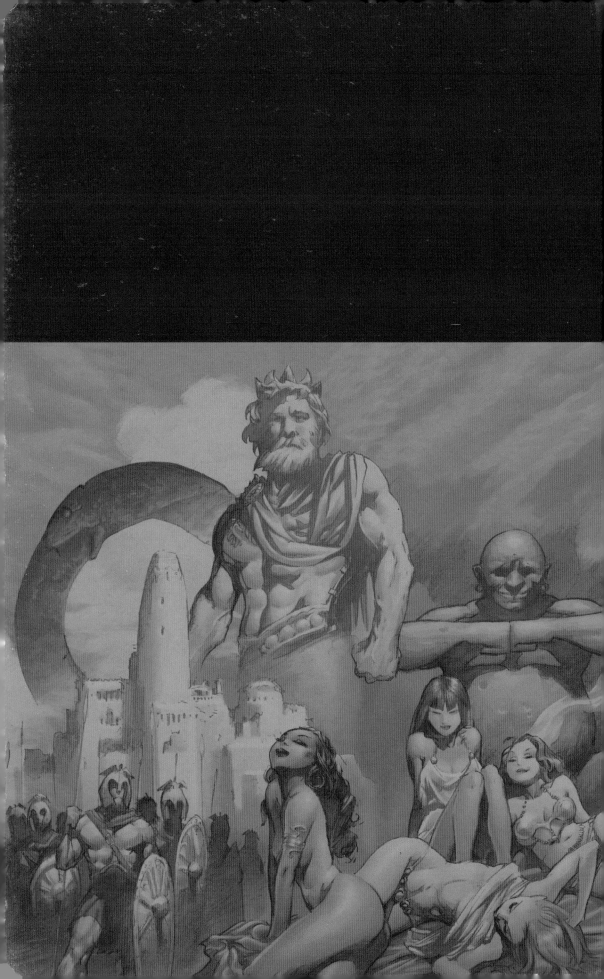

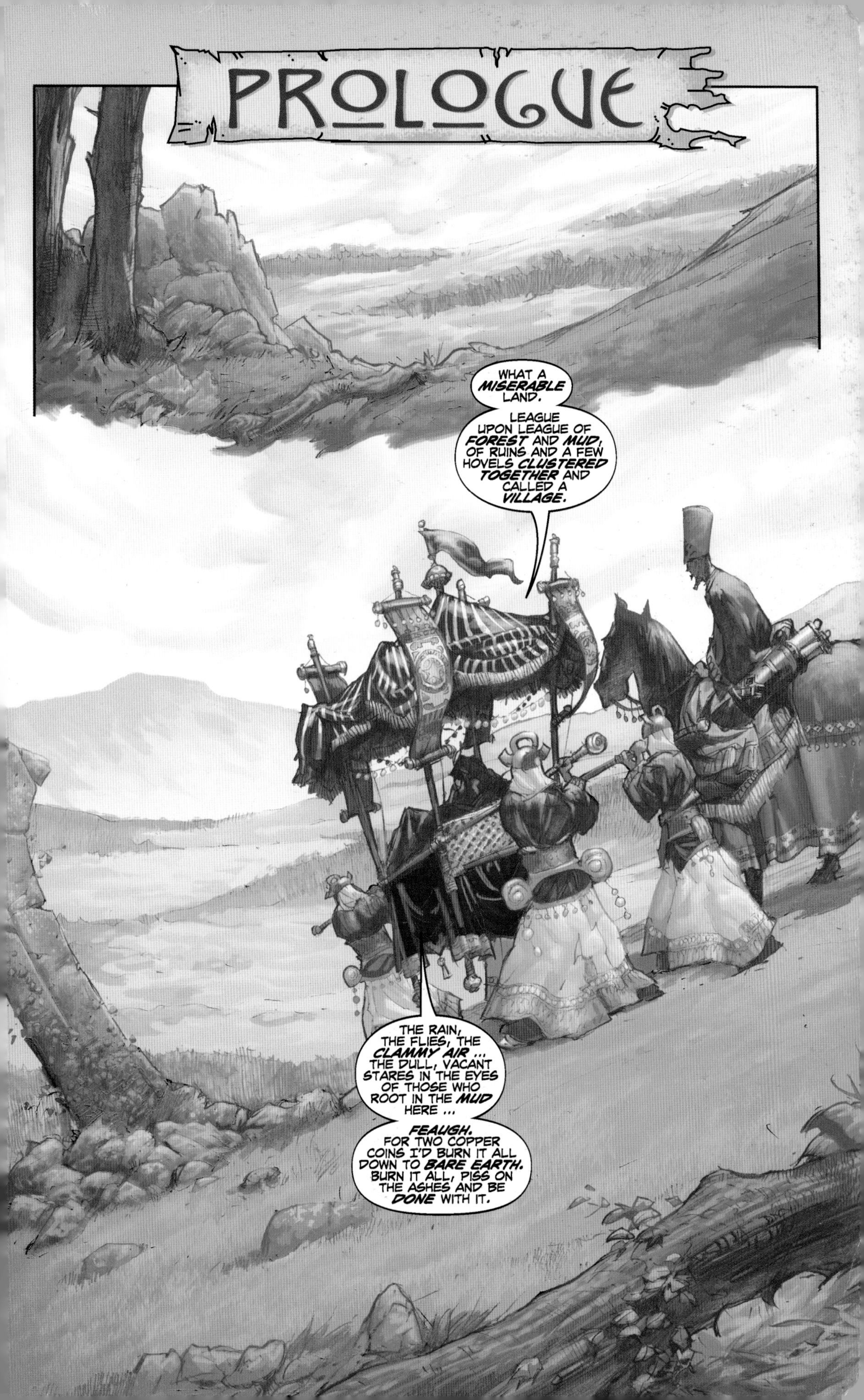
PROLOGUE
WHAT A MISERABLE LAND.
LEAGUE UPON LEAGUE OF FOREST AND MUD, OF RUINS AND A FEW HOVELS CLUSTERED TOGETHER AND CALLED A VILLAGE.
THE RAIN, THE FLIES, THE CLAMMY AIR ... THE DULL, VACANT STARES IN THE EYES OF THOSE WHO ROOT IN THE MUD HERE ...
FEAUGH. FOR TWO COPPER COINS I'D BURN IT ALL DOWN TO BARE EARTH. BURN IT ALL, PISS ON THE ASHES AND BE DONE WITH IT.

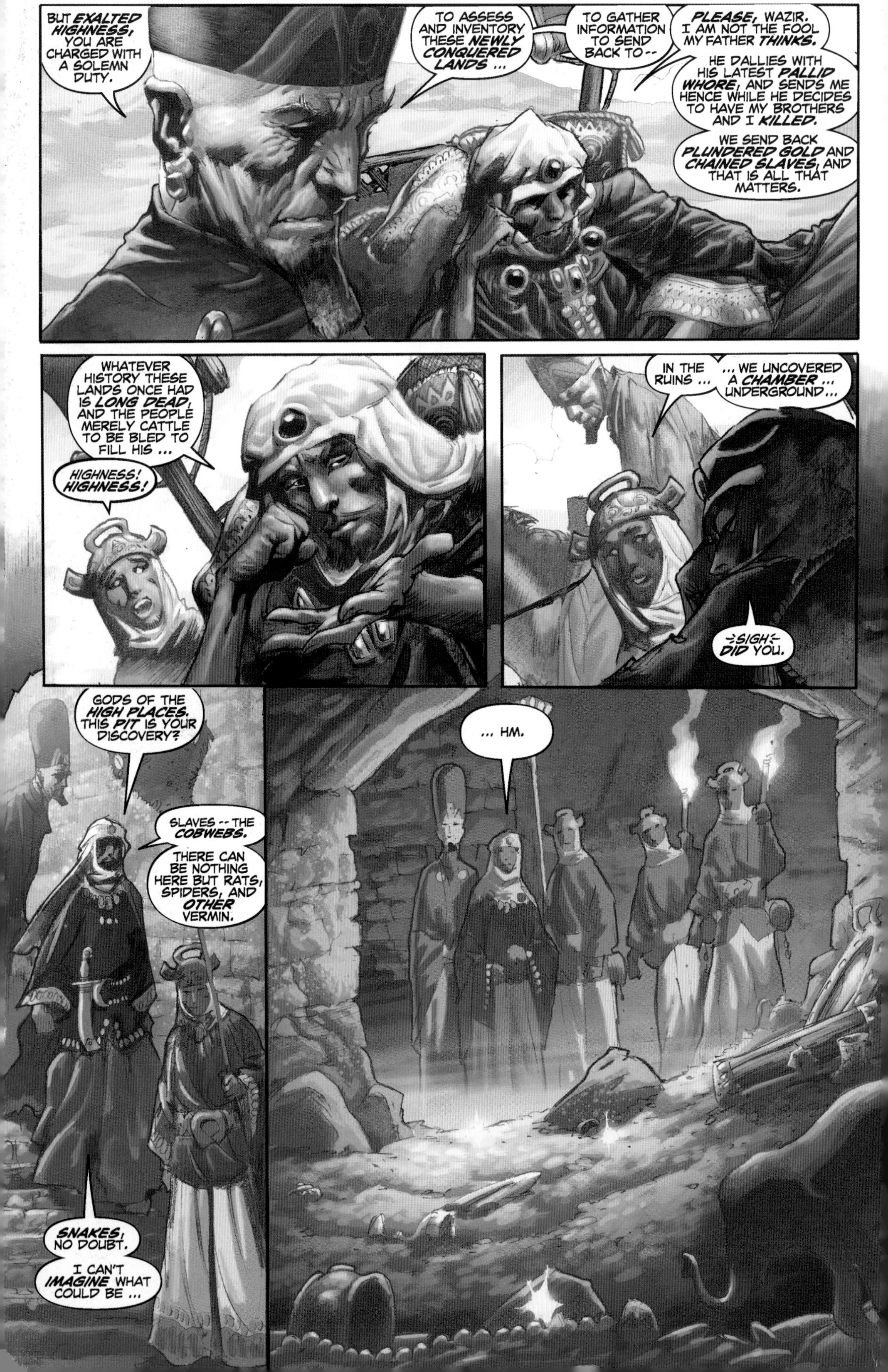

BUT EXALTED HIGHNESS, YOU ARE CHARGED WITH A SOLEMN DUTY.
TO ASSESS AND INVENTORY THESE NEWLY CONQUERED LANDS ...
TO GATHER INFORMATION TO SEND BACK TO --
PLEASE, WAZIR. I AM NOT THE FOOL MY FATHER THINKS.
HE DALLIES WITH HIS LATEST PALLID WHORE, AND SENDS ME HENCE WHILE HE DECIDES TO HAVE MY BROTHERS AND I KILLED.
WE SEND BACK PLUNDERED GOLD AND CHAINED SLAVES, AND THAT IS ALL THAT MATTERS.
WHATEVER HISTORY THESE LANDS ONCE HAD IS LONG DEAD, AND THE PEOPLE MERELY CATTLE TO BE BLED TO FILL HIS ...
HIGHNESS! HIGHNESS!
IN THE RUINS ...
... WE UNCOVERED A CHAMBER ... UNDERGROUND ...
-SIGH- DID YOU.
GODS OF THE HIGH PLACES. THIS PIT IS YOUR DISCOVERY?
SLAVES -- THE COBWEBS.
THERE CAN BE NOTHING HERE BUT RATS, SPIDERS, AND OTHER VERMIN.
SNAKES, NO DOUBT.
I CAN'T IMAGINE WHAT COULD BE ...
... HM.

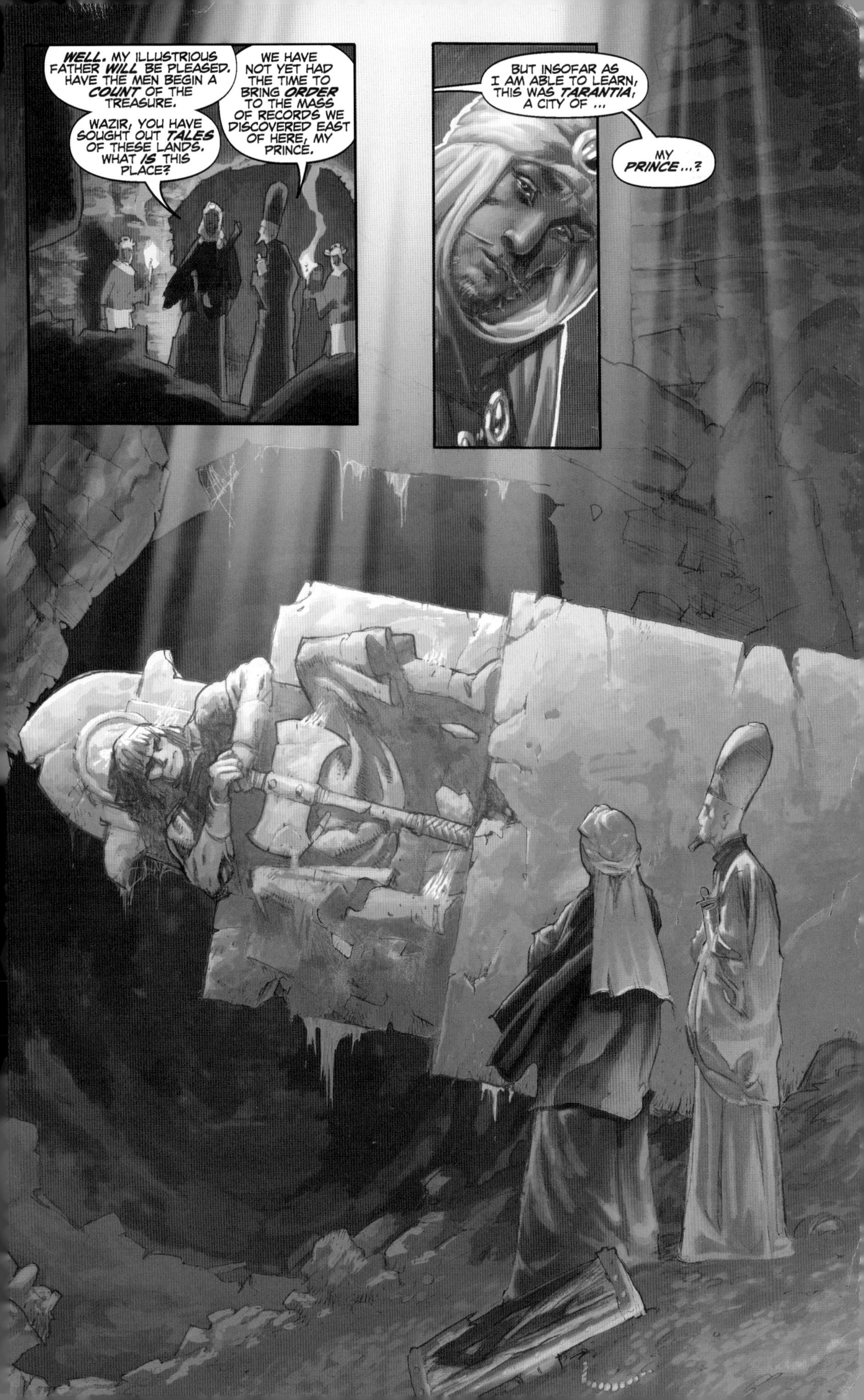
WELL. MY ILLUSTRIOUS FATHER WILL BE PLEASED. HAVE THE MEN BEGIN A COUNT OF THE TREASURE.
WAZIR, YOU HAVE SOUGHT OUT TALES OF THESE LANDS. WHAT IS THIS PLACE?
WE HAVE NOT YET HAD THE TIME TO BRING ORDER TO THE MASS OF RECORDS WE DISCOVERED EAST OF HERE, MY PRINCE.
BUT INSOFAR AS I AM ABLE TO LEARN, THIS WAS TARANTIA, A CITY OF ...
MY PRINCE...?

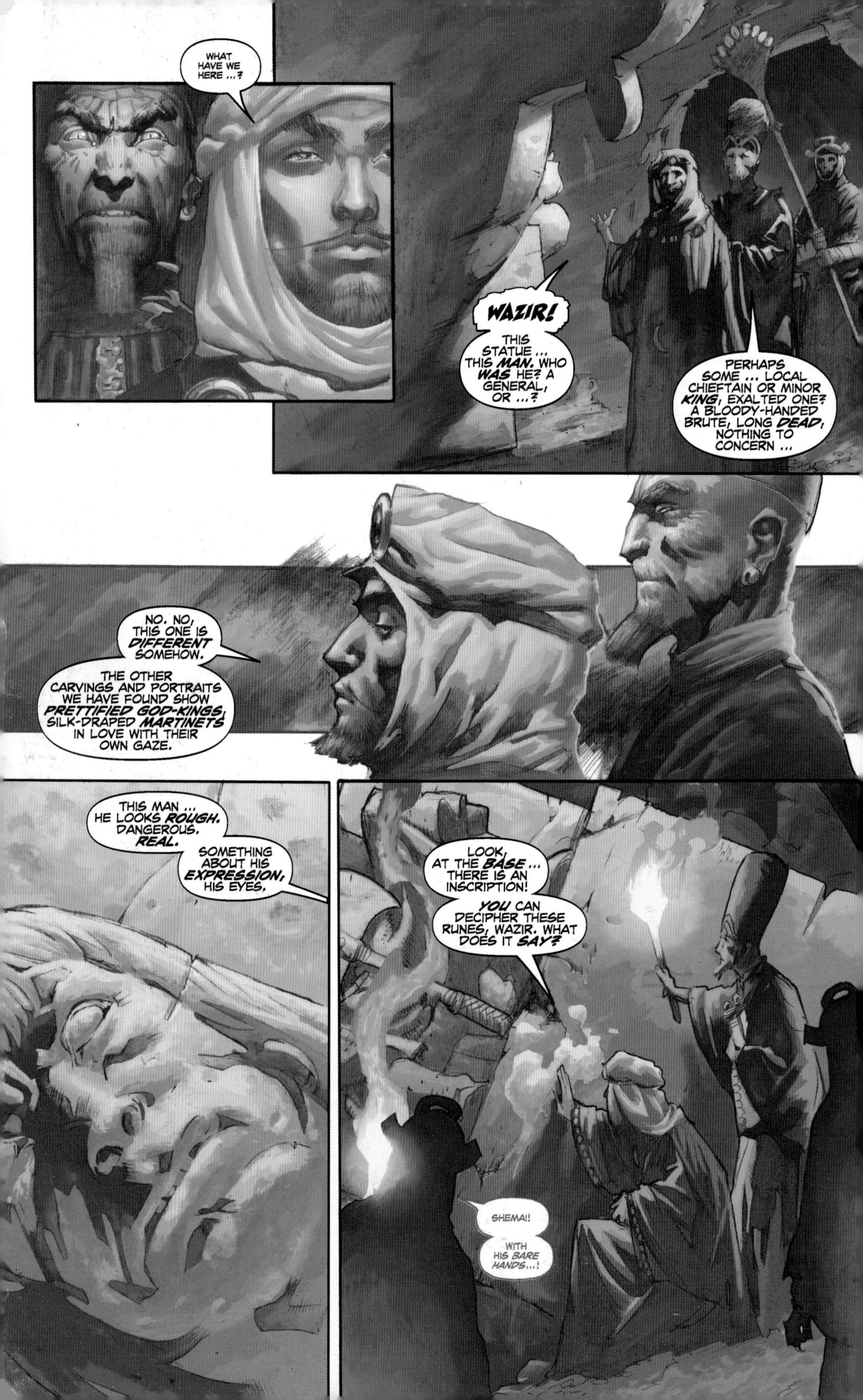

WHAT HAVE WE HERE ...?
WAZIR!
THIS STATUE ... THIS MAN. WHO WAS HE? A GENERAL, OR ...?
PERHAPS SOME ... LOCAL CHIEFTAIN OR MINOR KING, EXALTED ONE? A BLOODY-HANDED BRUTE, LONG DEAD, NOTHING TO CONCERN ...
NO. NO, THIS ONE IS DIFFERENT SOMEHOW.
THE OTHER CARVINGS AND PORTRAITS WE HAVE FOUND SHOW PRETTIFIED GOD-KINGS, SILK-DRAPED MARTINETS IN LOVE WITH THEIR OWN GAZE.
THIS MAN ... HE LOOKS ROUGH. DANGEROUS. REAL.
SOMETHING ABOUT HIS EXPRESSION, HIS EYES.
LOOK, AT THE BASE ... THERE IS AN INSCRIPTION!
YOU CAN DECIPHER THESE RUNES, WAZIR. WHAT DOES IT SAY?
SHEMAI!
WITH HIS BARE HANDS...!

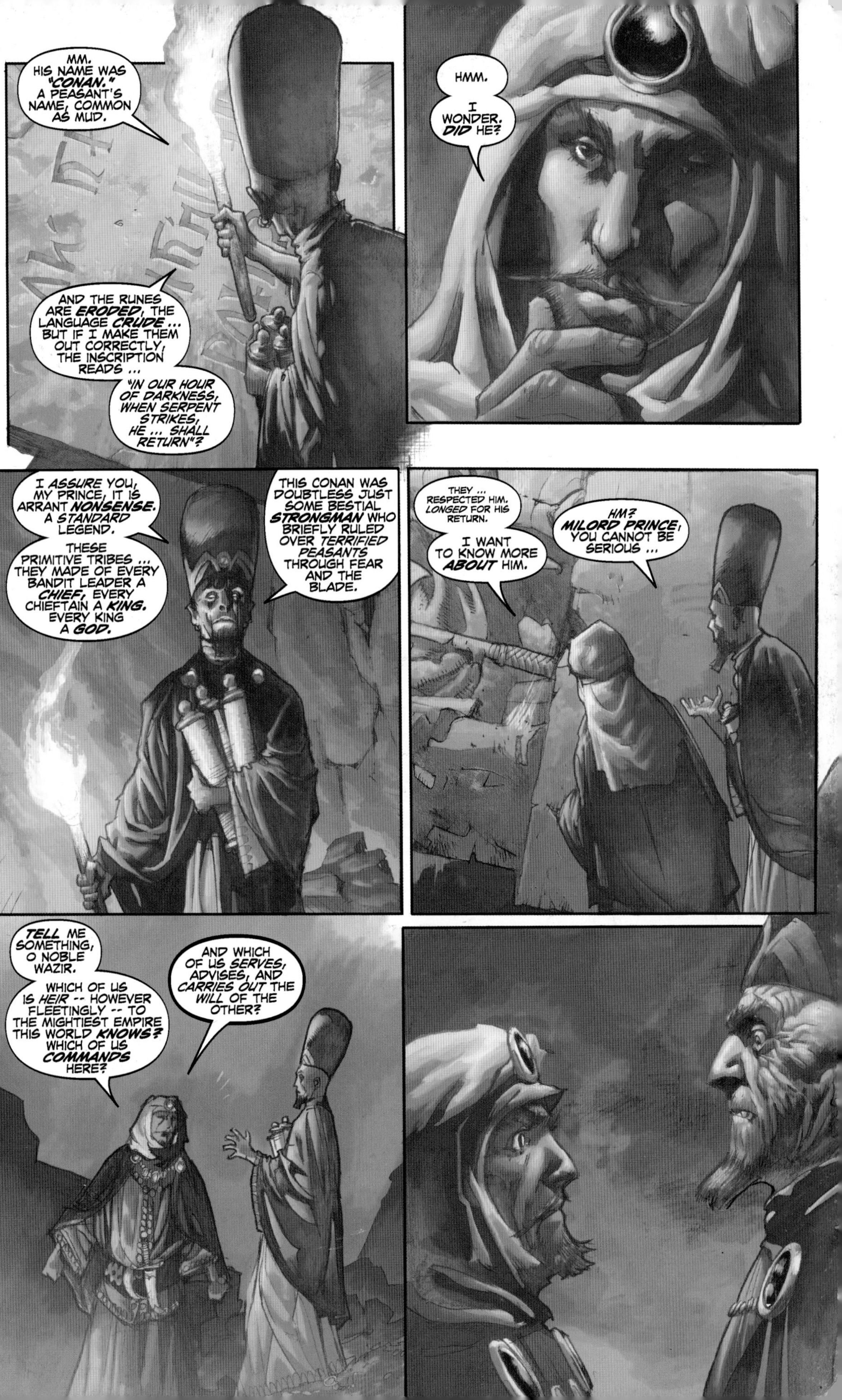
MM. HIS NAME WAS "CONAN." A PEASANT'S NAME, COMMON AS MUD.
AND THE RUNES ARE ERODED, THE LANGUAGE CRUDE ... BUT IF I MAKE THEM OUT CORRECTLY, THE INSCRIPTION READS ...
"IN OUR HOUR OF DARKNESS, WHEN SERPENT STRIKES, HE ... SHALL RETURN"?
HMM.
I WONDER. DID HE?
I ASSURE YOU, MY PRINCE, IT IS ARRANT NONSENSE. A STANDARD LEGEND.
THESE PRIMITIVE TRIBES ... THEY MADE OF EVERY BANDIT LEADER A CHIEF, EVERY CHIEFTAIN A KING. EVERY KING A GOD.
THIS CONAN WAS DOUBTLESS JUST SOME BESTIAL STRONGMAN WHO BRIEFLY RULED OVER TERRIFIED PEASANTS THROUGH FEAR AND THE BLADE.
THEY ... RESPECTED HIM. LONGED FOR HIS RETURN.
I WANT TO KNOW MORE ABOUT HIM.
HM? MILORD PRINCE, YOU CANNOT BE SERIOUS ...
TELL ME SOMETHING, O NOBLE WAZIR.
WHICH OF US IS HEIR -- HOWEVER FLEETINGLY -- TO THE MIGHTIEST EMPIRE THIS WORLD KNOWS? WHICH OF US COMMANDS HERE?
AND WHICH OF US SERVES, ADVISES, AND CARRIES OUT THE WILL OF THE OTHER?

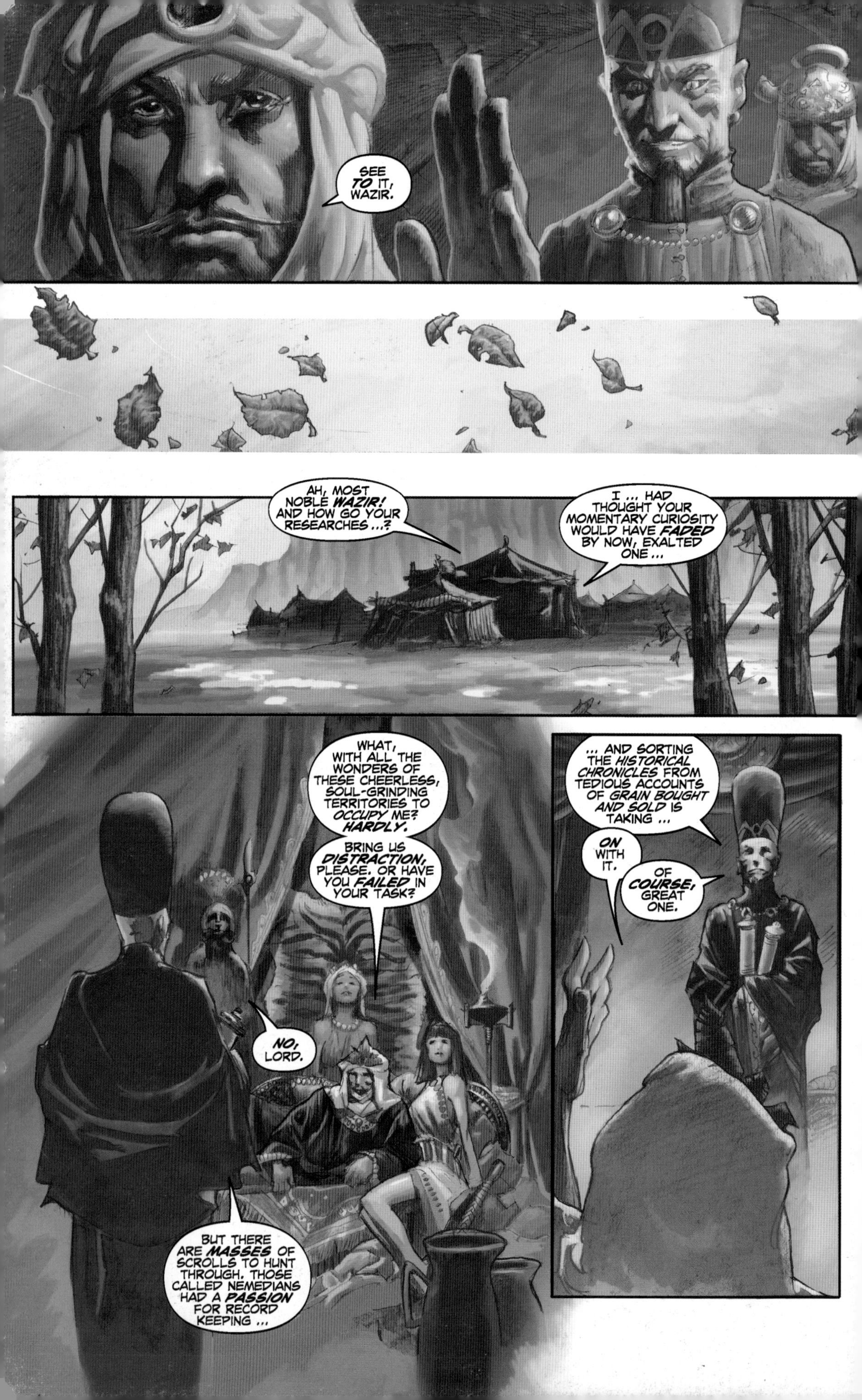
SEE TO IT, WAZIR.
AH, MOST NOBLE WAZIR! AND HOW GO YOUR RESEARCHES ...?
I ... HAD THOUGHT YOUR MOMENTARY CURIOSITY WOULD HAVE FADED BY NOW, EXALTED ONE ...
WHAT, WITH ALL THE WONDERS OF THESE CHEERLESS, SOUL-GRINDING TERRITORIES TO OCCUPY ME? HARDLY.
BRING US DISTRACTION, PLEASE. OR HAVE YOU FAILED IN YOUR TASK?
NO, LORD.
BUT THERE ARE MASSES OF SCROLLS TO HUNT THROUGH. THOSE CALLED NEMEDIANS HAD A PASSION FOR RECORD KEEPING ...
... AND SORTING THE HISTORICAL CHRONICLES FROM TEDIOUS ACCOUNTS OF GRAIN BOUGHT AND SOLD IS TAKING ...
ON WITH IT.
OF COURSE, GREAT ONE.

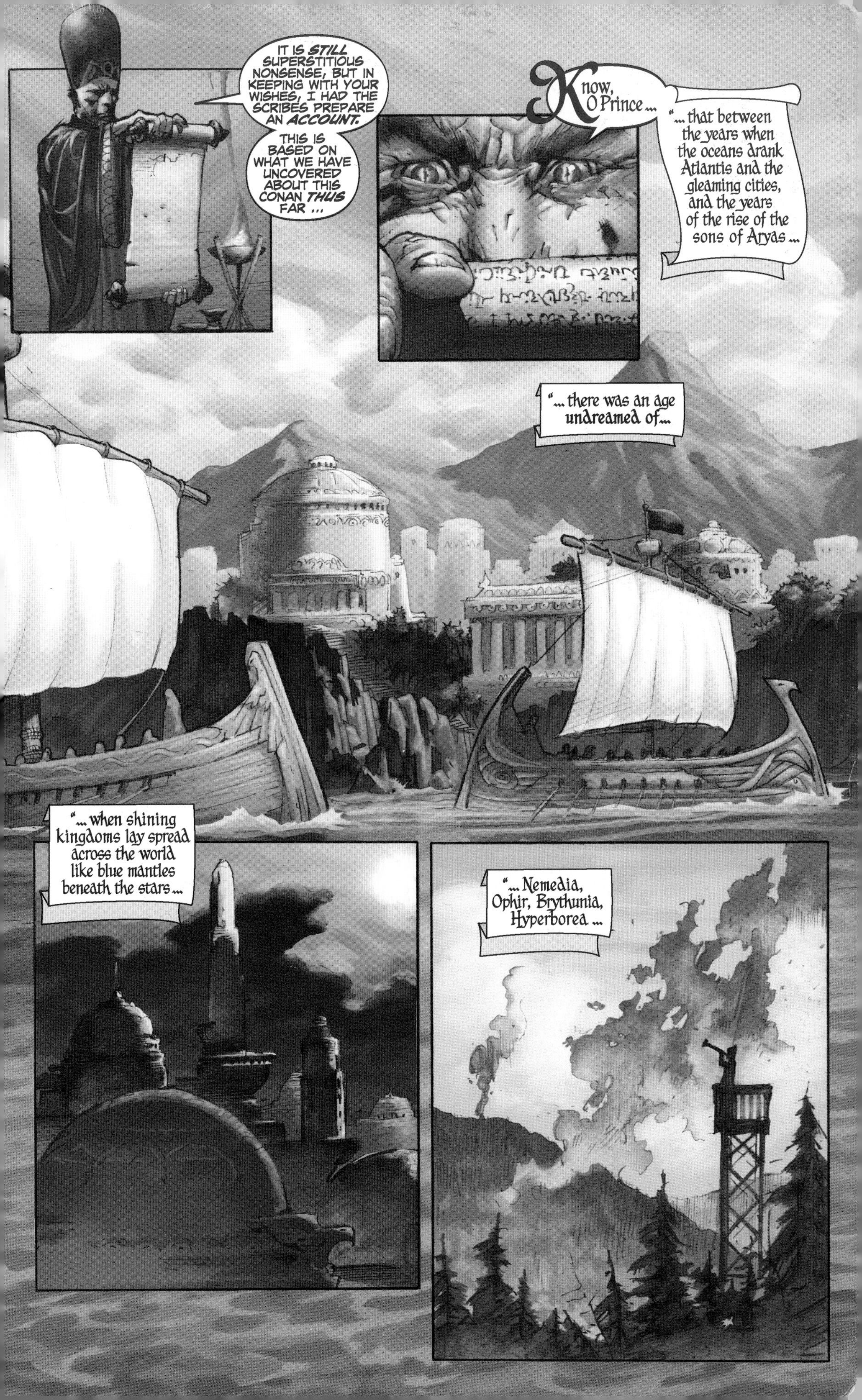
IT IS STILL SUPERSTITIOUS NONSENSE, BUT IN KEEPING WITH YOUR WISHES, I HAD THE SCRIBES PREPARE AN ACCOUNT.
THIS IS BASED ON WHAT WE HAVE UNCOVERED ABOUT THIS CONAN THUS FAR ...
Know, O Prince ...
"... that between the years when the oceans drank Atlantis and the gleaming cities, and the years of the rise of the sons of Aryas ...
"... there was an age undreamed of...
"... when shining kingdoms lay spread across the world like blue mantles beneath the stars ...
"... Nemedia, Ophir, Brythunia, Hyperborea ...

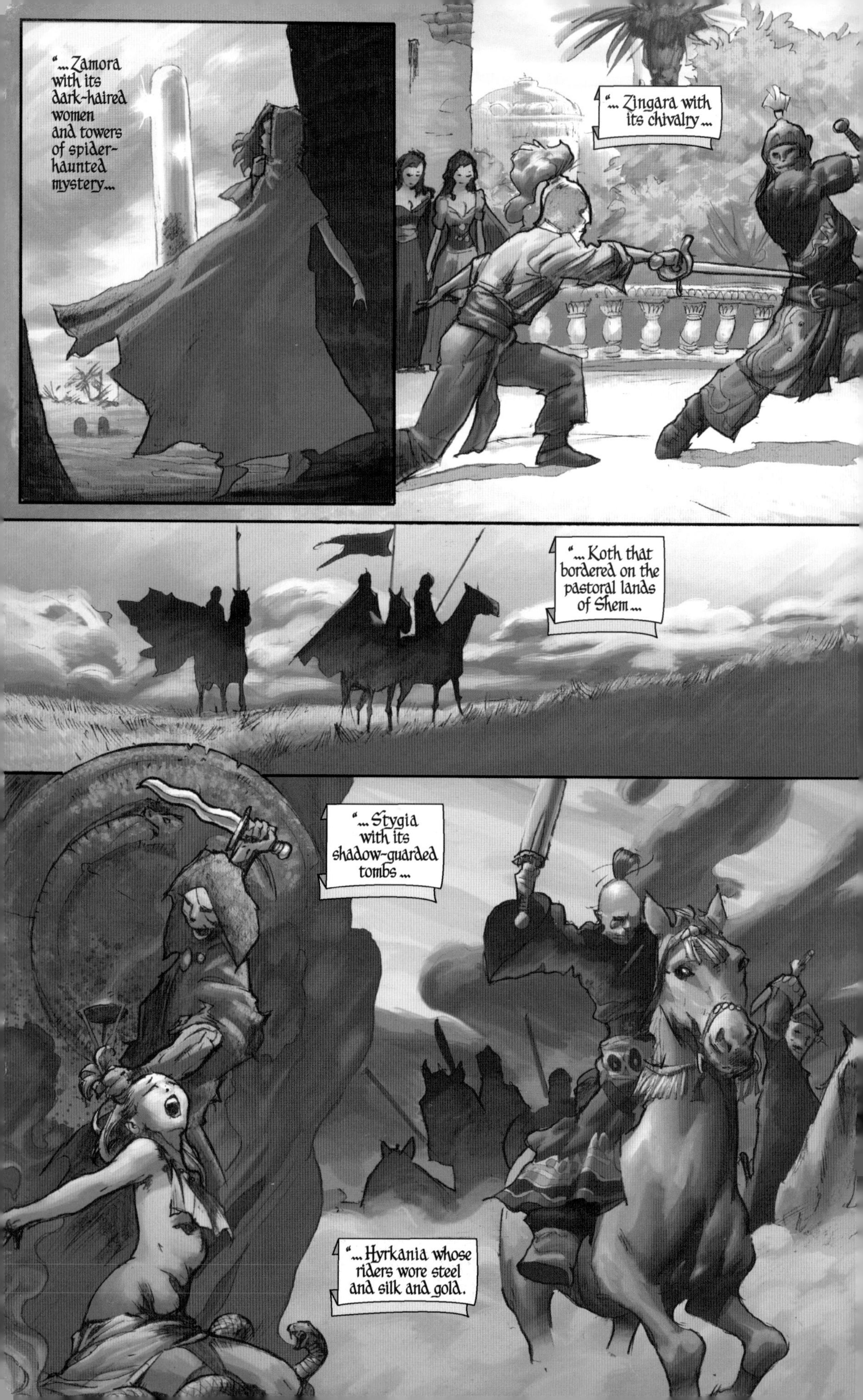
"...Zamora with its dark-haired women and towers of spider-haunted mystery...
"...Zingara with its chivalry...
"...Koth that bordered on the pastoral lands of Shem...
"...Stygia with its shadow-guarded tombs...
"...Hyrkania whose riders wore steel and silk and gold.

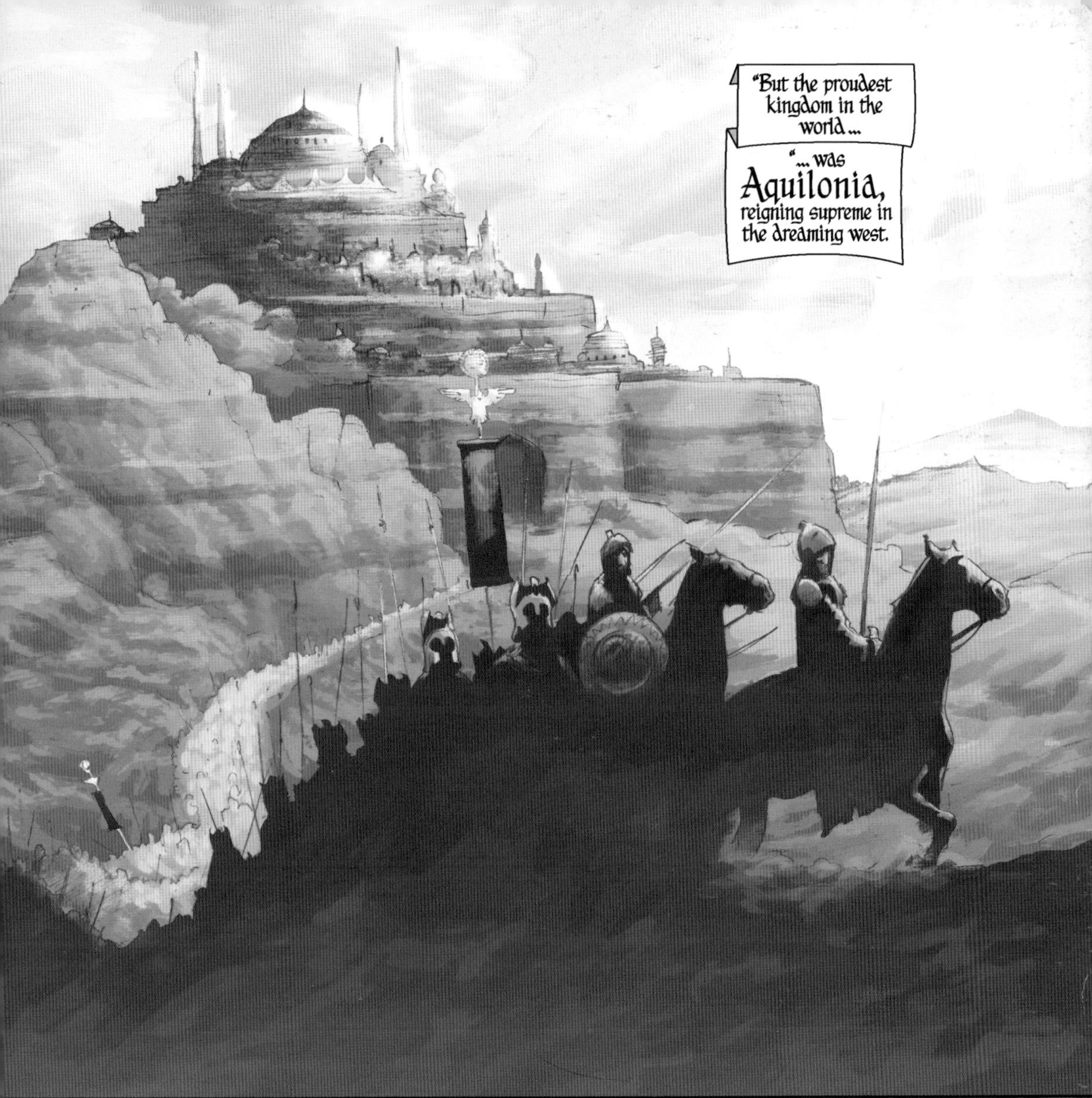
"But the proudest kingdom in the world...
"...was Aquilonia, reigning supreme in the dreaming west.
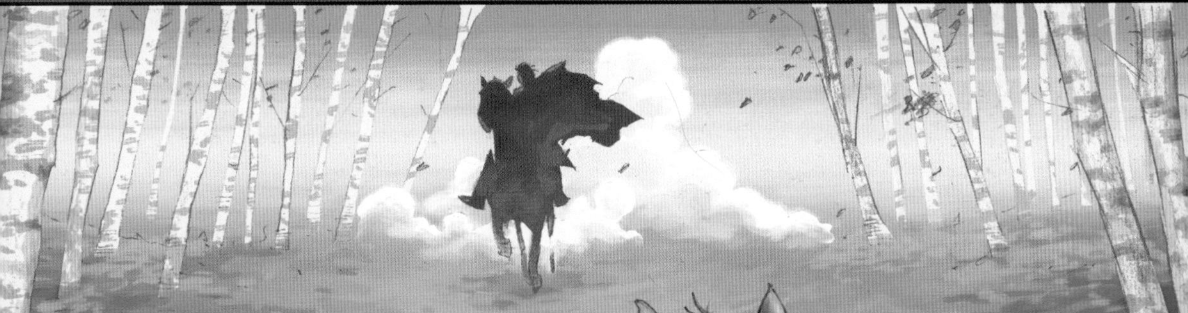
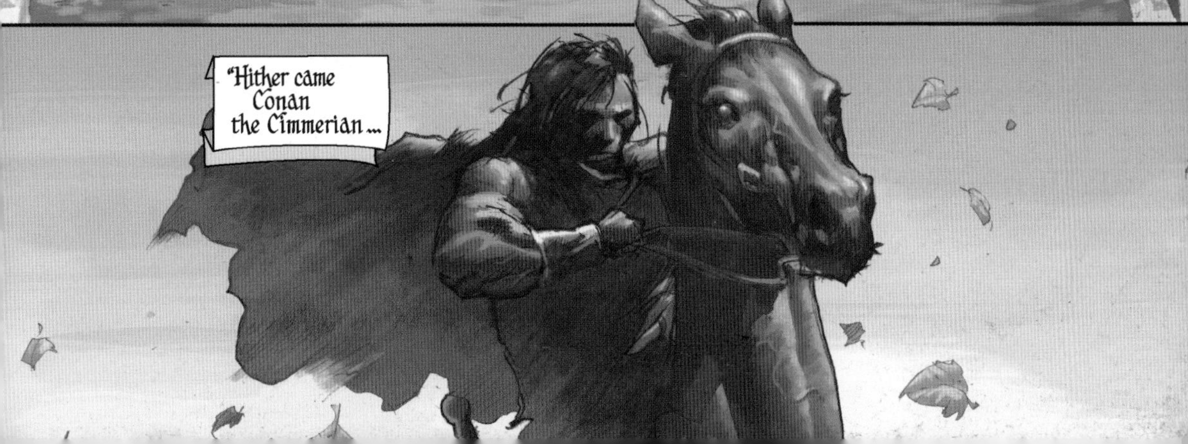
"Hither came Conan the Cimmerian...

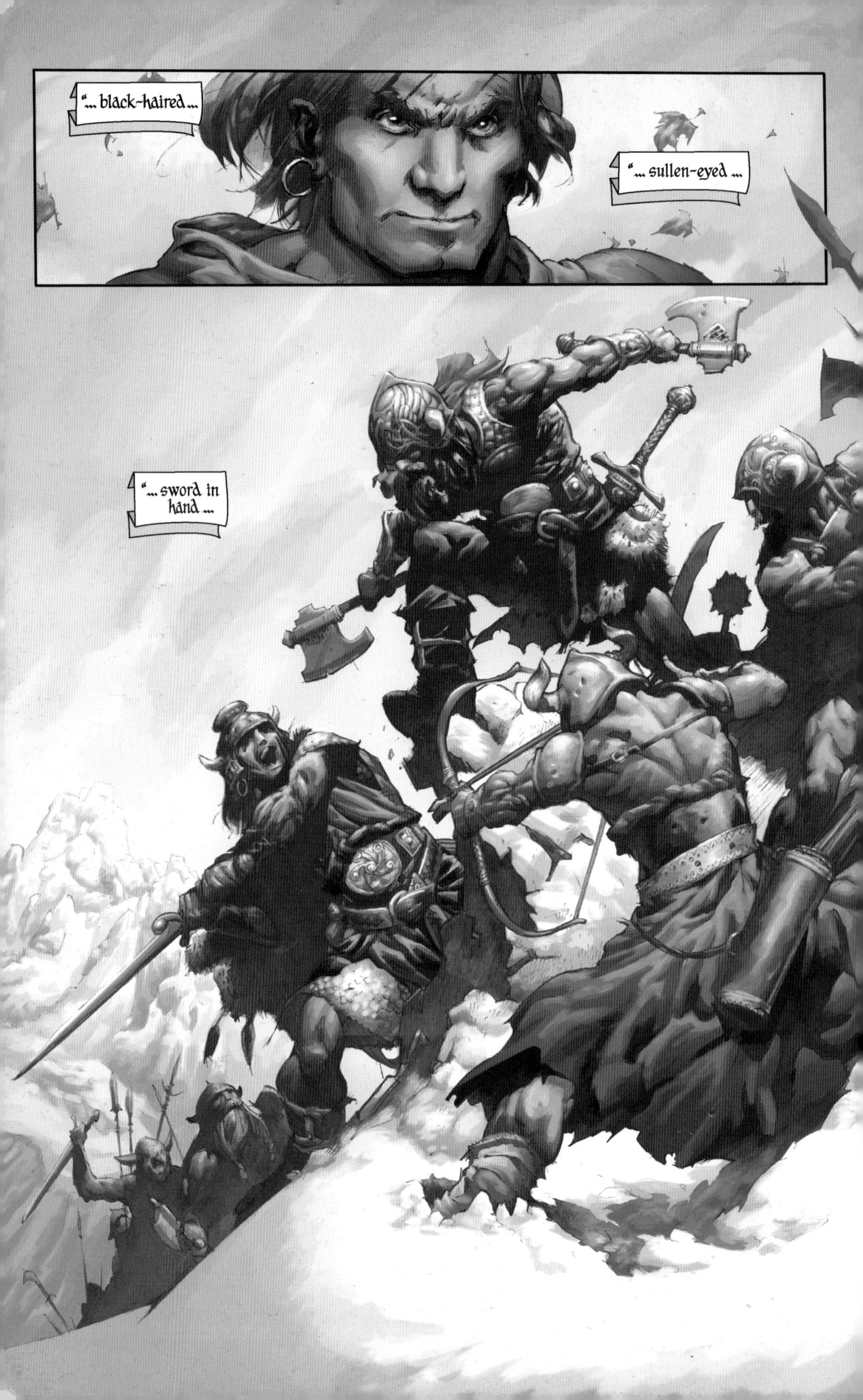
"... black-haired ...
"... sullen-eyed ...
"... sword in hand ...

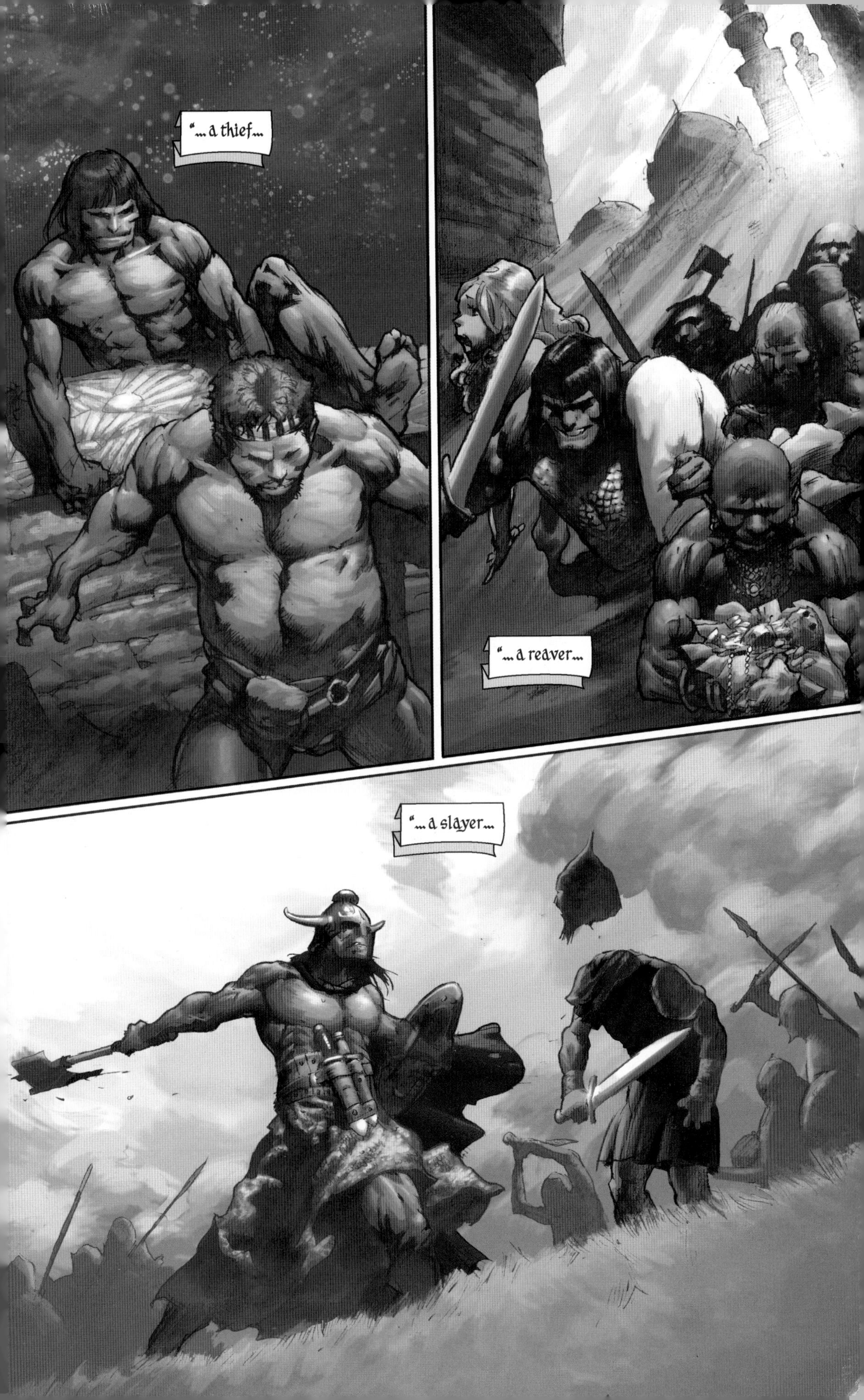
"...a thief...
"...a reaver...
"...a slayer...

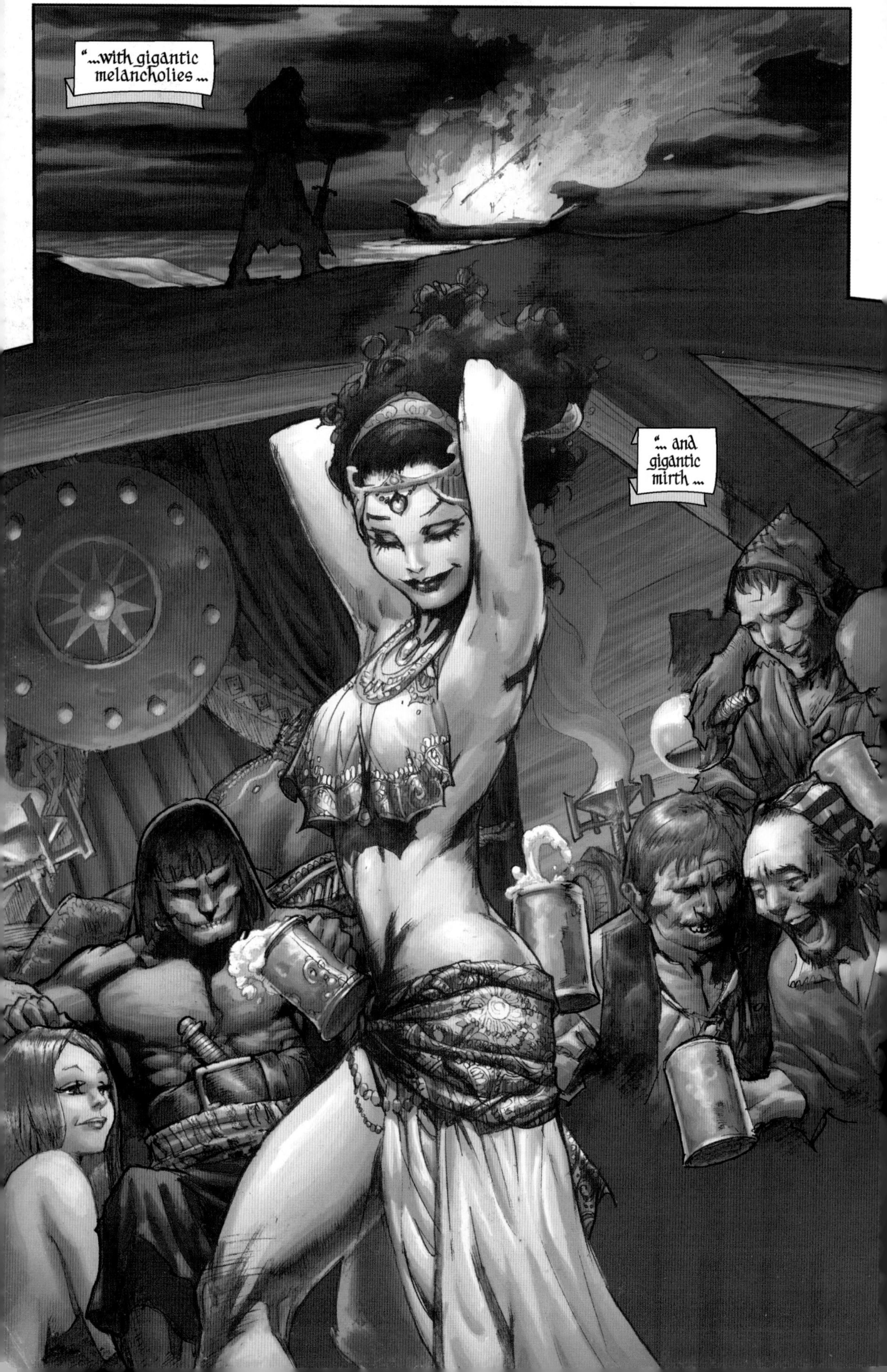
"...with gigantic melancholies ...
"... and gigantic mirth ...

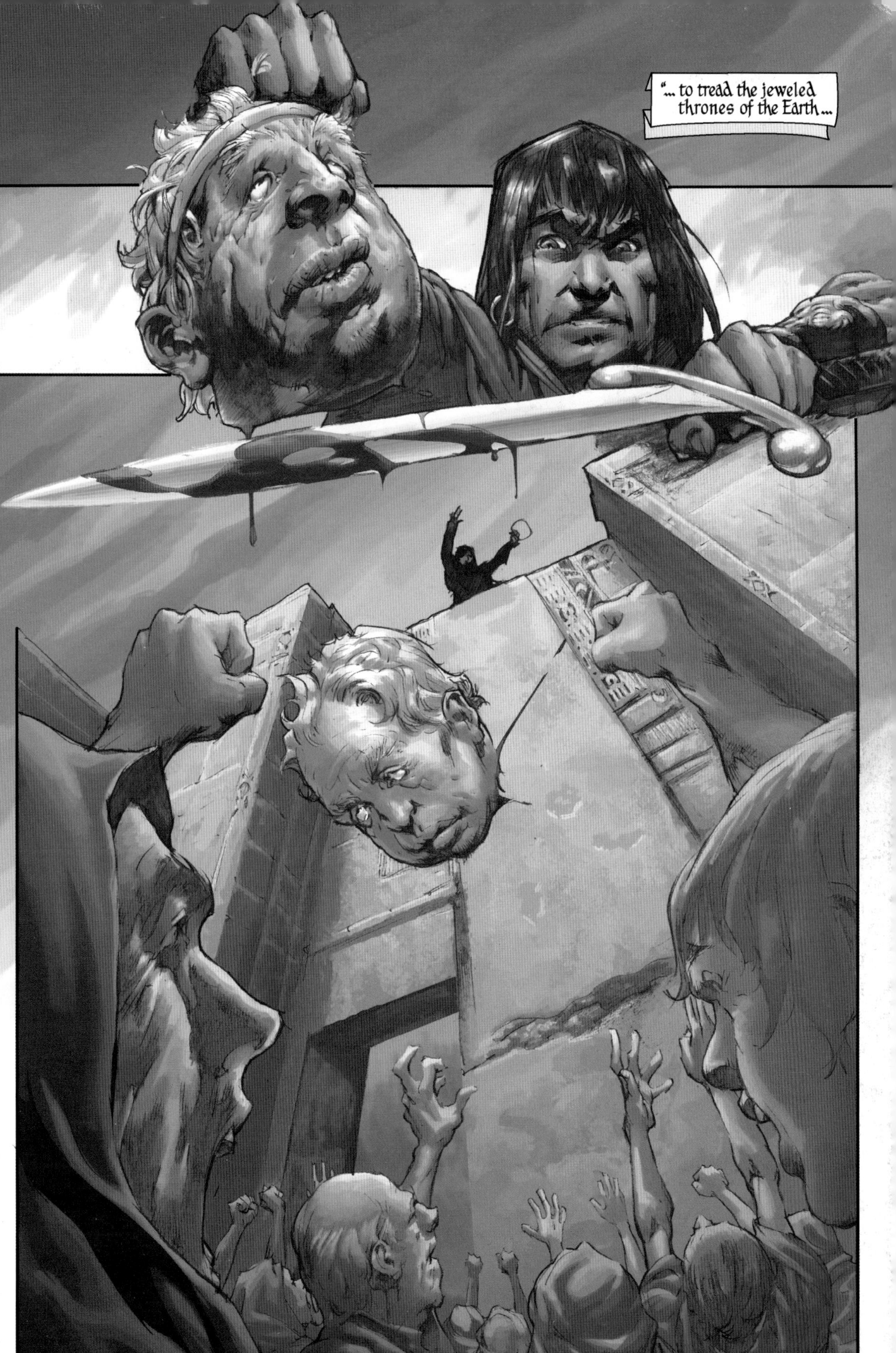
"... to tread the jeweled thrones of the Earth ...

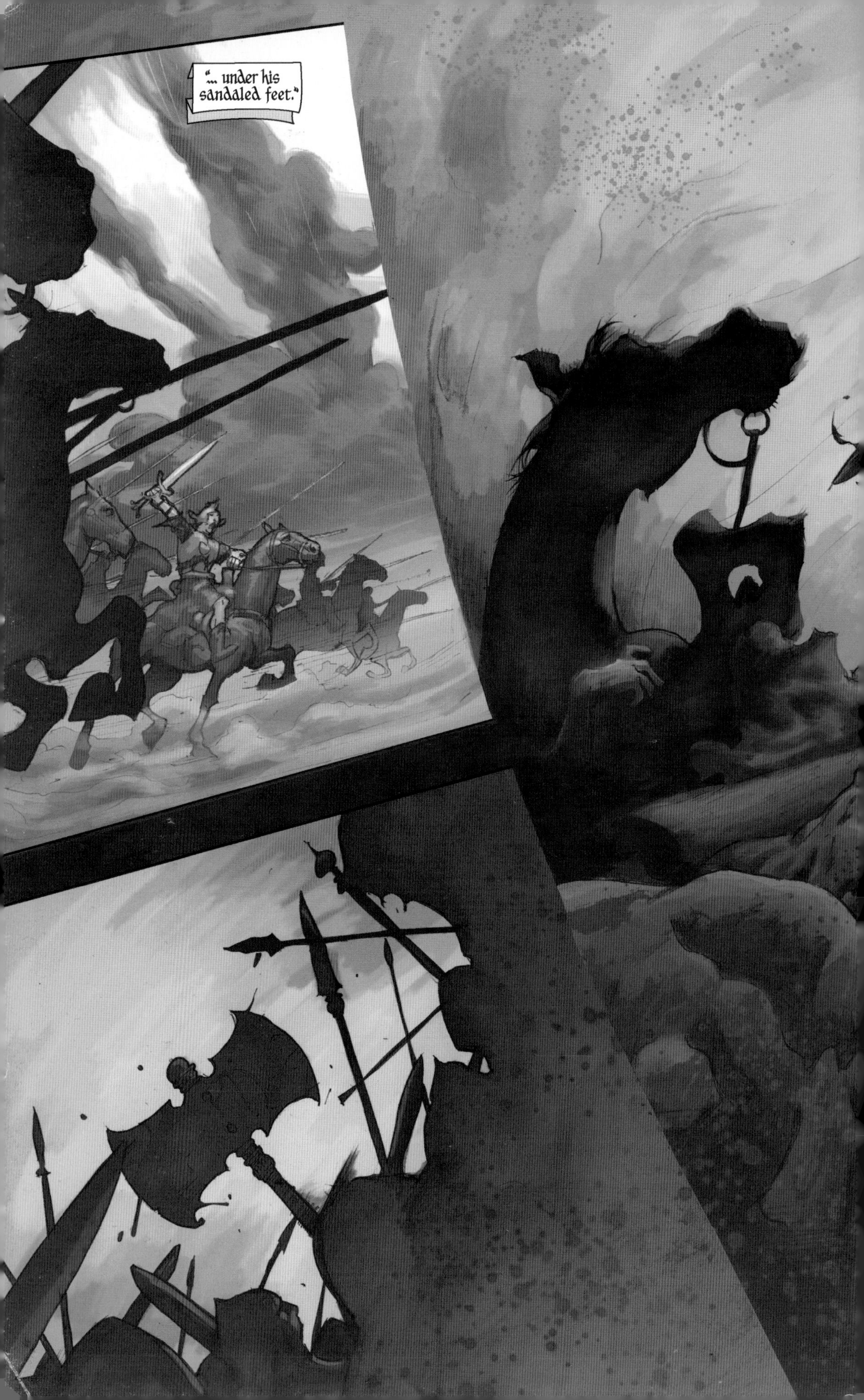
"... under his sandaled feet."

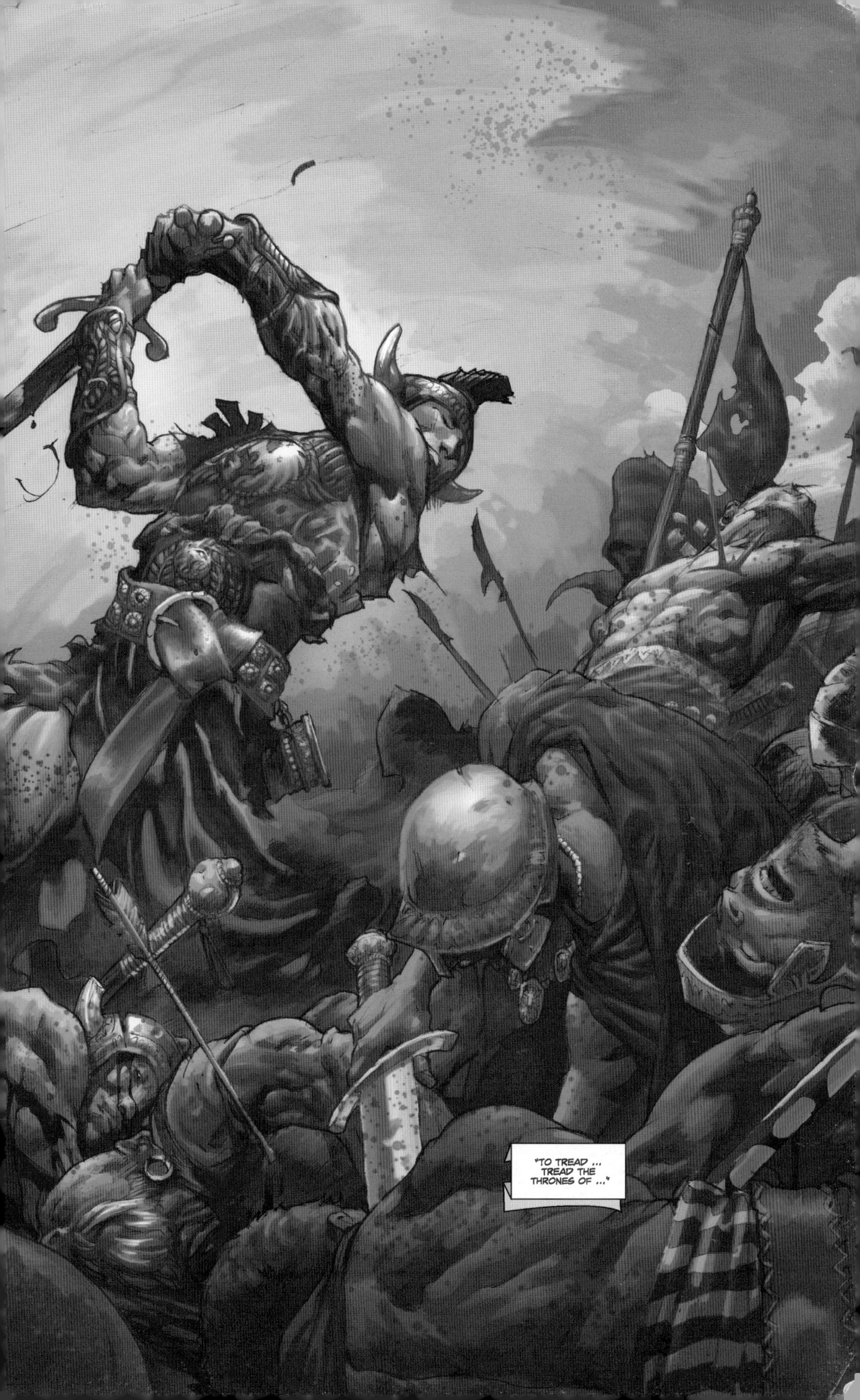
"TO TREAD ... TREAD THE THRONES OF ..."

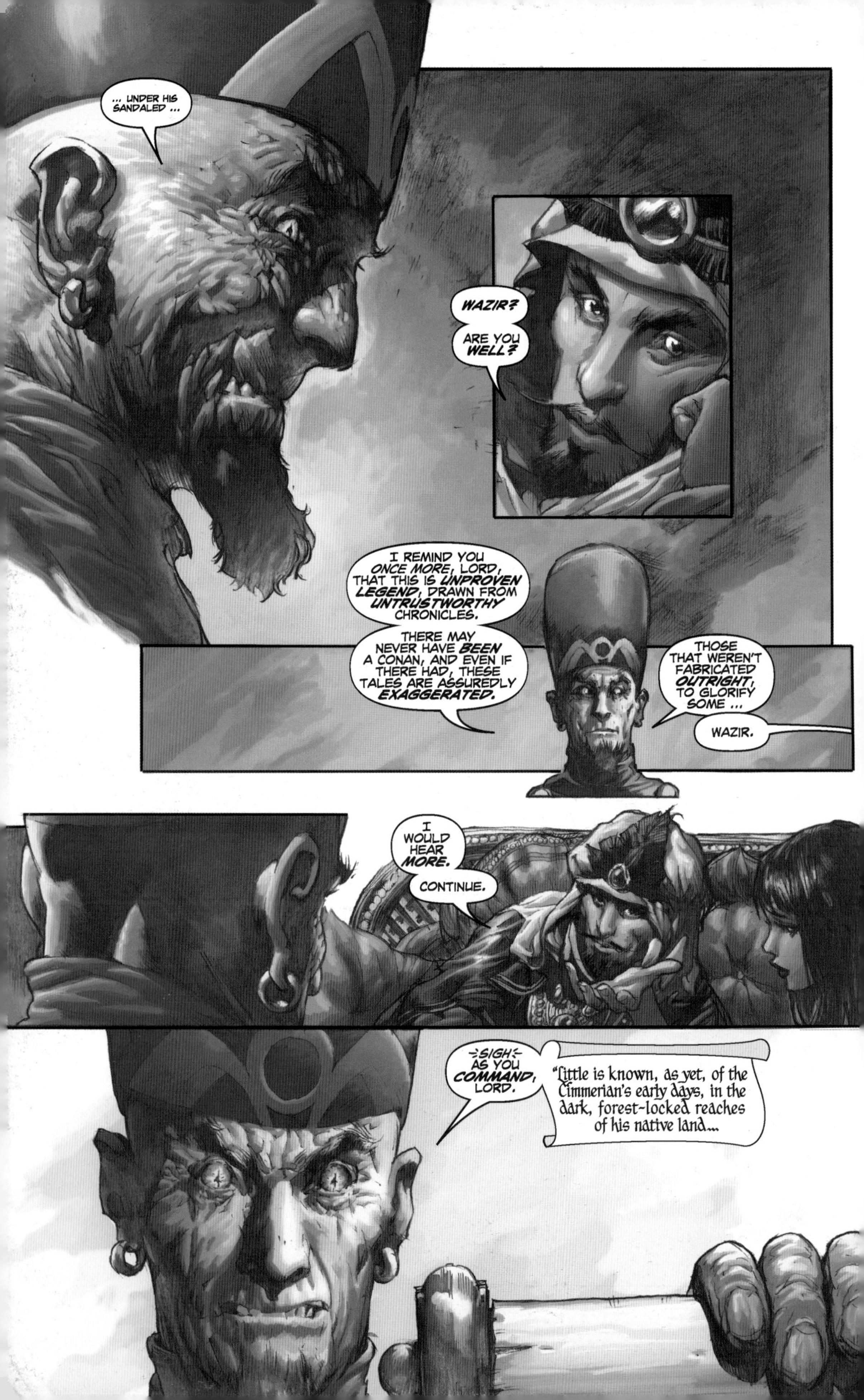
... UNDER HIS SANDALED ...
WAZIR?
ARE YOU WELL?
I REMIND YOU ONCE MORE, LORD, THAT THIS IS UNPROVEN LEGEND, DRAWN FROM UNTRUSTWORTHY CHRONICLES.
THERE MAY NEVER HAVE BEEN A CONAN, AND EVEN IF THERE HAD, THESE TALES ARE ASSUREDLY EXAGGERATED.
THOSE THAT WEREN'T FABRICATED OUTRIGHT, TO GLORIFY SOME ...
WAZIR.
I WOULD HEAR MORE.
CONTINUE.
-SIGH- AS YOU COMMAND, LORD.
"Little is known, as yet, of the Cimmerian's early days, in the dark, forest-locked reaches of his native land...

CHAPTER ONE

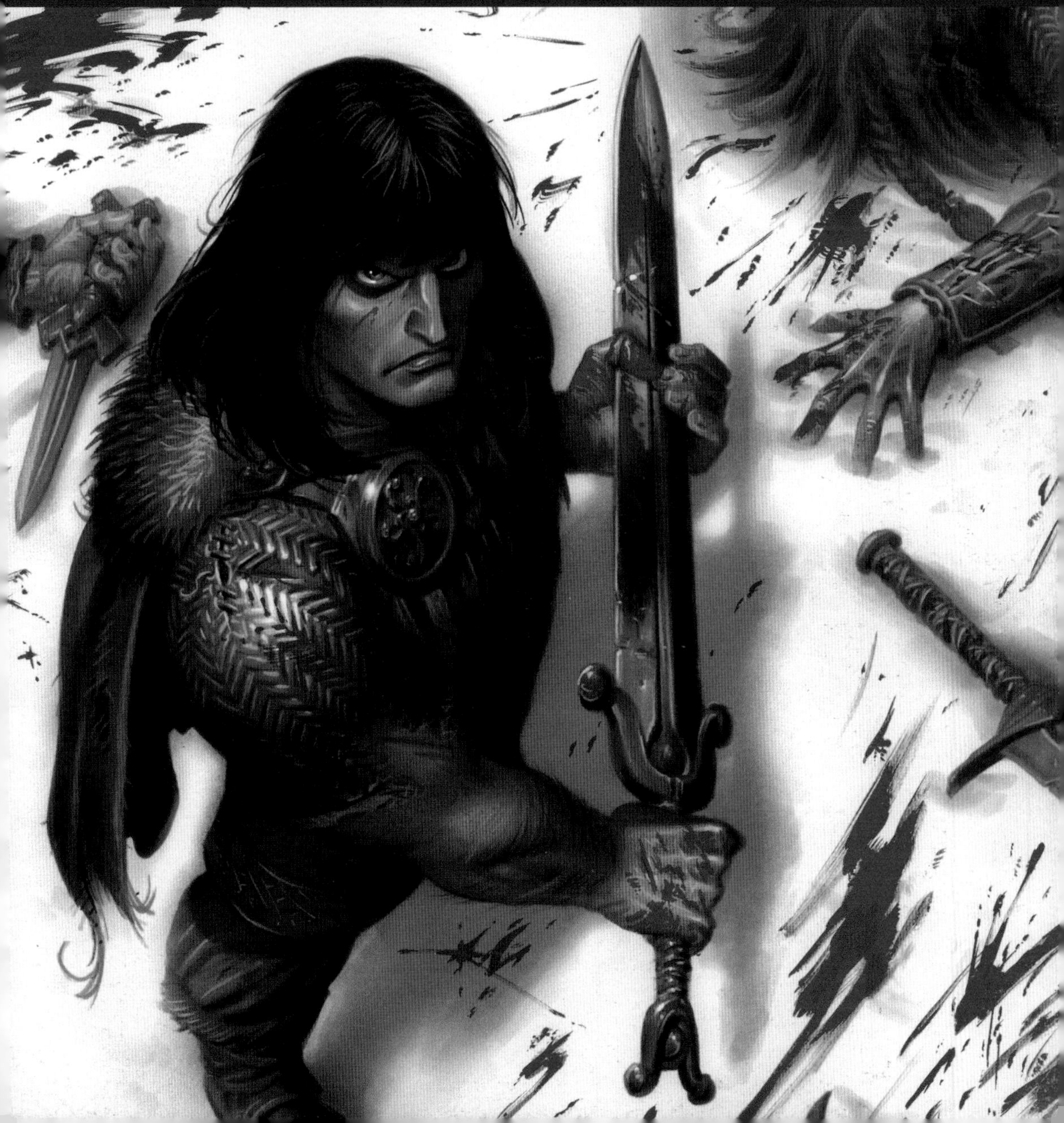

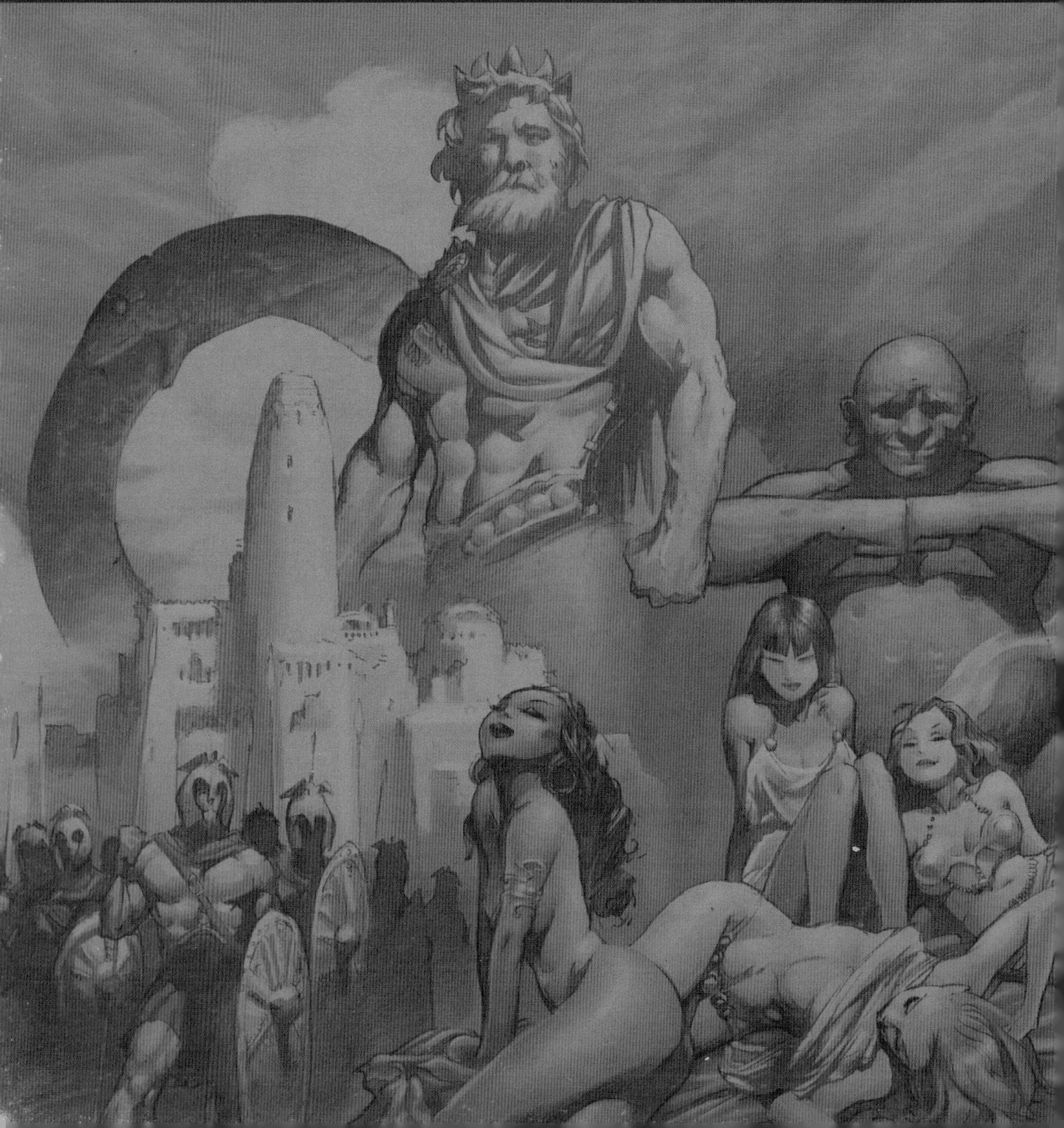

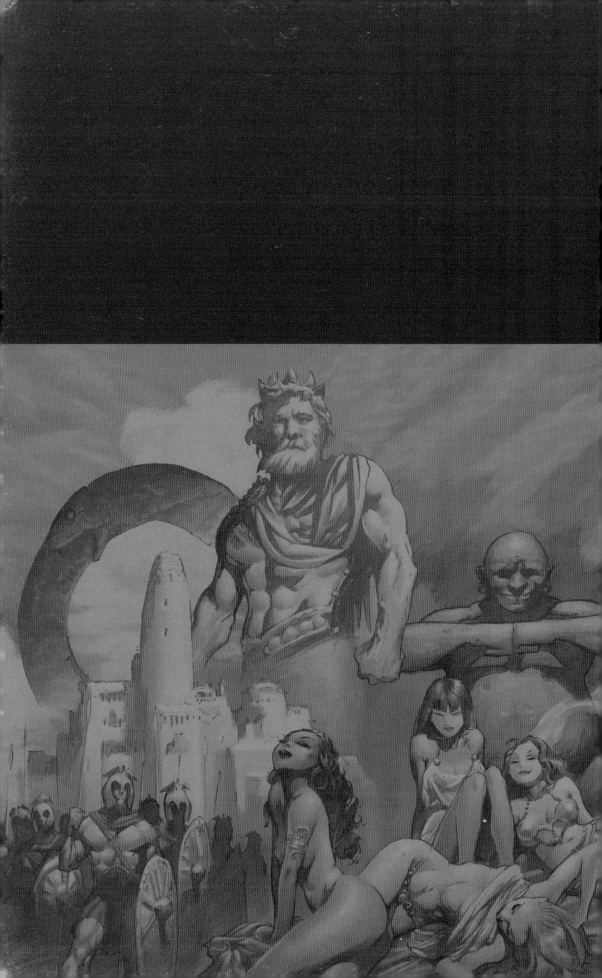

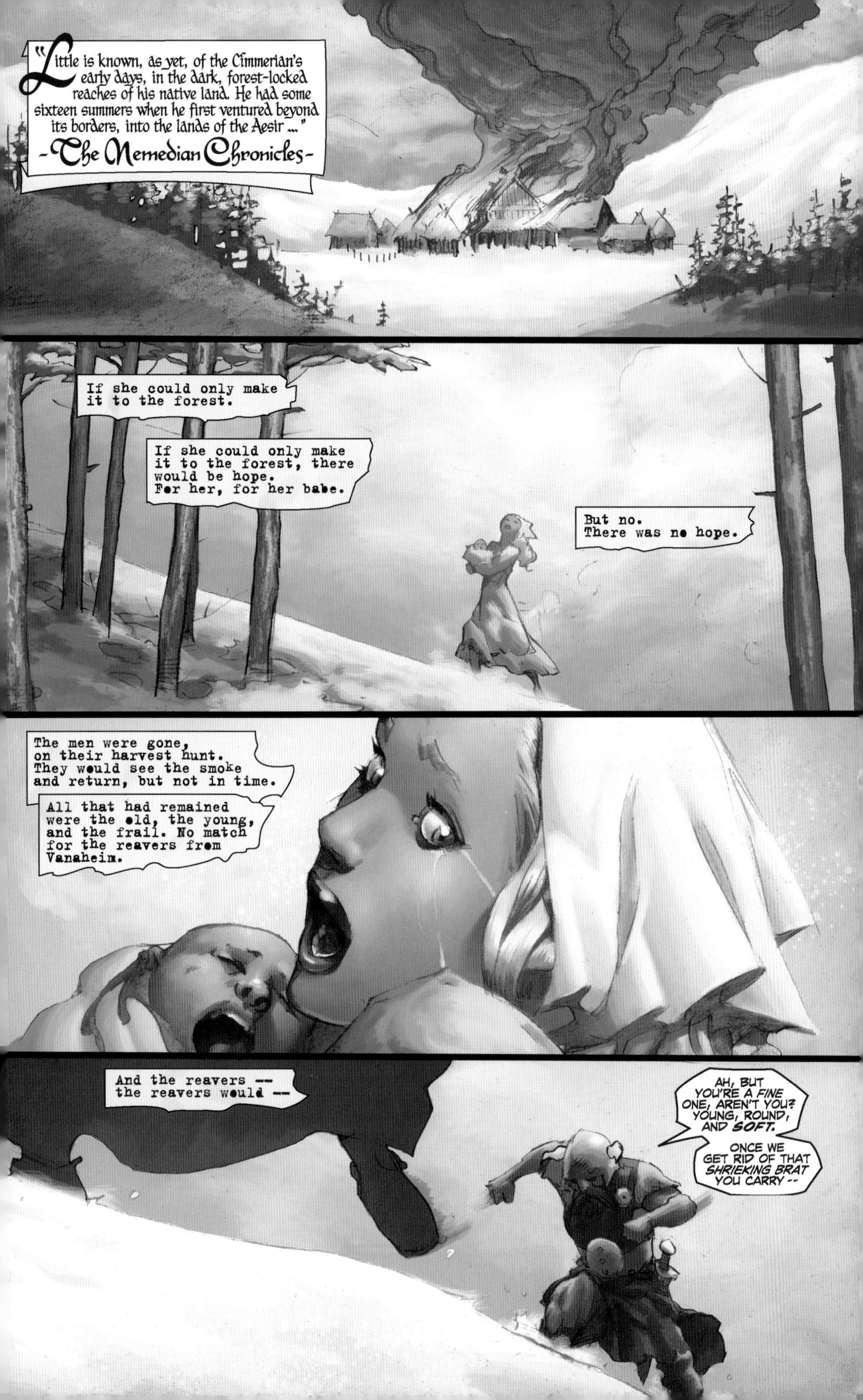
"Little is known, as yet, of the Cimmerian's early days, in the dark, forest-locked reaches of his native land. He had some sixteen summers when he first ventured beyond its borders, into the lands of the Aesir ..."
-The Nemedian Chronicles-
If she could only make it to the forest.
If she could only make it to the forest, there would be hope. For her, for her babe.
But no. There was no hope.
The men were gone, on their harvest hunt. They would see the smoke and return, but not in time.
All that had remained were the old, the young, and the frail. No match for the reavers from Vanaheim.
And the reavers — the reavers would —
AH, BUT YOU'RE A *FINE* ONE, AREN'T YOU? YOUNG, ROUND, AND *SOFT.*
ONCE WE GET RID OF THAT *SHRIEKING BRAT* YOU CARRY --

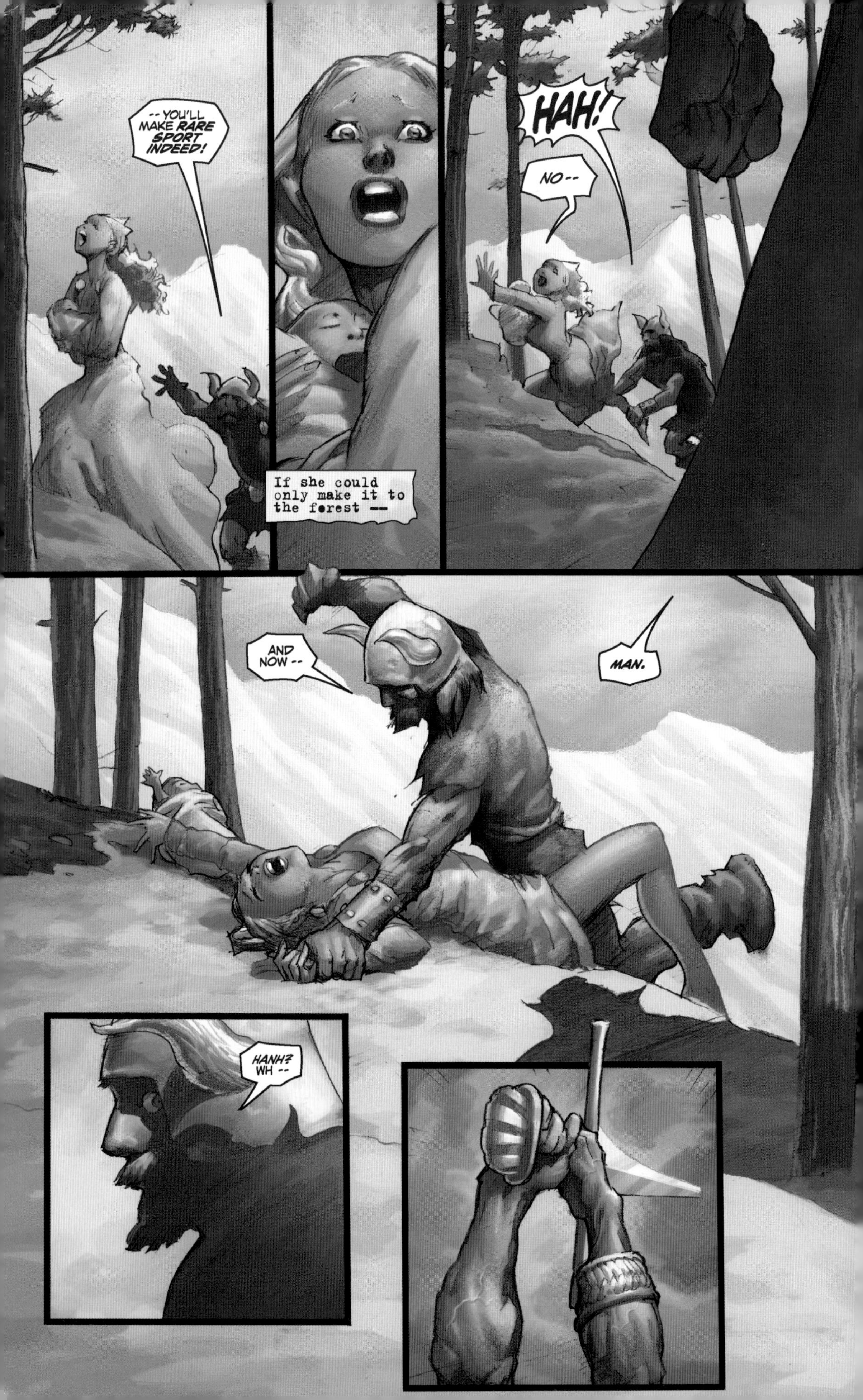
-- YOU'LL MAKE RARE SPORT INDEED!
If she could only make it to the forest --
HAH!
NO --
AND NOW --
MAN.
HANH? WH --

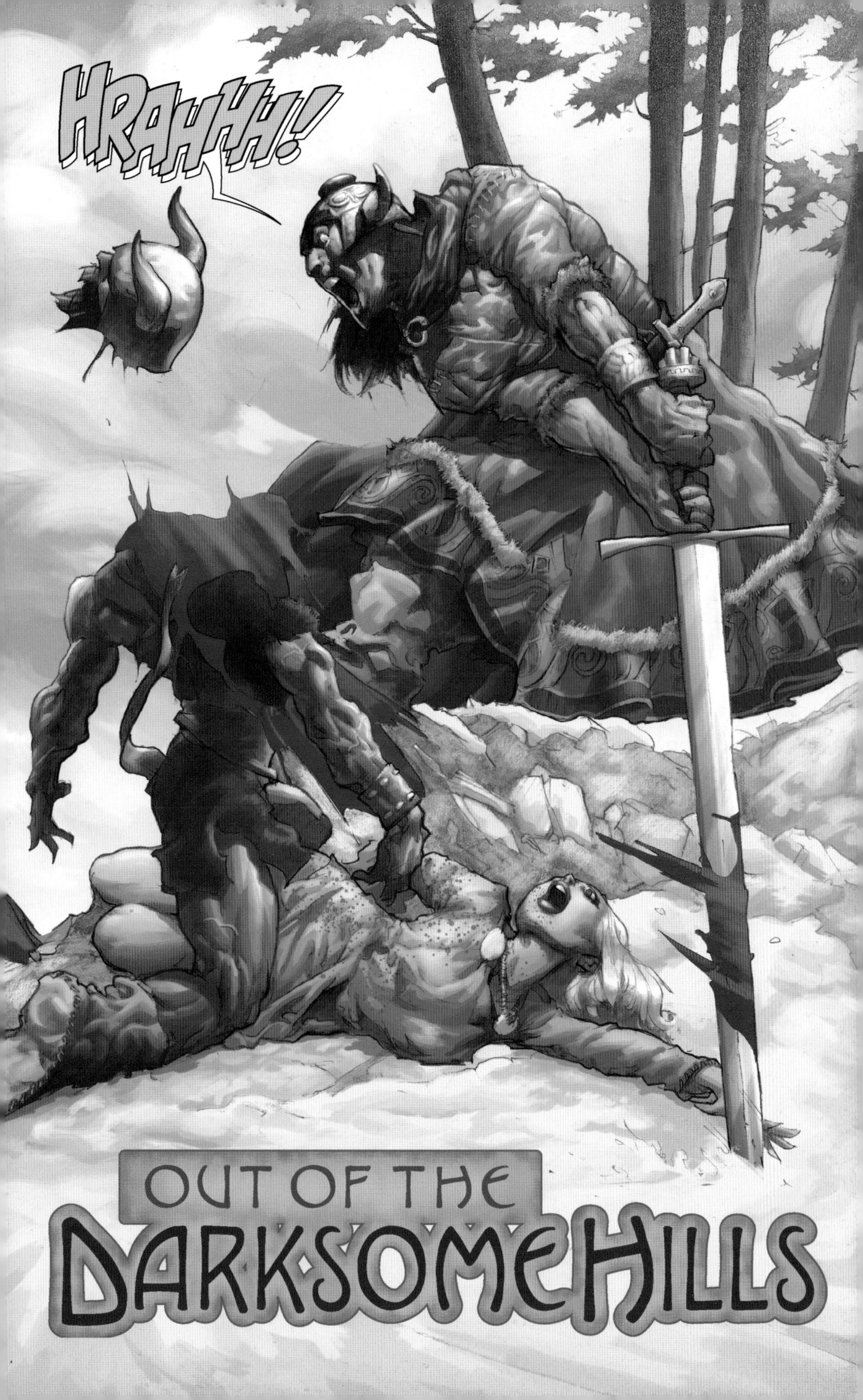
HRAHHH!
OUT OF THE
DARKSOME HILLS

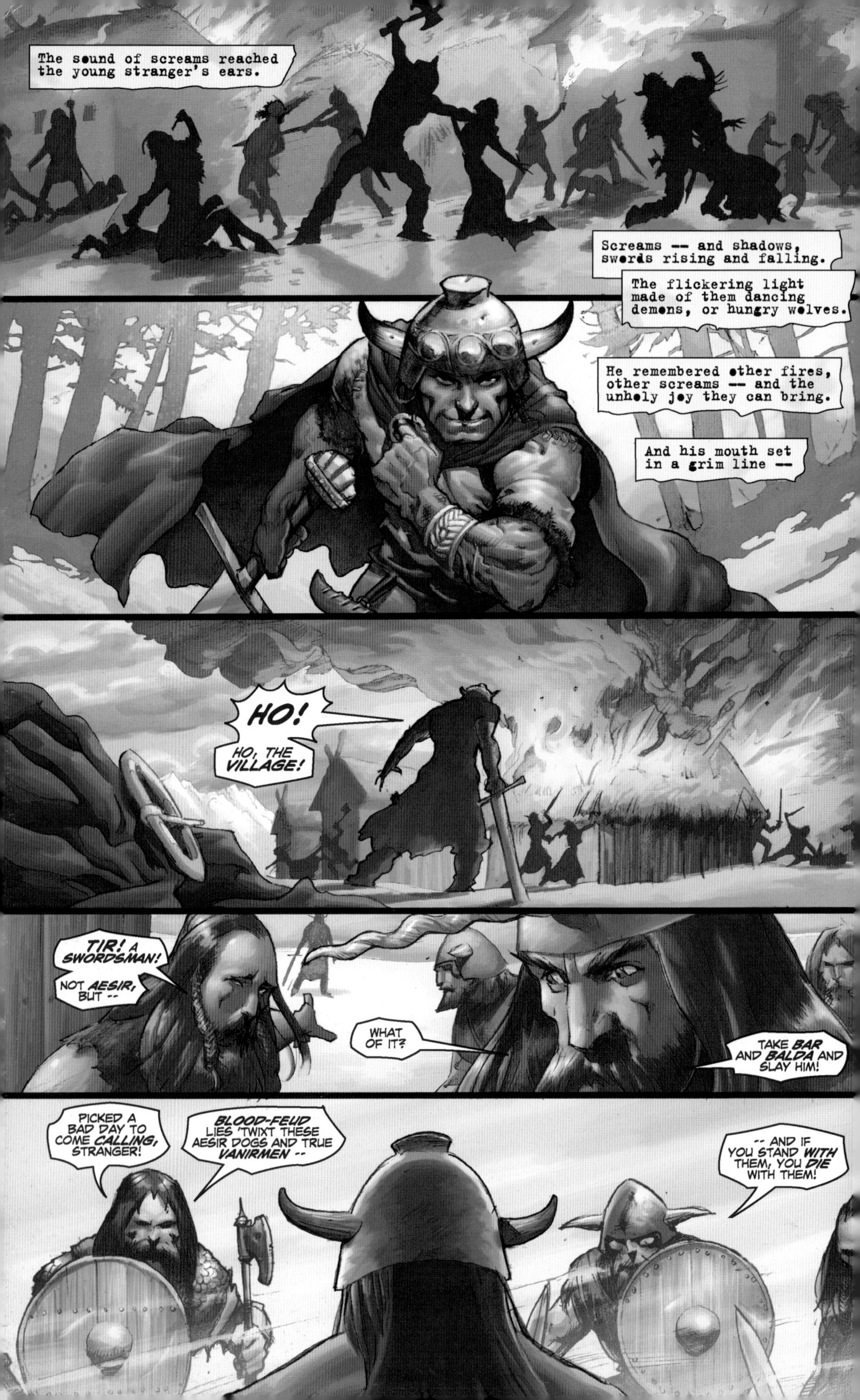

The sound of screams reached the young stranger's ears.
Screams -- and shadows, swords rising and falling.
The flickering light made of them dancing demons, or hungry wolves.
He remembered other fires, other screams -- and the unholy joy they can bring.
And his mouth set in a grim line --
HO!
HO, THE VILLAGE!
TIR! A SWORDSMAN!
NOT AESIR, BUT --
WHAT OF IT?
TAKE BAR AND BALDA AND SLAY HIM!
PICKED A BAD DAY TO COME CALLING, STRANGER!
BLOOD-FEUD LIES 'TWIXT THESE AESIR DOGS AND TRUE VANIRMEN --
-- AND IF YOU STAND WITH THEM, YOU DIE WITH THEM!

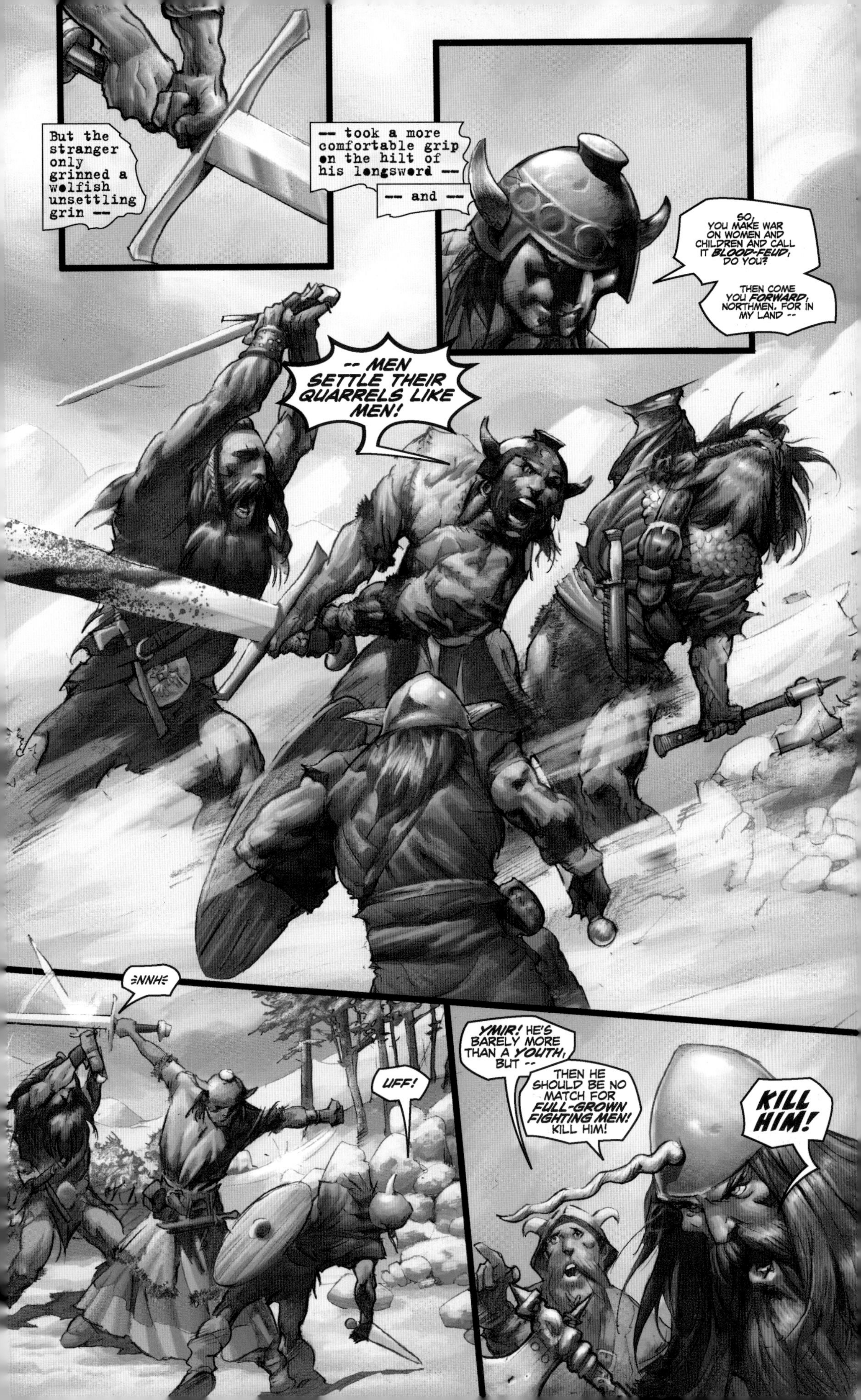
But the stranger only grinned a wolfish unsettling grin --
-- took a more comfortable grip on the hilt of his longsword --
-- and --
SO, YOU MAKE WAR ON WOMEN AND CHILDREN AND CALL IT BLOOD-FEUD, DO YOU?
THEN COME YOU FORWARD, NORTHMEN. FOR IN MY LAND --
-- MEN SETTLE THEIR QUARRELS LIKE MEN!
NNH
UFF!
YMIR! HE'S BARELY MORE THAN A YOUTH, BUT --
THEN HE SHOULD BE NO MATCH FOR FULL-GROWN FIGHTING MEN! KILL HIM!
KILL HIM!

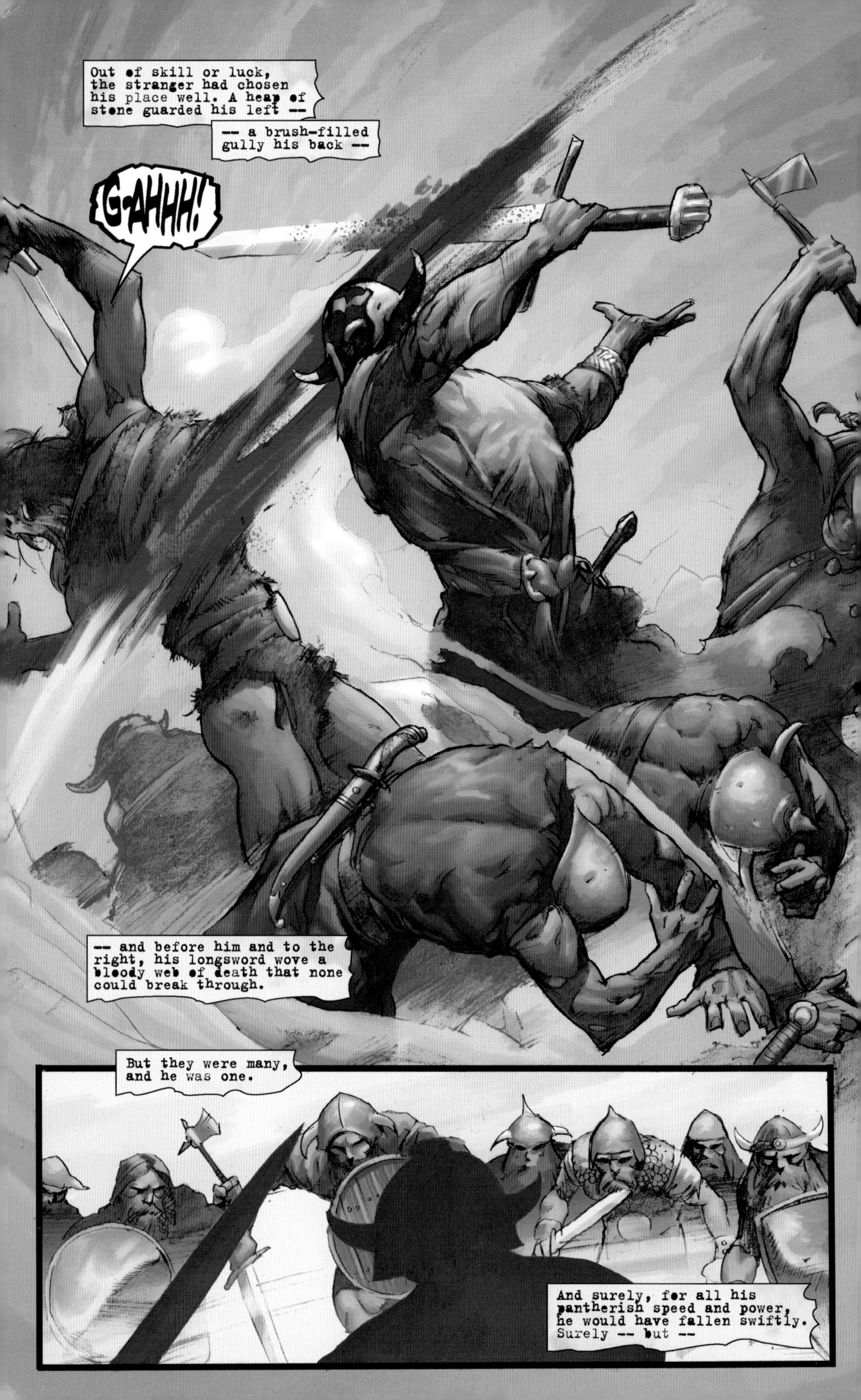
Out of skill or luck, the stranger had chosen his place well. A heap of stone guarded his left --
-- a brush-filled gully his back --
G-AHHH!
-- and before him and to the right, his longsword wove a bloody web of death that none could break through.
But they were many, and he was one.
And surely, for all his pantherish speed and power, he would have fallen swiftly. Surely -- but --

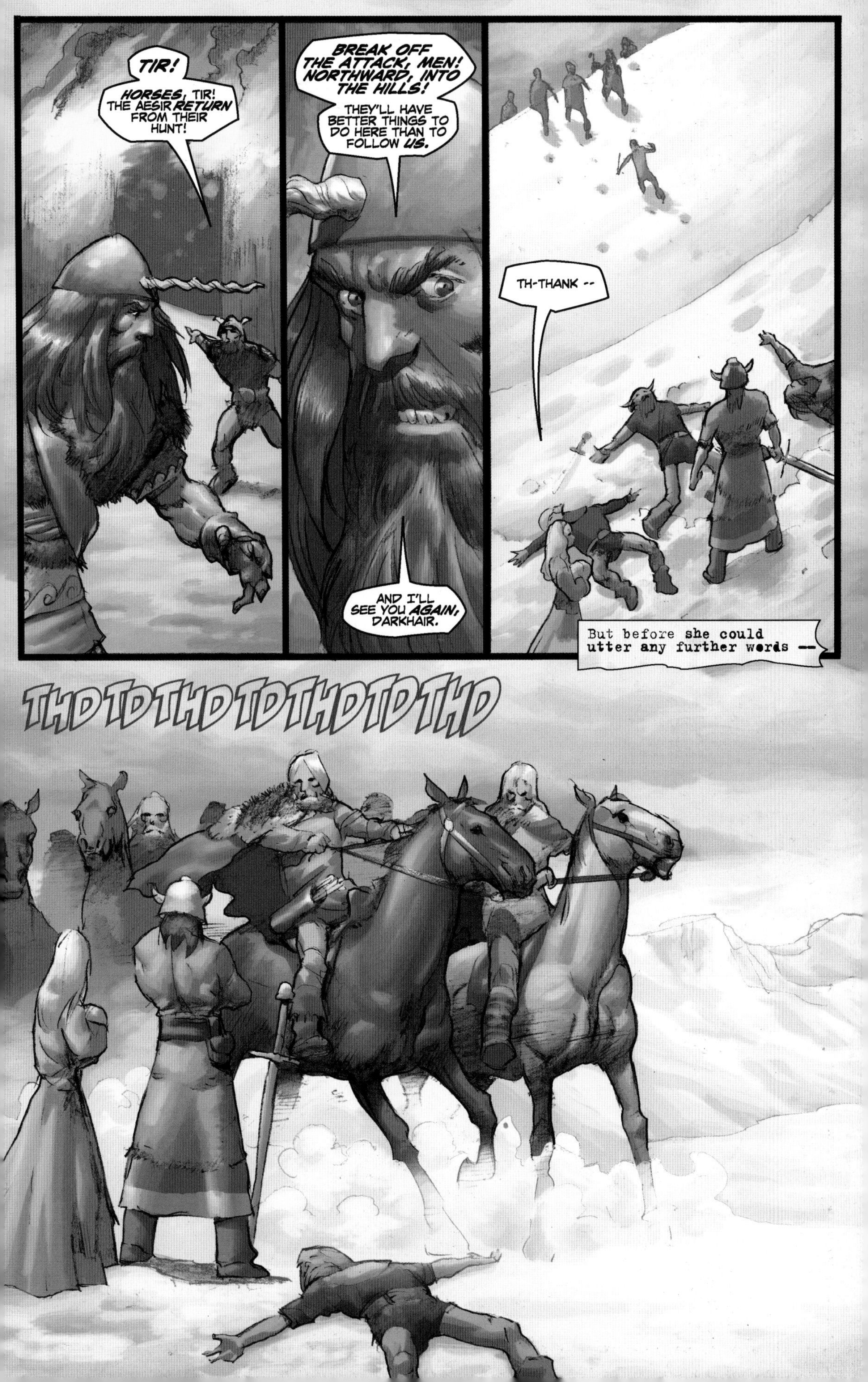
TIR!
HORSES, TIR! THE AESIR RETURN FROM THEIR HUNT!
BREAK OFF THE ATTACK, MEN! NORTHWARD, INTO THE HILLS!
THEY'LL HAVE BETTER THINGS TO DO HERE THAN TO FOLLOW US.
AND I'LL SEE YOU AGAIN, DARKHAIR.
TH-THANK --
But before she could utter any further words --
THDTDTHDTDTHDTDTHD

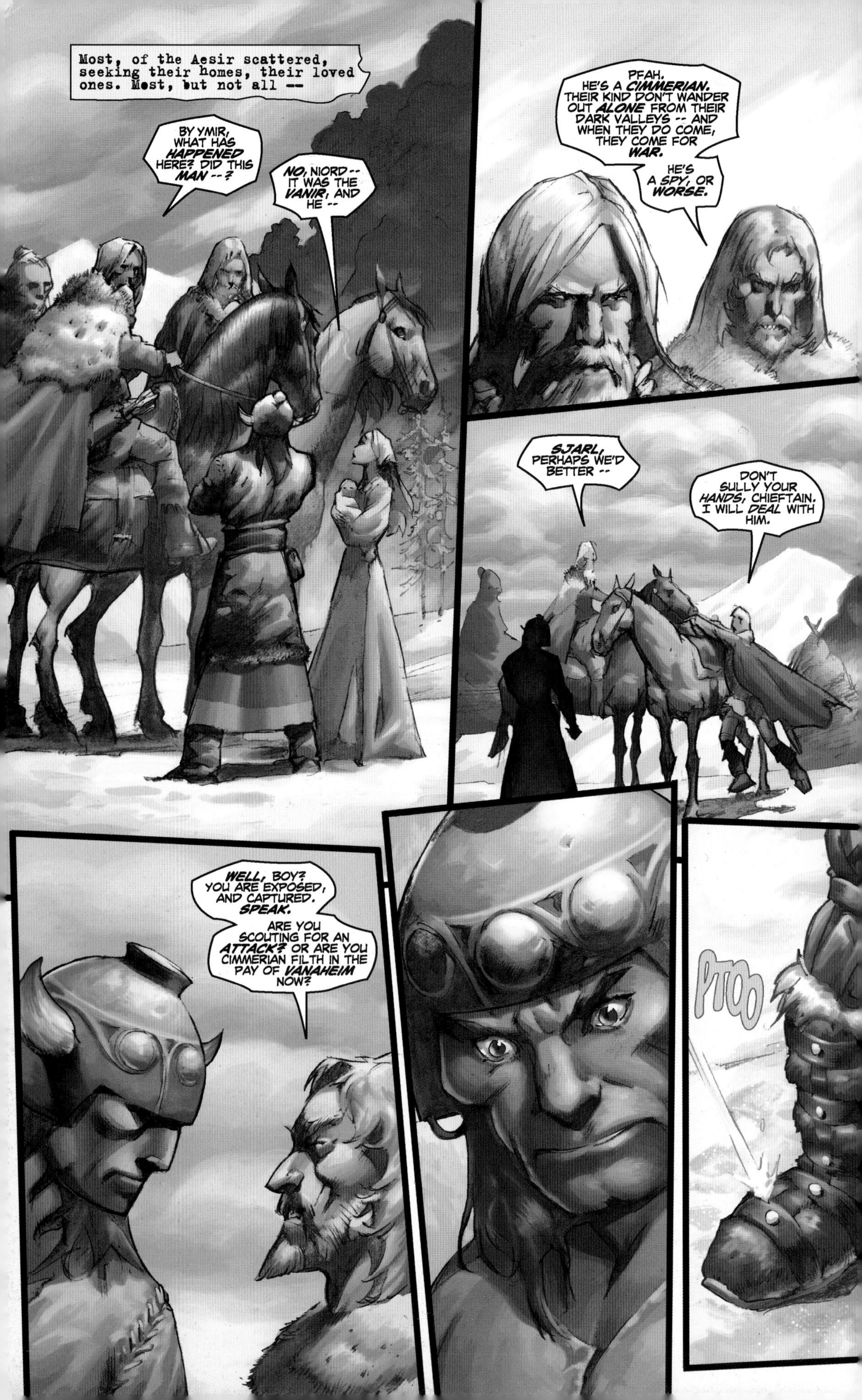
Most, of the Aesir scattered, seeking their homes, their loved ones. Most, but not all --
BY YMIR, WHAT HAS HAPPENED HERE? DID THIS MAN -- ?
NO, NIORD -- IT WAS THE VANIR, AND HE --
PFAH. HE'S A CIMMERIAN. THEIR KIND DON'T WANDER OUT ALONE FROM THEIR DARK VALLEYS -- AND WHEN THEY DO COME, THEY COME FOR WAR.
HE'S A SPY, OR WORSE.
SJARL, PERHAPS WE'D BETTER --
DON'T SULLY YOUR HANDS, CHIEFTAIN. I WILL DEAL WITH HIM.
WELL, BOY? YOU ARE EXPOSED, AND CAPTURED. SPEAK.
ARE YOU SCOUTING FOR AN ATTACK? OR ARE YOU CIMMERIAN FILTH IN THE PAY OF VANAHEIM NOW?
PTOO

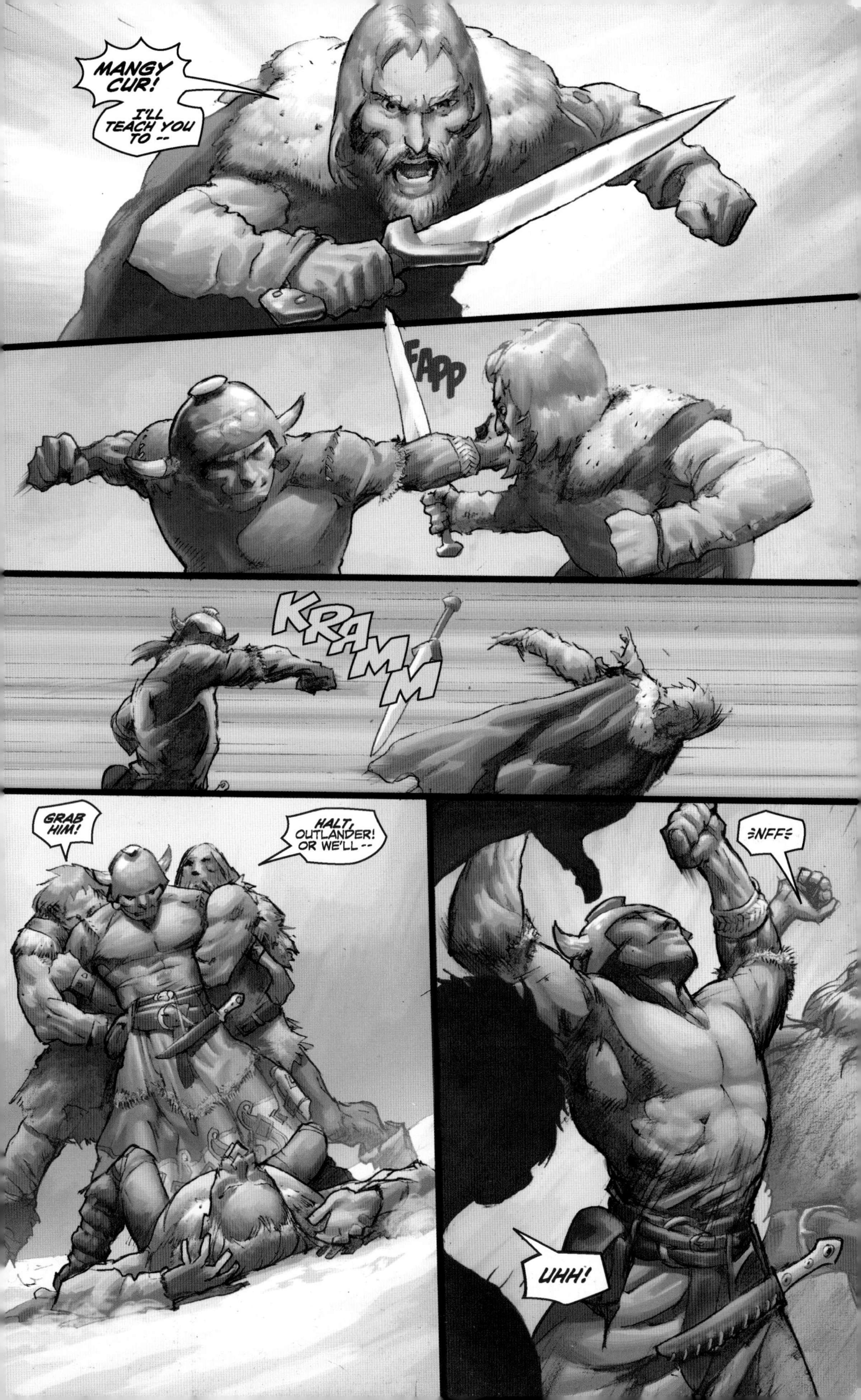
MANGY CUR!
I'LL TEACH YOU TO --
FAPP
KRAMM
GRAB HIM!
HALT, OUTLANDER! OR WE'LL --
NFF
UHH!

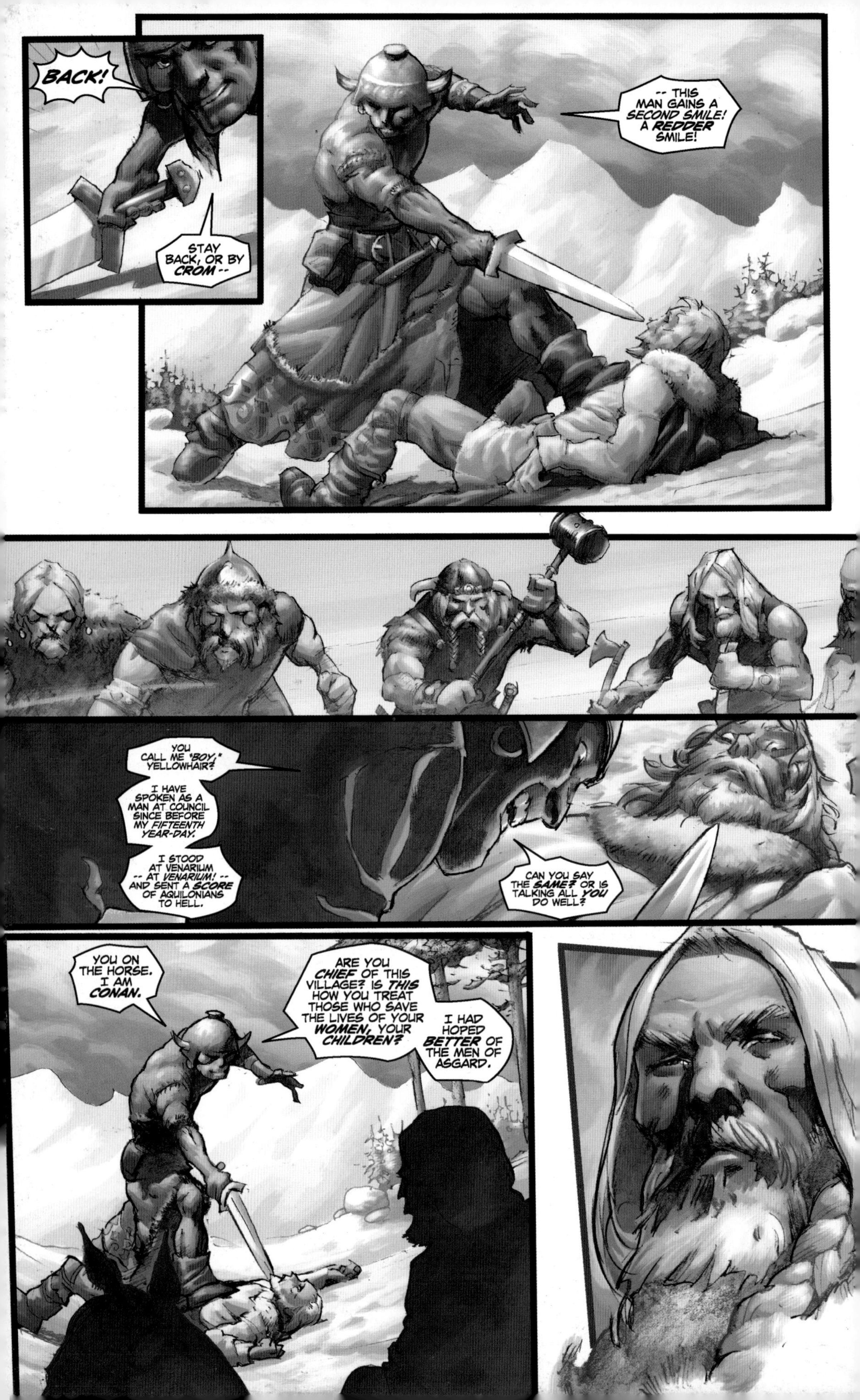
BACK!
STAY BACK, OR BY CROM --
-- THIS MAN GAINS A SECOND SMILE! A REDDER SMILE!
YOU CALL ME "BOY," YELLOWHAIR?
I HAVE SPOKEN AS A MAN AT COUNCIL SINCE BEFORE MY FIFTEENTH YEAR-DAY.
I STOOD AT VENARIUM -- AT VENARIUM! -- AND SENT A SCORE OF AQUILONIANS TO HELL.
CAN YOU SAY THE SAME? OR IS TALKING ALL YOU DO WELL?
YOU ON THE HORSE. I AM CONAN.
ARE YOU CHIEF OF THIS VILLAGE? IS THIS HOW YOU TREAT THOSE WHO SAVE THE LIVES OF YOUR WOMEN, YOUR CHILDREN?
I HAD HOPED BETTER OF THE MEN OF ASGARD.

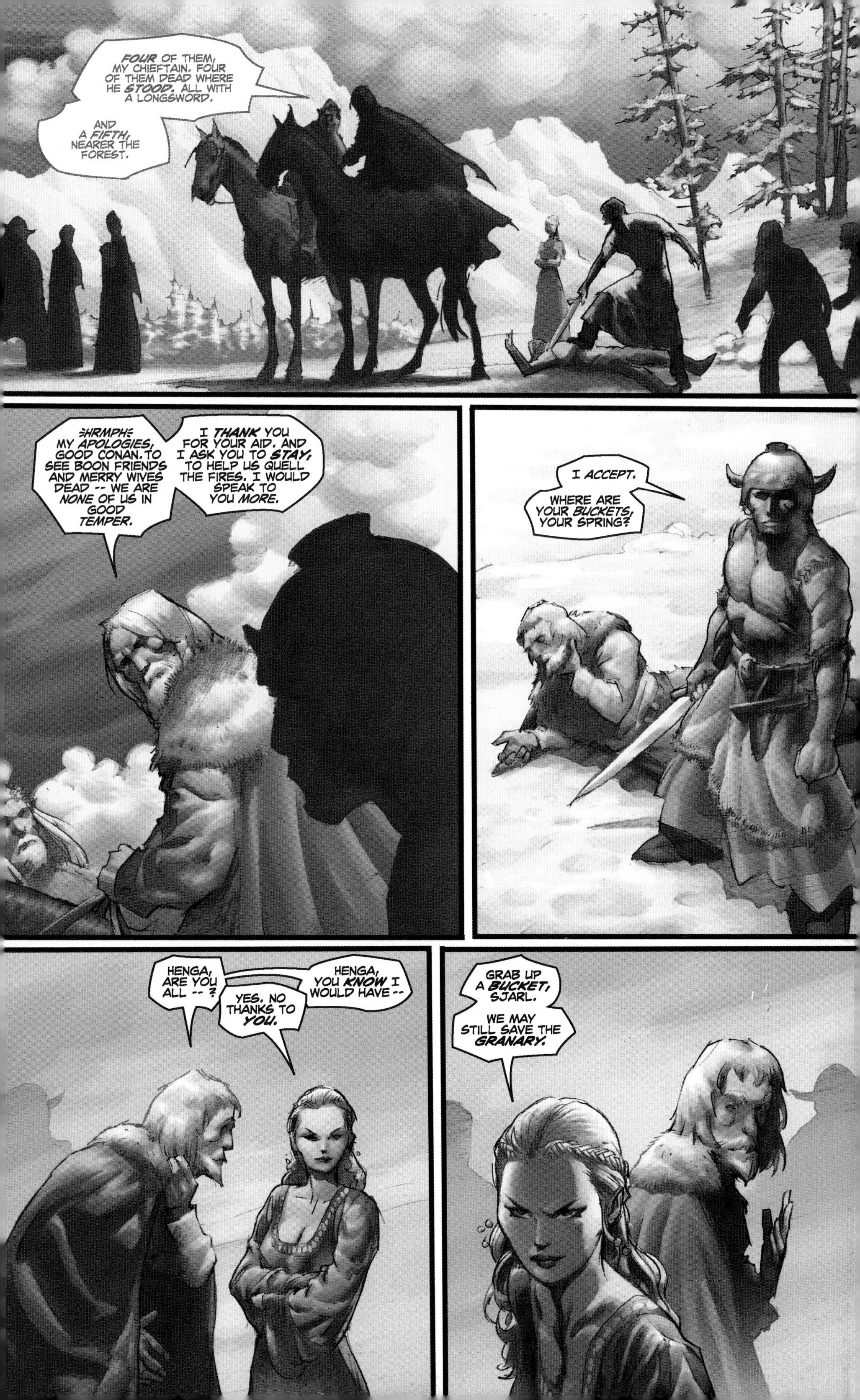
FOUR OF THEM, MY CHIEFTAIN. FOUR OF THEM DEAD WHERE HE STOOD. ALL WITH A LONGSWORD.
AND A FIFTH, NEARER THE FOREST.
HRMPH
MY APOLOGIES, GOOD CONAN. TO SEE BOON FRIENDS AND MERRY WIVES DEAD -- WE ARE NONE OF US IN GOOD TEMPER.
I THANK YOU FOR YOUR AID. AND I ASK YOU TO STAY, TO HELP US QUELL THE FIRES. I WOULD SPEAK TO YOU MORE.
I ACCEPT.
WHERE ARE YOUR BUCKETS, YOUR SPRING?
HENGA, ARE YOU ALL -- ?
YES. NO THANKS TO YOU.
HENGA, YOU KNOW I WOULD HAVE --
GRAB UP A BUCKET, SJARL.
WE MAY STILL SAVE THE GRANARY.

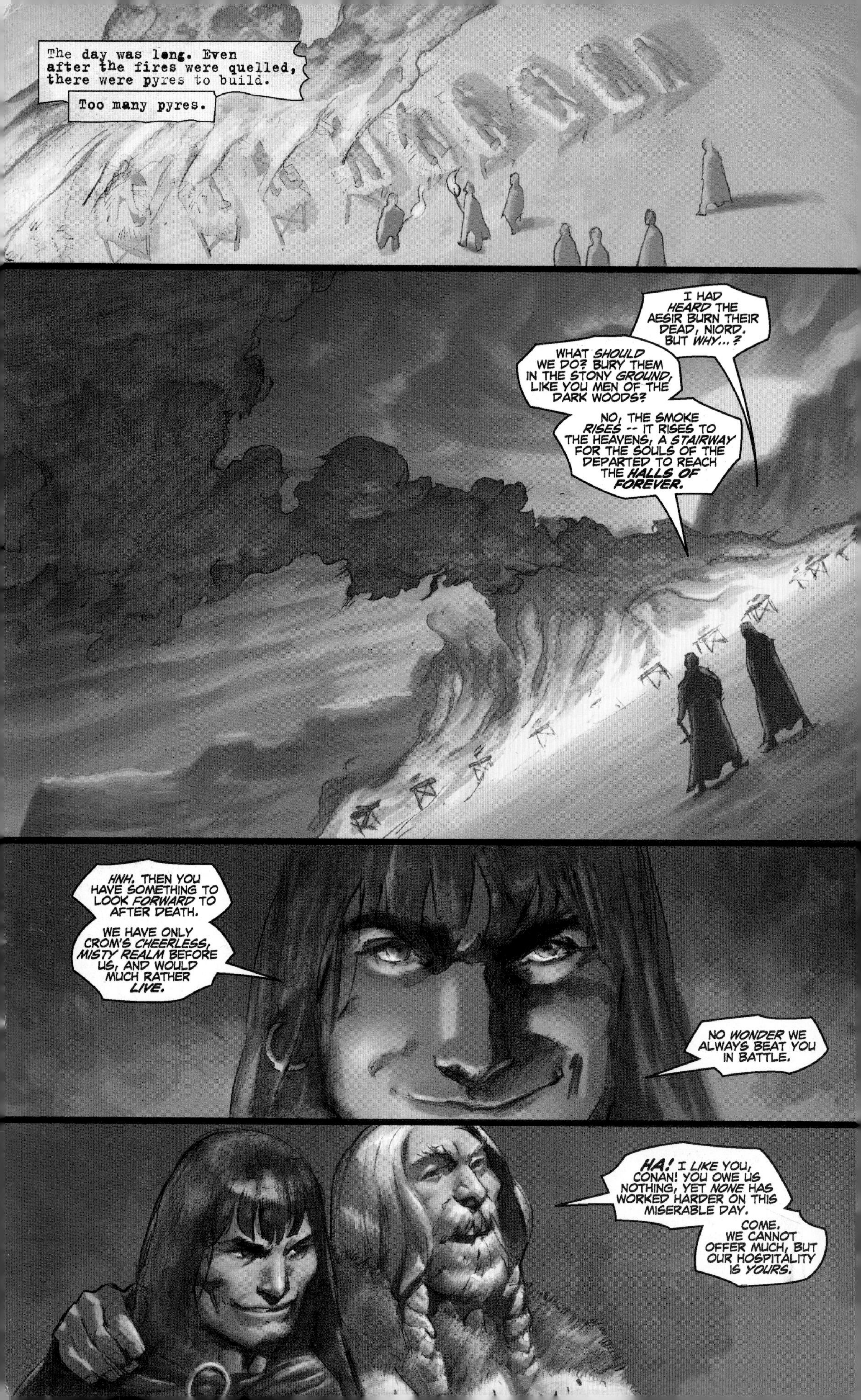

The day was long. Even after the fires were quelled, there were pyres to build.
Too many pyres.
I HAD HEARD THE AESIR BURN THEIR DEAD, NIORD. BUT WHY...?
WHAT SHOULD WE DO? BURY THEM IN THE STONY GROUND, LIKE YOU MEN OF THE DARK WOODS?
NO, THE SMOKE RISES -- IT RISES TO THE HEAVENS, A STAIRWAY FOR THE SOULS OF THE DEPARTED TO REACH THE HALLS OF FOREVER.
HNH. THEN YOU HAVE SOMETHING TO LOOK FORWARD TO AFTER DEATH.
WE HAVE ONLY CROM'S CHEERLESS, MISTY REALM BEFORE US, AND WOULD MUCH RATHER LIVE.
NO WONDER WE ALWAYS BEAT YOU IN BATTLE.
HA! I LIKE YOU, CONAN! YOU OWE US NOTHING, YET NONE HAS WORKED HARDER ON THIS MISERABLE DAY.
COME. WE CANNOT OFFER MUCH, BUT OUR HOSPITALITY IS YOURS.

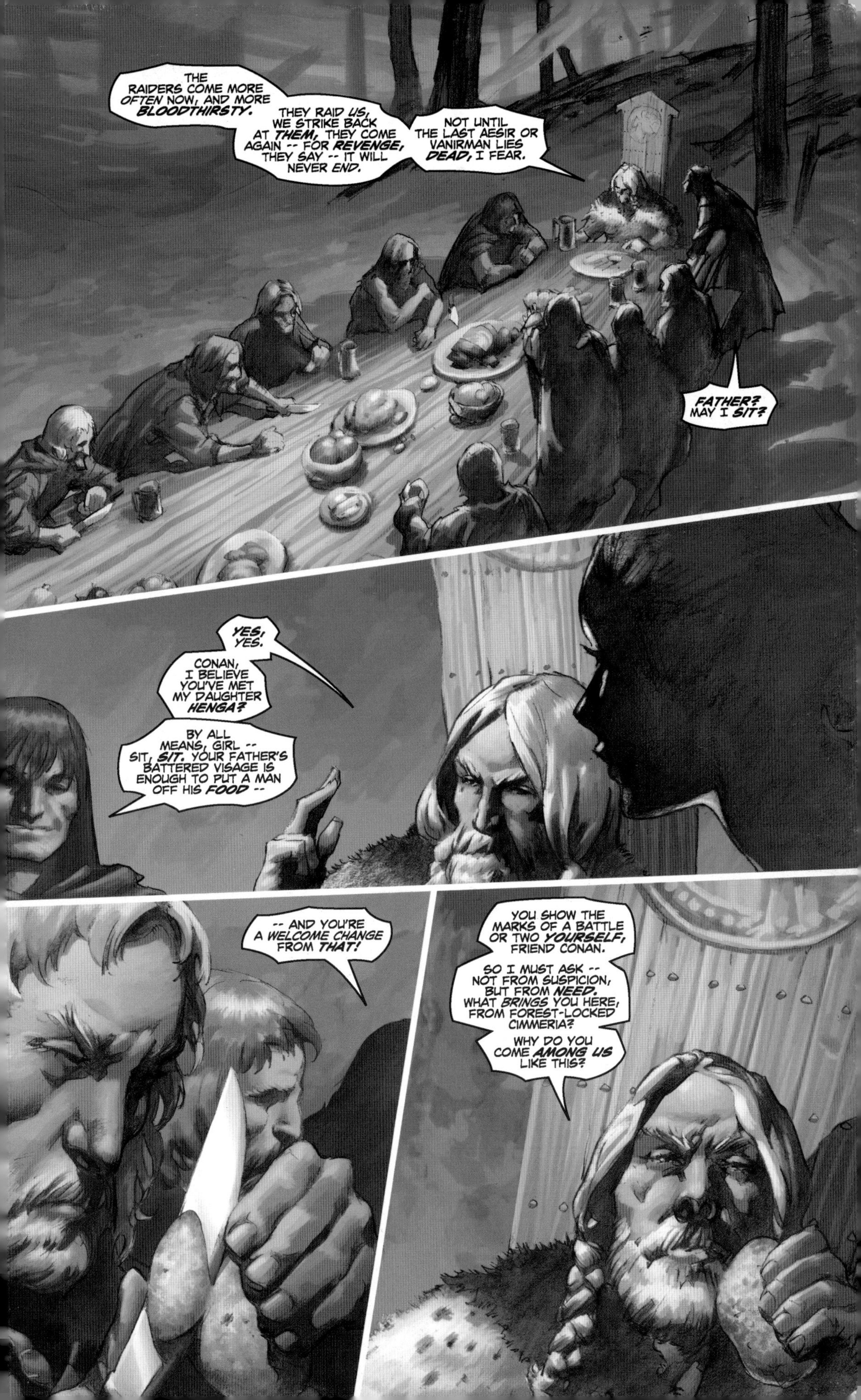
THE RAIDERS COME MORE OFTEN NOW, AND MORE BLOODTHIRSTY.
THEY RAID US, WE STRIKE BACK AT THEM, THEY COME AGAIN -- FOR REVENGE, THEY SAY -- IT WILL NEVER END.
NOT UNTIL THE LAST AESIR OR VANIRMAN LIES DEAD, I FEAR.
FATHER? MAY I SIT?
YES, YES.
CONAN, I BELIEVE YOU'VE MET MY DAUGHTER HENGA?
BY ALL MEANS, GIRL -- SIT, SIT. YOUR FATHER'S BATTERED VISAGE IS ENOUGH TO PUT A MAN OFF HIS FOOD --
-- AND YOU'RE A WELCOME CHANGE FROM THAT!
YOU SHOW THE MARKS OF A BATTLE OR TWO YOURSELF, FRIEND CONAN.
SO I MUST ASK -- NOT FROM SUSPICION, BUT FROM NEED. WHAT BRINGS YOU HERE, FROM FOREST-LOCKED CIMMERIA?
WHY DO YOU COME AMONG US LIKE THIS?

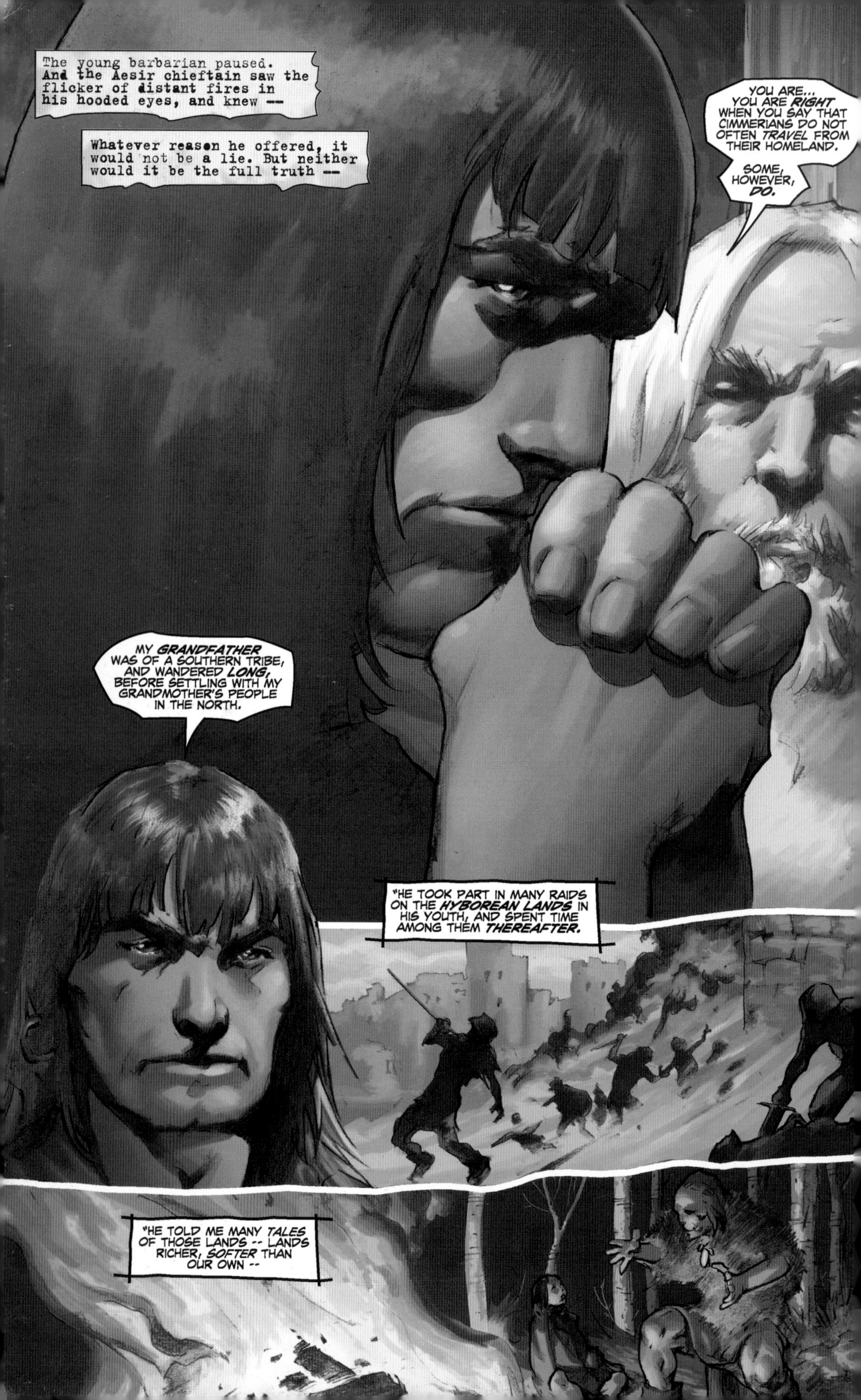
The young barbarian paused. And the Aesir chieftain saw the flicker of distant fires in his hooded eyes, and knew --
Whatever reason he offered, it would not be a lie. But neither would it be the full truth --
YOU ARE... YOU ARE RIGHT WHEN YOU SAY THAT CIMMERIANS DO NOT OFTEN TRAVEL FROM THEIR HOMELAND.
SOME, HOWEVER, DO.
MY GRANDFATHER WAS OF A SOUTHERN TRIBE, AND WANDERED LONG, BEFORE SETTLING WITH MY GRANDMOTHER'S PEOPLE IN THE NORTH.
"HE TOOK PART IN MANY RAIDS ON THE HYBOREAN LANDS IN HIS YOUTH, AND SPENT TIME AMONG THEM THEREAFTER.
"HE TOLD ME MANY TALES OF THOSE LANDS -- LANDS RICHER, SOFTER THAN OUR OWN --

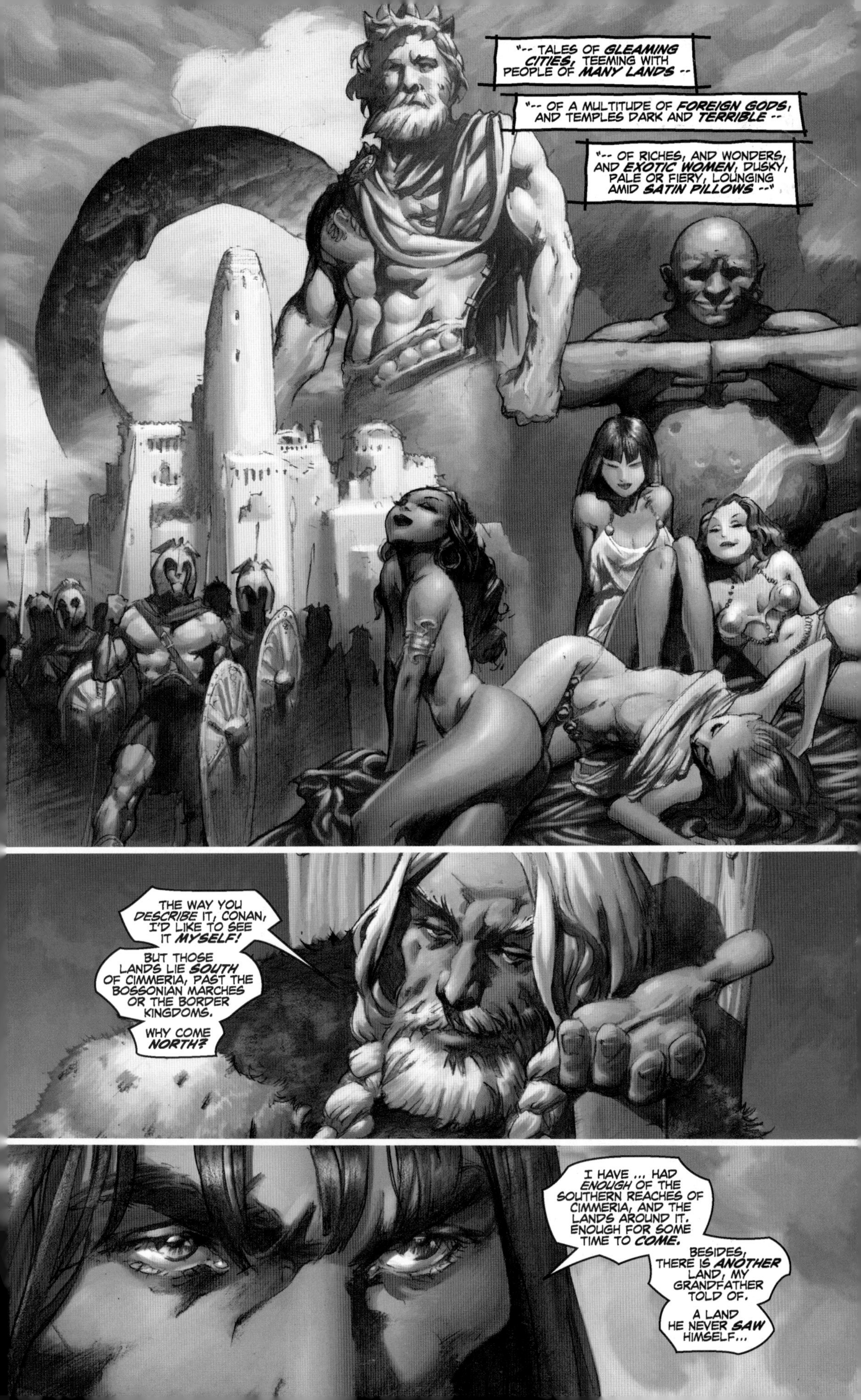
"-- TALES OF GLEAMING CITIES, TEEMING WITH PEOPLE OF MANY LANDS --
"-- OF A MULTITUDE OF FOREIGN GODS, AND TEMPLES DARK AND TERRIBLE --
"-- OF RICHES, AND WONDERS, AND EXOTIC WOMEN, DUSKY, PALE OR FIERY, LOUNGING AMID SATIN PILLOWS --"
THE WAY YOU DESCRIBE IT, CONAN, I'D LIKE TO SEE IT MYSELF!
BUT THOSE LANDS LIE SOUTH OF CIMMERIA, PAST THE BOSSONIAN MARCHES OR THE BORDER KINGDOMS.
WHY COME NORTH?
I HAVE ... HAD ENOUGH OF THE SOUTHERN REACHES OF CIMMERIA, AND THE LANDS AROUND IT. ENOUGH FOR SOME TIME TO COME.
BESIDES, THERE IS ANOTHER LAND, MY GRANDFATHER TOLD OF.
A LAND HE NEVER SAW HIMSELF...

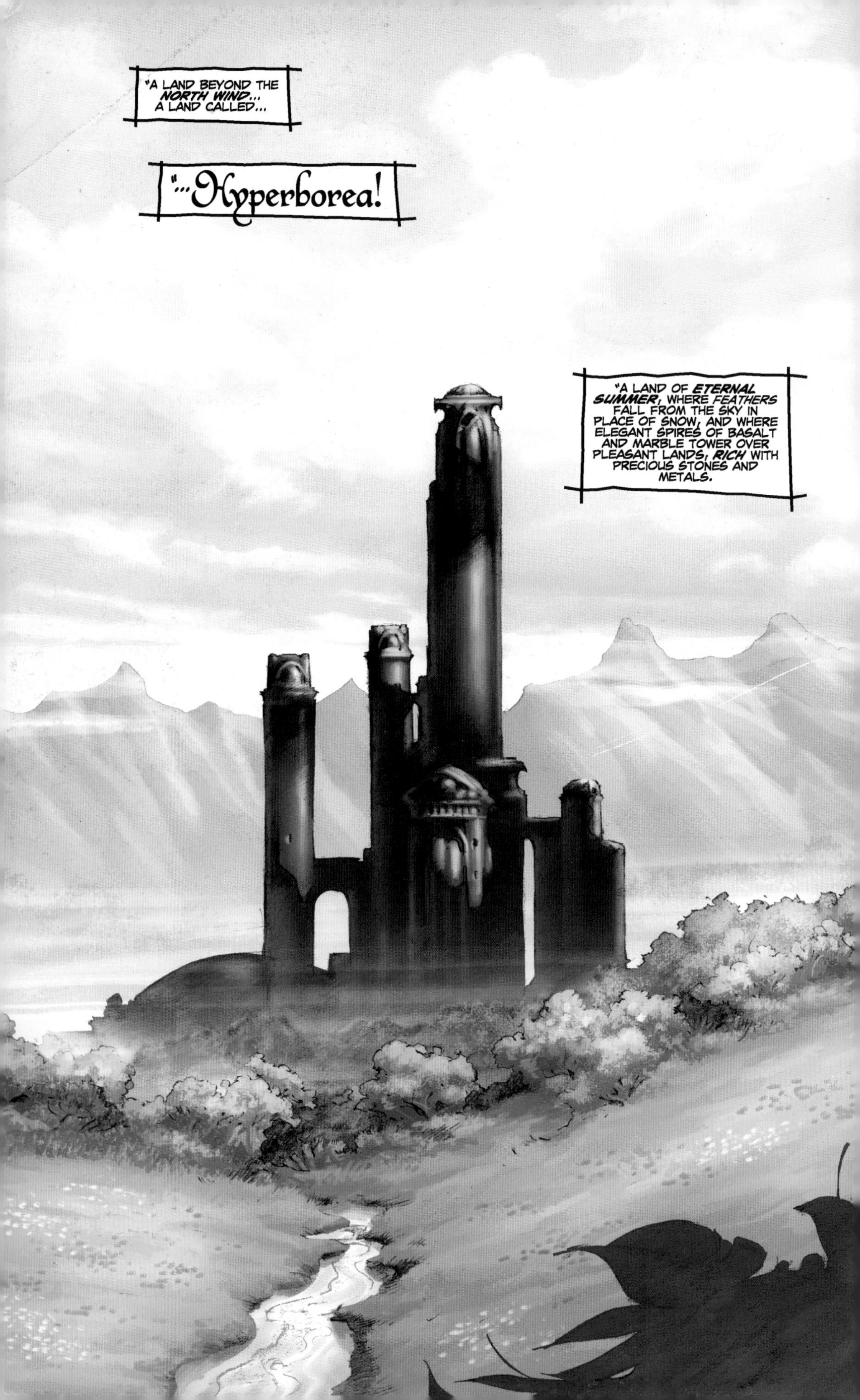
"A LAND BEYOND THE NORTH WIND... A LAND CALLED...
"...Hyperborea!
"A LAND OF ETERNAL SUMMER, WHERE FEATHERS FALL FROM THE SKY IN PLACE OF SNOW, AND WHERE ELEGANT SPIRES OF BASALT AND MARBLE TOWER OVER PLEASANT LANDS, RICH WITH PRECIOUS STONES AND METALS.

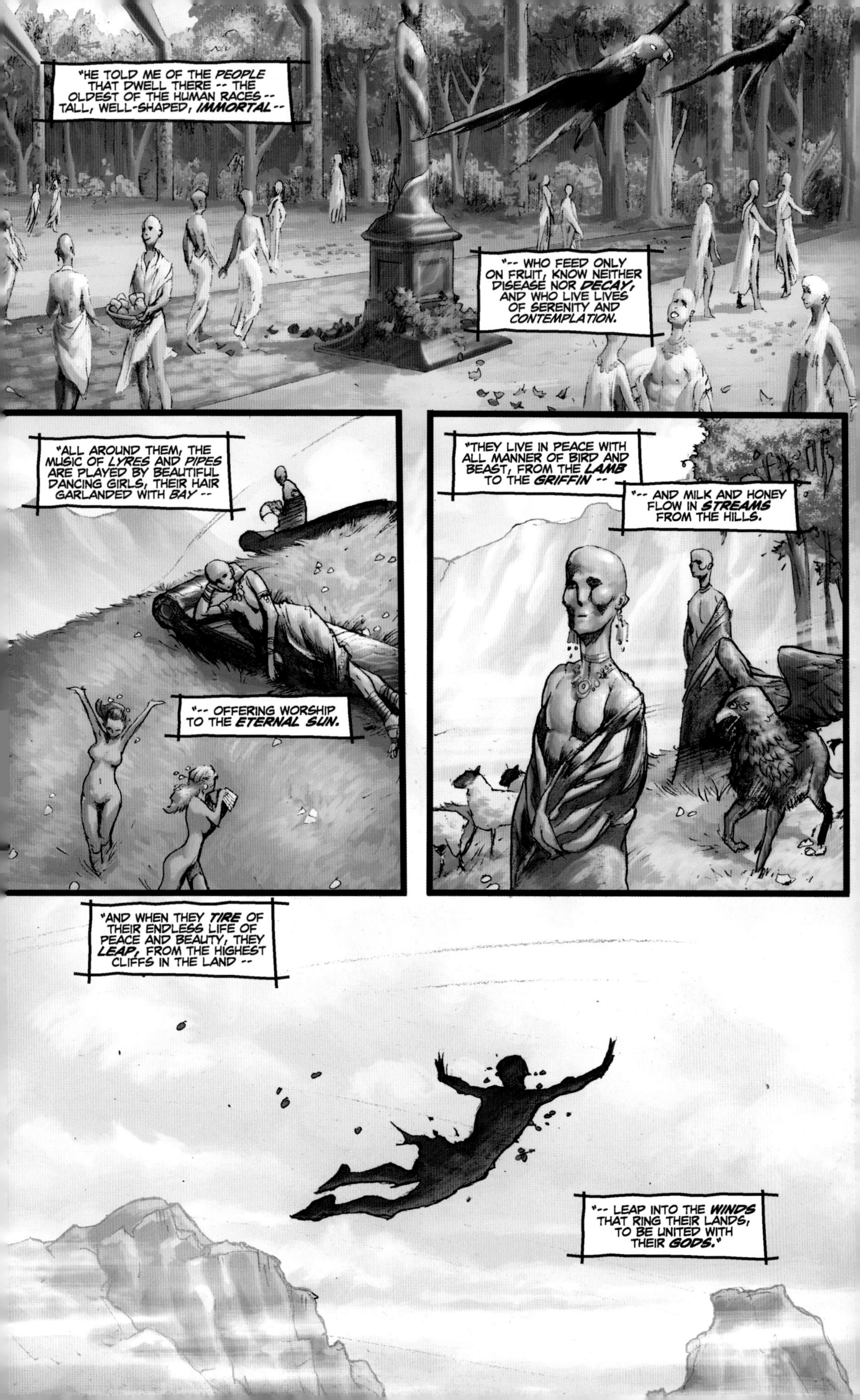
"HE TOLD ME OF THE PEOPLE THAT DWELL THERE -- THE OLDEST OF THE HUMAN RACES -- TALL, WELL-SHAPED, IMMORTAL --
"-- WHO FEED ONLY ON FRUIT, KNOW NEITHER DISEASE NOR DECAY, AND WHO LIVE LIVES OF SERENITY AND CONTEMPLATION.
"ALL AROUND THEM, THE MUSIC OF LYRES AND PIPES ARE PLAYED BY BEAUTIFUL DANCING GIRLS, THEIR HAIR GARLANDED WITH BAY --
"-- OFFERING WORSHIP TO THE ETERNAL SUN.
"THEY LIVE IN PEACE WITH ALL MANNER OF BIRD AND BEAST, FROM THE LAMB TO THE GRIFFIN --
"-- AND MILK AND HONEY FLOW IN STREAMS FROM THE HILLS.
"AND WHEN THEY TIRE OF THEIR ENDLESS LIFE OF PEACE AND BEAUTY, THEY LEAP, FROM THE HIGHEST CLIFFS IN THE LAND --
"-- LEAP INTO THE WINDS THAT RING THEIR LANDS, TO BE UNITED WITH THEIR GODS."

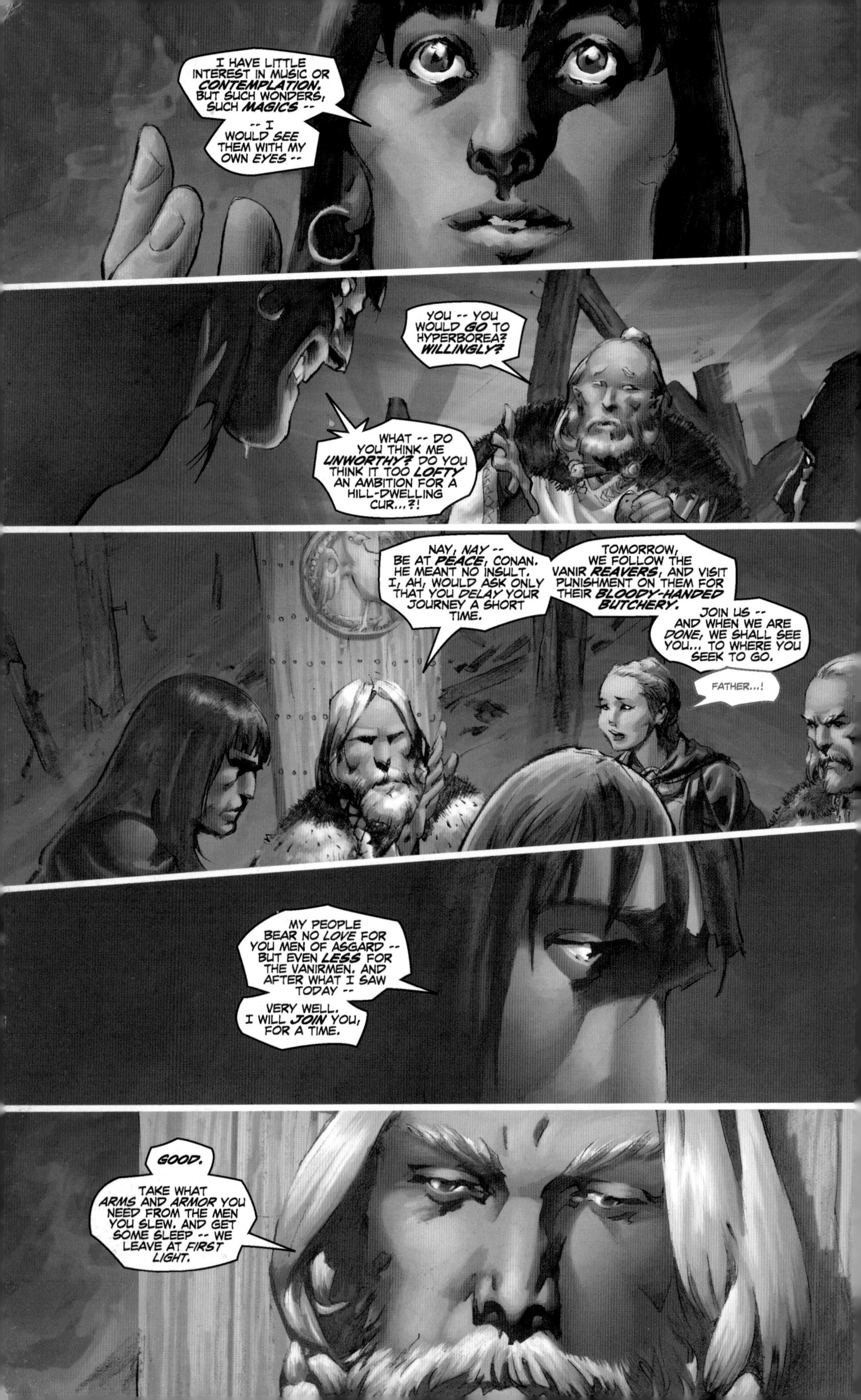
I HAVE LITTLE INTEREST IN MUSIC OR CONTEMPLATION. BUT SUCH WONDERS, SUCH MAGICS --
-- I WOULD SEE THEM WITH MY OWN EYES --
YOU -- YOU WOULD GO TO HYPERBOREA? WILLINGLY?
WHAT -- DO YOU THINK ME UNWORTHY? DO YOU THINK IT TOO LOFTY AN AMBITION FOR A HILL-DWELLING CUR...?!
NAY, NAY -- BE AT PEACE, CONAN. HE MEANT NO INSULT. I, AH, WOULD ASK ONLY THAT YOU DELAY YOUR JOURNEY A SHORT TIME.
TOMORROW, WE FOLLOW THE VANIR REAVERS, AND VISIT PUNISHMENT ON THEM FOR THEIR BLOODY-HANDED BUTCHERY.
JOIN US -- AND WHEN WE ARE DONE, WE SHALL SEE YOU... TO WHERE YOU SEEK TO GO.
FATHER...!
MY PEOPLE BEAR NO LOVE FOR YOU MEN OF ASGARD -- BUT EVEN LESS FOR THE VANIRMEN. AND AFTER WHAT I SAW TODAY --
VERY WELL. I WILL JOIN YOU, FOR A TIME.
GOOD.
TAKE WHAT ARMS AND ARMOR YOU NEED FROM THE MEN YOU SLEW. AND GET SOME SLEEP -- WE LEAVE AT FIRST LIGHT.

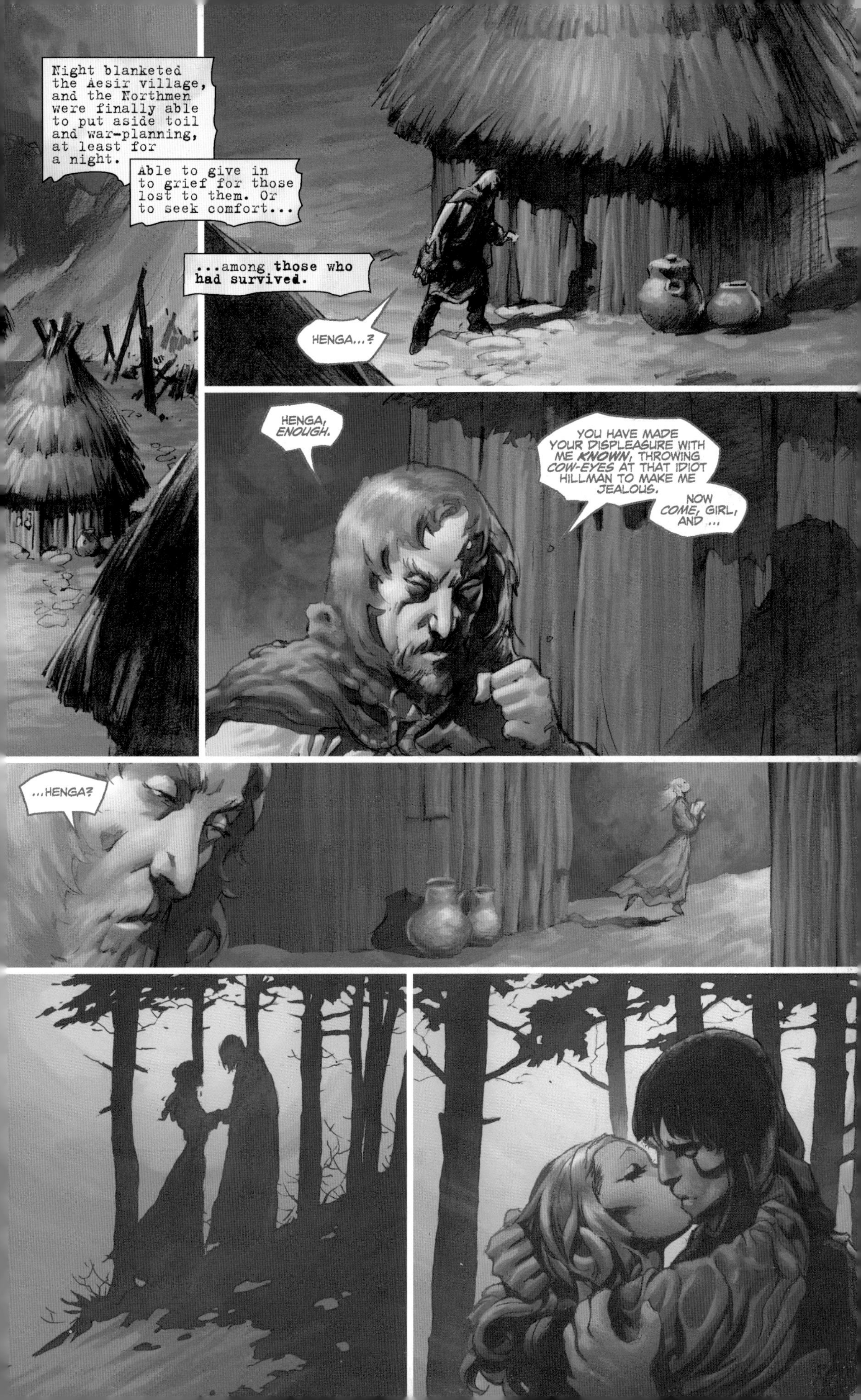
Night blanketed the Aesir village, and the Northmen were finally able to put aside toil and war-planning, at least for a night.
Able to give in to grief for those lost to them. Or to seek comfort...
...among those who had survived.
HENGA...?
HENGA, ENOUGH.
YOU HAVE MADE YOUR DISPLEASURE WITH ME KNOWN, THROWING COW-EYES AT THAT IDIOT HILLMAN TO MAKE ME JEALOUS.
NOW COME, GIRL, AND ...
...HENGA?

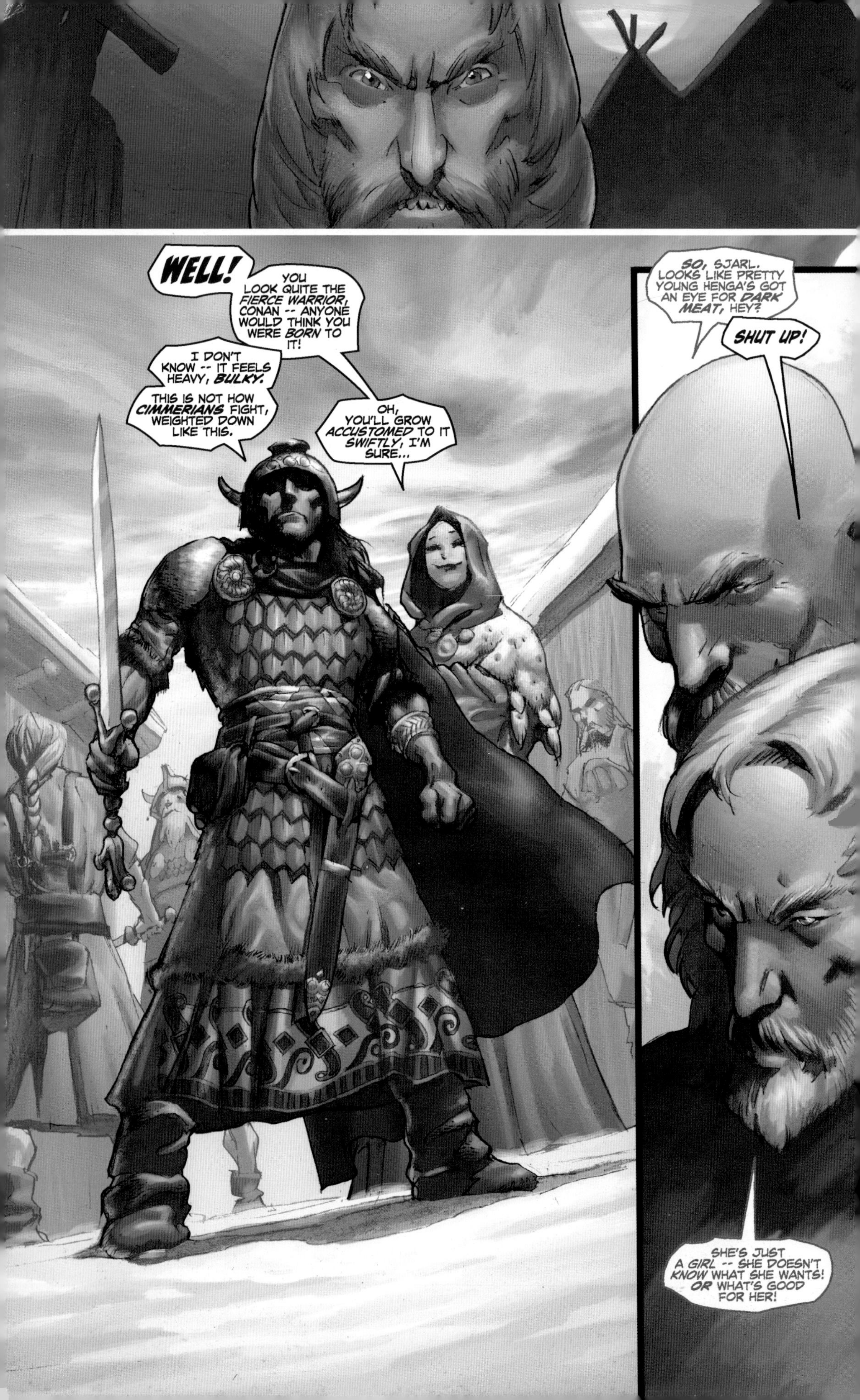
WELL!
YOU LOOK QUITE THE FIERCE WARRIOR, CONAN -- ANYONE WOULD THINK YOU WERE BORN TO IT!
I DON'T KNOW -- IT FEELS HEAVY, BULKY.
THIS IS NOT HOW CIMMERIANS FIGHT, WEIGHTED DOWN LIKE THIS.
OH, YOU'LL GROW ACCUSTOMED TO IT SWIFTLY, I'M SURE...
SO, SJARL. LOOKS LIKE PRETTY YOUNG HENGA'S GOT AN EYE FOR DARK MEAT, HEY?
SHUT UP!
SHE'S JUST A GIRL -- SHE DOESN'T KNOW WHAT SHE WANTS! OR WHAT'S GOOD FOR HER!

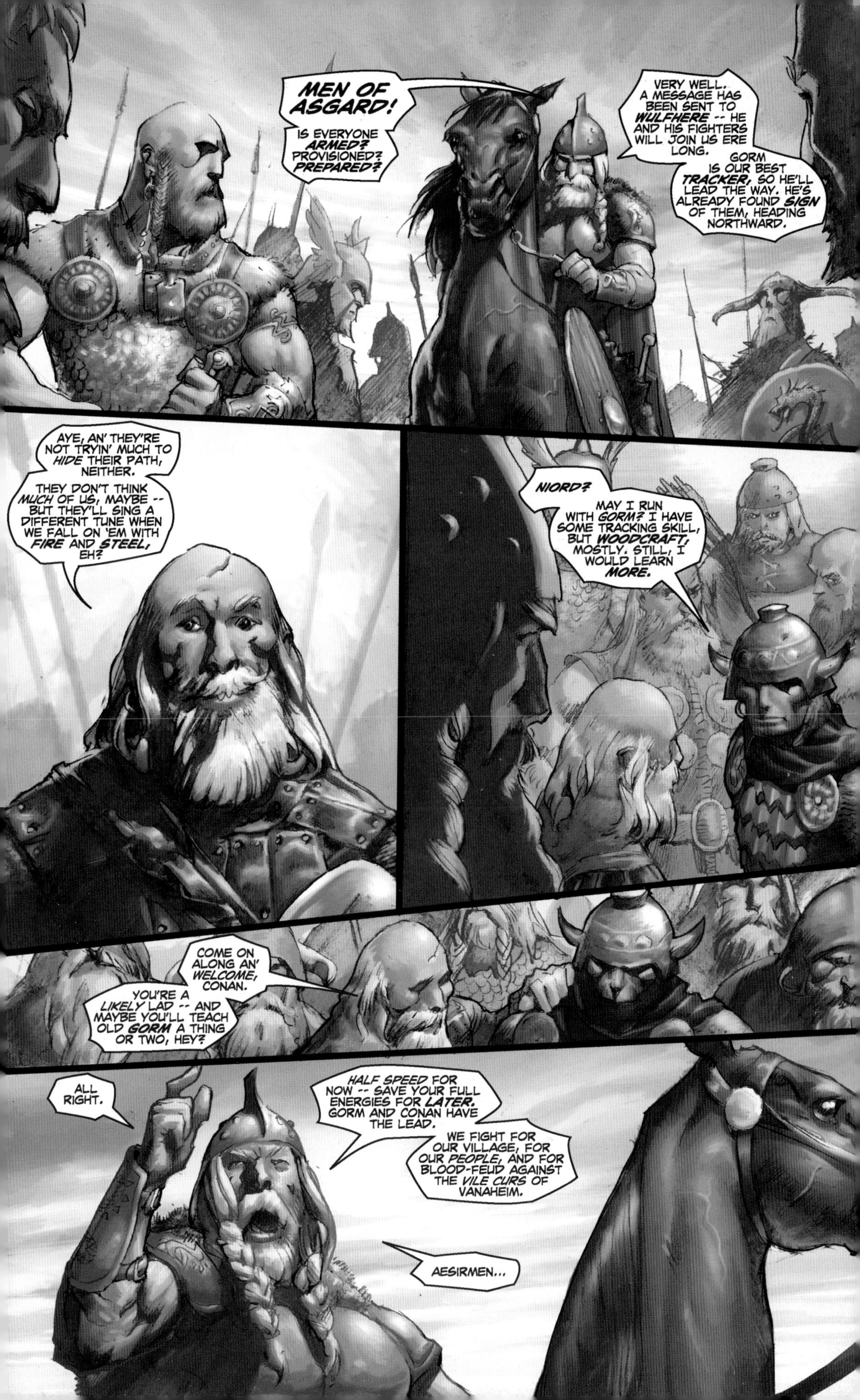
MEN OF ASGARD!
IS EVERYONE ARMED? PROVISIONED? PREPARED?
VERY WELL. A MESSAGE HAS BEEN SENT TO WULFHERE -- HE AND HIS FIGHTERS WILL JOIN US ERE LONG.
GORM IS OUR BEST TRACKER, SO HE'LL LEAD THE WAY. HE'S ALREADY FOUND SIGN OF THEM, HEADING NORTHWARD.
AYE, AN' THEY'RE NOT TRYIN' MUCH TO HIDE THEIR PATH, NEITHER.
THEY DON'T THINK MUCH OF US, MAYBE -- BUT THEY'LL SING A DIFFERENT TUNE WHEN WE FALL ON 'EM WITH FIRE AND STEEL, EH?
NIORD?
MAY I RUN WITH GORM? I HAVE SOME TRACKING SKILL, BUT WOODCRAFT, MOSTLY. STILL, I WOULD LEARN MORE.
COME ON ALONG AN' WELCOME, CONAN.
YOU'RE A LIKELY LAD -- AND MAYBE YOU'LL TEACH OLD GORM A THING OR TWO, HEY?
ALL RIGHT.
HALF SPEED FOR NOW -- SAVE YOUR FULL ENERGIES FOR LATER. GORM AND CONAN HAVE THE LEAD.
WE FIGHT FOR OUR VILLAGE, FOR OUR PEOPLE, AND FOR BLOOD-FEUD AGAINST THE VILE CURS OF VANAHEIM.
AESIRMEN...

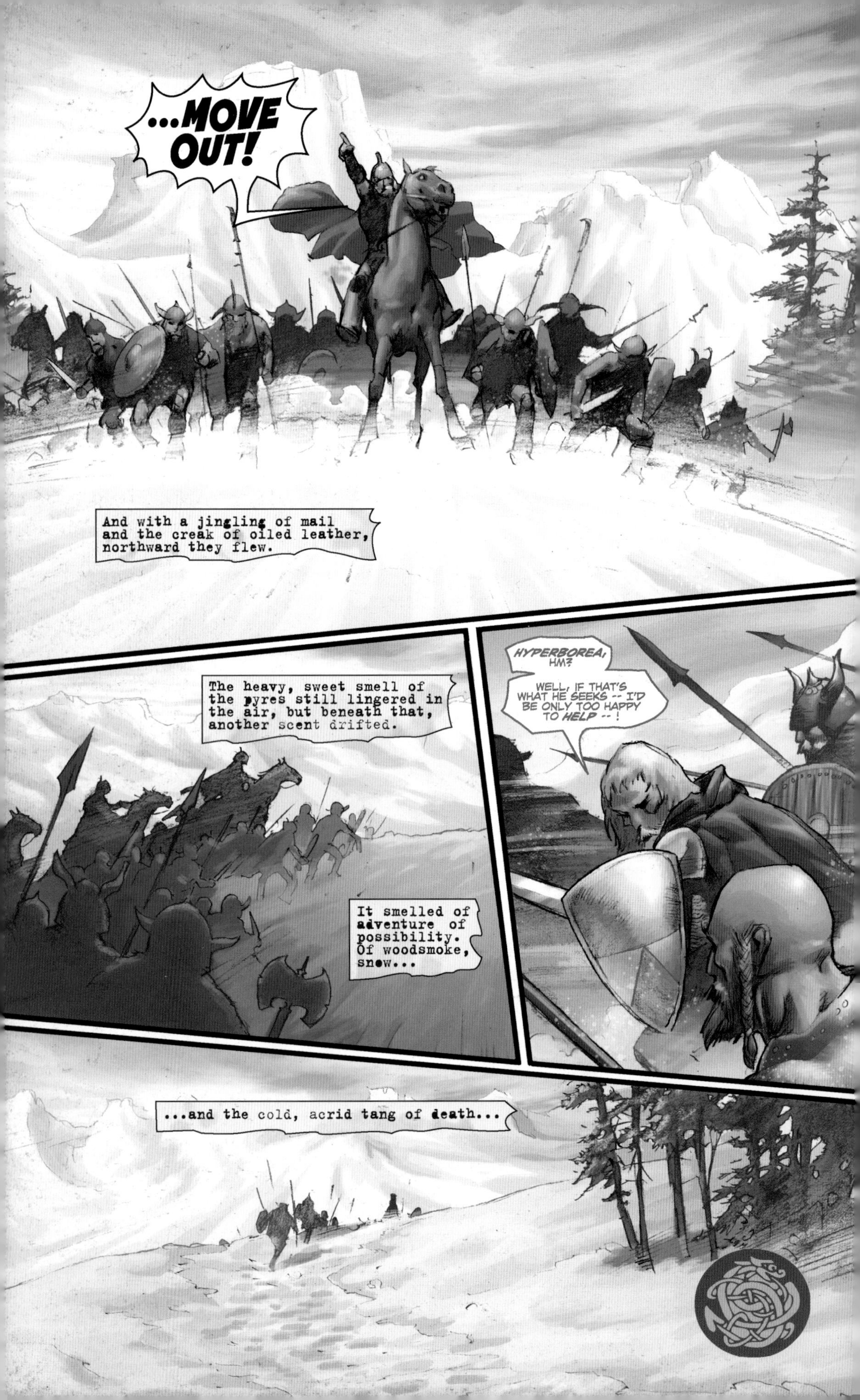
...MOVE OUT!
And with a jingling of mail and the creak of oiled leather, northward they flew.
The heavy, sweet smell of the pyres still lingered in the air, but beneath that, another scent drifted.
It smelled of adventure of possibility. Of woodsmoke, snow...
HYPERBOREA, HM?
WELL, IF THAT'S WHAT HE SEEKS -- I'D BE ONLY TOO HAPPY TO HELP -- !
...and the cold, acrid tang of death...

CHAPTER TWO

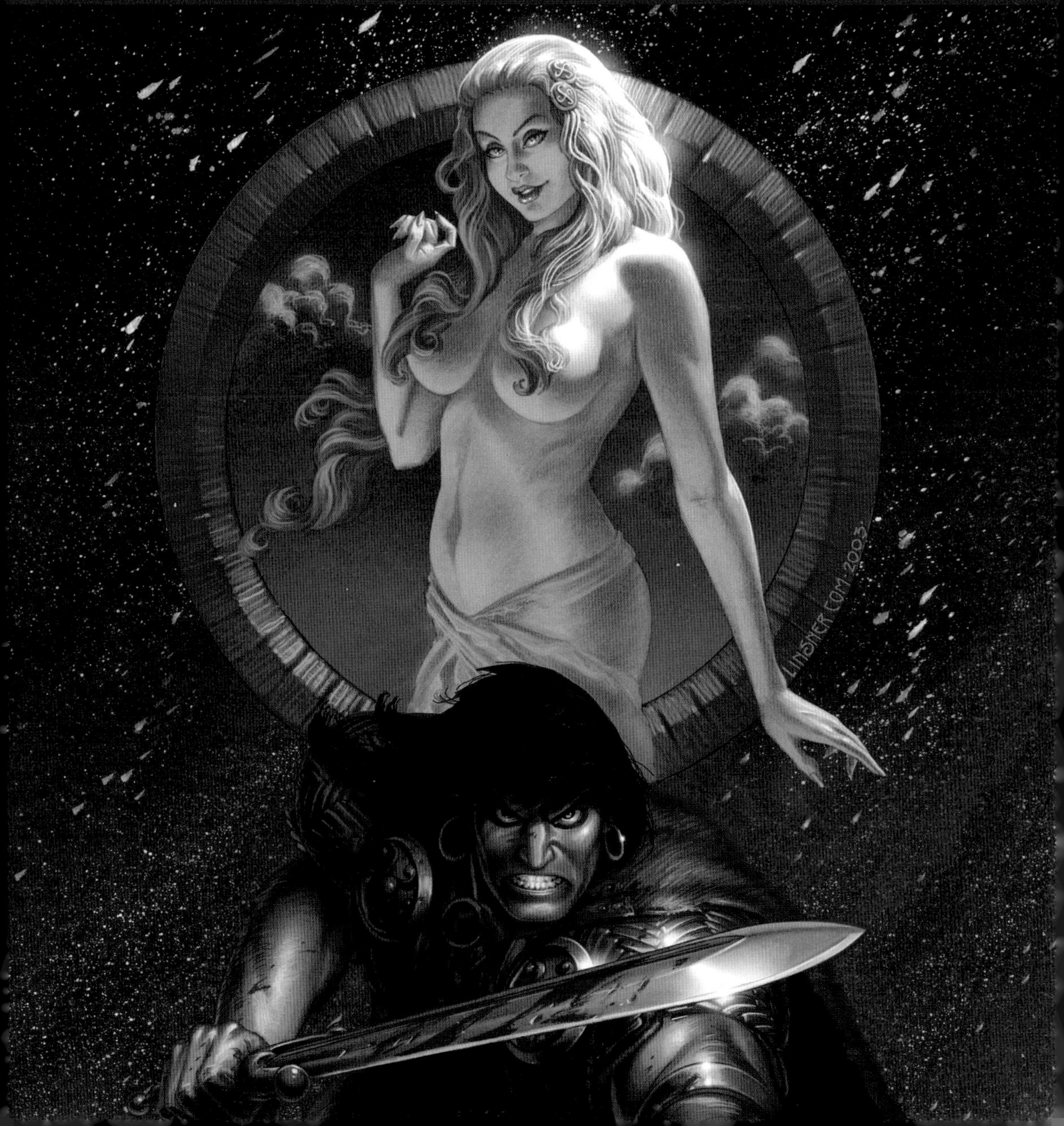
LINDNER.COM·2003

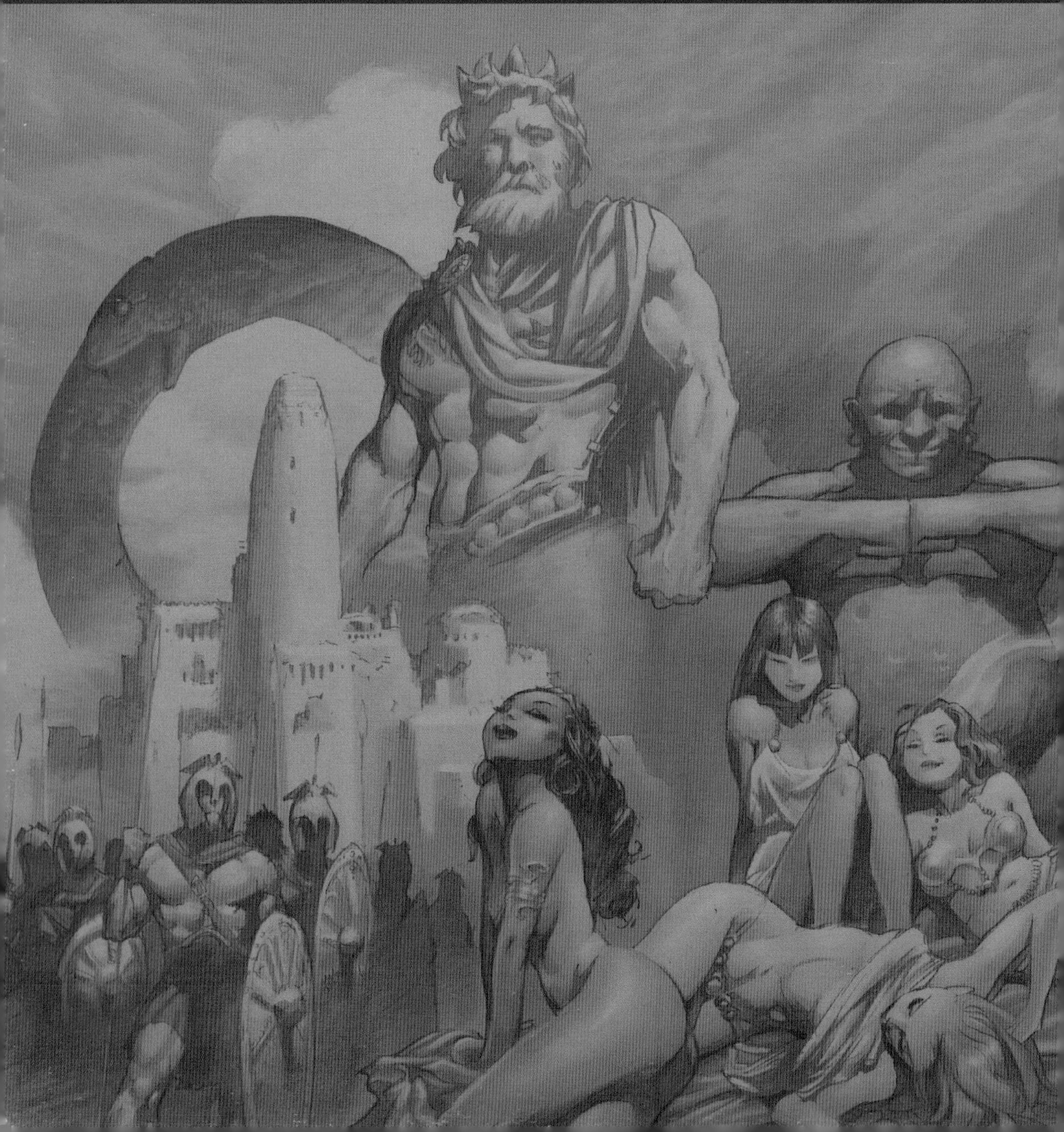

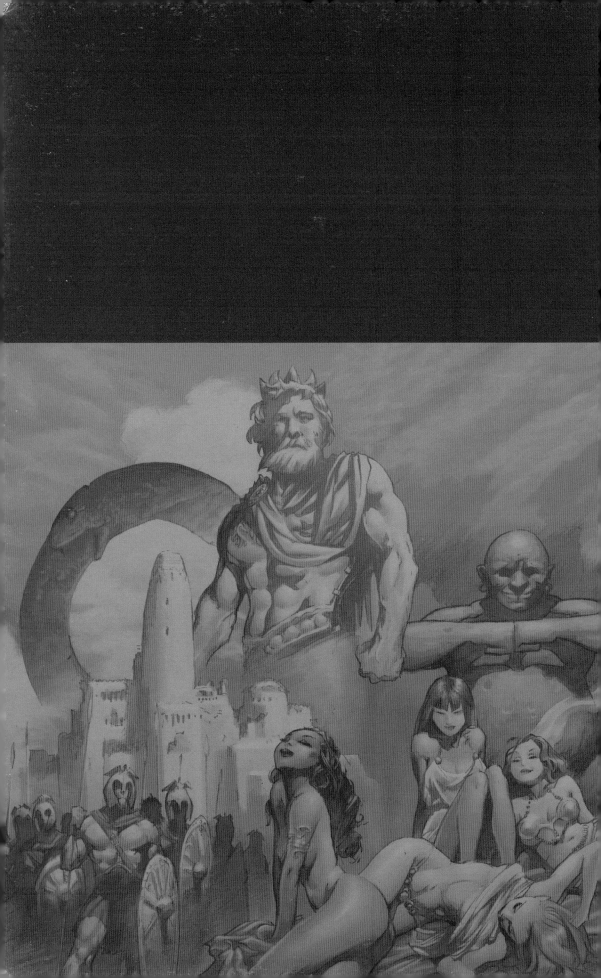

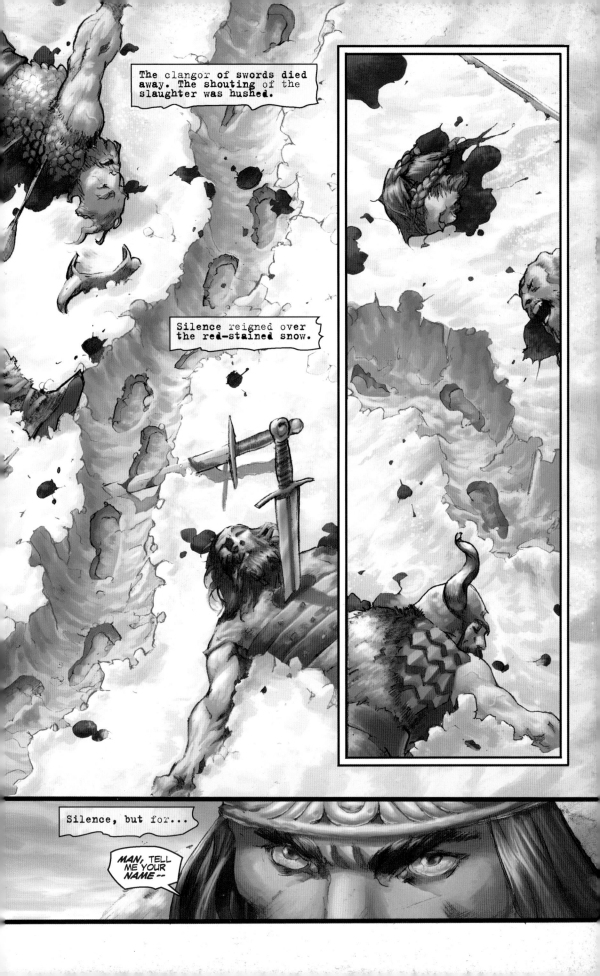

The clangor of swords died away. The shouting of the slaughter was hushed.

Silence reigned over the red-stained snow.

Silence, but for...

MAN, TELL ME YOUR NAME --

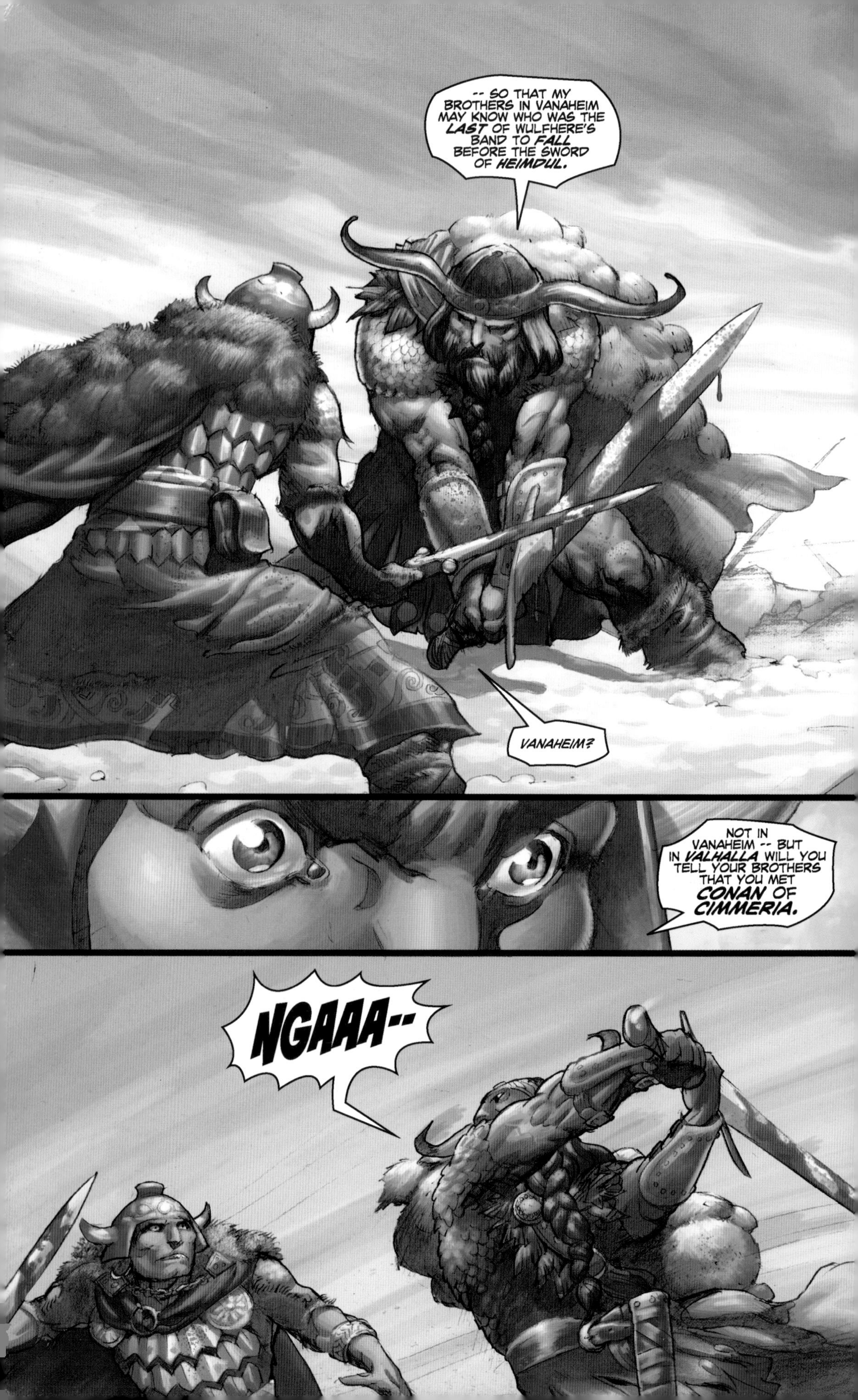
-- SO THAT MY BROTHERS IN VANAHEIM MAY KNOW WHO WAS THE LAST OF WULFHERE'S BAND TO FALL BEFORE THE SWORD OF HEIMDUL.
VANAHEIM?
NOT IN VANAHEIM -- BUT IN VALHALLA WILL YOU TELL YOUR BROTHERS THAT YOU MET CONAN OF CIMMERIA.
NGAAA--

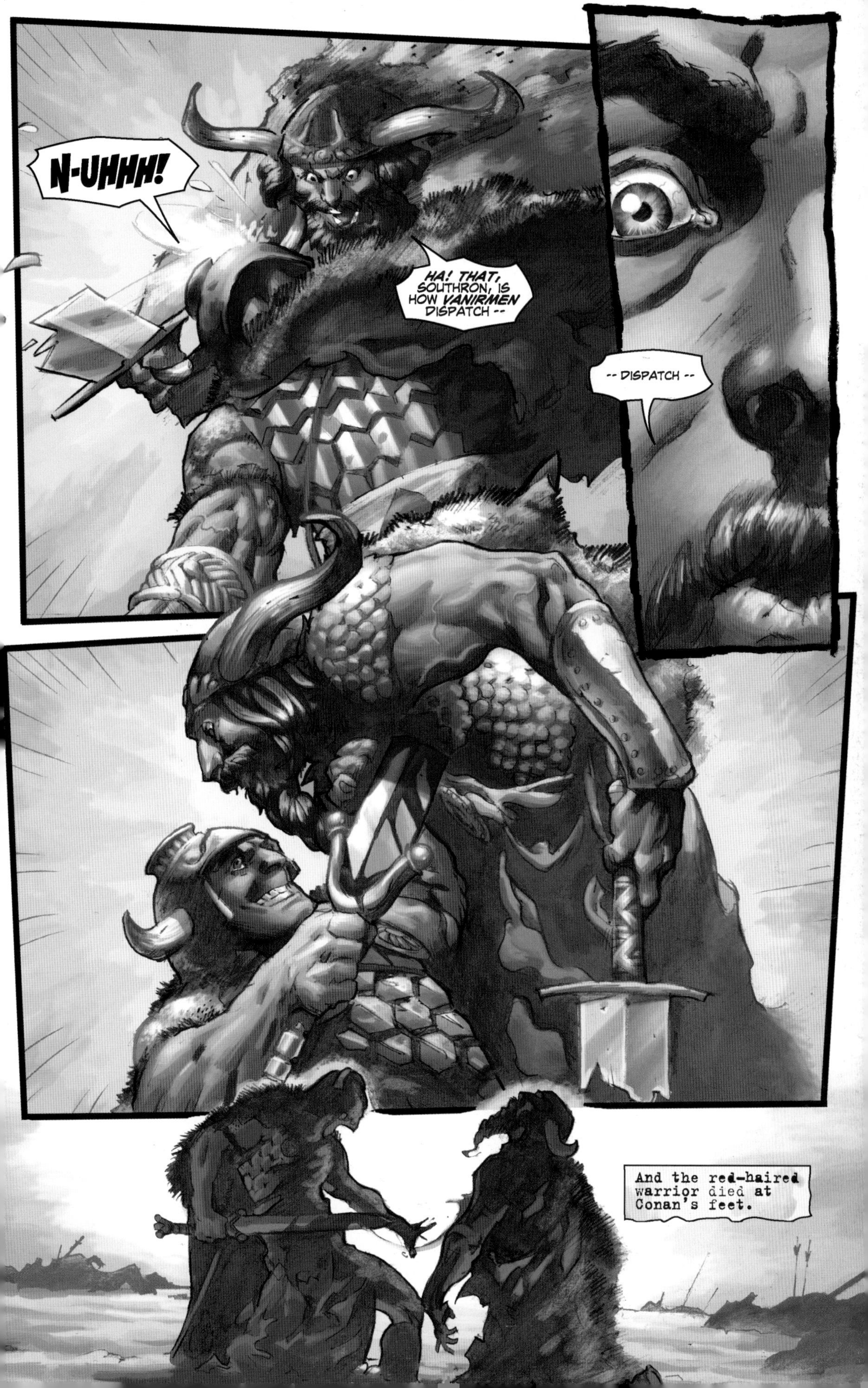
N-UHHH!
HA! THAT, SOUTHRON, IS HOW VANIRMEN DISPATCH --
-- DISPATCH --
And the red-haired warrior died at Conan's feet.

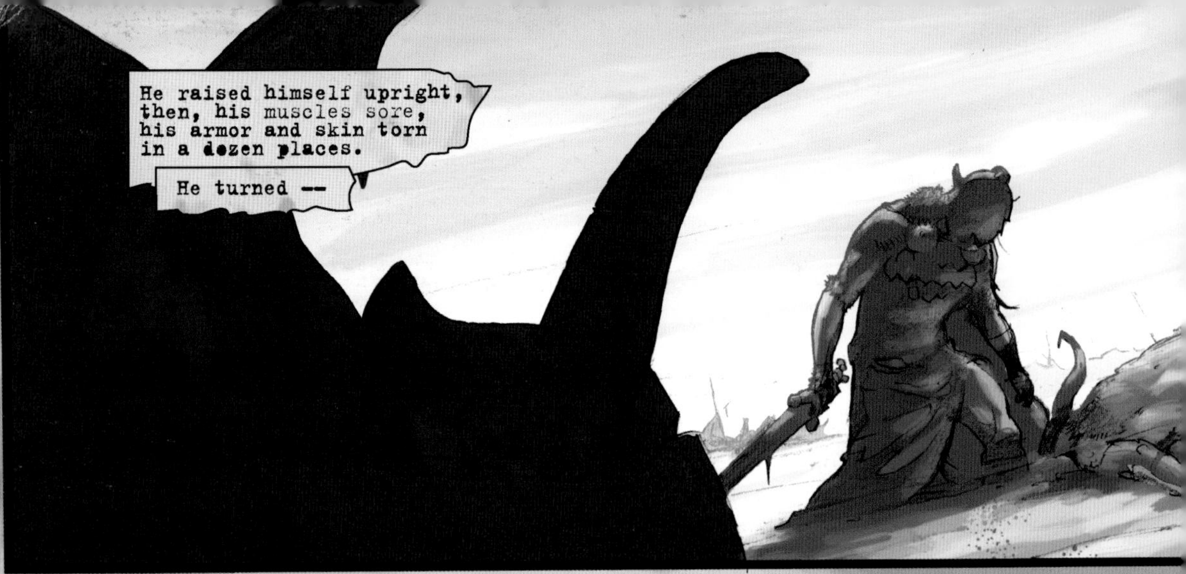
He raised himself upright, then, his muscles sore, his armor and skin torn in a dozen places.
He turned --

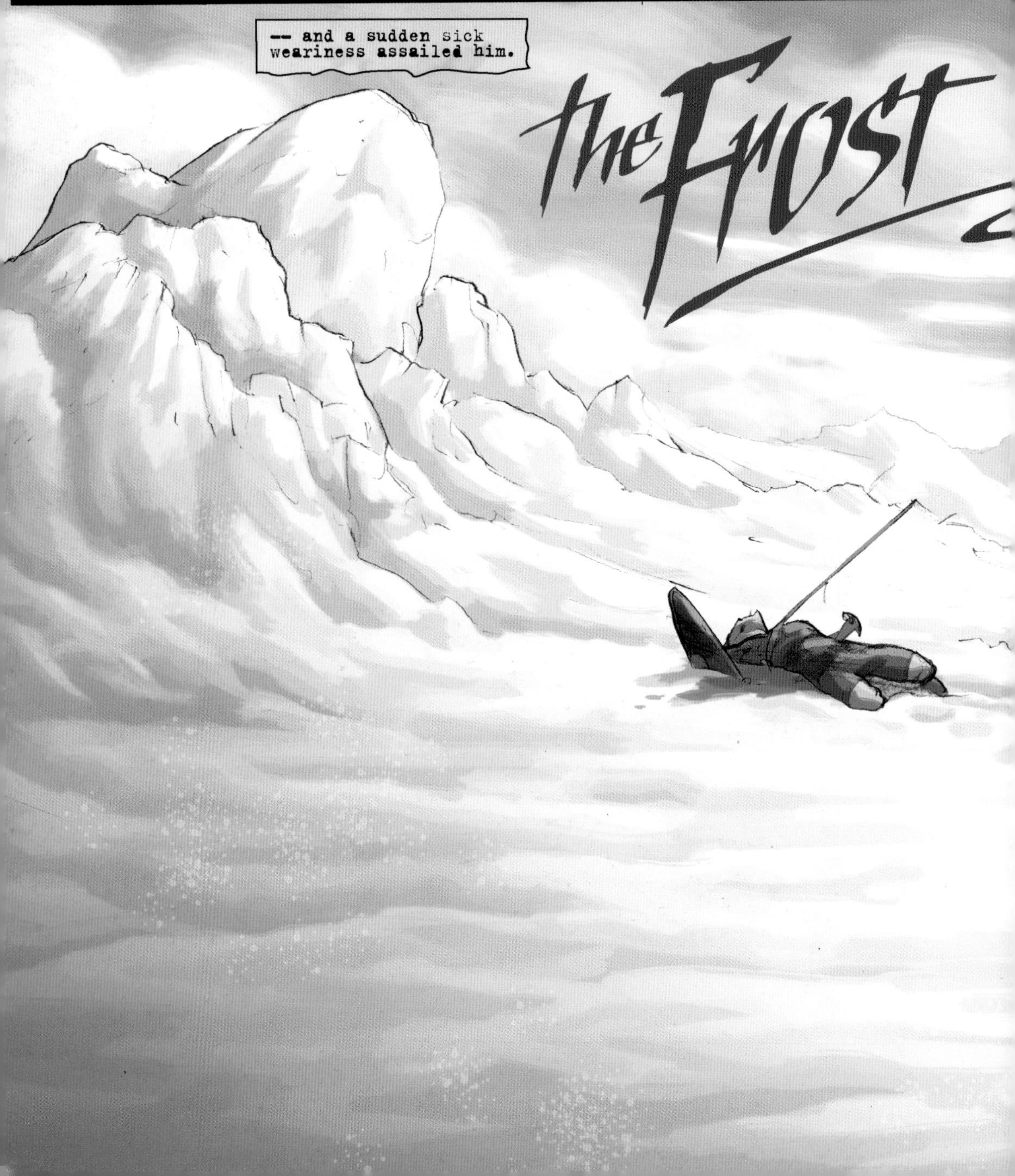
-- and a sudden sick weariness assailed him.
the Frost

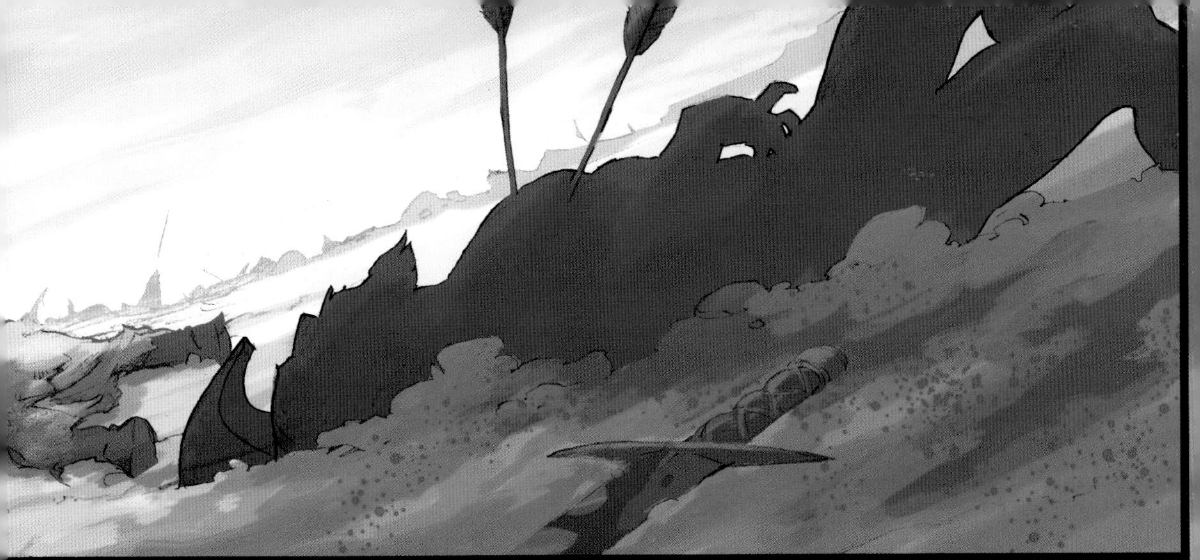

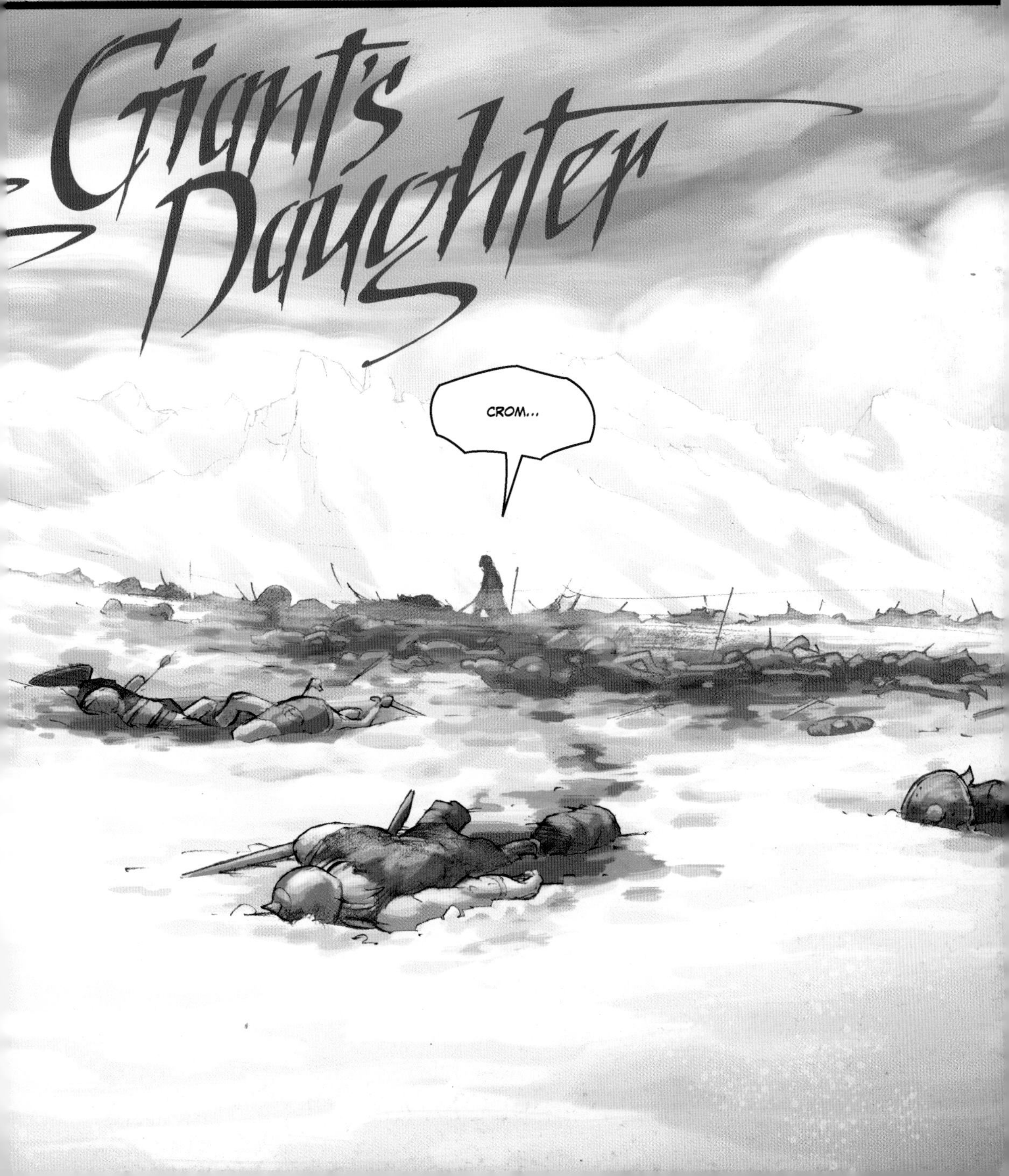
Giant's Daughter
CROM...

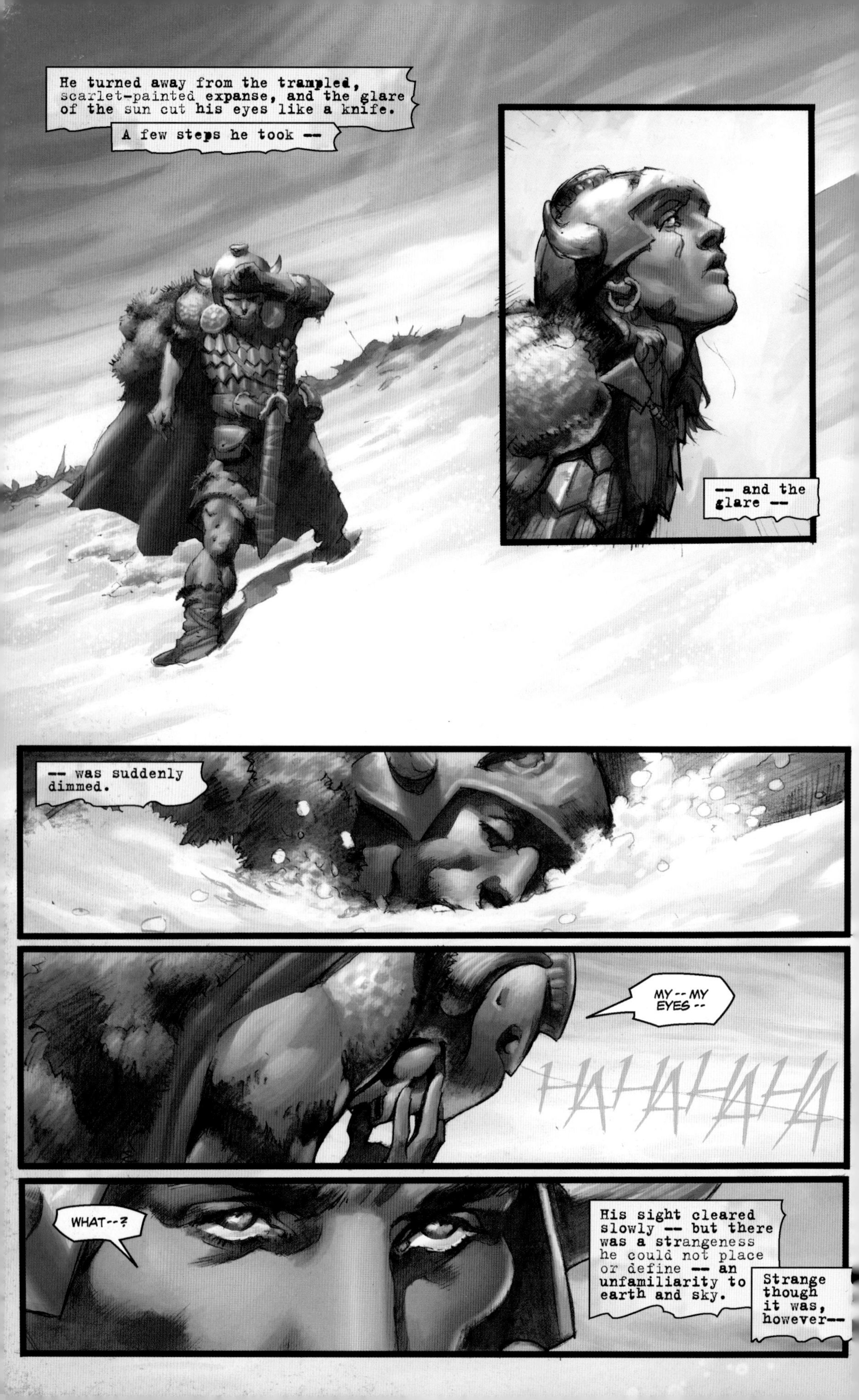
He turned away from the trampled, scarlet-painted expanse, and the glare of the sun cut his eyes like a knife.
A few steps he took --
-- and the glare --
-- was suddenly dimmed.
MY -- MY EYES --
HAHAHAHA
WHAT--?
His sight cleared slowly -- but there was a strangeness he could not place or define -- an unfamiliarity to earth and sky.
Strange though it was, however--

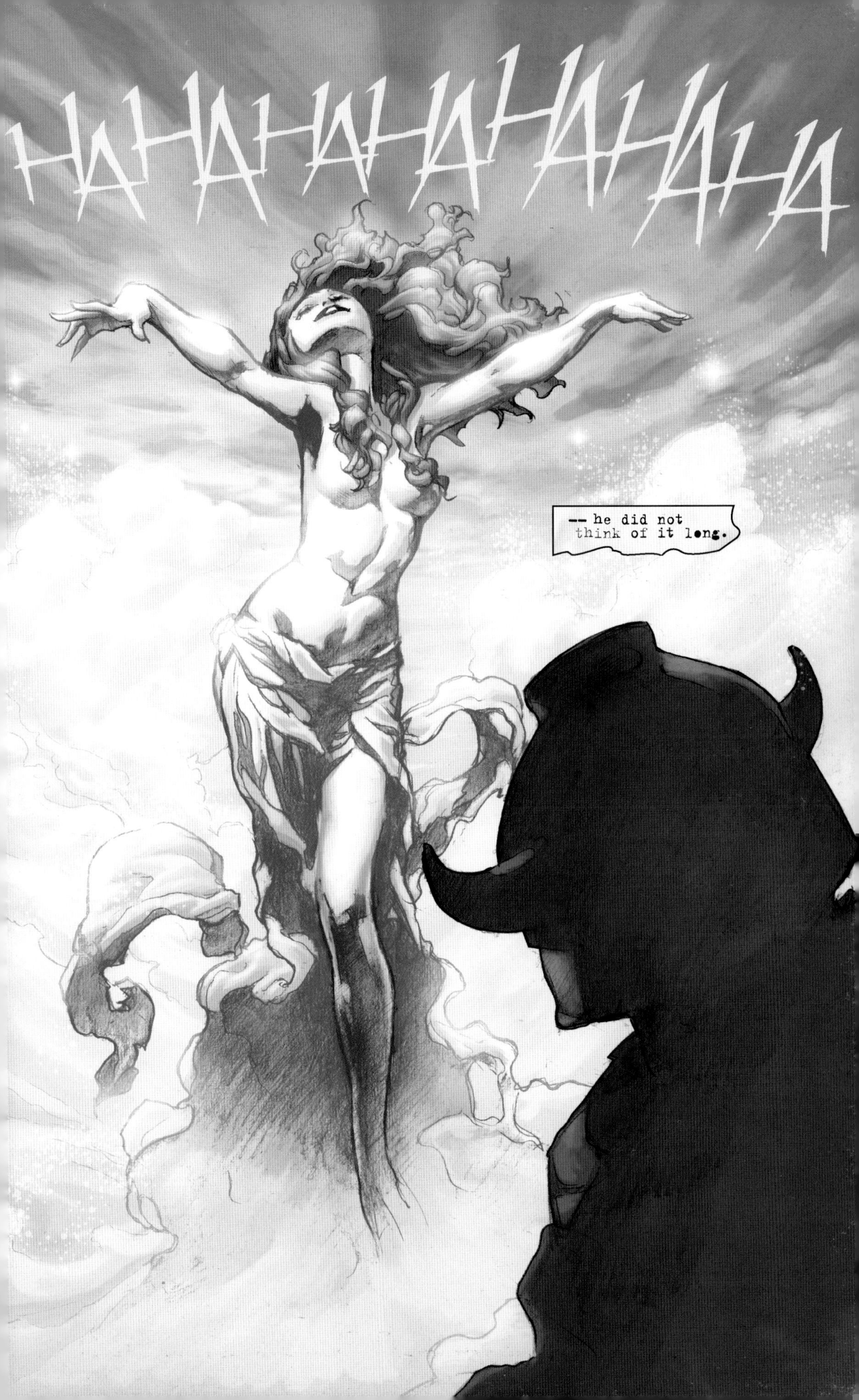
HAHAHAHAHAHAHAHA
-- he did not think of it long.

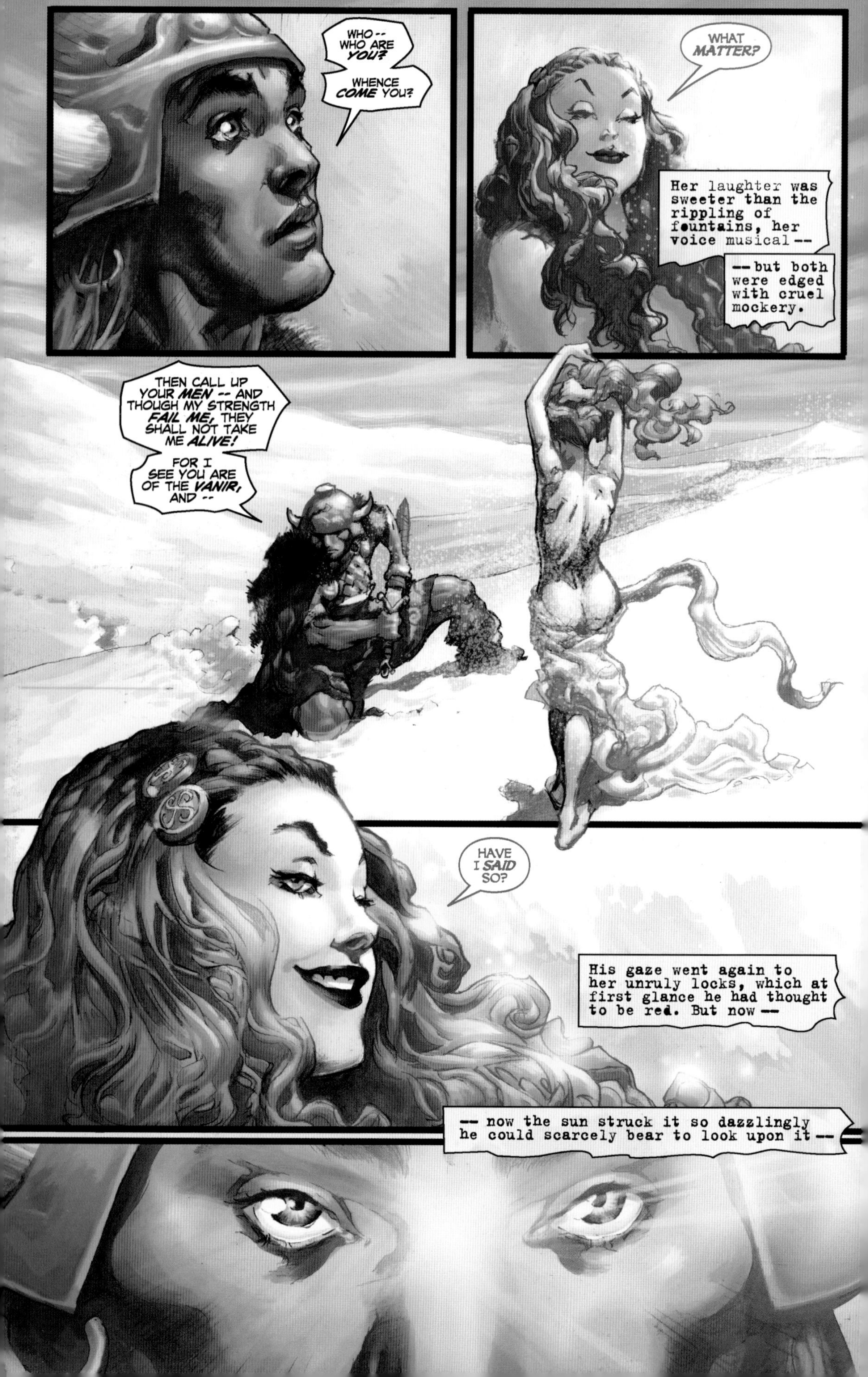
WHO -- WHO ARE YOU?
WHENCE COME YOU?
WHAT MATTER?
Her laughter was sweeter than the rippling of fountains, her voice musical --
-- but both were edged with cruel mockery.
THEN CALL UP YOUR MEN -- AND THOUGH MY STRENGTH FAIL ME, THEY SHALL NOT TAKE ME ALIVE!
FOR I SEE YOU ARE OF THE VANIR, AND --
HAVE I SAID SO?
His gaze went again to her unruly locks, which at first glance he had thought to be red. But now --
-- now the sun struck it so dazzlingly he could scarcely bear to look upon it --

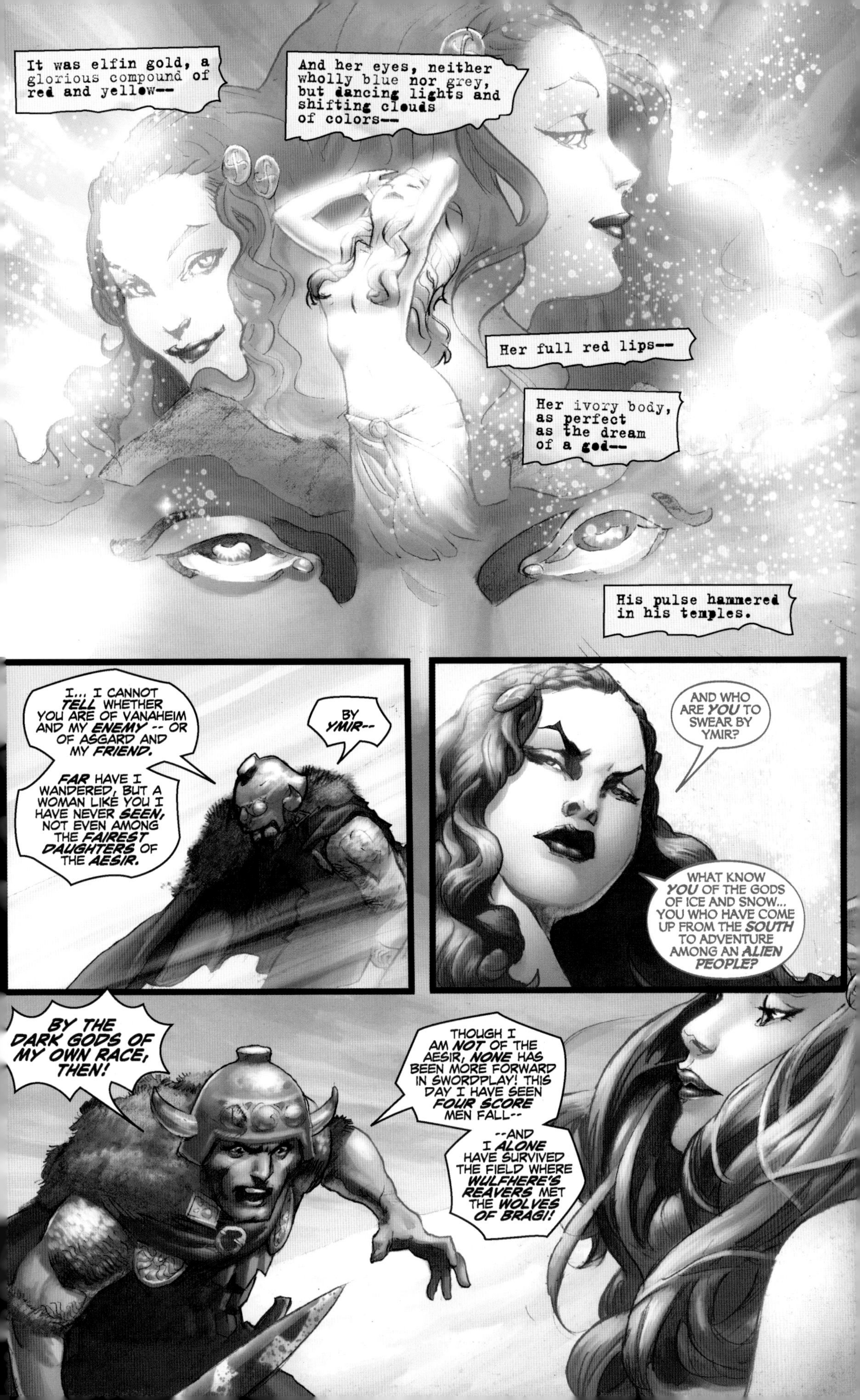
It was elfin gold, a glorious compound of red and yellow--
And her eyes, neither wholly blue nor grey, but dancing lights and shifting clouds of colors--
Her full red lips--
Her ivory body, as perfect as the dream of a god--
His pulse hammered in his temples.
I... I CANNOT TELL WHETHER YOU ARE OF VANAHEIM AND MY ENEMY -- OR OF ASGARD AND MY FRIEND.
FAR HAVE I WANDERED, BUT A WOMAN LIKE YOU I HAVE NEVER SEEN, NOT EVEN AMONG THE FAIREST DAUGHTERS OF THE AESIR.
BY YMIR--
AND WHO ARE YOU TO SWEAR BY YMIR?
WHAT KNOW YOU OF THE GODS OF ICE AND SNOW... YOU WHO HAVE COME UP FROM THE SOUTH TO ADVENTURE AMONG AN ALIEN PEOPLE?
BY THE DARK GODS OF MY OWN RACE, THEN!
THOUGH I AM NOT OF THE AESIR, NONE HAS BEEN MORE FORWARD IN SWORDPLAY! THIS DAY I HAVE SEEN FOUR SCORE MEN FALL--
--AND I ALONE HAVE SURVIVED THE FIELD WHERE WULFHERE'S REAVERS MET THE WOLVES OF BRAGI!

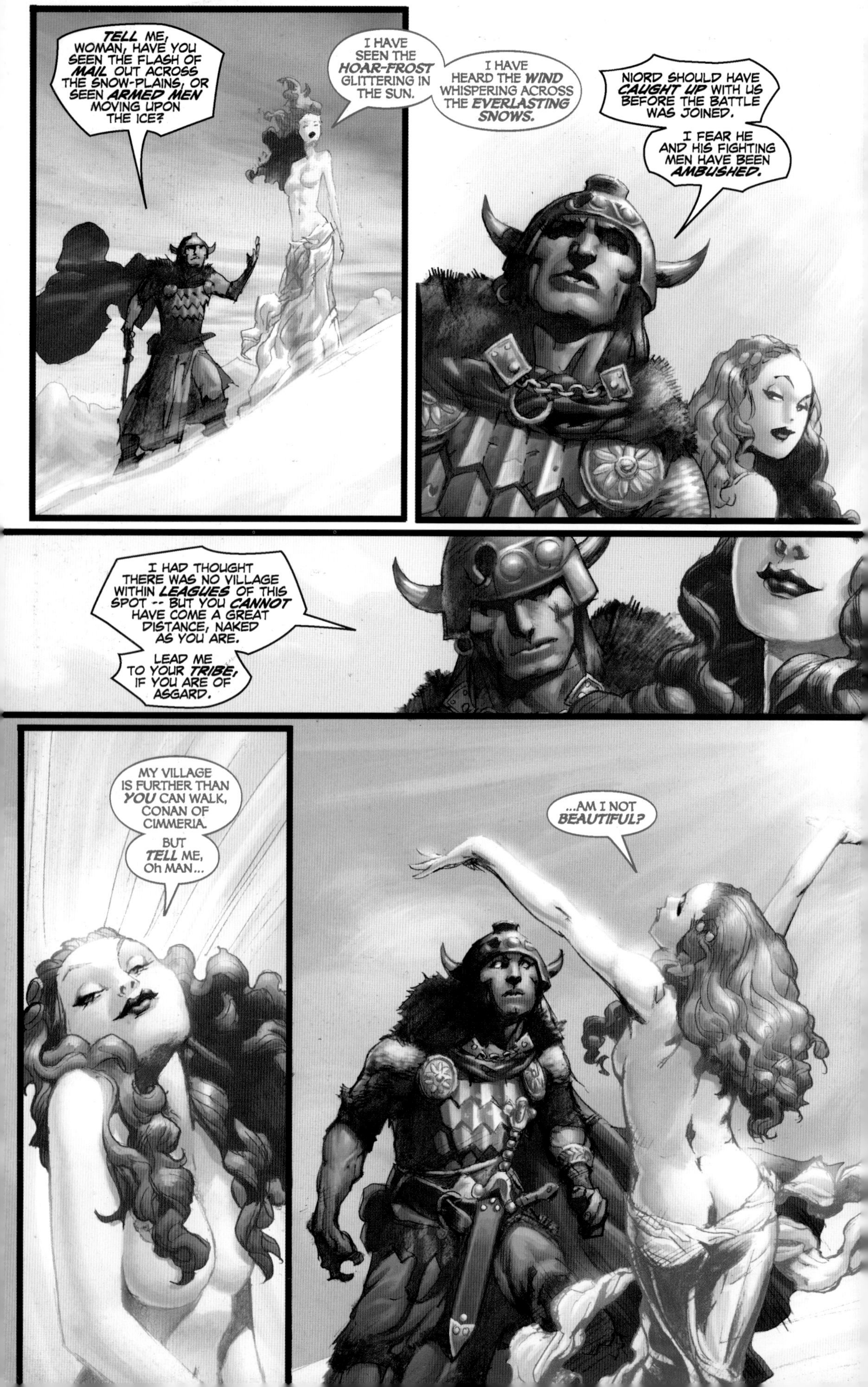
TELL ME, WOMAN, HAVE YOU SEEN THE FLASH OF MAIL OUT ACROSS THE SNOW-PLAINS, OR SEEN ARMED MEN MOVING UPON THE ICE?
I HAVE SEEN THE HOAR-FROST GLITTERING IN THE SUN.
I HAVE HEARD THE WIND WHISPERING ACROSS THE EVERLASTING SNOWS.
NIORD SHOULD HAVE CAUGHT UP WITH US BEFORE THE BATTLE WAS JOINED.
I FEAR HE AND HIS FIGHTING MEN HAVE BEEN AMBUSHED.
I HAD THOUGHT THERE WAS NO VILLAGE WITHIN LEAGUES OF THIS SPOT -- BUT YOU CANNOT HAVE COME A GREAT DISTANCE, NAKED AS YOU ARE.
LEAD ME TO YOUR TRIBE, IF YOU ARE OF ASGARD.
MY VILLAGE IS FURTHER THAN YOU CAN WALK, CONAN OF CIMMERIA.
BUT TELL ME, Oh MAN...
...AM I NOT BEAUTIFUL?

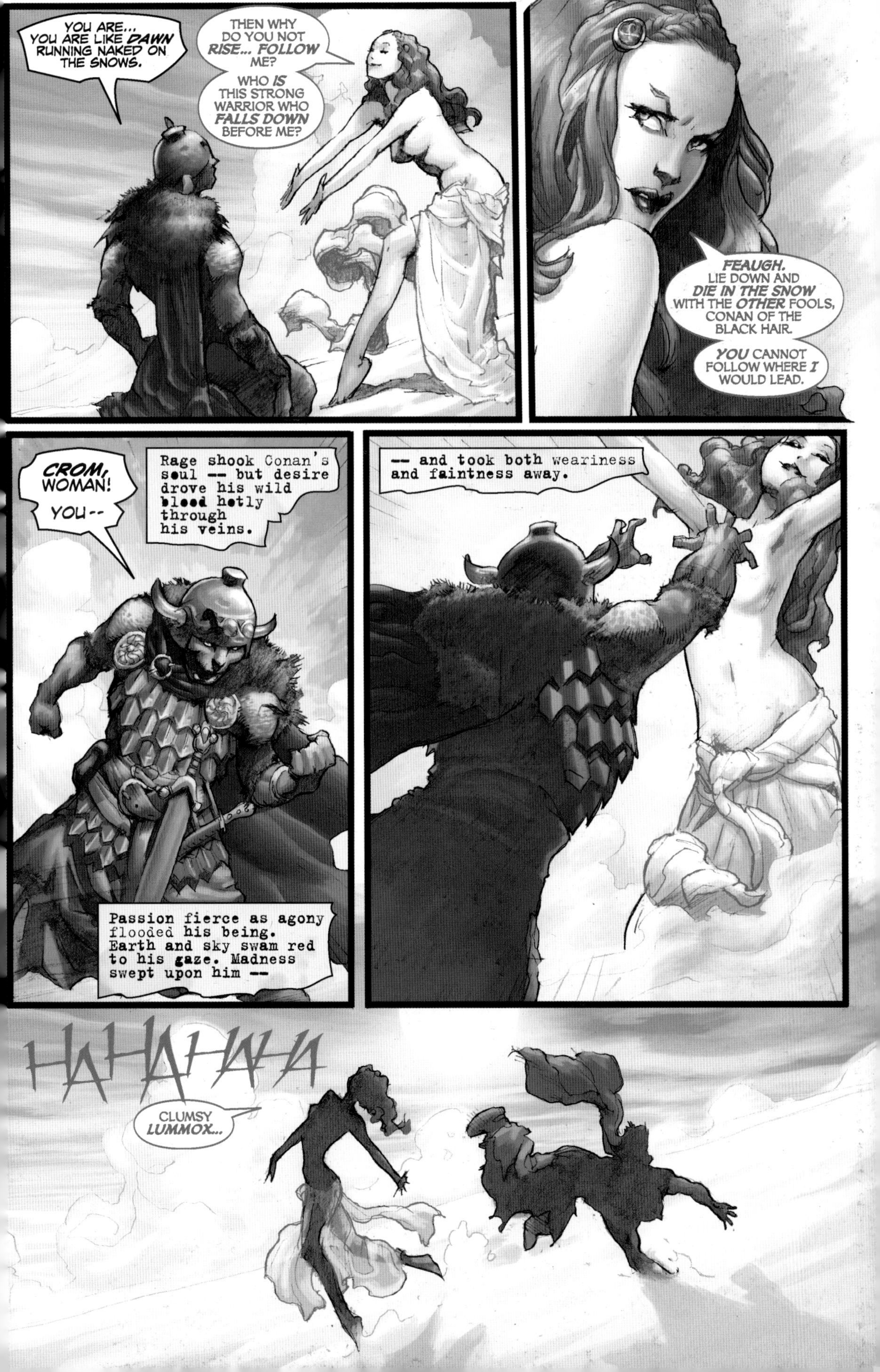
YOU ARE... YOU ARE LIKE DAWN RUNNING NAKED ON THE SNOWS.
THEN WHY DO YOU NOT RISE... FOLLOW ME?
WHO IS THIS STRONG WARRIOR WHO FALLS DOWN BEFORE ME?
FEAUGH. LIE DOWN AND DIE IN THE SNOW WITH THE OTHER FOOLS, CONAN OF THE BLACK HAIR.
YOU CANNOT FOLLOW WHERE I WOULD LEAD.
CROM, WOMAN!
YOU--
Rage shook Conan's soul -- but desire drove his wild blood hotly through his veins.
Passion fierce as agony flooded his being. Earth and sky swam red to his gaze. Madness swept upon him --
-- and took both weariness and faintness away.
HAHAHAHA
CLUMSY LUMMOX...

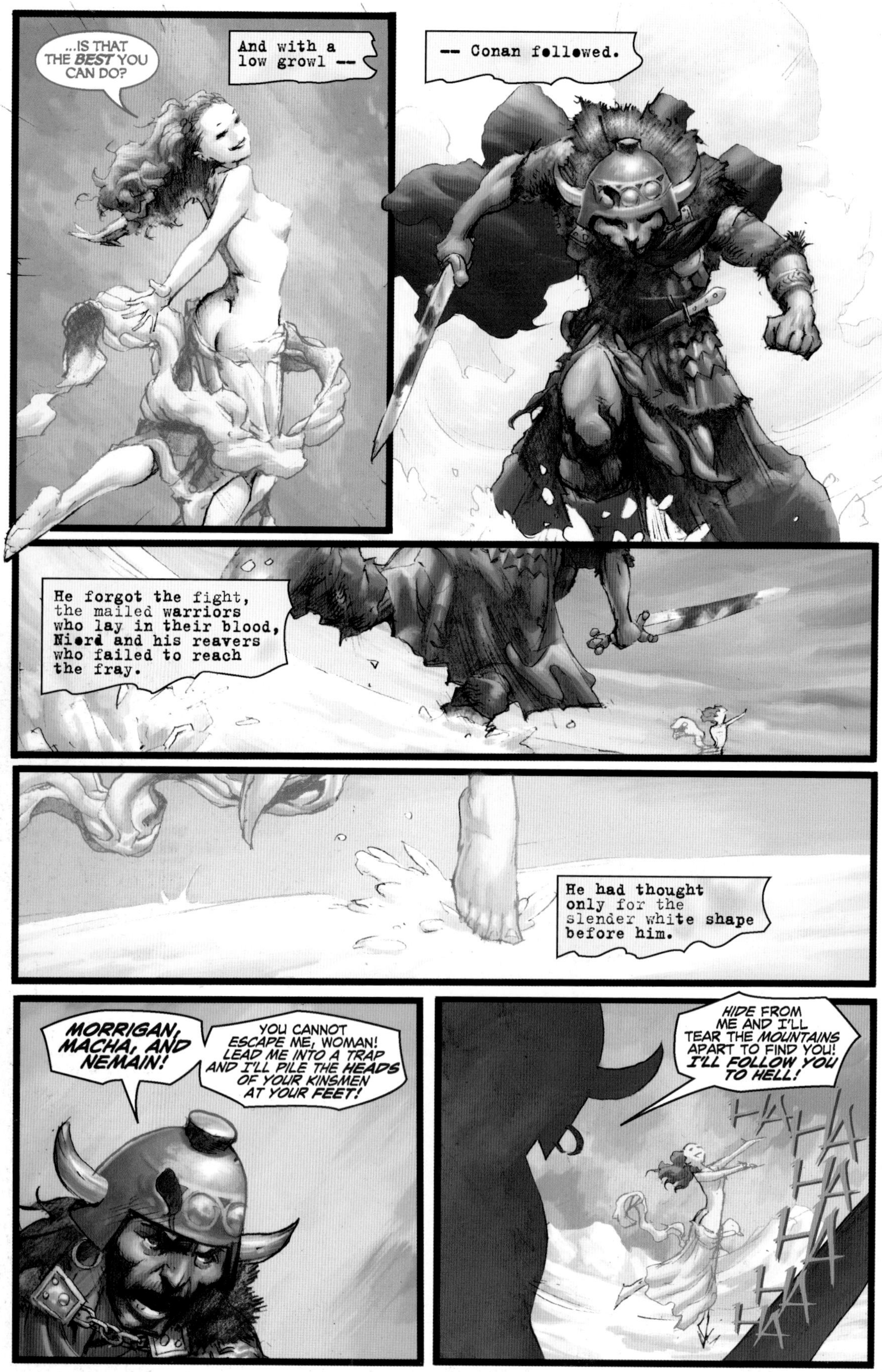
...IS THAT THE BEST YOU CAN DO?
And with a low growl --
-- Conan followed.
He forgot the fight, the mailed warriors who lay in their blood, Niord and his reavers who failed to reach the fray.
He had thought only for the slender white shape before him.
MORRIGAN, MACHA, AND NEMAIN!
YOU CANNOT ESCAPE ME, WOMAN! LEAD ME INTO A TRAP AND I'LL PILE THE HEADS OF YOUR KINSMEN AT YOUR FEET!
HIDE FROM ME AND I'LL TEAR THE MOUNTAINS APART TO FIND YOU! I'LL FOLLOW YOU TO HELL!
HA HA HA HA HA HA

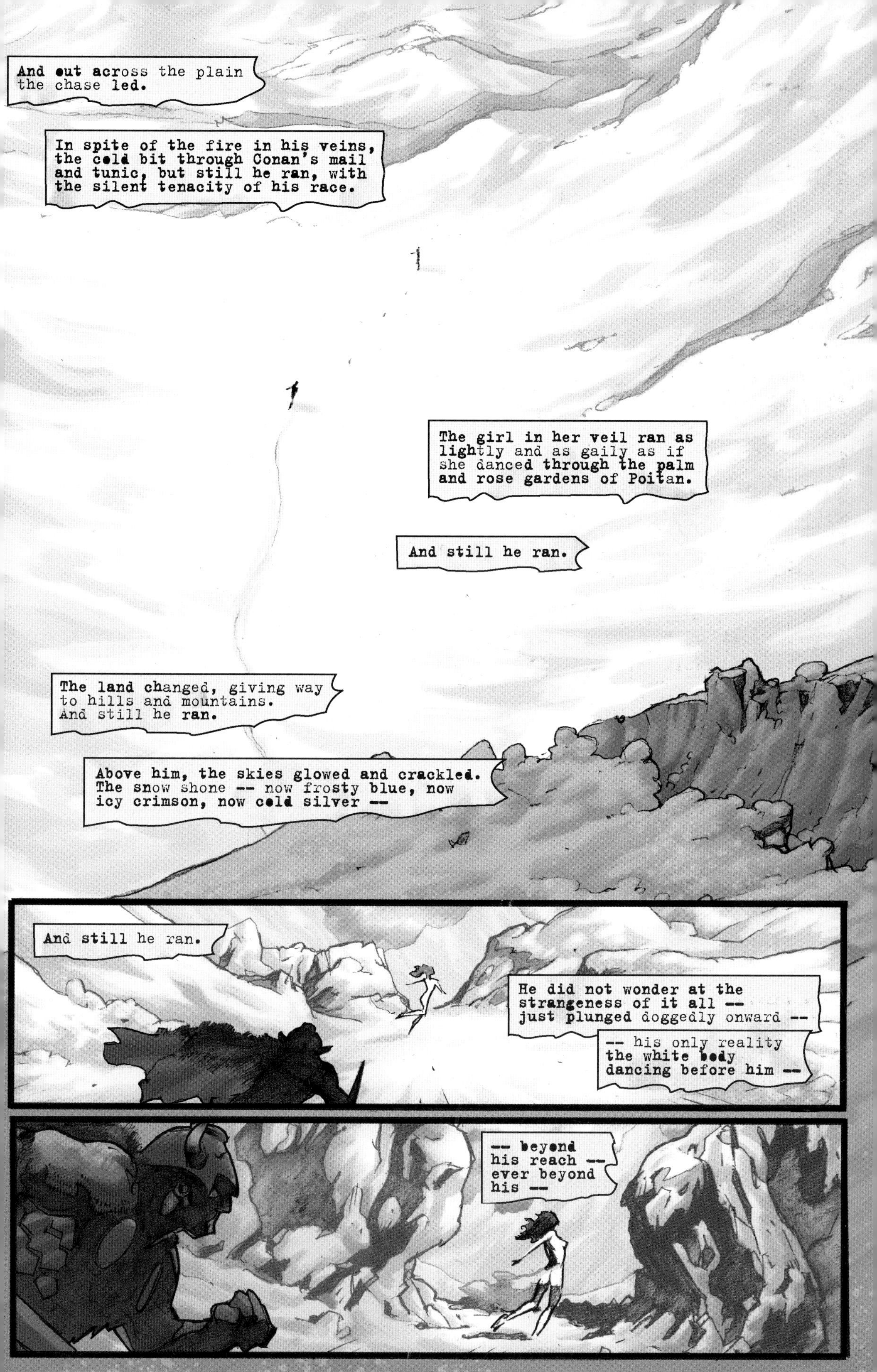
And out across the plain the chase led.
In spite of the fire in his veins, the cold bit through Conan's mail and tunic, but still he ran, with the silent tenacity of his race.
The girl in her veil ran as lightly and as gaily as if she danced through the palm and rose gardens of Poitan.
And still he ran.
The land changed, giving way to hills and mountains. And still he ran.
Above him, the skies glowed and crackled. The snow shone -- now frosty blue, now icy crimson, now cold silver --
And still he ran.
He did not wonder at the strangeness of it all -- just plunged doggedly onward --
-- his only reality the white body dancing before him --
-- beyond his reach -- ever beyond his --

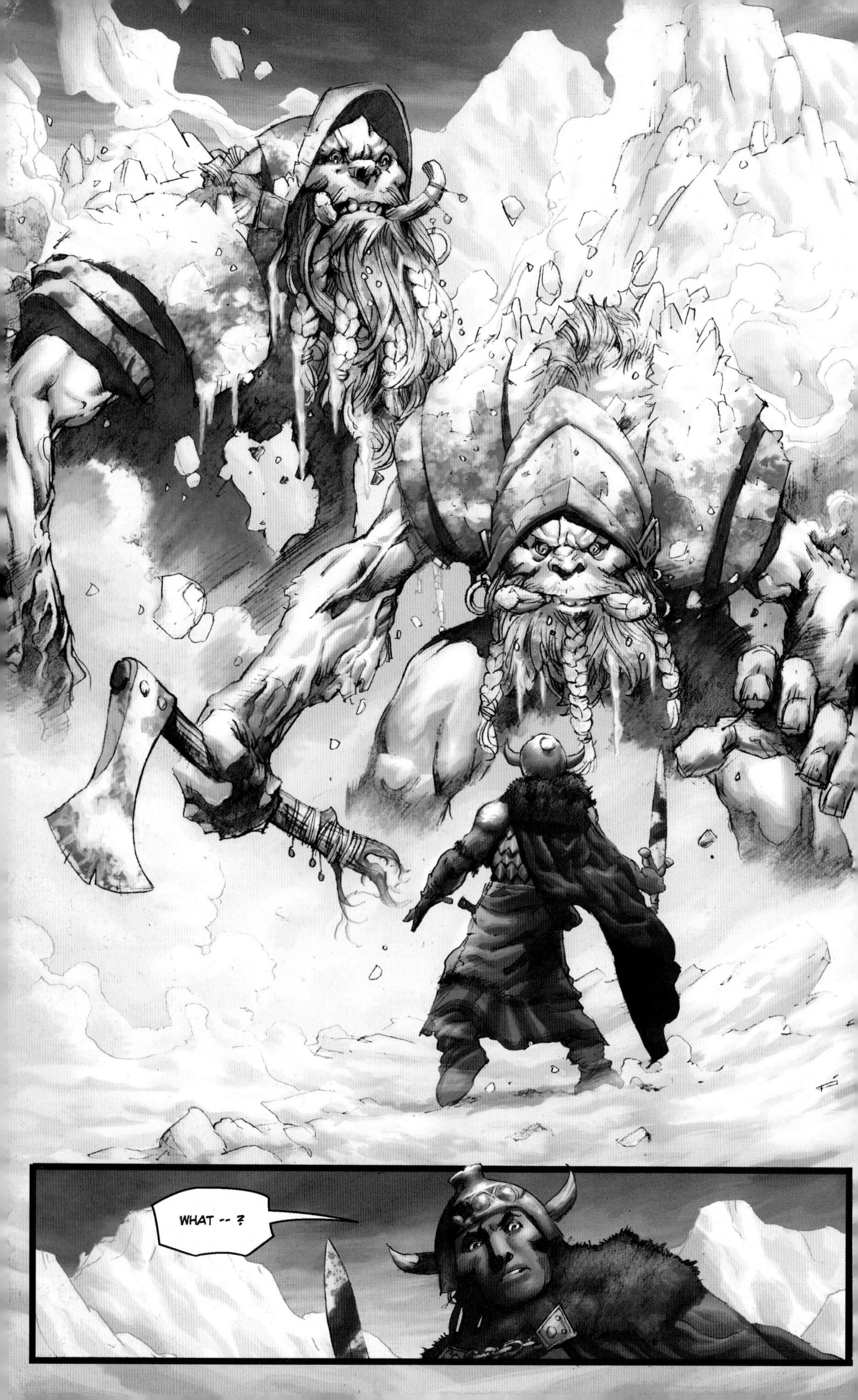
WHAT -- ?

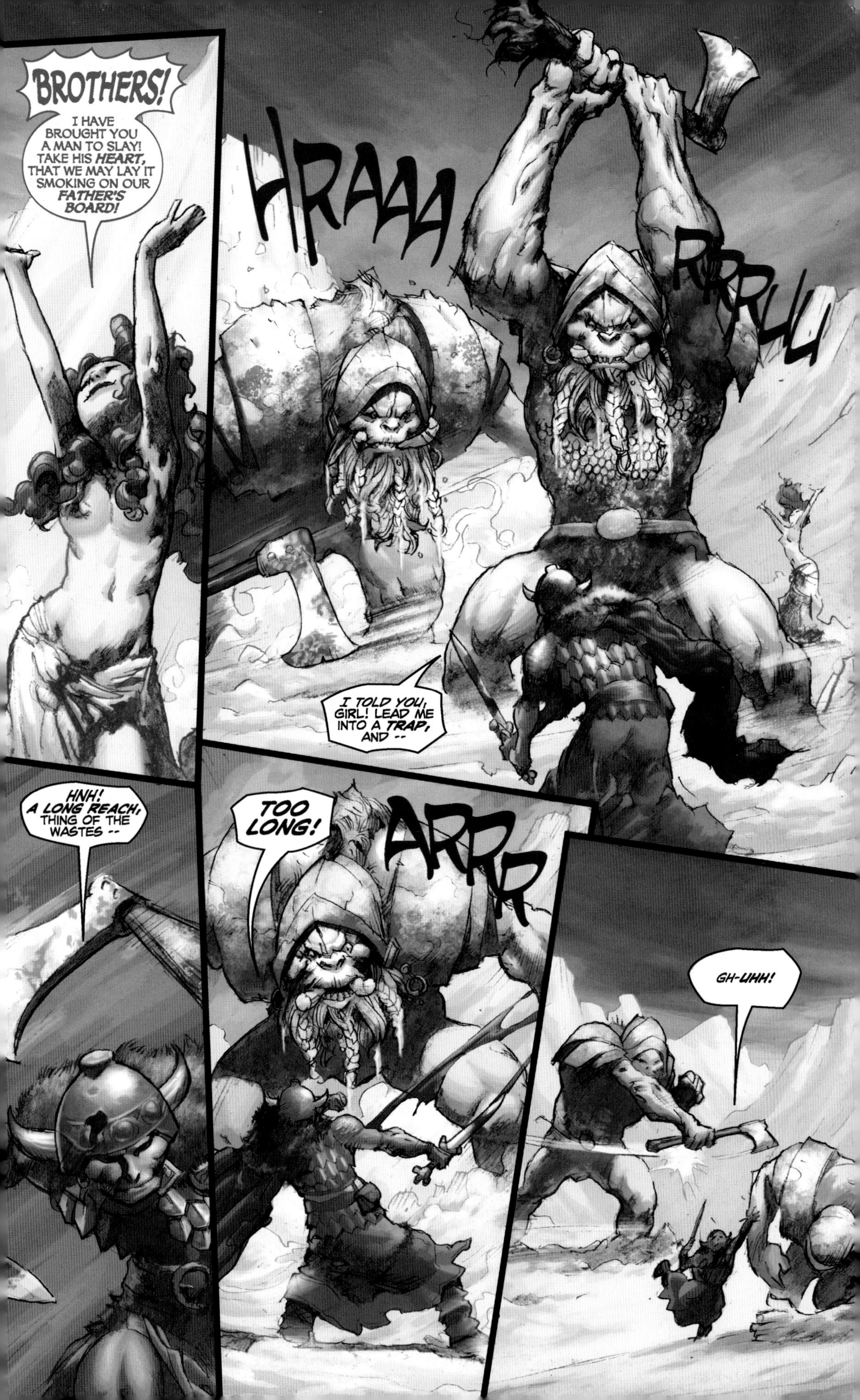
BROTHERS!
I HAVE BROUGHT YOU A MAN TO SLAY! TAKE HIS HEART, THAT WE MAY LAY IT SMOKING ON OUR FATHER'S BOARD!
HRAAAA
RRRRUU
I TOLD YOU, GIRL! LEAD ME INTO A TRAP, AND --
HNH! A LONG REACH, THING OF THE WASTES --
TOO LONG!
ARRR
GH-UHH!

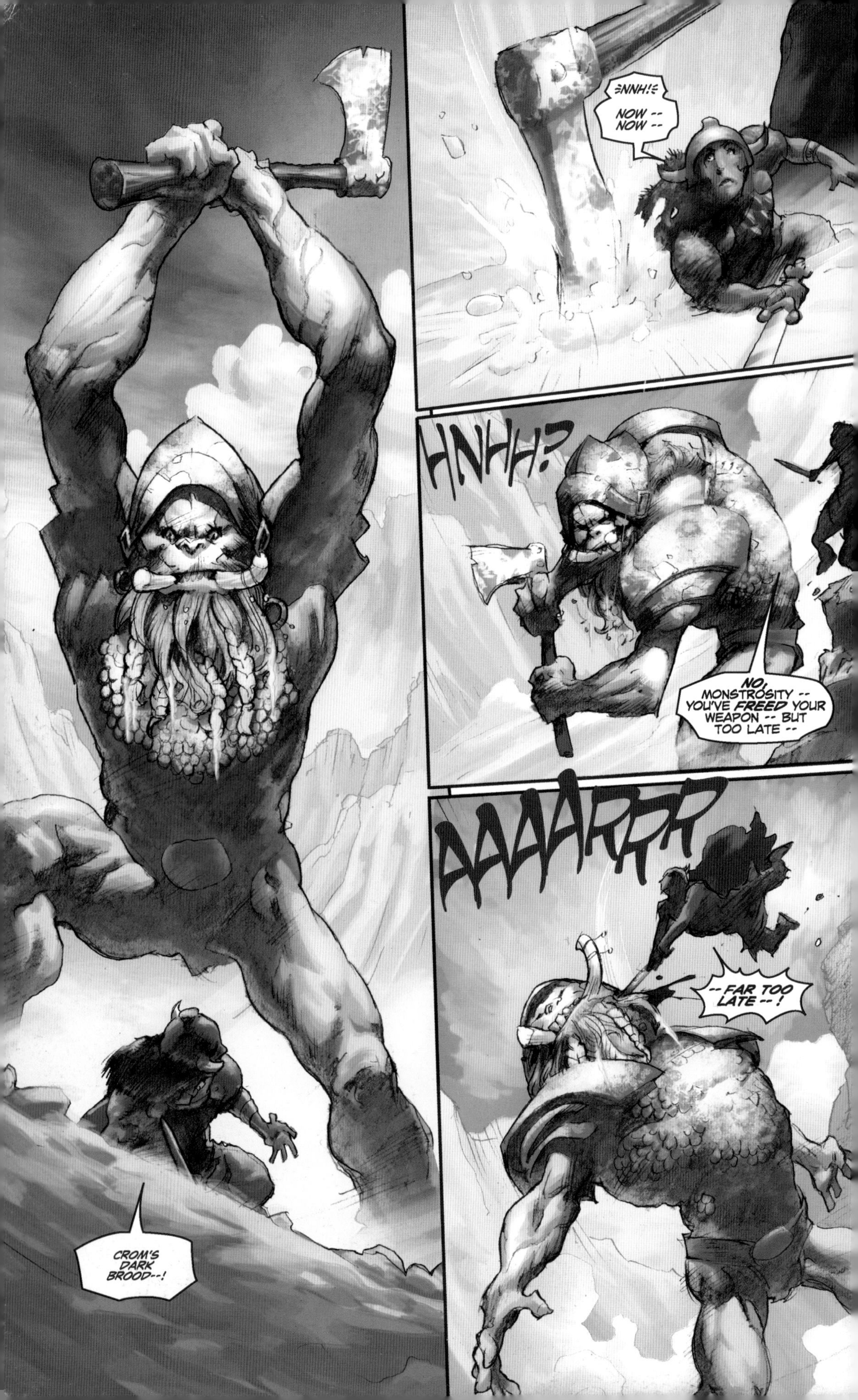
CROM'S DARK BROOD--!
=NNH!=
NOW -- NOW --
HNHH?
NO, MONSTROSITY -- YOU'VE FREED YOUR WEAPON -- BUT TOO LATE --
AAAARRR
-- FAR TOO LATE -- !

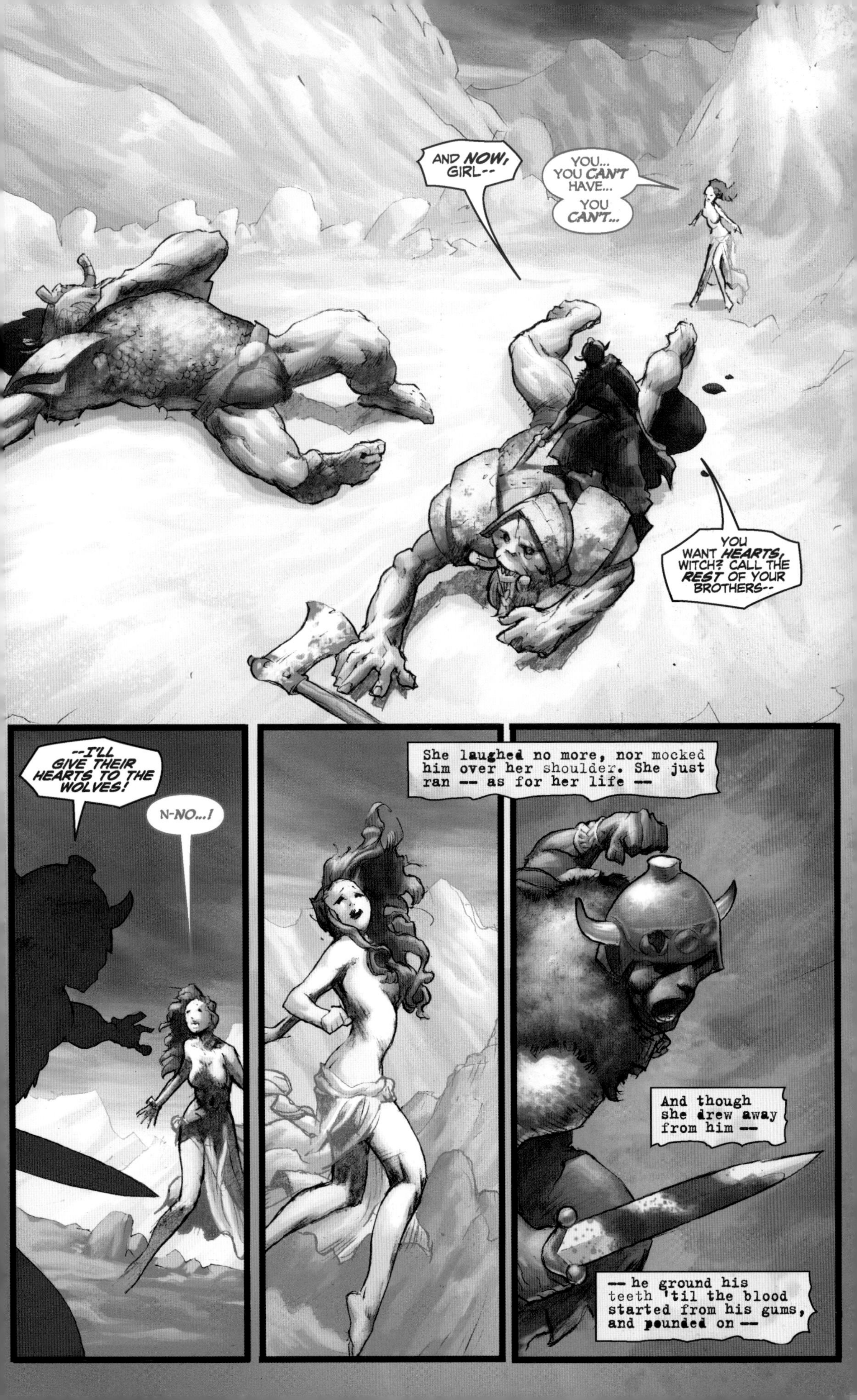
AND NOW, GIRL--
YOU... YOU CAN'T HAVE... YOU CAN'T...
YOU WANT HEARTS, WITCH? CALL THE REST OF YOUR BROTHERS--
--I'LL GIVE THEIR HEARTS TO THE WOLVES!
N-NO...!
She laughed no more, nor mocked him over her shoulder. She just ran -- as for her life --
And though she drew away from him --
-- he ground his teeth 'til the blood started from his gums, and pounded on --

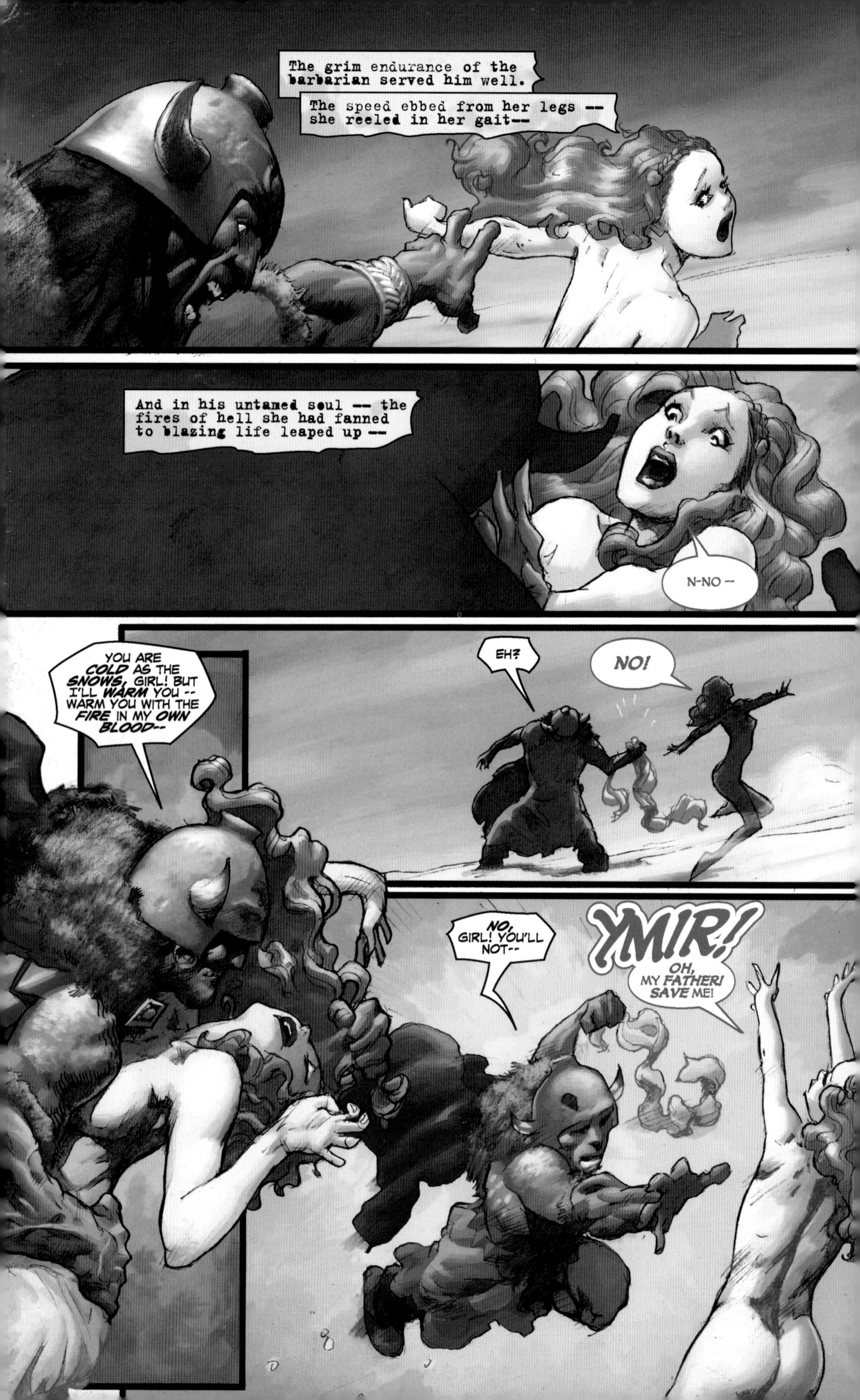
The grim endurance of the barbarian served him well.
The speed ebbed from her legs -- she reeled in her gait--
And in his untamed soul -- the fires of hell she had fanned to blazing life leaped up --
N-NO --
YOU ARE COLD AS THE SNOWS, GIRL! BUT I'LL WARM YOU -- WARM YOU WITH THE FIRE IN MY OWN BLOOD--
EH?
NO!
NO, GIRL! YOU'LL NOT--
YMIR!
OH, MY FATHER! SAVE ME!

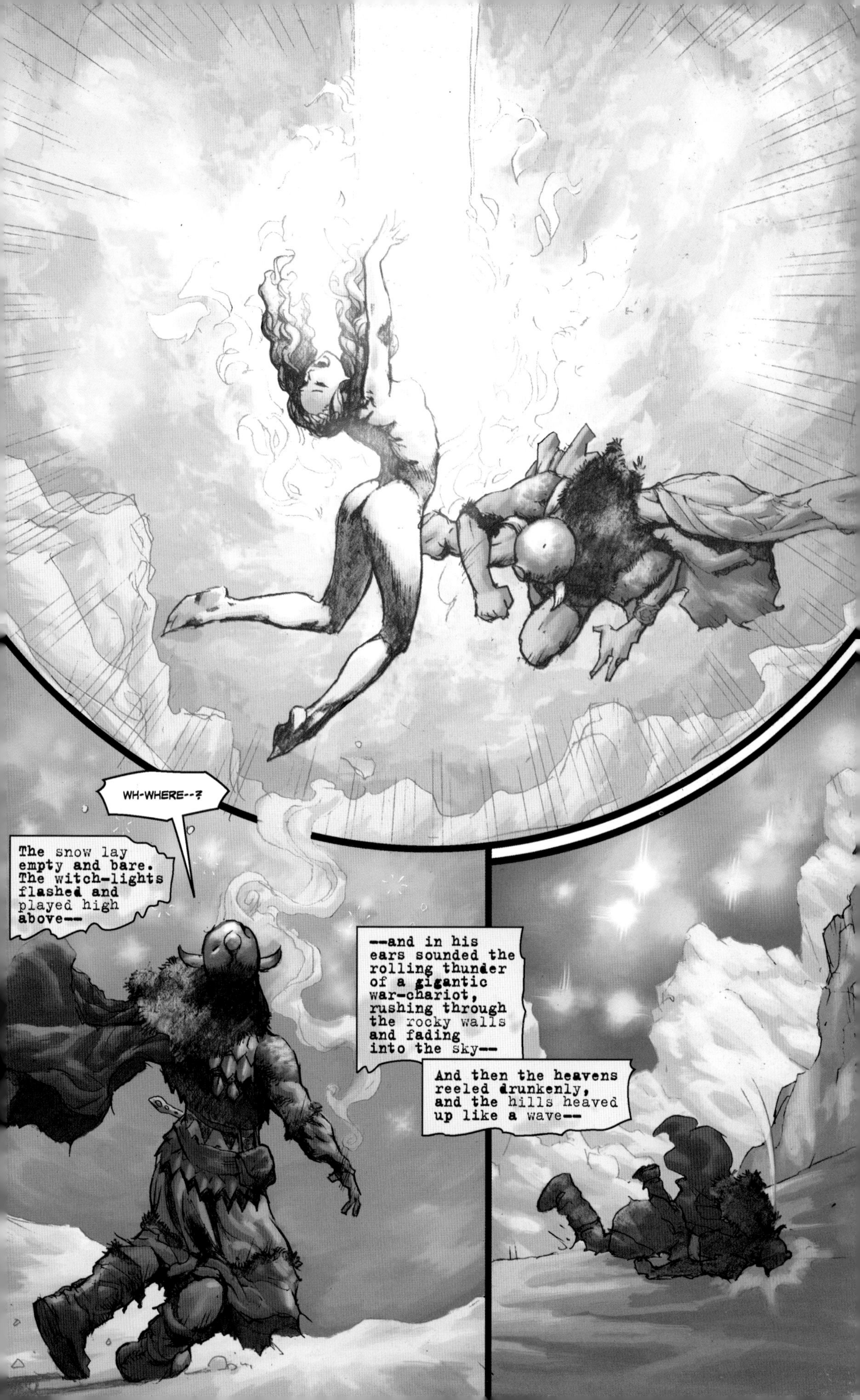
WH-WHERE--?
The snow lay empty and bare. The witch-lights flashed and played high above--
--and in his ears sounded the rolling thunder of a gigantic war-chariot, rushing through the rocky walls and fading into the sky--
And then the heavens reeled drunkenly, and the hills heaved up like a wave--

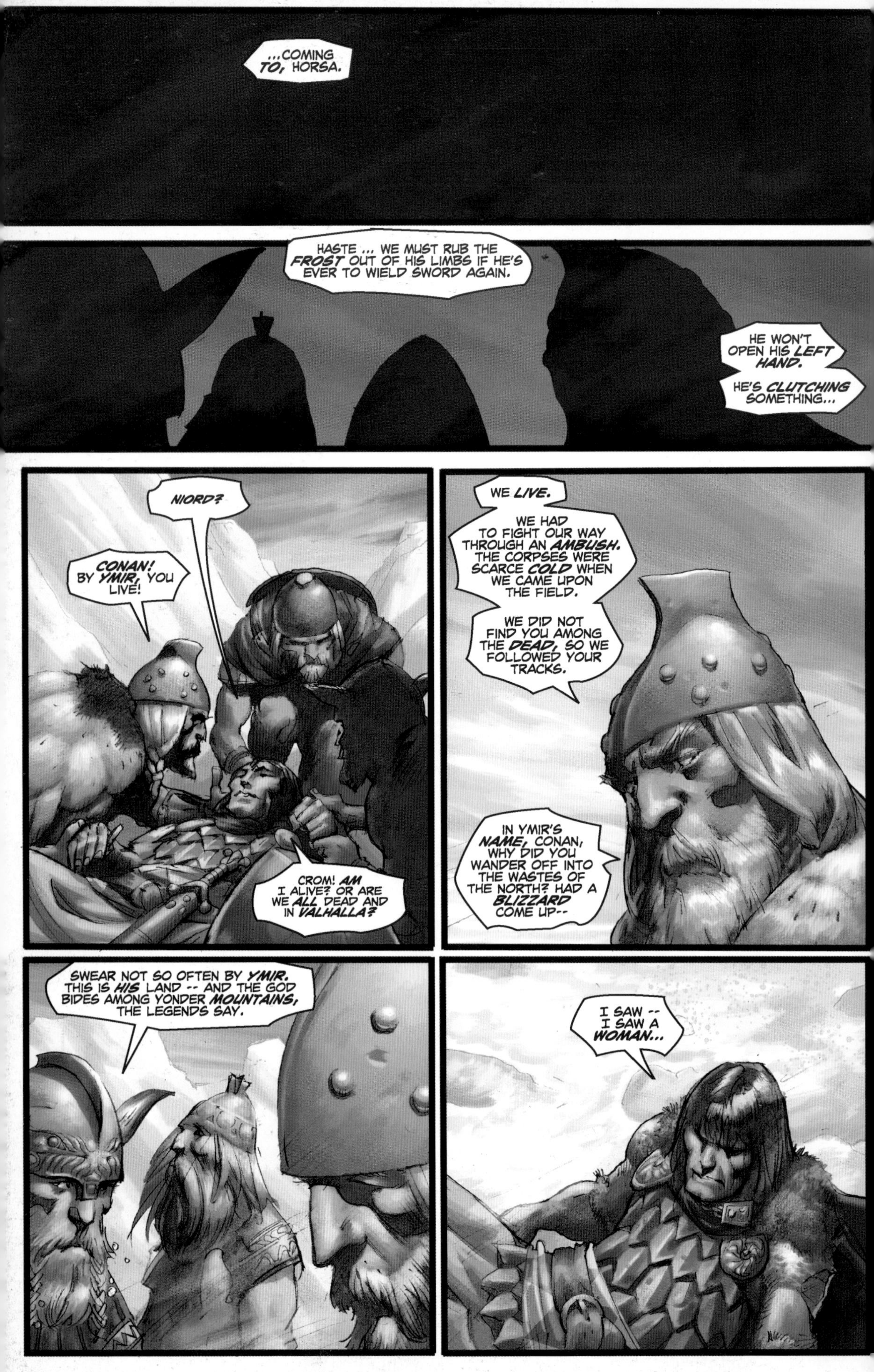
...COMING TO, HORSA.
HASTE ... WE MUST RUB THE FROST OUT OF HIS LIMBS IF HE'S EVER TO WIELD SWORD AGAIN.
HE WON'T OPEN HIS LEFT HAND.
HE'S CLUTCHING SOMETHING...
NIORD?
CONAN! BY YMIR, YOU LIVE!
CROM! AM I ALIVE? OR ARE WE ALL DEAD AND IN VALHALLA?
WE LIVE.
WE HAD TO FIGHT OUR WAY THROUGH AN AMBUSH. THE CORPSES WERE SCARCE COLD WHEN WE CAME UPON THE FIELD.
WE DID NOT FIND YOU AMONG THE DEAD, SO WE FOLLOWED YOUR TRACKS.
IN YMIR'S NAME, CONAN, WHY DID YOU WANDER OFF INTO THE WASTES OF THE NORTH? HAD A BLIZZARD COME UP--
SWEAR NOT SO OFTEN BY YMIR. THIS IS HIS LAND -- AND THE GOD BIDES AMONG YONDER MOUNTAINS, THE LEGENDS SAY.
I SAW -- I SAW A WOMAN...

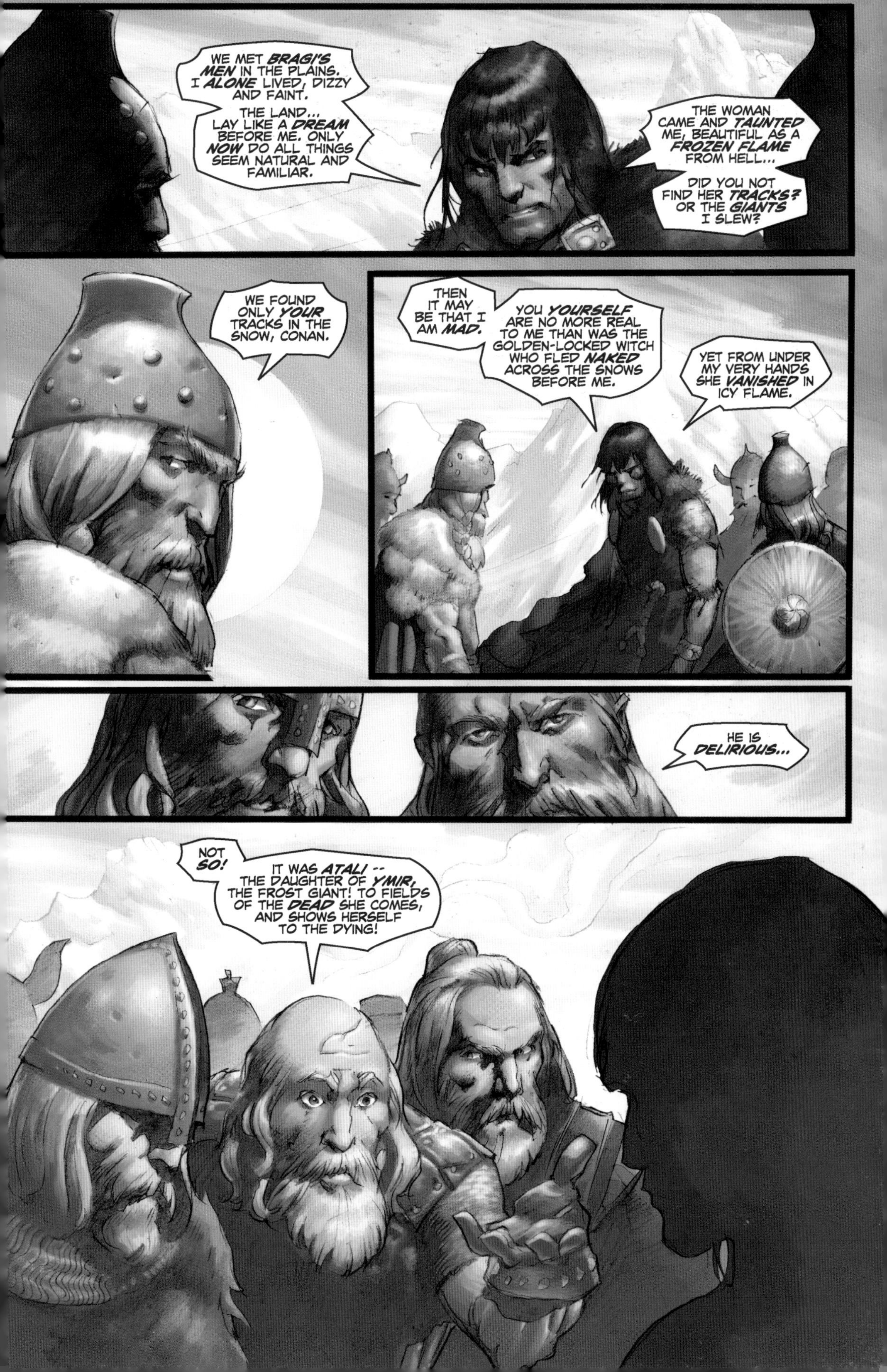
WE MET BRAGI'S MEN IN THE PLAINS. I ALONE LIVED, DIZZY AND FAINT.
THE LAND... LAY LIKE A DREAM BEFORE ME. ONLY NOW DO ALL THINGS SEEM NATURAL AND FAMILIAR.
THE WOMAN CAME AND TAUNTED ME, BEAUTIFUL AS A FROZEN FLAME FROM HELL...
DID YOU NOT FIND HER TRACKS? OR THE GIANTS I SLEW?
WE FOUND ONLY YOUR TRACKS IN THE SNOW, CONAN.
THEN IT MAY BE THAT I AM MAD.
YOU YOURSELF ARE NO MORE REAL TO ME THAN WAS THE GOLDEN-LOCKED WITCH WHO FLED NAKED ACROSS THE SNOWS BEFORE ME.
YET FROM UNDER MY VERY HANDS SHE VANISHED IN ICY FLAME.
HE IS DELIRIOUS...
NOT SO!
IT WAS ATALI -- THE DAUGHTER OF YMIR, THE FROST GIANT! TO FIELDS OF THE DEAD SHE COMES, AND SHOWS HERSELF TO THE DYING!

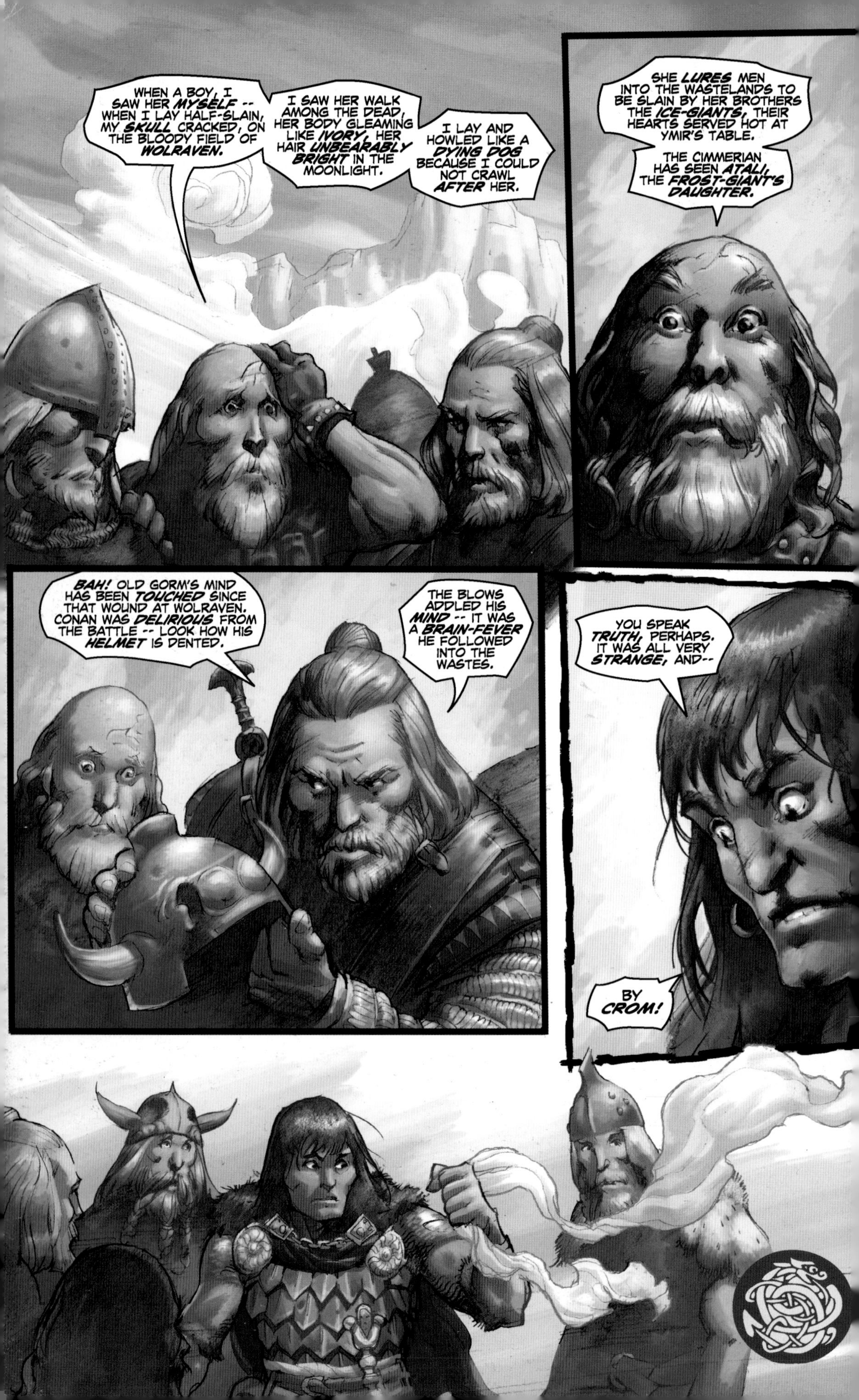

WHEN A BOY, I SAW HER MYSELF -- WHEN I LAY HALF-SLAIN, MY SKULL CRACKED, ON THE BLOODY FIELD OF WOLRAVEN.
I SAW HER WALK AMONG THE DEAD, HER BODY GLEAMING LIKE IVORY, HER HAIR UNBEARABLY BRIGHT IN THE MOONLIGHT.
I LAY AND HOWLED LIKE A DYING DOG BECAUSE I COULD NOT CRAWL AFTER HER.
SHE LURES MEN INTO THE WASTELANDS TO BE SLAIN BY HER BROTHERS THE ICE-GIANTS, THEIR HEARTS SERVED HOT AT YMIR'S TABLE.
THE CIMMERIAN HAS SEEN ATALI, THE FROST-GIANT'S DAUGHTER.
BAH! OLD GORM'S MIND HAS BEEN TOUCHED SINCE THAT WOUND AT WOLRAVEN. CONAN WAS DELIRIOUS FROM THE BATTLE -- LOOK HOW HIS HELMET IS DENTED.
THE BLOWS ADDLED HIS MIND -- IT WAS A BRAIN-FEVER HE FOLLOWED INTO THE WASTES.
YOU SPEAK TRUTH, PERHAPS. IT WAS ALL VERY STRANGE, AND--
BY CROM!

CHAPTER THREE

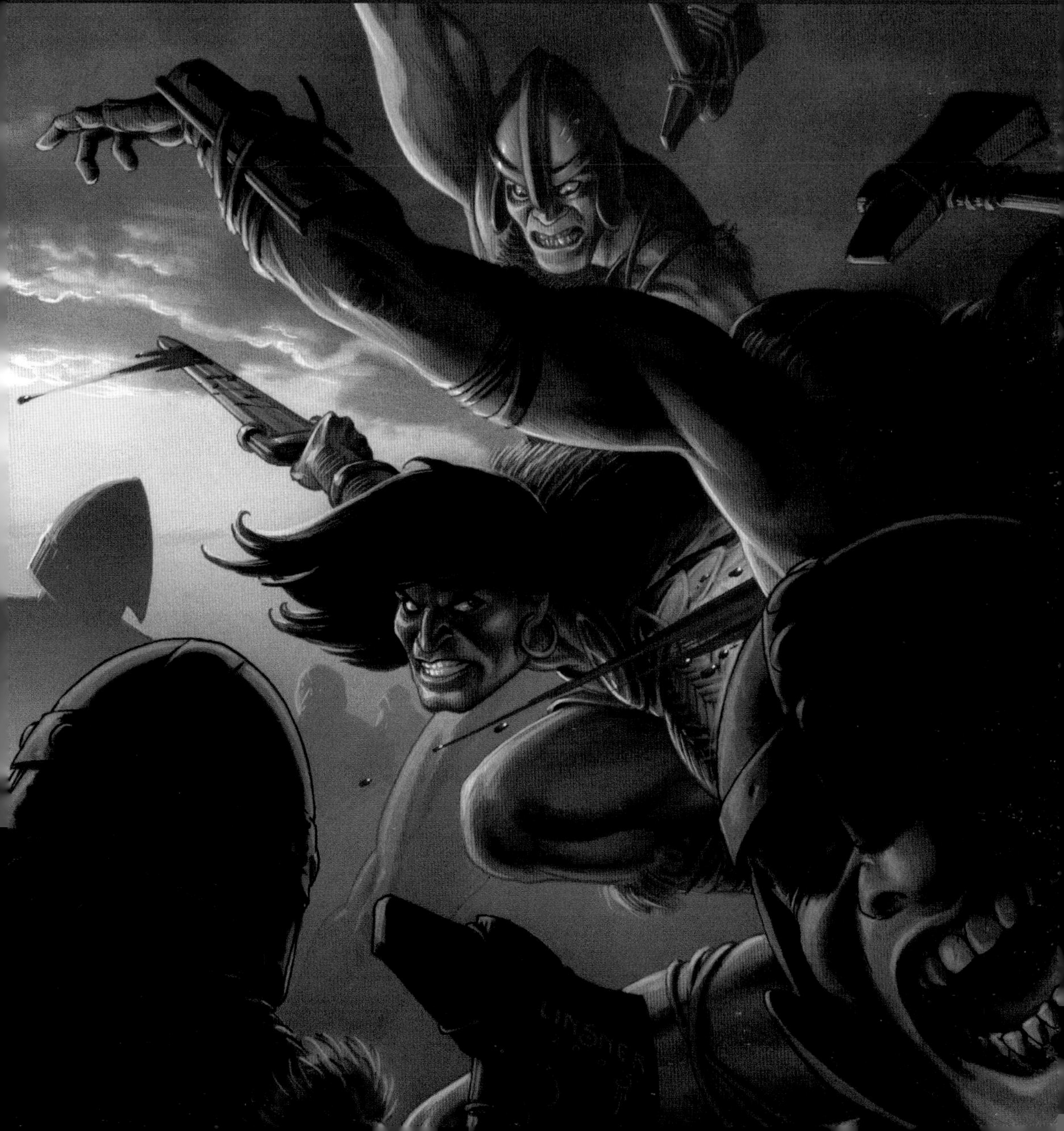

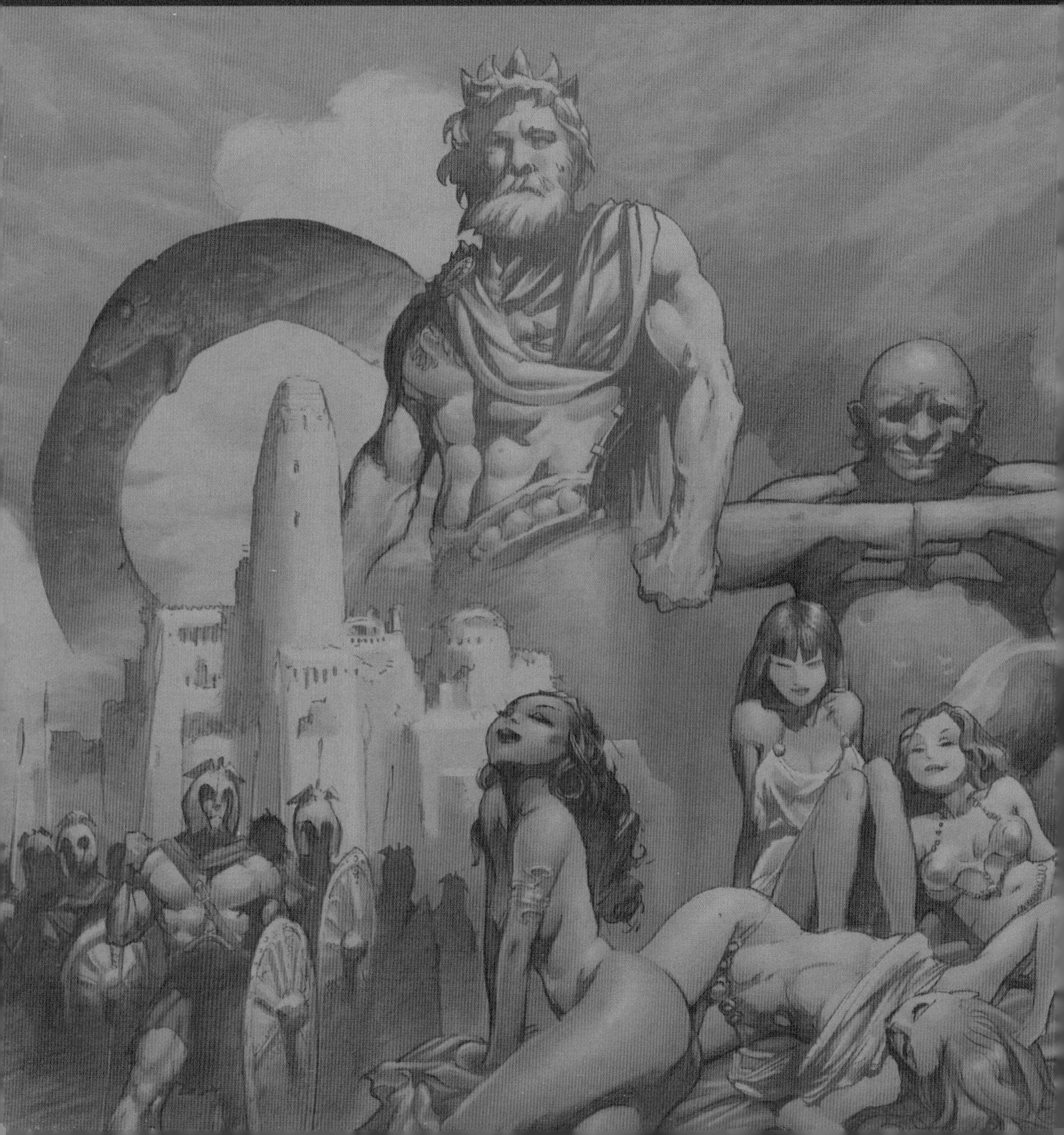

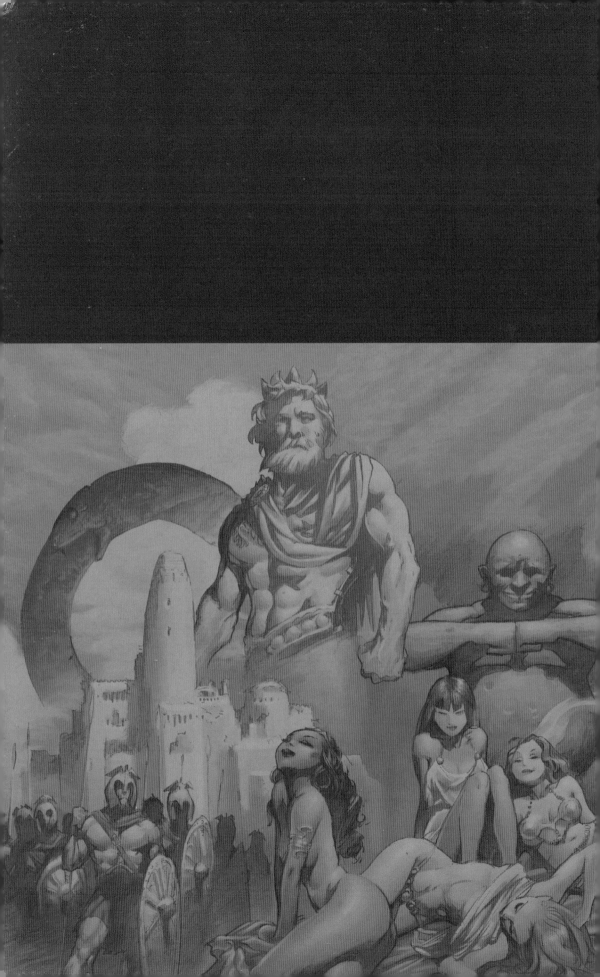

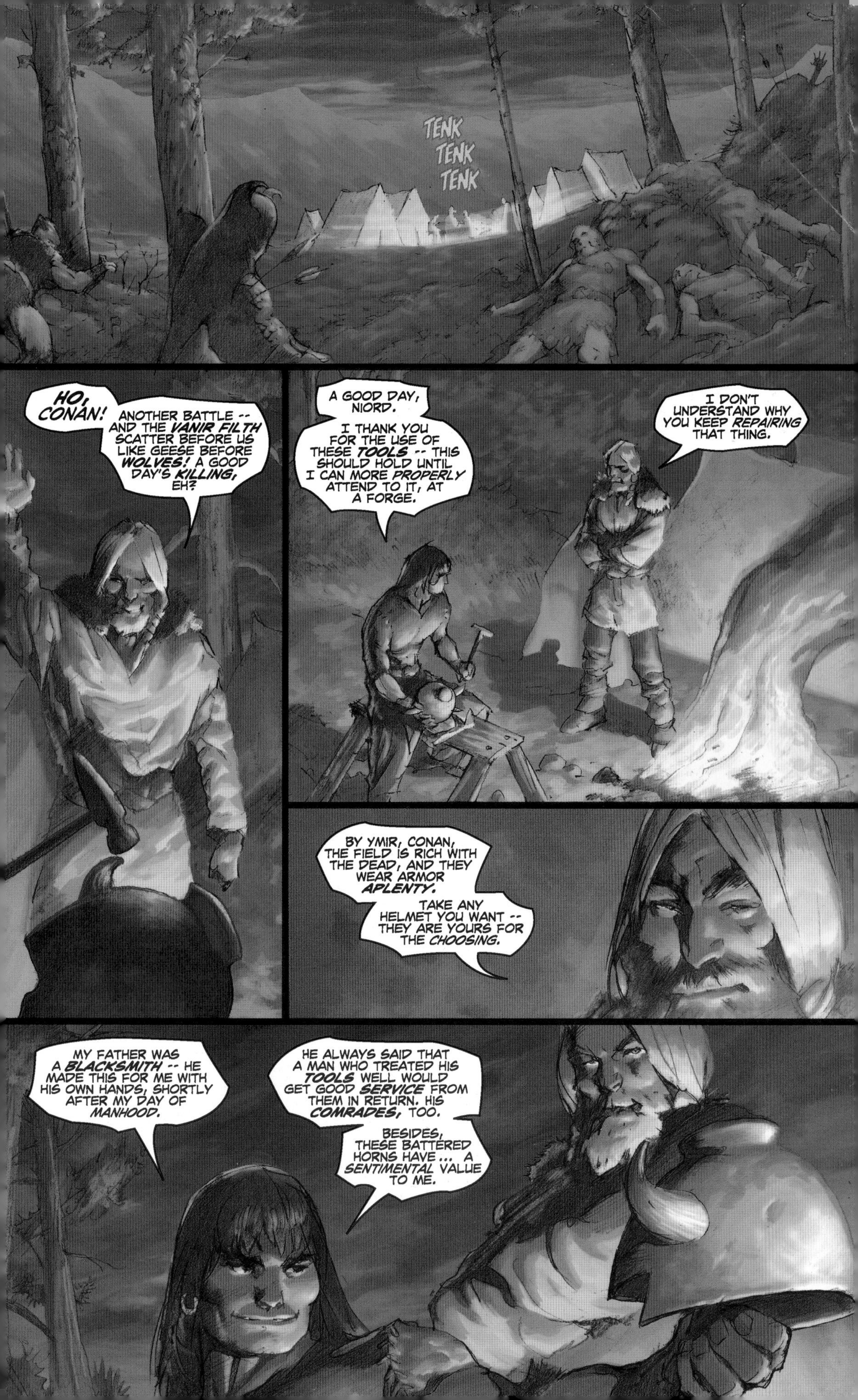
TENK TENK TENK
HO, CONAN!
ANOTHER BATTLE -- AND THE VANIR FILTH SCATTER BEFORE US LIKE GEESE BEFORE WOLVES! A GOOD DAY'S KILLING, EH?
A GOOD DAY, NIORD.
I THANK YOU FOR THE USE OF THESE TOOLS -- THIS SHOULD HOLD UNTIL I CAN MORE PROPERLY ATTEND TO IT, AT A FORGE.
I DON'T UNDERSTAND WHY YOU KEEP REPAIRING THAT THING.
BY YMIR, CONAN, THE FIELD IS RICH WITH THE DEAD, AND THEY WEAR ARMOR APLENTY.
TAKE ANY HELMET YOU WANT -- THEY ARE YOURS FOR THE CHOOSING.
MY FATHER WAS A BLACKSMITH -- HE MADE THIS FOR ME WITH HIS OWN HANDS, SHORTLY AFTER MY DAY OF MANHOOD.
HE ALWAYS SAID THAT A MAN WHO TREATED HIS TOOLS WELL WOULD GET GOOD SERVICE FROM THEM IN RETURN. HIS COMRADES, TOO.
BESIDES, THESE BATTERED HORNS HAVE... A SENTIMENTAL VALUE TO ME.

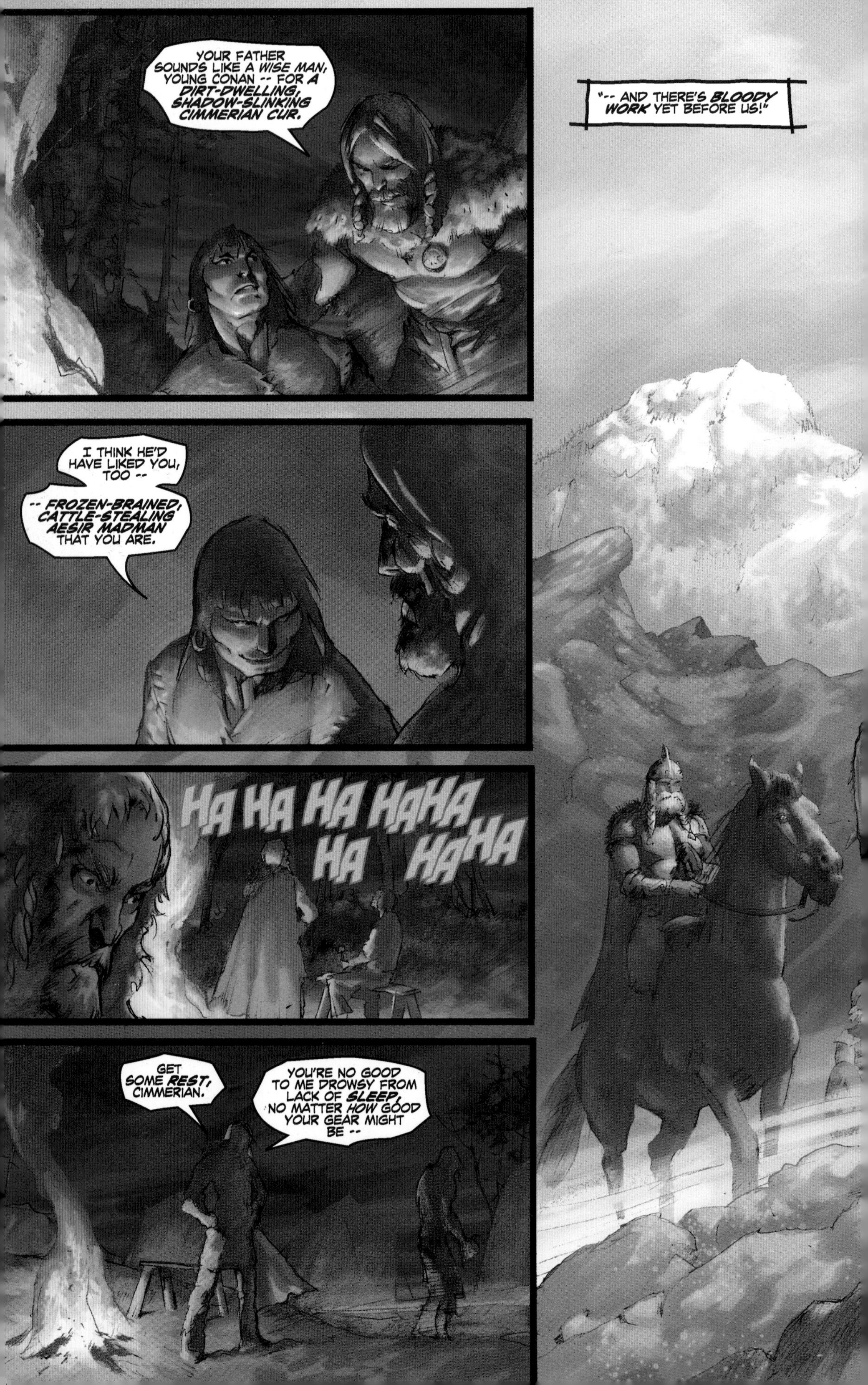
YOUR FATHER SOUNDS LIKE A WISE MAN, YOUNG CONAN -- FOR A DIRT-DWELLING, SHADOW-SLINKING CIMMERIAN CUR.
"-- AND THERE'S BLOODY WORK YET BEFORE US!"
I THINK HE'D HAVE LIKED YOU, TOO --
-- FROZEN-BRAINED, CATTLE-STEALING AESIR MADMAN THAT YOU ARE.
HA HA HA HAHA HA HAHA
GET SOME REST, CIMMERIAN.
YOU'RE NO GOOD TO ME DROWSY FROM LACK OF SLEEP, NO MATTER HOW GOOD YOUR GEAR MIGHT BE --

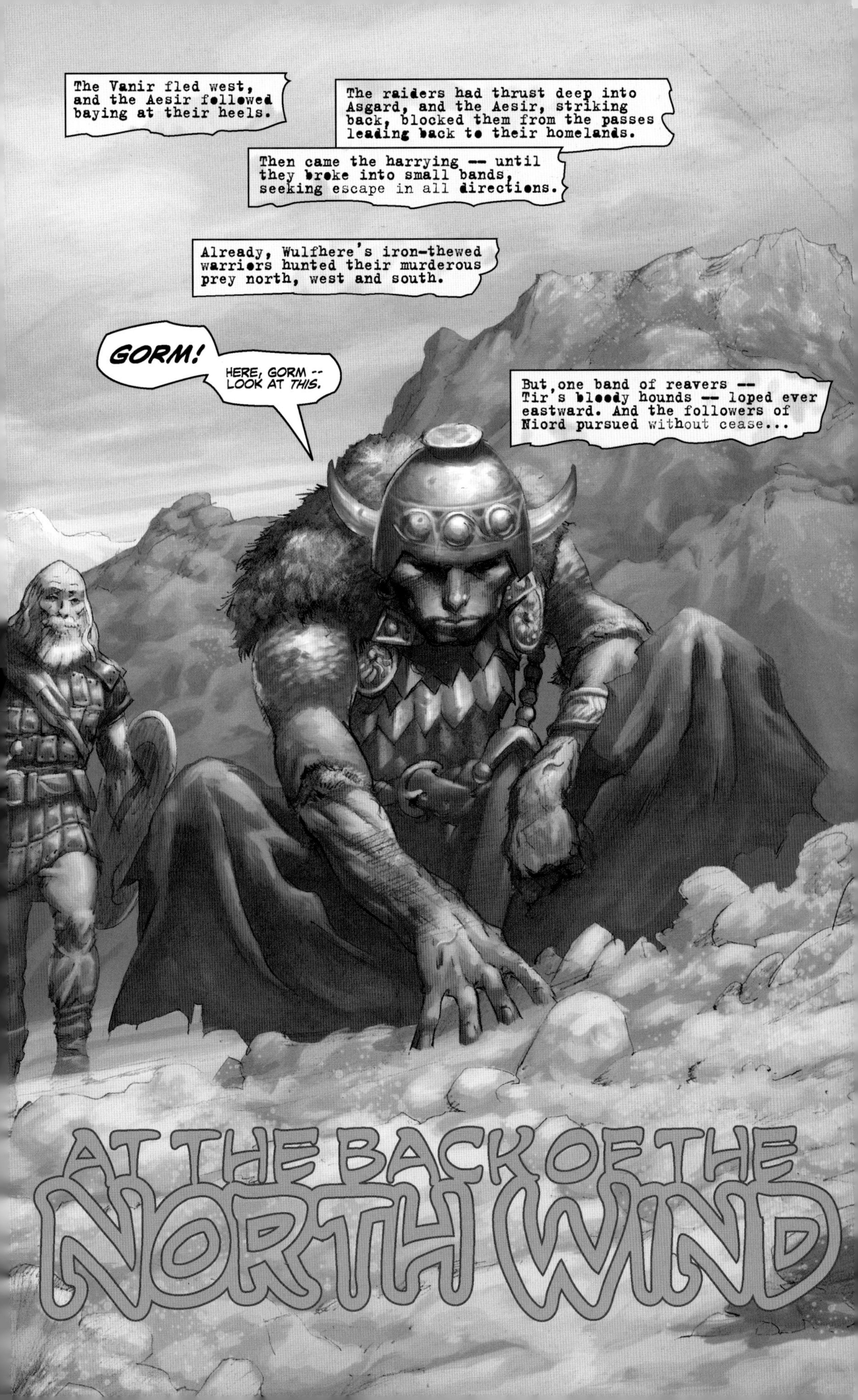
The Vanir fled west, and the Aesir followed baying at their heels.
The raiders had thrust deep into Asgard, and the Aesir, striking back, blocked them from the passes leading back to their homelands.
Then came the harrying -- until they broke into small bands, seeking escape in all directions.
Already, Wulfhere's iron-thewed warriors hunted their murderous prey north, west and south.
GORM!
HERE, GORM -- LOOK AT *THIS.*
But, one band of reavers -- Tir's bloody hounds -- loped ever eastward. And the followers of Niord pursued without cease...
AT THE BACK OF THE NORTH WIND

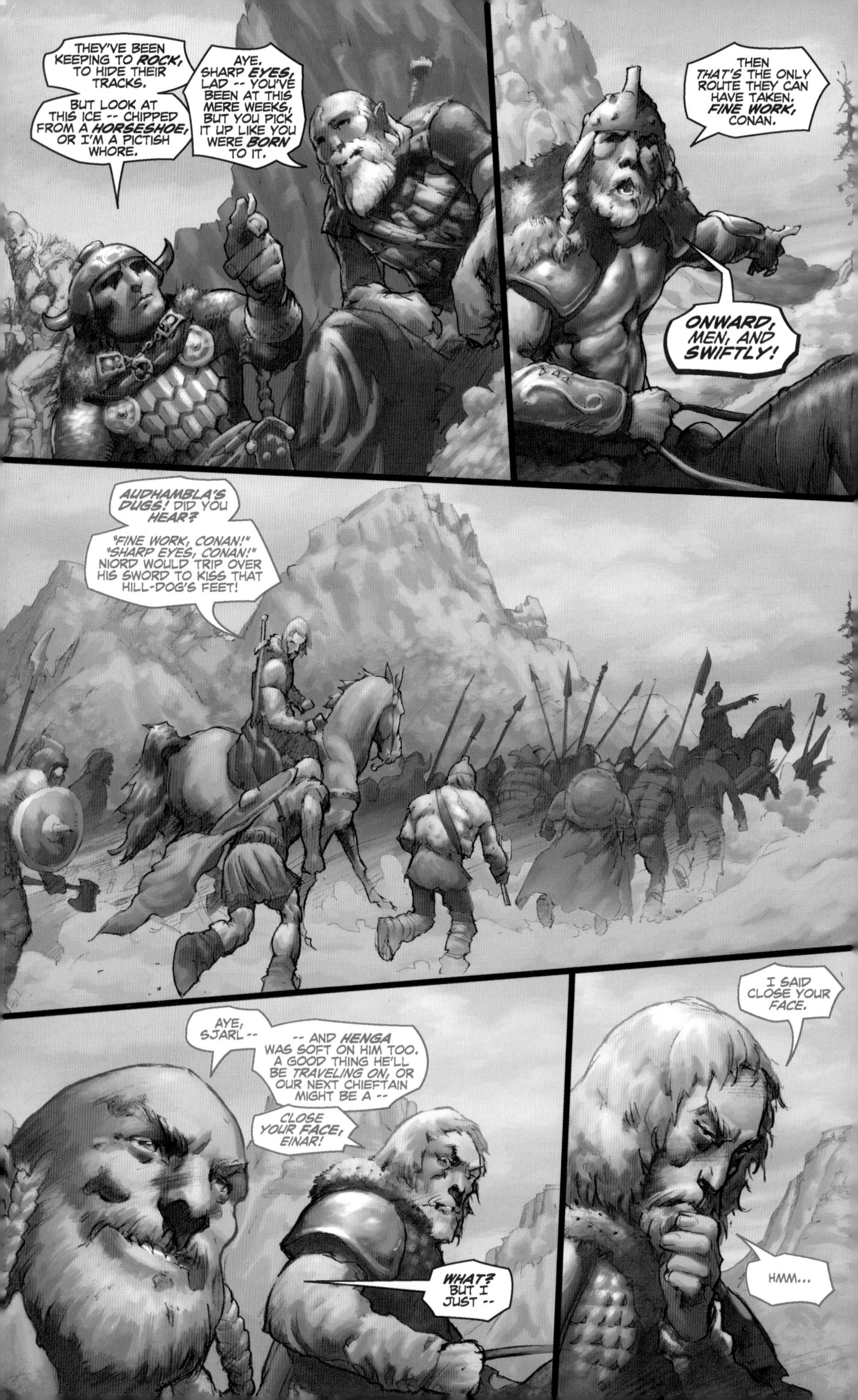
THEY'VE BEEN KEEPING TO ROCK, TO HIDE THEIR TRACKS.
BUT LOOK AT THIS ICE -- CHIPPED FROM A HORSESHOE, OR I'M A PICTISH WHORE.
AYE. SHARP EYES, LAD -- YOU'VE BEEN AT THIS MERE WEEKS, BUT YOU PICK IT UP LIKE YOU WERE BORN TO IT.
THEN THAT'S THE ONLY ROUTE THEY CAN HAVE TAKEN. FINE WORK, CONAN.
ONWARD, MEN, AND SWIFTLY!
AUDHAMBLA'S DUGS! DID YOU HEAR?
"FINE WORK, CONAN!" "SHARP EYES, CONAN!" NIORD WOULD TRIP OVER HIS SWORD TO KISS THAT HILL-DOG'S FEET!
AYE, SJARL --
-- AND HENGA WAS SOFT ON HIM TOO. A GOOD THING HE'LL BE TRAVELING ON, OR OUR NEXT CHIEFTAIN MIGHT BE A --
CLOSE YOUR FACE, EINAR!
WHAT? BUT I JUST --
I SAID CLOSE YOUR FACE.
HMM...

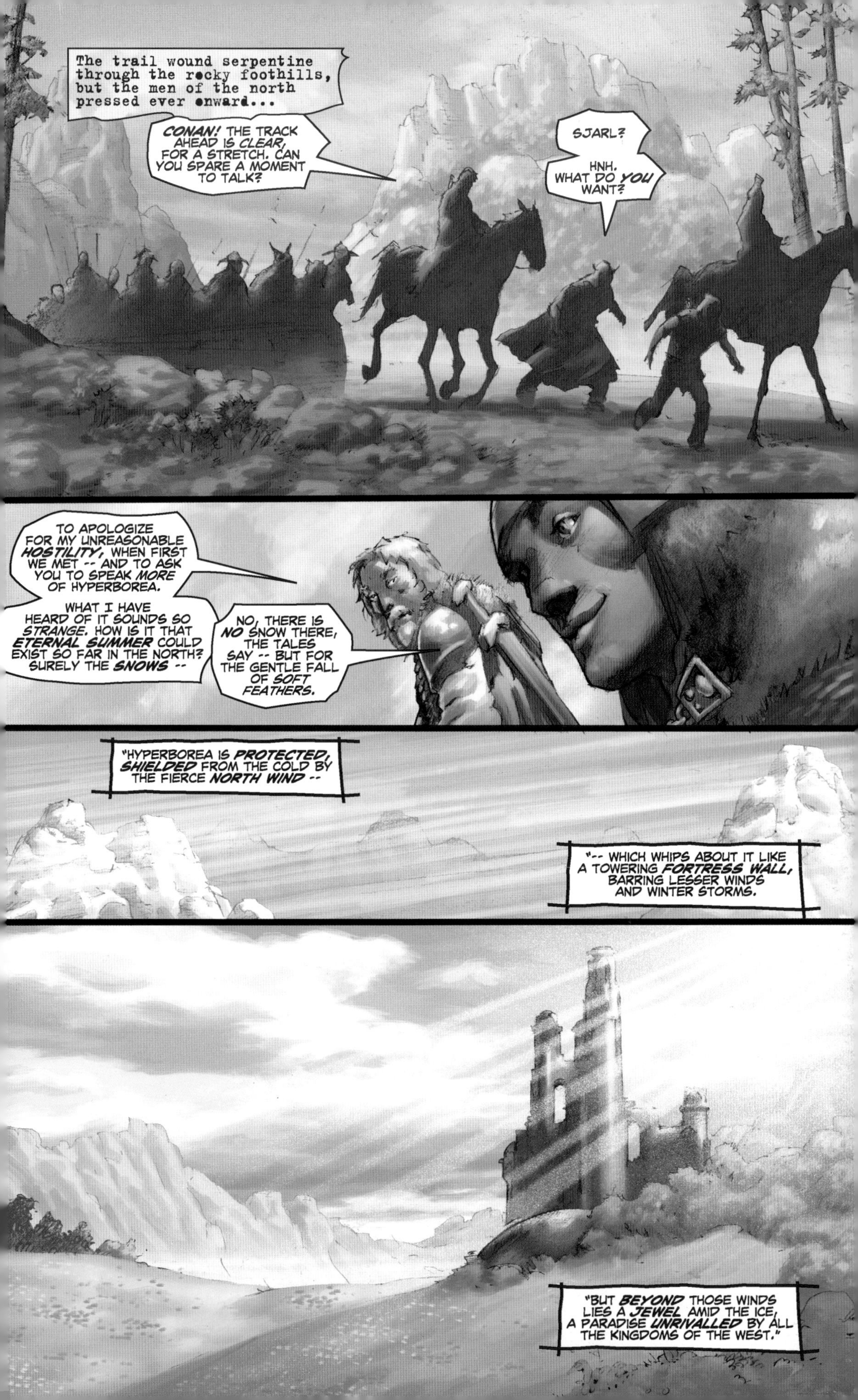
The trail wound serpentine through the rocky foothills, but the men of the north pressed ever onward...
CONAN! THE TRACK AHEAD IS CLEAR, FOR A STRETCH. CAN YOU SPARE A MOMENT TO TALK?
SJARL?
HNH. WHAT DO YOU WANT?
TO APOLOGIZE FOR MY UNREASONABLE HOSTILITY, WHEN FIRST WE MET -- AND TO ASK YOU TO SPEAK MORE OF HYPERBOREA.
WHAT I HAVE HEARD OF IT SOUNDS SO STRANGE. HOW IS IT THAT ETERNAL SUMMER COULD EXIST SO FAR IN THE NORTH? SURELY THE SNOWS --
NO, THERE IS NO SNOW THERE, THE TALES SAY -- BUT FOR THE GENTLE FALL OF SOFT FEATHERS.
"HYPERBOREA IS PROTECTED, SHIELDED FROM THE COLD BY THE FIERCE NORTH WIND --
"-- WHICH WHIPS ABOUT IT LIKE A TOWERING FORTRESS WALL, BARRING LESSER WINDS AND WINTER STORMS.
"BUT BEYOND THOSE WINDS LIES A JEWEL AMID THE ICE, A PARADISE UNRIVALLED BY ALL THE KINGDOMS OF THE WEST."

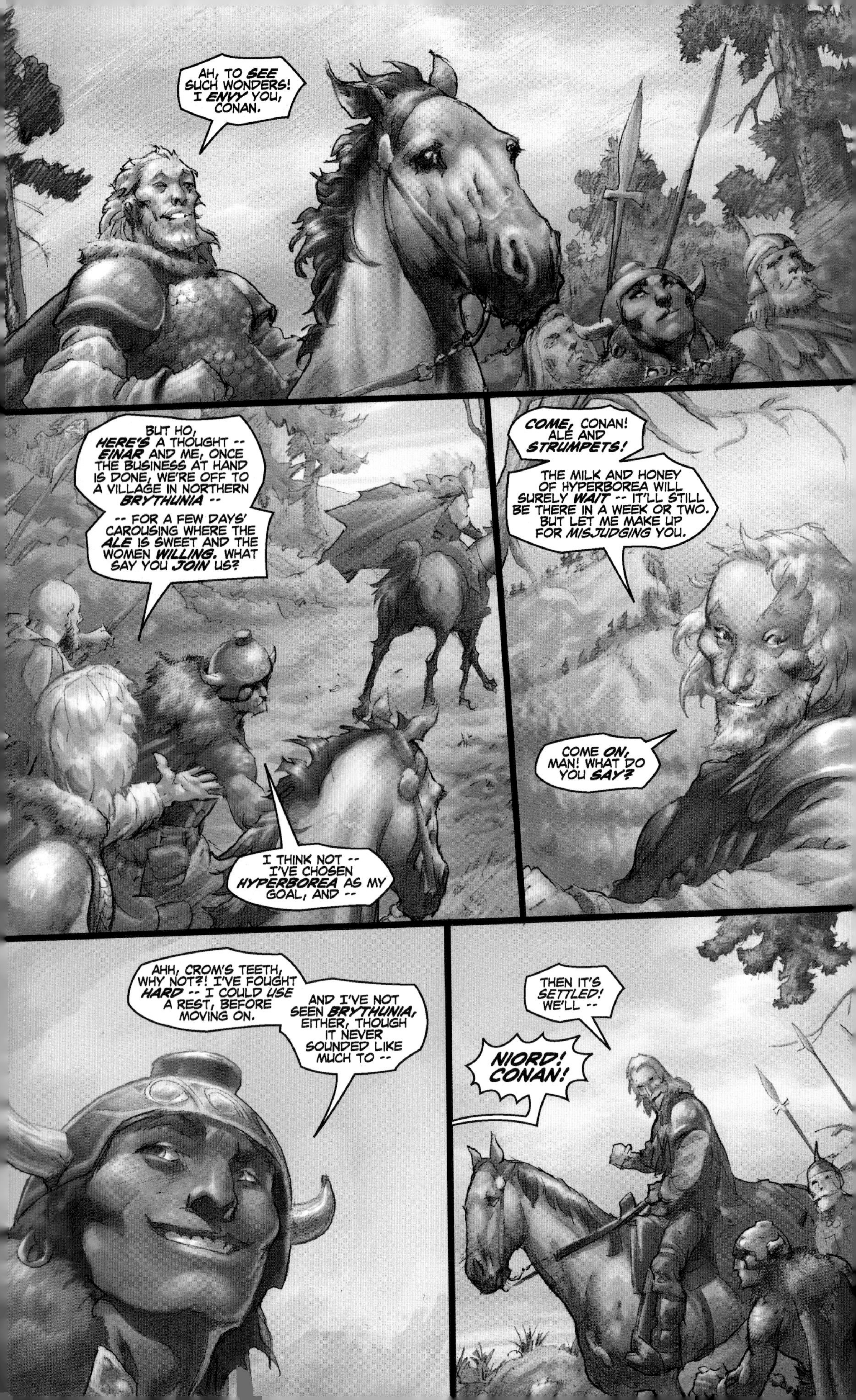
AH, TO SEE SUCH WONDERS! I ENVY YOU, CONAN.
BUT HO, HERE'S A THOUGHT -- EINAR AND ME, ONCE THE BUSINESS AT HAND IS DONE, WE'RE OFF TO A VILLAGE IN NORTHERN BRYTHUNIA --
-- FOR A FEW DAYS' CAROUSING WHERE THE ALE IS SWEET AND THE WOMEN WILLING. WHAT SAY YOU JOIN US?
I THINK NOT -- I'VE CHOSEN HYPERBOREA AS MY GOAL, AND --
COME, CONAN! ALE AND STRUMPETS!
THE MILK AND HONEY OF HYPERBOREA WILL SURELY WAIT -- IT'LL STILL BE THERE IN A WEEK OR TWO. BUT LET ME MAKE UP FOR MISJUDGING YOU.
COME ON, MAN! WHAT DO YOU SAY?
AHH, CROM'S TEETH, WHY NOT?! I'VE FOUGHT HARD -- I COULD USE A REST, BEFORE MOVING ON.
AND I'VE NOT SEEN BRYTHUNIA, EITHER, THOUGH IT NEVER SOUNDED LIKE MUCH TO --
THEN IT'S SETTLED! WE'LL --
NIORD! CONAN!

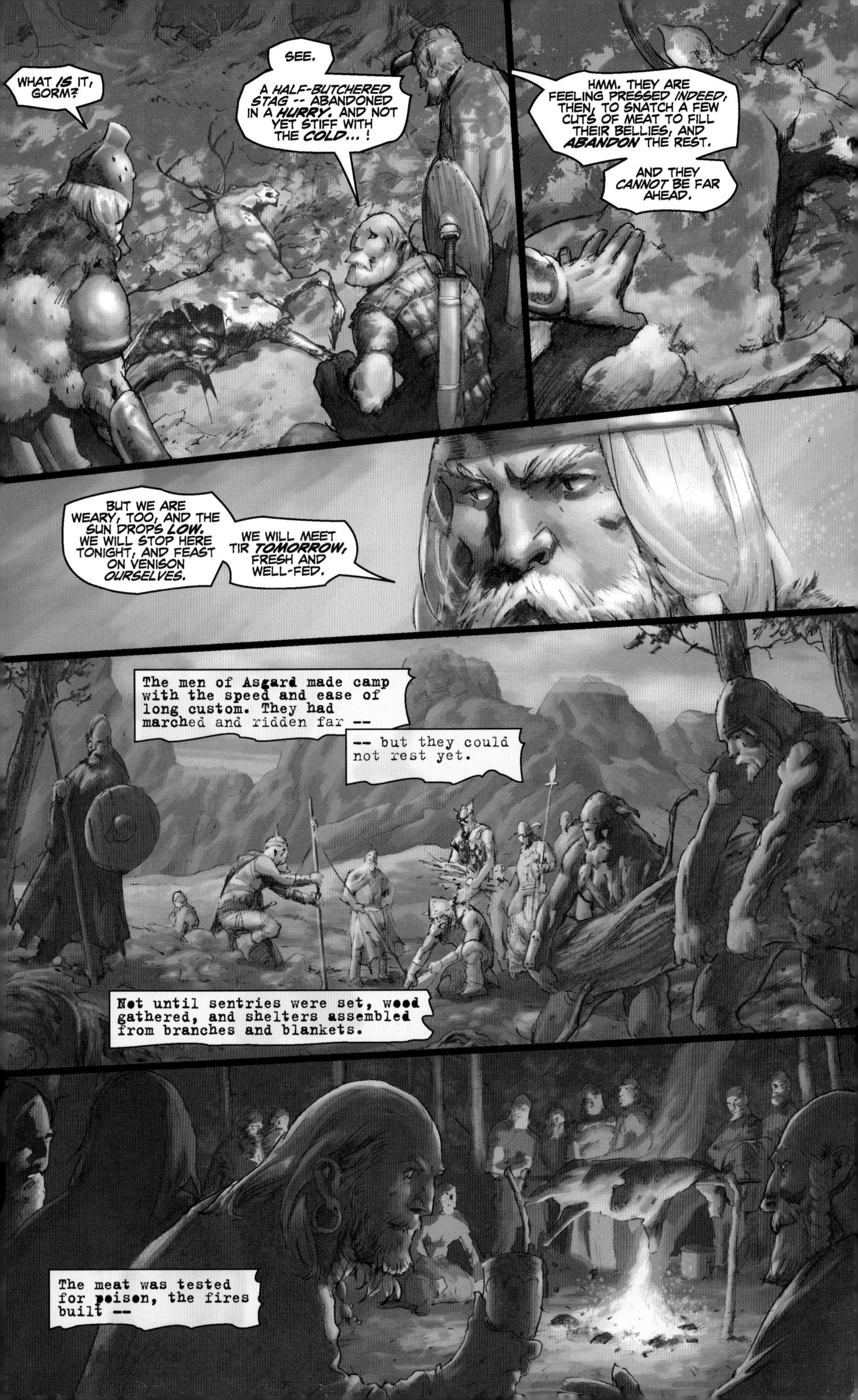
WHAT IS IT, GORM?
SEE.
A HALF-BUTCHERED STAG -- ABANDONED IN A HURRY. AND NOT YET STIFF WITH THE COLD... !
HMM. THEY ARE FEELING PRESSED INDEED, THEN, TO SNATCH A FEW CUTS OF MEAT TO FILL THEIR BELLIES, AND ABANDON THE REST.
AND THEY CANNOT BE FAR AHEAD.
BUT WE ARE WEARY, TOO, AND THE SUN DROPS LOW. WE WILL STOP HERE TONIGHT, AND FEAST ON VENISON OURSELVES.
WE WILL MEET TIR TOMORROW, FRESH AND WELL-FED.
The men of Asgard made camp with the speed and ease of long custom. They had marched and ridden far --
-- but they could not rest yet.
Not until sentries were set, wood gathered, and shelters assembled from branches and blankets.
The meat was tested for poison, the fires built --

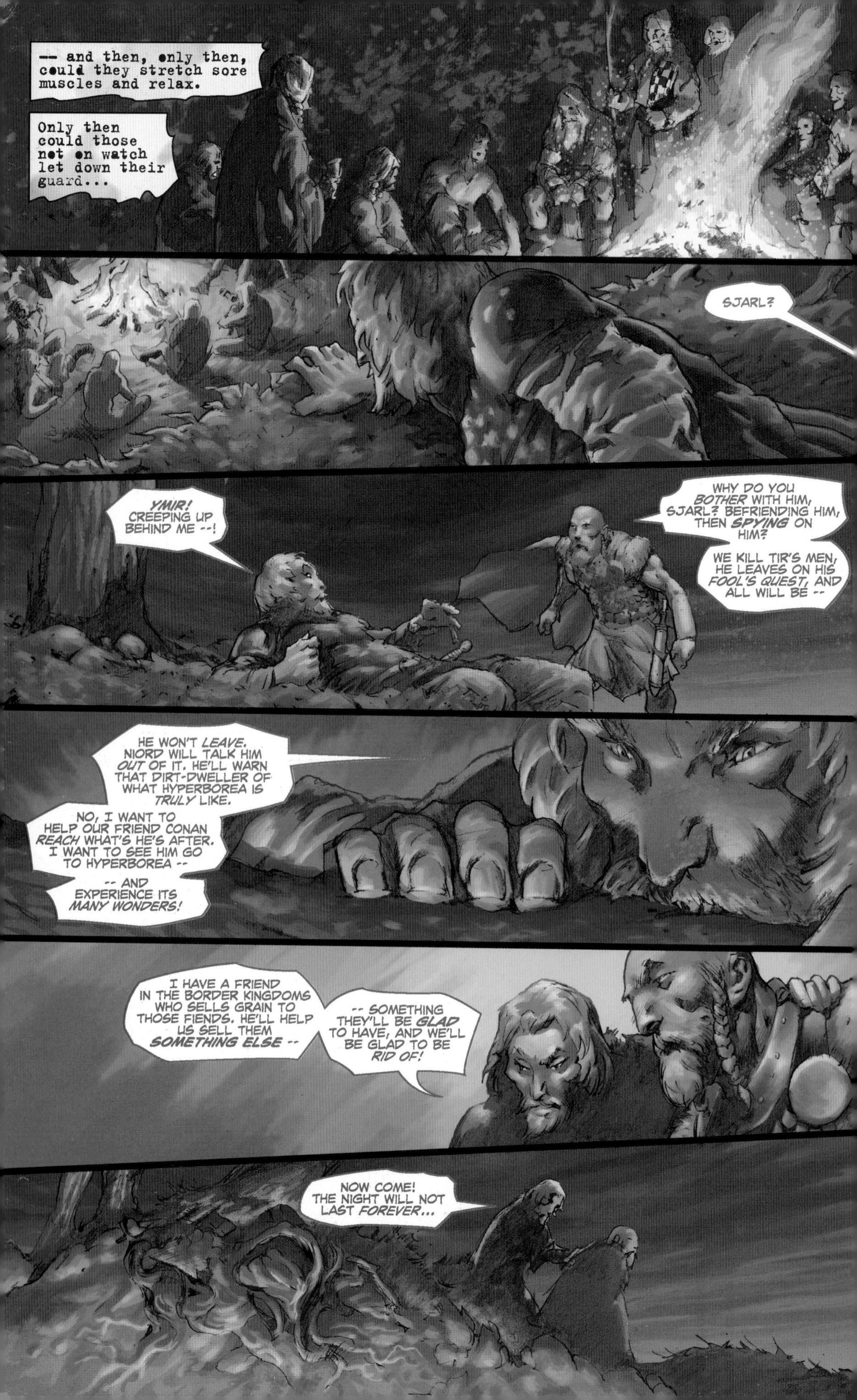
-- and then, only then, could they stretch sore muscles and relax.
Only then could those not on watch let down their guard...
SJARL?
YMIR! CREEPING UP BEHIND ME --!
WHY DO YOU BOTHER WITH HIM, SJARL? BEFRIENDING HIM, THEN SPYING ON HIM?
WE KILL TIR'S MEN, HE LEAVES ON HIS FOOL'S QUEST, AND ALL WILL BE --
HE WON'T LEAVE. NIORD WILL TALK HIM OUT OF IT. HE'LL WARN THAT DIRT-DWELLER OF WHAT HYPERBOREA IS TRULY LIKE.
NO, I WANT TO HELP OUR FRIEND CONAN REACH WHAT'S HE'S AFTER. I WANT TO SEE HIM GO TO HYPERBOREA --
-- AND EXPERIENCE ITS MANY WONDERS!
I HAVE A FRIEND IN THE BORDER KINGDOMS WHO SELLS GRAIN TO THOSE FIENDS. HE'LL HELP US SELL THEM SOMETHING ELSE --
-- SOMETHING THEY'LL BE GLAD TO HAVE, AND WE'LL BE GLAD TO BE RID OF!
NOW COME! THE NIGHT WILL NOT LAST FOREVER...

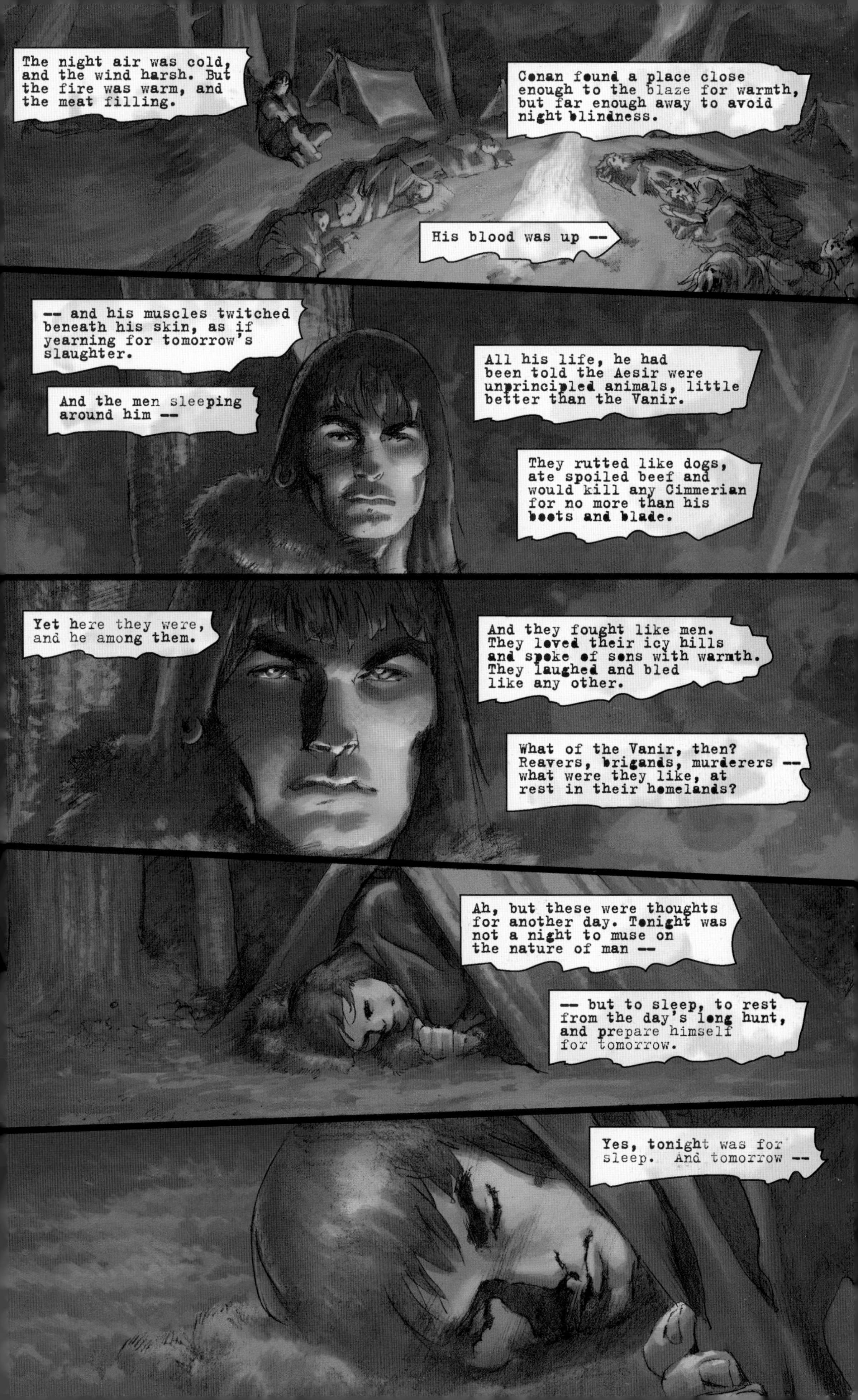
The night air was cold, and the wind harsh. But the fire was warm, and the meat filling.
Conan found a place close enough to the blaze for warmth, but far enough away to avoid night blindness.
His blood was up --
-- and his muscles twitched beneath his skin, as if yearning for tomorrow's slaughter.
And the men sleeping around him --
All his life, he had been told the Aesir were unprincipled animals, little better than the Vanir.
They rutted like dogs, ate spoiled beef and would kill any Cimmerian for no more than his boots and blade.
Yet here they were, and he among them.
And they fought like men. They loved their icy hills and spoke of sons with warmth. They laughed and bled like any other.
What of the Vanir, then? Reavers, brigands, murderers -- what were they like, at rest in their homelands?
Ah, but these were thoughts for another day. Tonight was not a night to muse on the nature of man --
-- but to sleep, to rest from the day's long hunt, and prepare himself for tomorrow.
Yes, tonight was for sleep. And tomorrow --

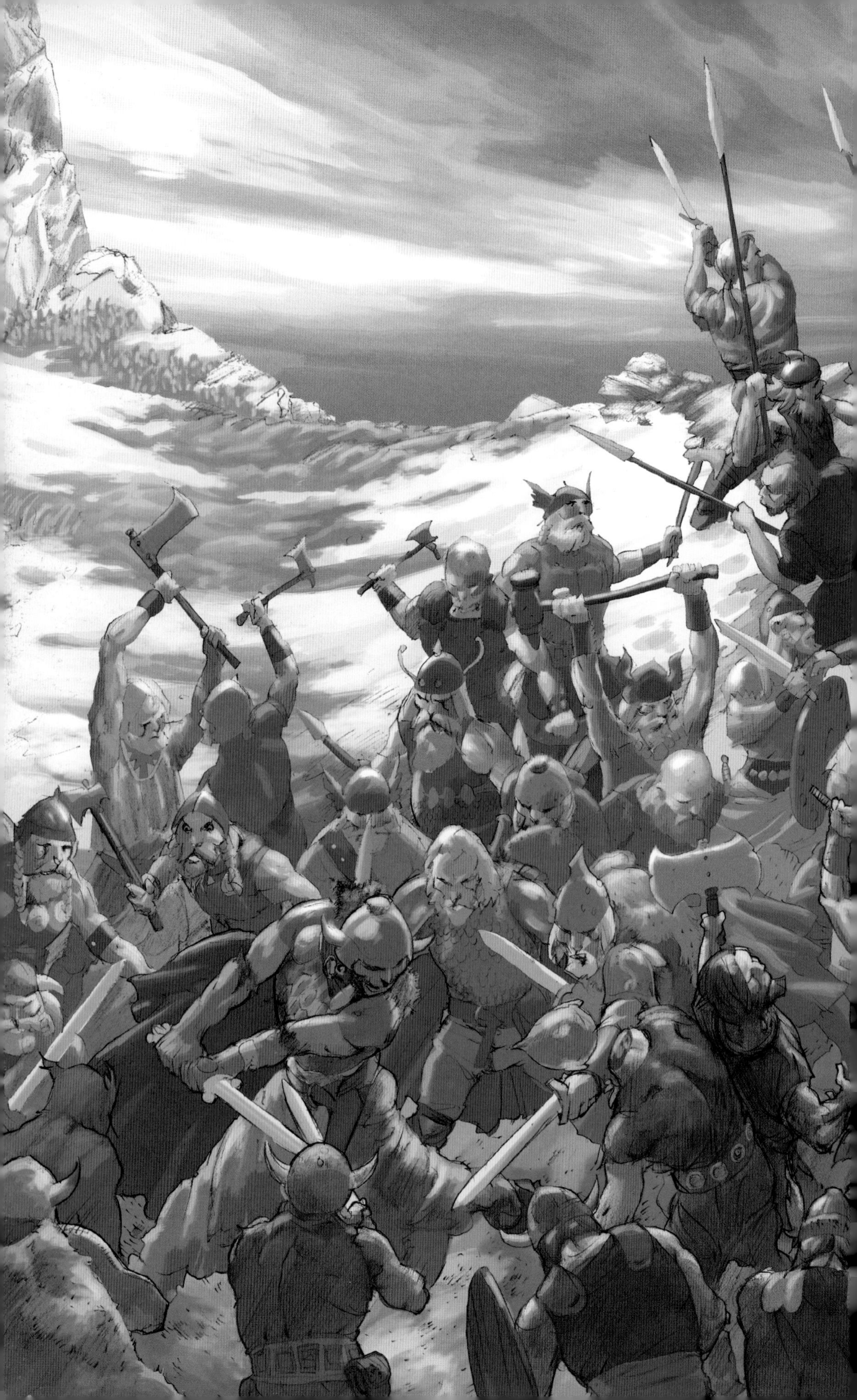

They fell on their foes an hour past daybreak.

The Vanir had been leading their steeds, their harnesses muffled, looking for a place to turn north -- and then west, for the long race home.

They fought desperately, knowing their only hope of survival was to win through.

But they were far from home, deep in a hostile land, and hope was swiftly flagging.

What they found was steel, and blood.

Still, it was in their eyes, in the set of their feet. Die they might, but they would fight -- fight right to the --

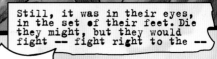

HOLD!

TRUCE, NIORD! A MOMENT'S TRUCE, I PRAY YOU!

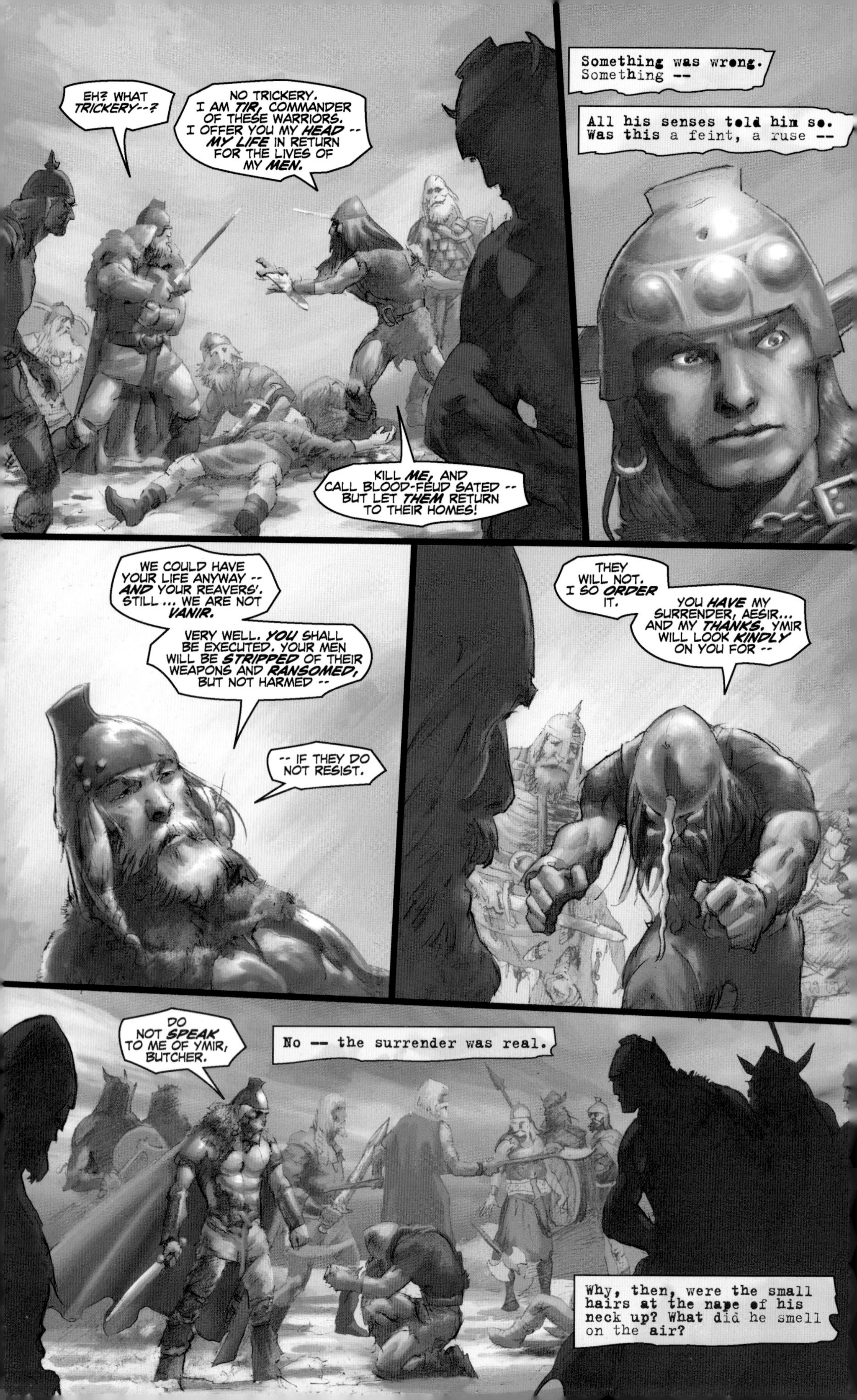
EH? WHAT TRICKERY--?
NO TRICKERY. I AM TIR, COMMANDER OF THESE WARRIORS. I OFFER YOU MY HEAD -- MY LIFE IN RETURN FOR THE LIVES OF MY MEN.
KILL ME, AND CALL BLOOD-FEUD SATED -- BUT LET THEM RETURN TO THEIR HOMES!
Something was wrong. Something --
All his senses told him so. Was this a feint, a ruse --
WE COULD HAVE YOUR LIFE ANYWAY -- AND YOUR REAVERS'. STILL ... WE ARE NOT VANIR.
VERY WELL. YOU SHALL BE EXECUTED. YOUR MEN WILL BE STRIPPED OF THEIR WEAPONS AND RANSOMED, BUT NOT HARMED --
-- IF THEY DO NOT RESIST.
THEY WILL NOT. I SO ORDER IT.
YOU HAVE MY SURRENDER, AESIR... AND MY THANKS. YMIR WILL LOOK KINDLY ON YOU FOR --
DO NOT SPEAK TO ME OF YMIR, BUTCHER.
No -- the surrender was real.
Why, then, were the small hairs at the nape of his neck up? What did he smell on the air?

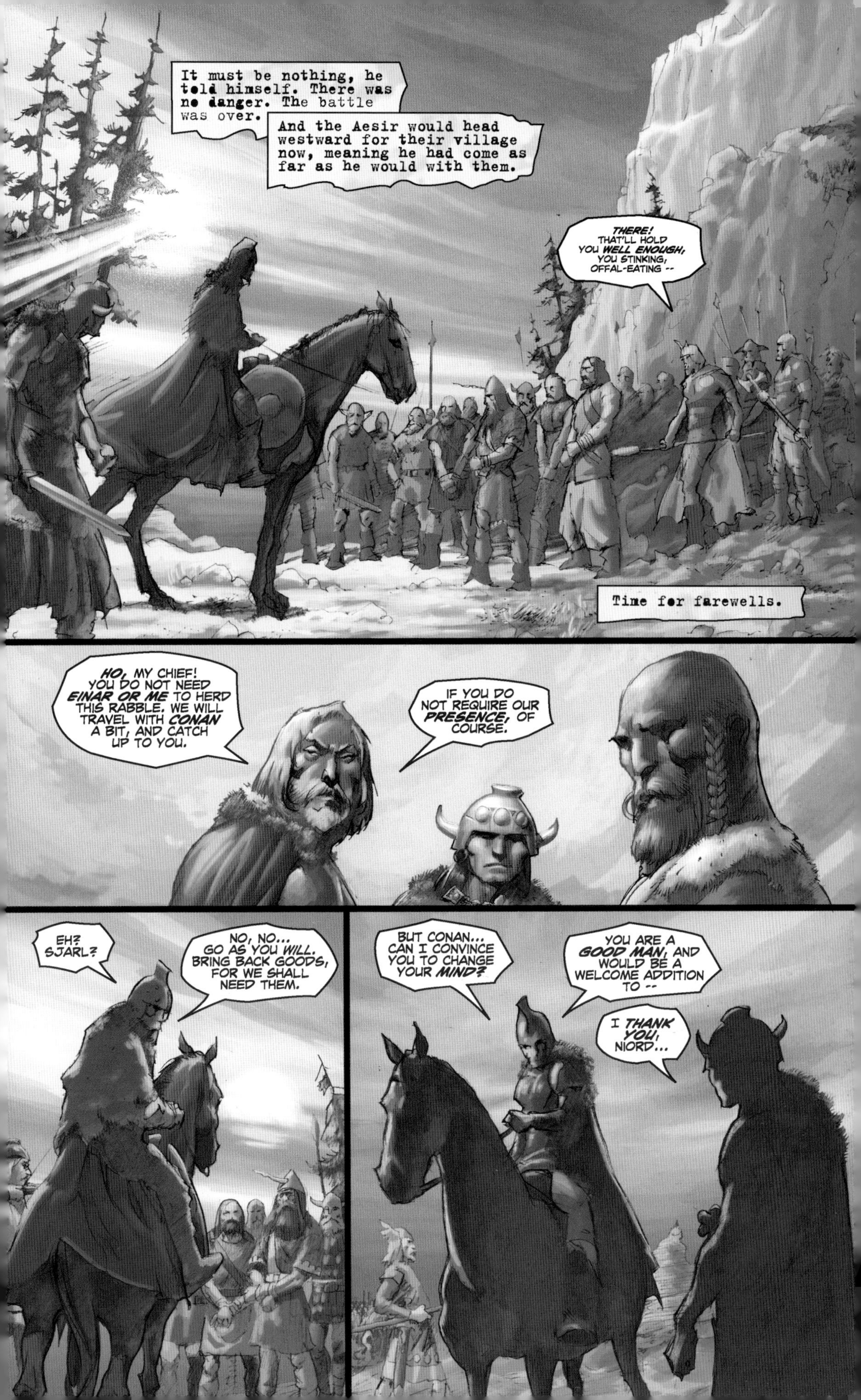
It must be nothing, he told himself. There was no danger. The battle was over.
And the Aesir would head westward for their village now, meaning he had come as far as he would with them.
THERE! THAT'LL HOLD YOU WELL ENOUGH, YOU STINKING, OFFAL-EATING --
Time for farewells.
HO, MY CHIEF! YOU DO NOT NEED EINAR OR ME TO HERD THIS RABBLE. WE WILL TRAVEL WITH CONAN A BIT, AND CATCH UP TO YOU.
IF YOU DO NOT REQUIRE OUR PRESENCE, OF COURSE.
EH? SJARL?
NO, NO... GO AS YOU WILL. BRING BACK GOODS, FOR WE SHALL NEED THEM.
BUT CONAN... CAN I CONVINCE YOU TO CHANGE YOUR MIND?
YOU ARE A GOOD MAN, AND WOULD BE A WELCOME ADDITION TO --
I THANK YOU, NIORD...

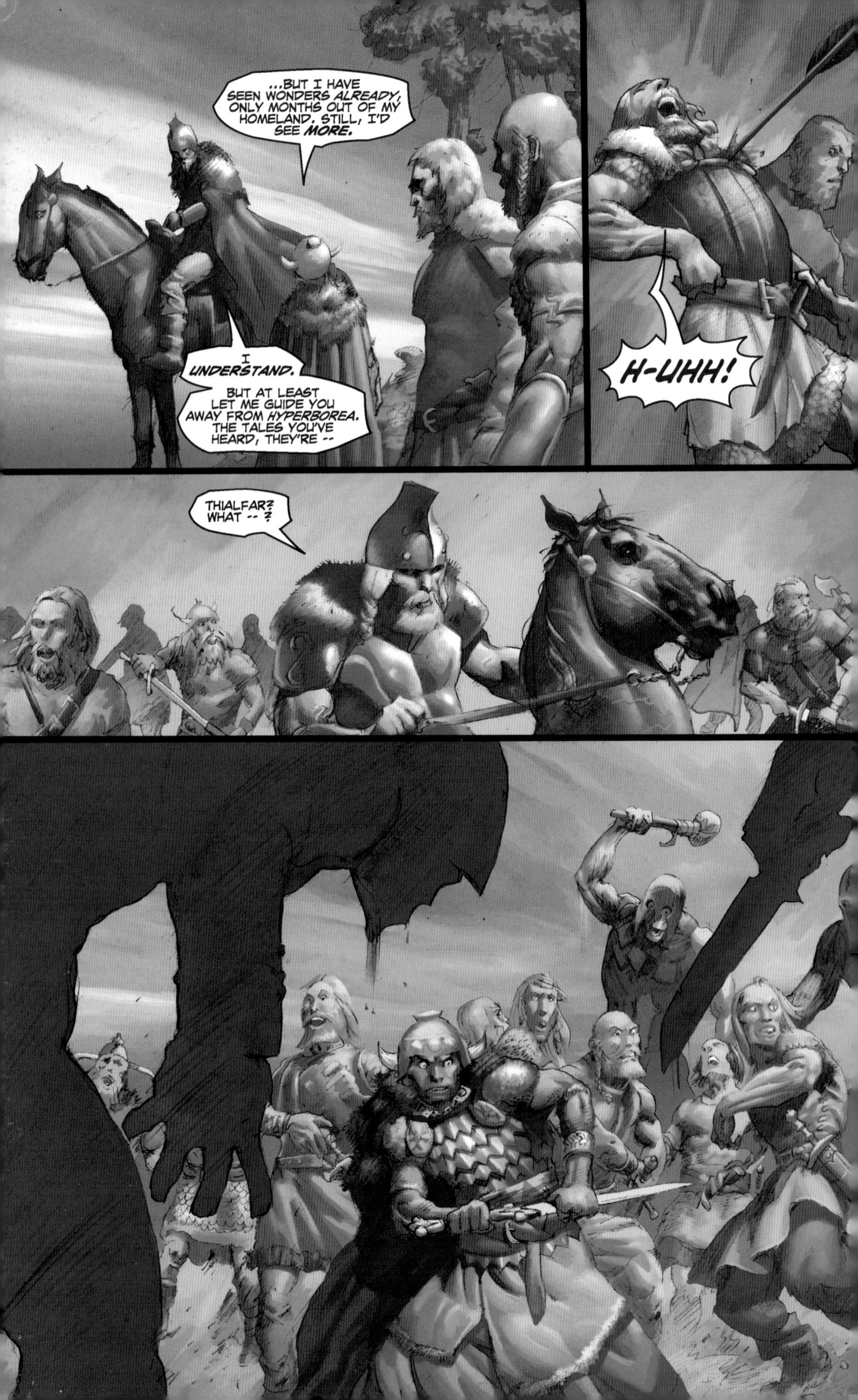
...BUT I HAVE SEEN WONDERS *ALREADY*, ONLY MONTHS OUT OF MY HOMELAND. STILL, I'D SEE ***MORE.***
I ***UNDERSTAND.***
BUT AT LEAST LET ME GUIDE YOU AWAY FROM *HYPERBOREA*. THE TALES YOU'VE HEARD, THEY'RE --
H-UHH!
THIALFAR? WHAT -- ?

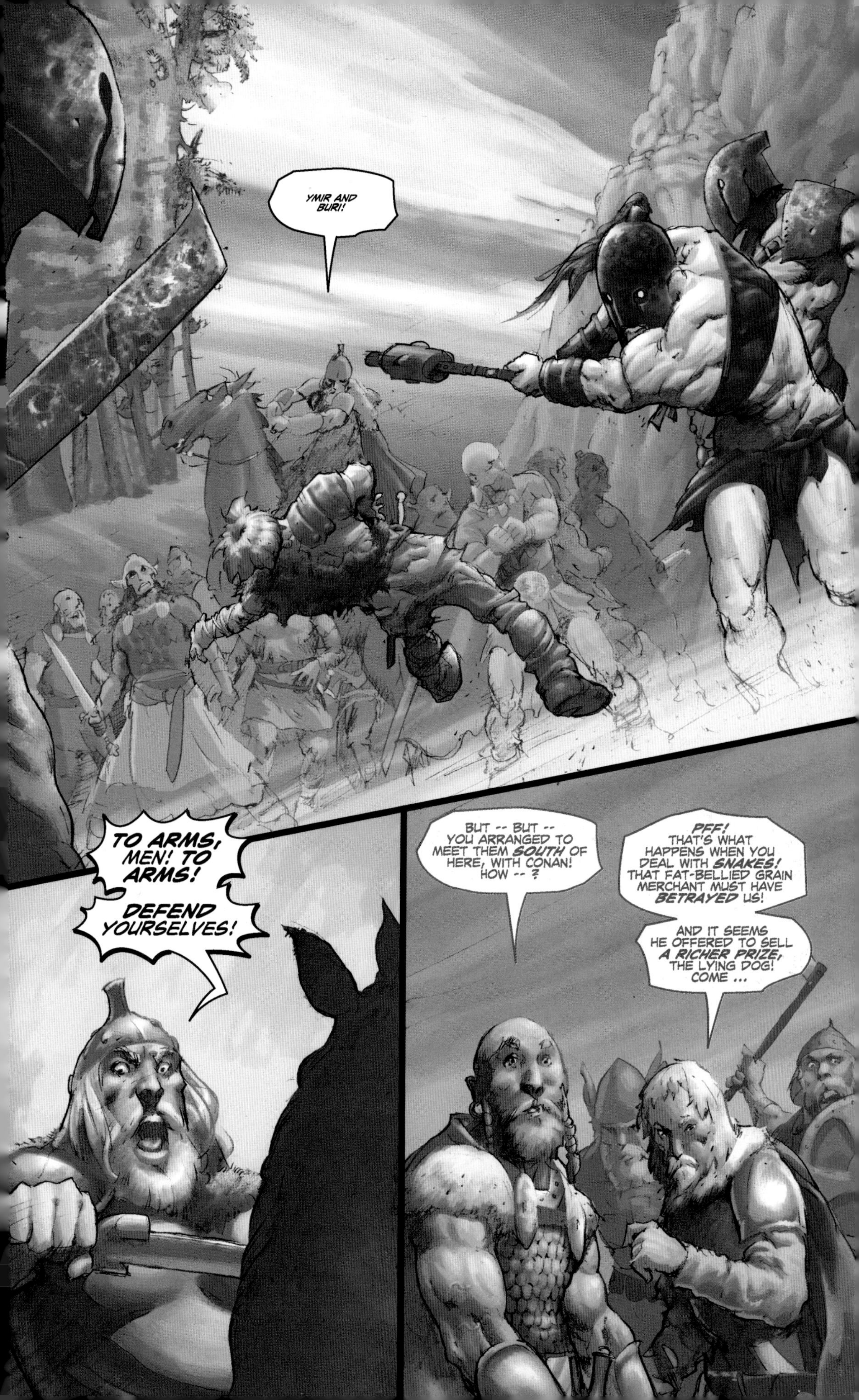
YMIR AND BURI!
TO ARMS, MEN! TO ARMS!
DEFEND YOURSELVES!
BUT -- BUT -- YOU ARRANGED TO MEET THEM SOUTH OF HERE, WITH CONAN! HOW -- ?
PFF! THAT'S WHAT HAPPENS WHEN YOU DEAL WITH SNAKES! THAT FAT-BELLIED GRAIN MERCHANT MUST HAVE BETRAYED US!
AND IT SEEMS HE OFFERED TO SELL A RICHER PRIZE, THE LYING DOG! COME ...

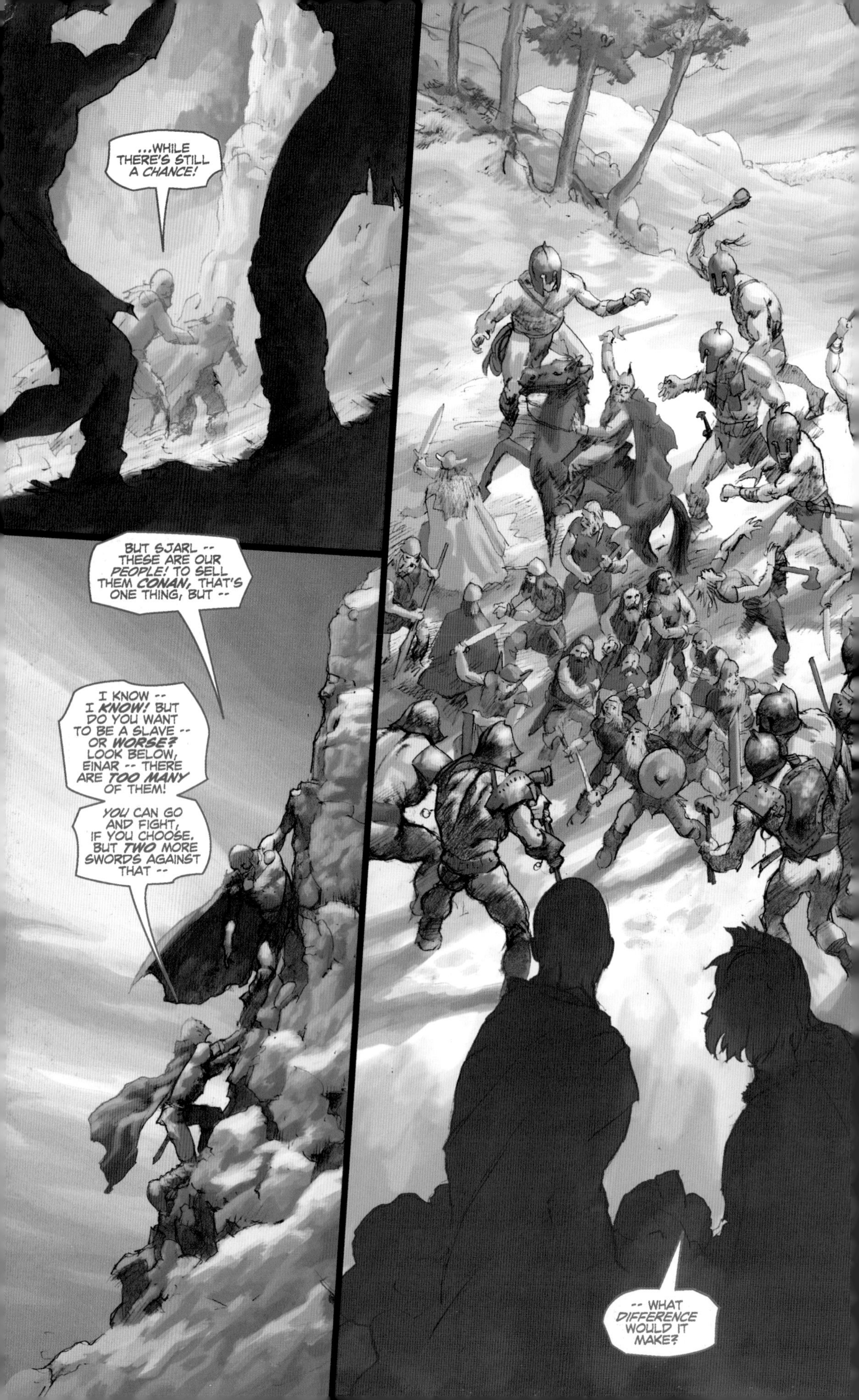
...WHILE THERE'S STILL A *CHANCE!*
BUT SJARL -- THESE ARE OUR *PEOPLE!* TO SELL THEM *CONAN,* THAT'S ONE THING, BUT --
I KNOW -- I ***KNOW!*** BUT DO YOU WANT TO BE A SLAVE -- OR ***WORSE?*** LOOK BELOW, EINAR -- THERE ARE ***TOO MANY*** OF THEM!
YOU CAN GO AND FIGHT, IF YOU CHOOSE. BUT ***TWO*** MORE SWORDS AGAINST THAT --
-- WHAT *DIFFERENCE* WOULD IT MAKE?

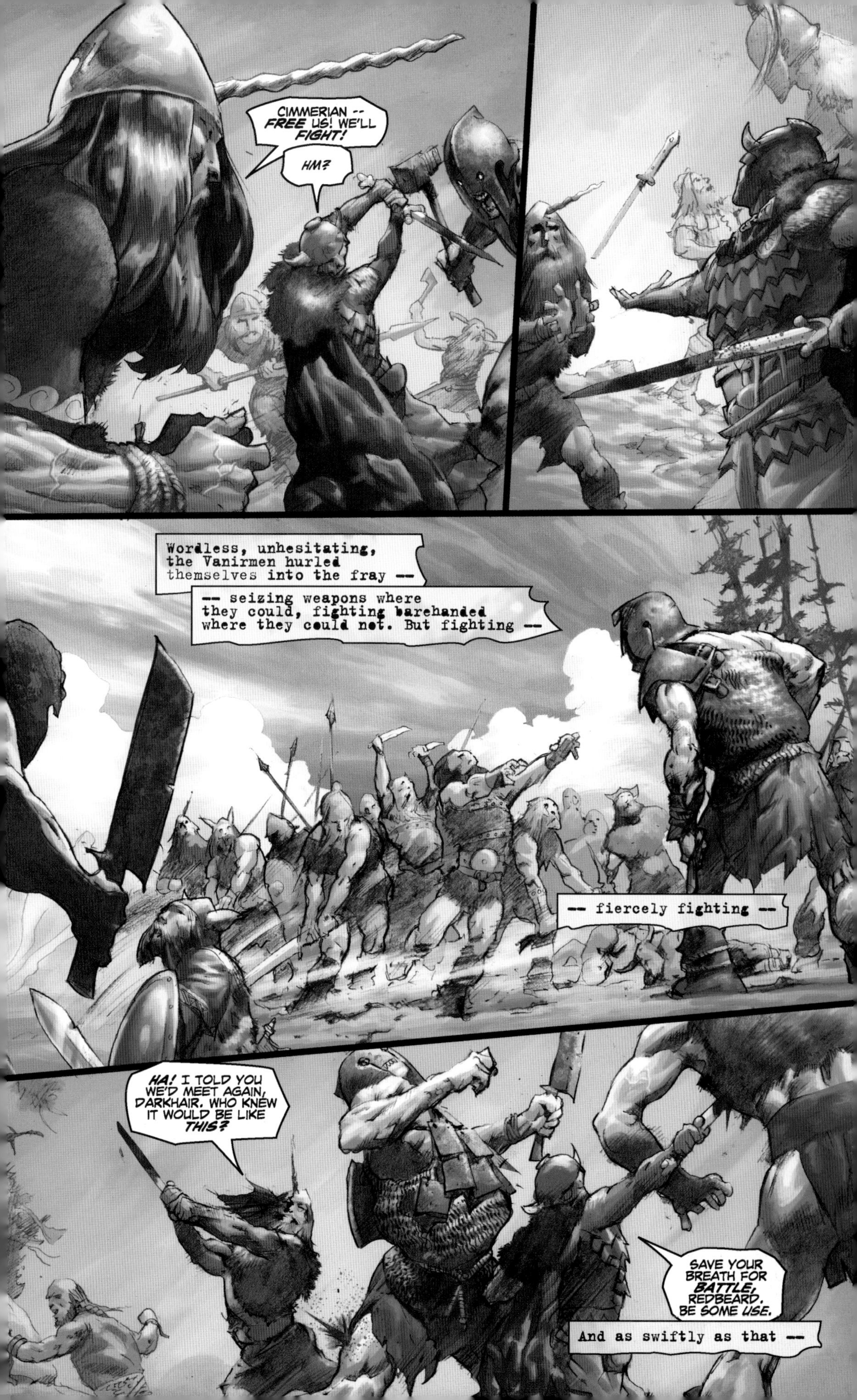
CIMMERIAN -- FREE US! WE'LL FIGHT!
HM?
Wordless, unhesitating, the Vanirmen hurled themselves into the fray --
-- seizing weapons where they could, fighting barehanded where they could not. But fighting --
-- fiercely fighting --
HA! I TOLD YOU WE'D MEET AGAIN, DARKHAIR. WHO KNEW IT WOULD BE LIKE THIS?
SAVE YOUR BREATH FOR BATTLE, REDBEARD. BE SOME USE.
And as swiftly as that --

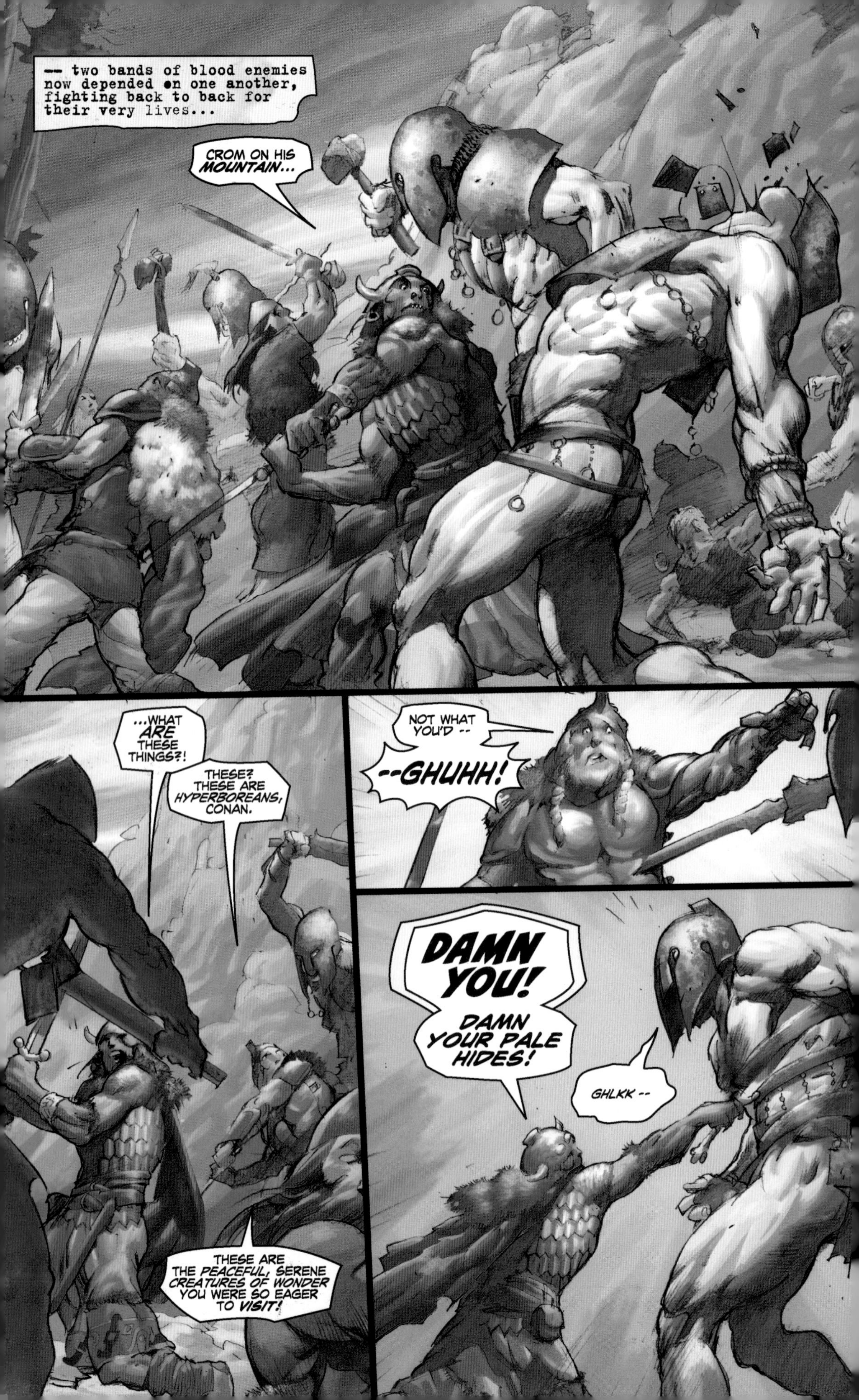

-- two bands of blood enemies now depended on one another, fighting back to back for their very lives...
CROM ON HIS MOUNTAIN...
...WHAT ARE THESE THINGS?!
THESE? THESE ARE HYPERBOREANS, CONAN.
THESE ARE THE PEACEFUL, SERENE CREATURES OF WONDER YOU WERE SO EAGER TO VISIT!
NOT WHAT YOU'D --
--GHUHH!
DAMN YOU!
DAMN YOUR PALE HIDES!
GHLKK --

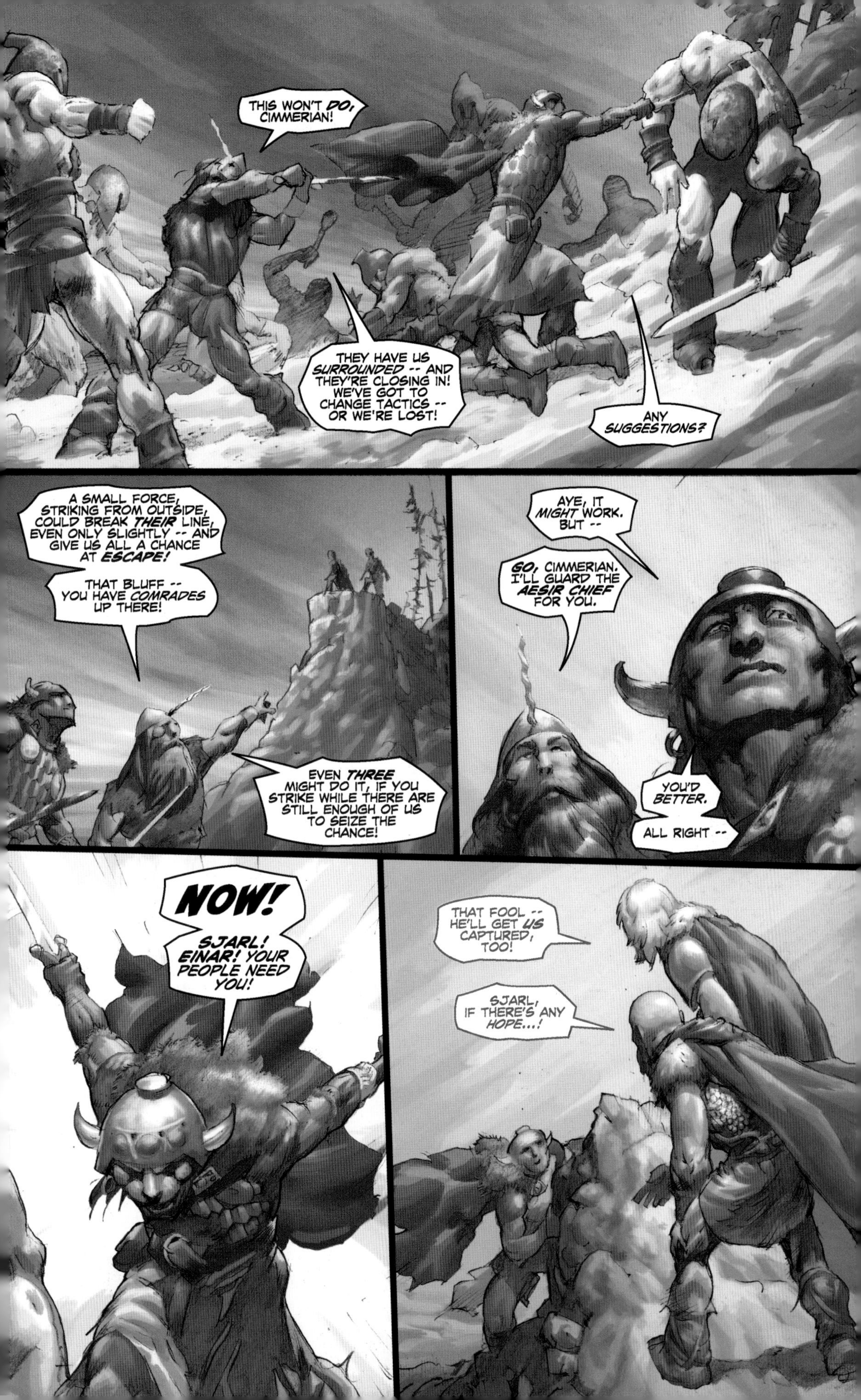
THIS WON'T DO, CIMMERIAN!
THEY HAVE US SURROUNDED -- AND THEY'RE CLOSING IN! WE'VE GOT TO CHANGE TACTICS -- OR WE'RE LOST!
ANY SUGGESTIONS?
A SMALL FORCE, STRIKING FROM OUTSIDE, COULD BREAK THEIR LINE, EVEN ONLY SLIGHTLY -- AND GIVE US ALL A CHANCE AT ESCAPE!
THAT BLUFF -- YOU HAVE COMRADES UP THERE!
EVEN THREE MIGHT DO IT, IF YOU STRIKE WHILE THERE ARE STILL ENOUGH OF US TO SEIZE THE CHANCE!
AYE, IT MIGHT WORK. BUT --
GO, CIMMERIAN. I'LL GUARD THE AESIR CHIEF FOR YOU.
YOU'D BETTER.
ALL RIGHT --
NOW!
SJARL! EINAR! YOUR PEOPLE NEED YOU!
THAT FOOL -- HE'LL GET US CAPTURED, TOO!
SJARL, IF THERE'S ANY HOPE...!

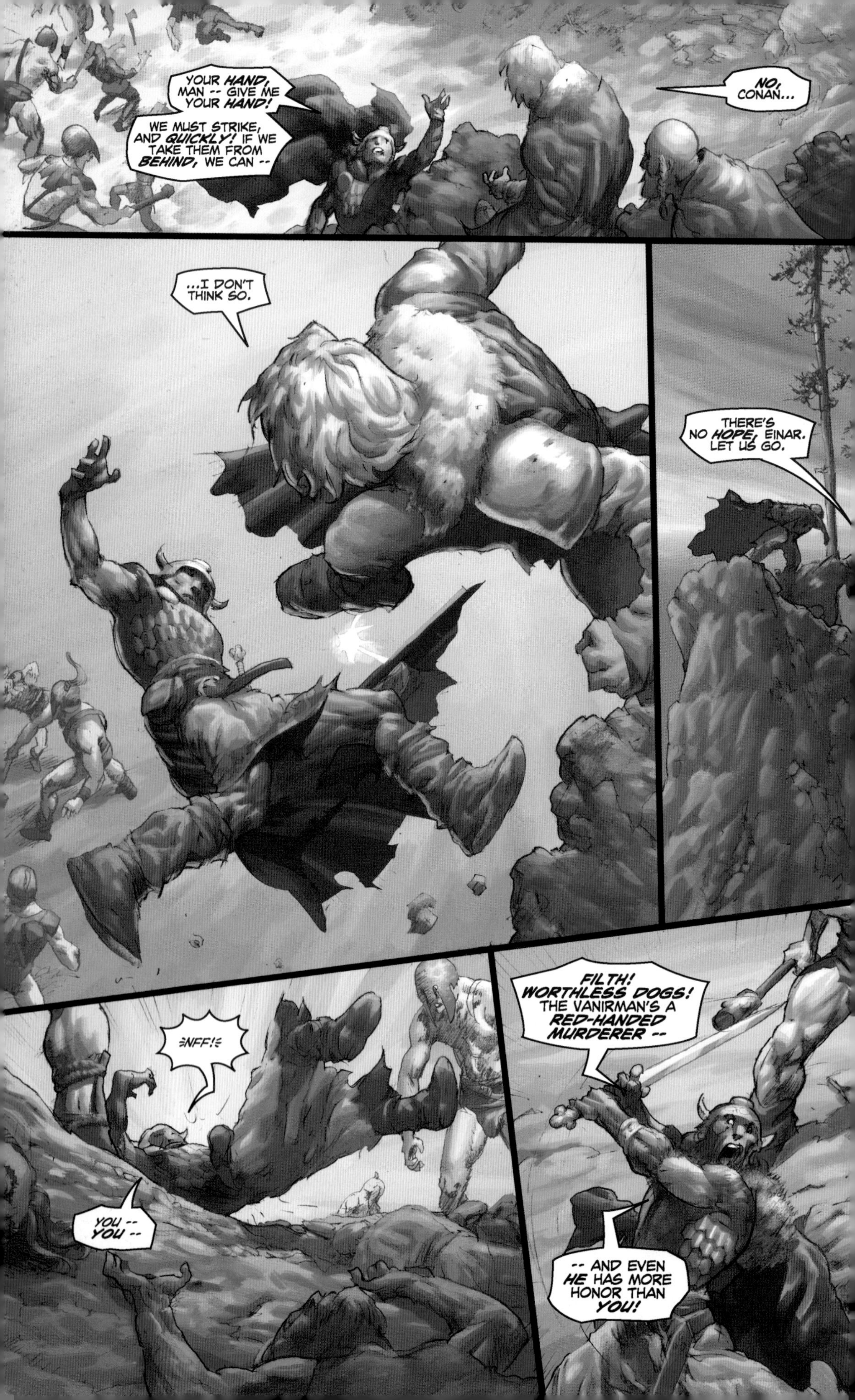
YOUR *HAND,* MAN -- GIVE ME YOUR *HAND!*
WE MUST STRIKE, AND *QUICKLY!* IF WE TAKE THEM FROM *BEHIND,* WE CAN --
NO, CONAN...
...I DON'T THINK SO.
THERE'S NO *HOPE,* EINAR. LET US GO.
NFF!
YOU -- *YOU* --
FILTH! WORTHLESS DOGS! THE VANIRMAN'S A *RED-HANDED MURDERER* --
-- AND EVEN *HE* HAS MORE HONOR THAN *YOU!*

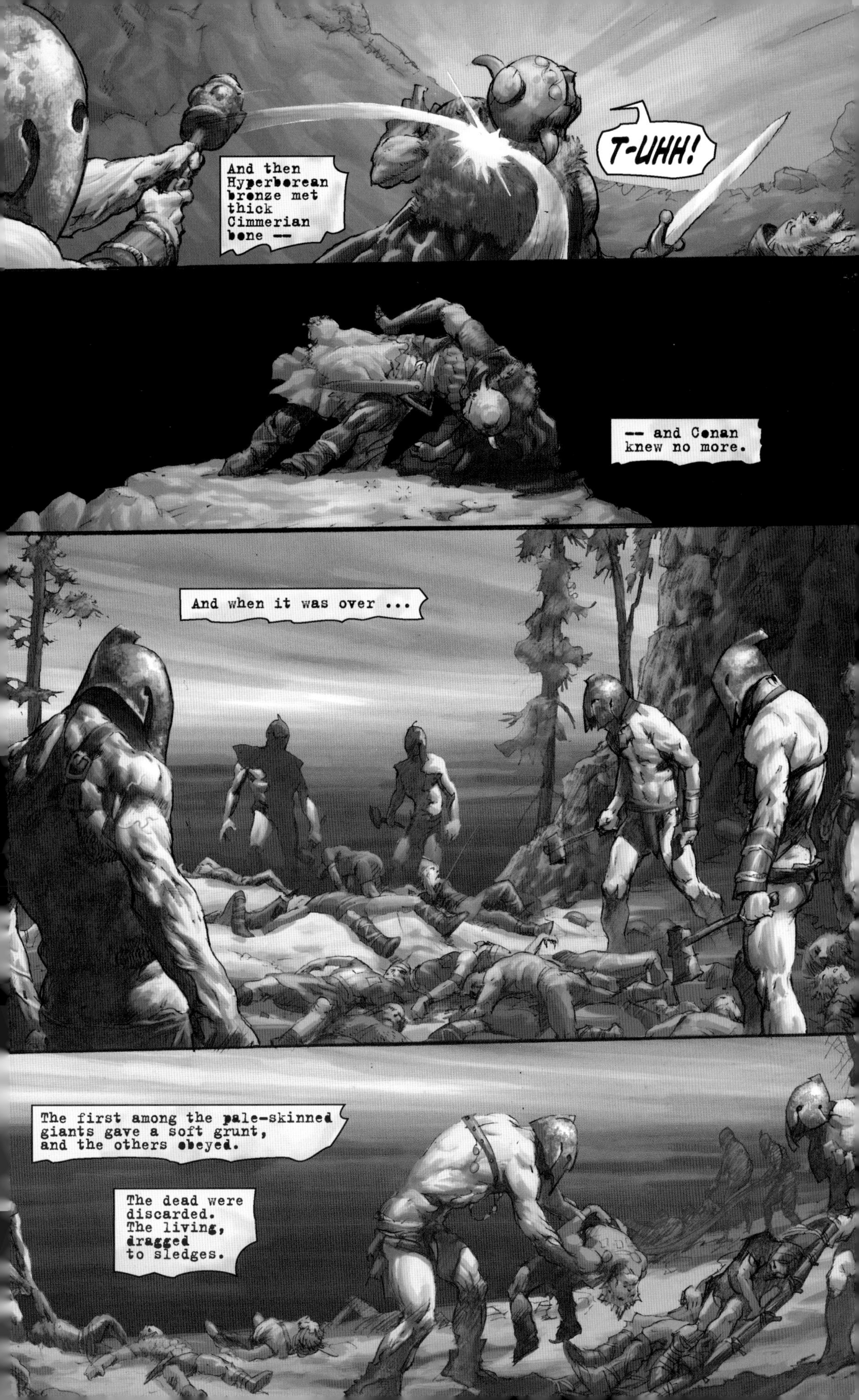
And then Hyperborean bronze met thick Cimmerian bone --
T-UHH!
-- and Conan knew no more.
And when it was over ...
The first among the pale-skinned giants gave a soft grunt, and the others obeyed.
The dead were discarded. The living, dragged to sledges.

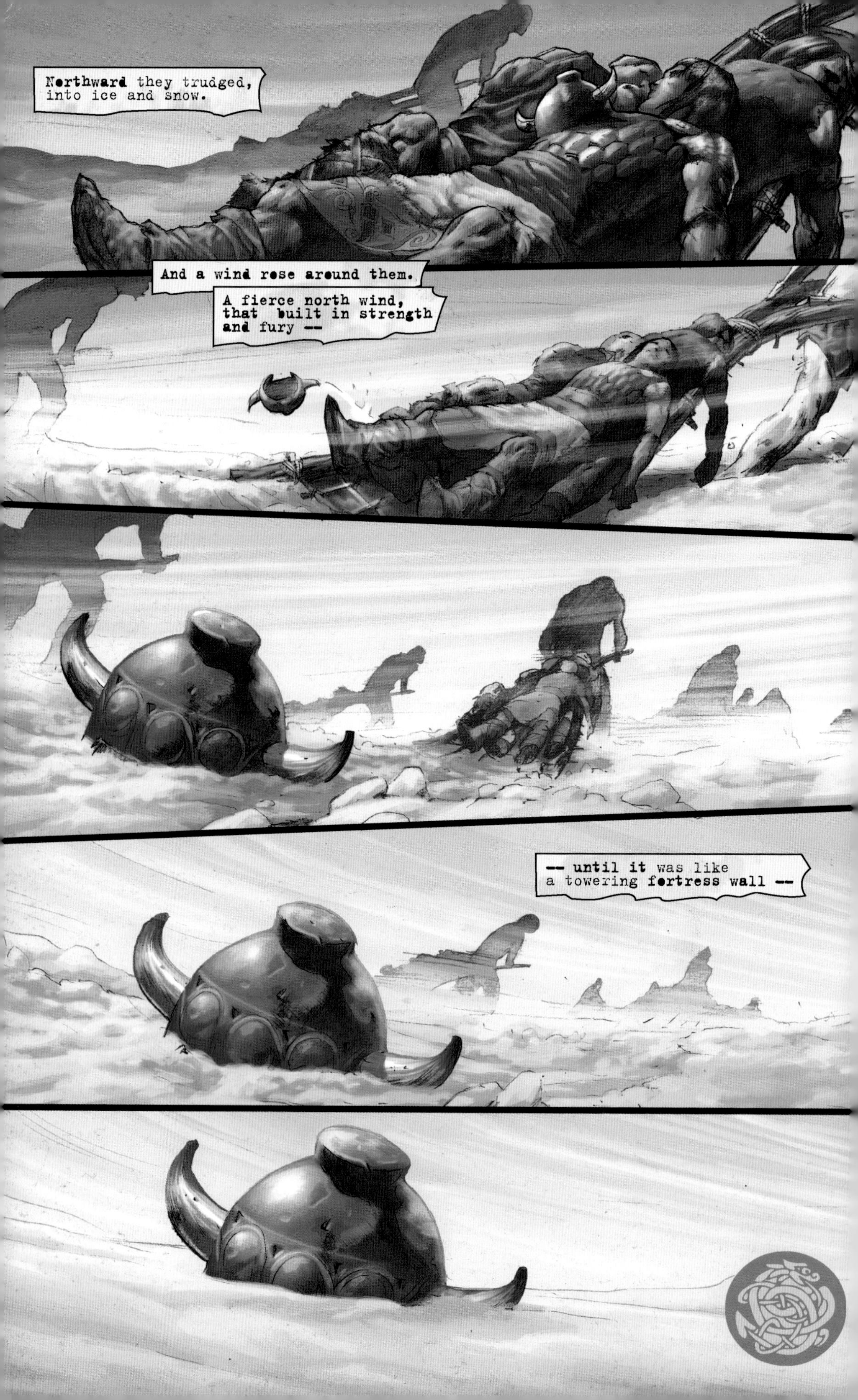
Northward they trudged, into ice and snow.
And a wind rose around them.
A fierce north wind, that built in strength and fury --
-- until it was like a towering fortress wall --

CHAPTER FOUR

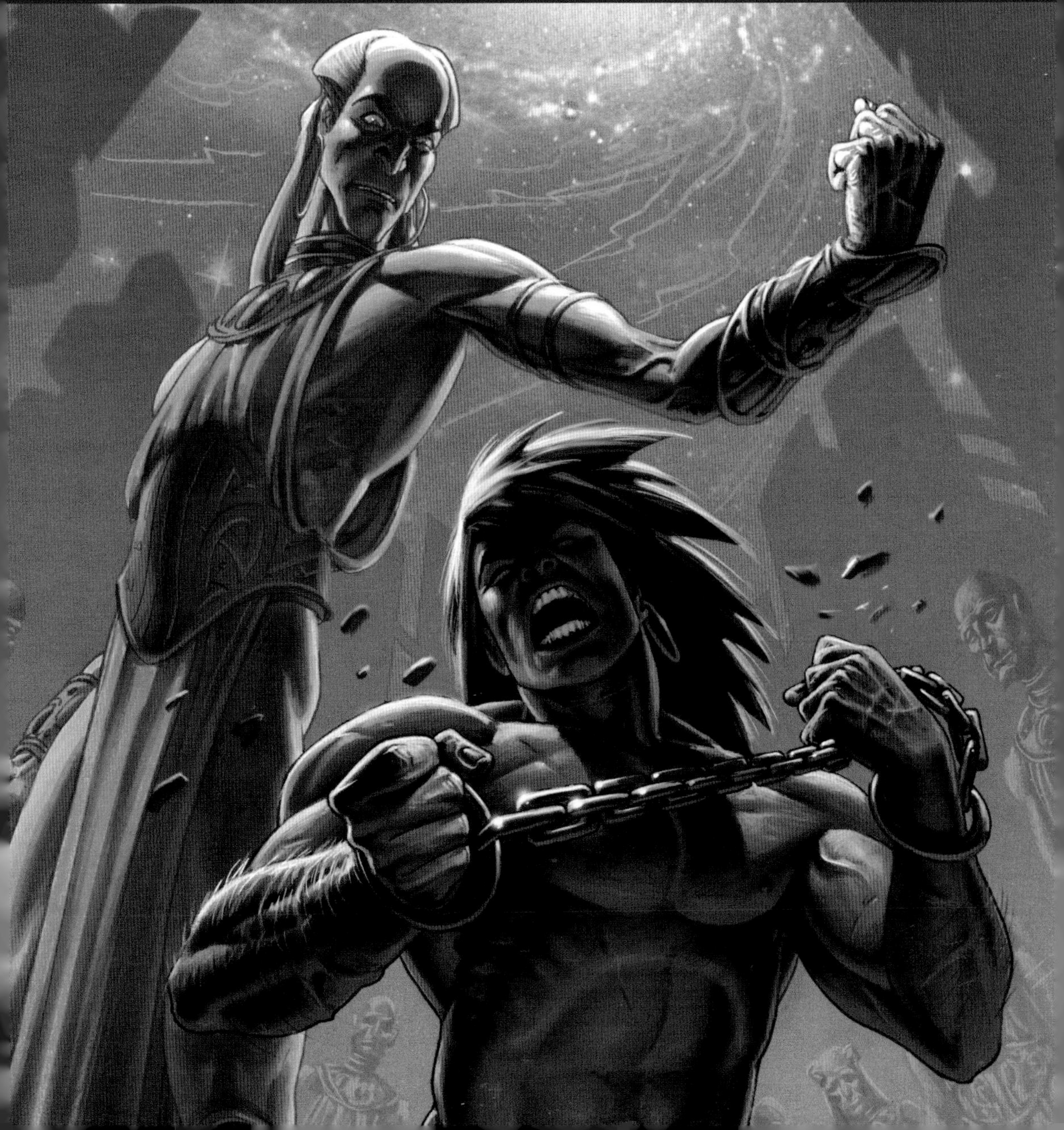

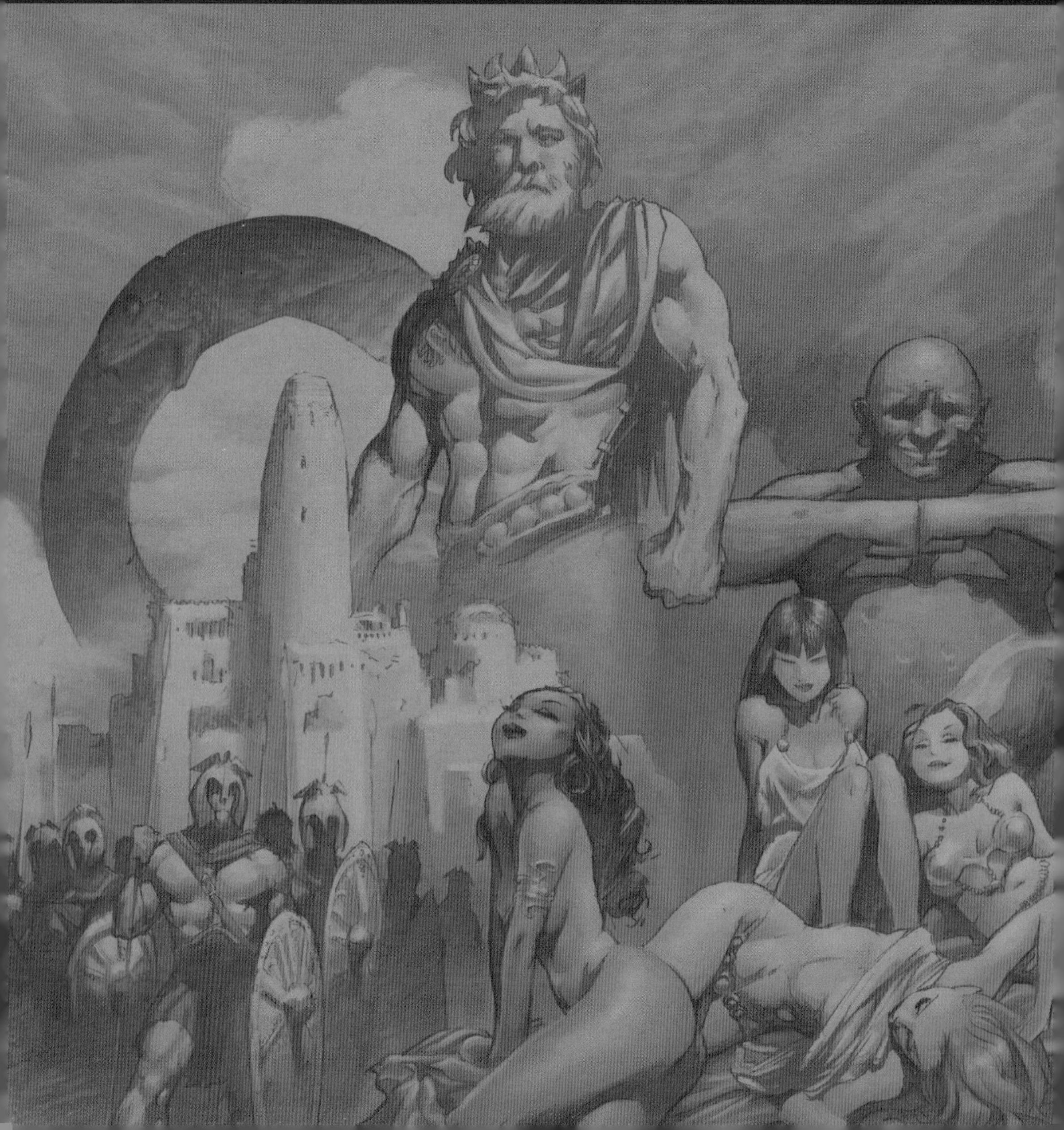

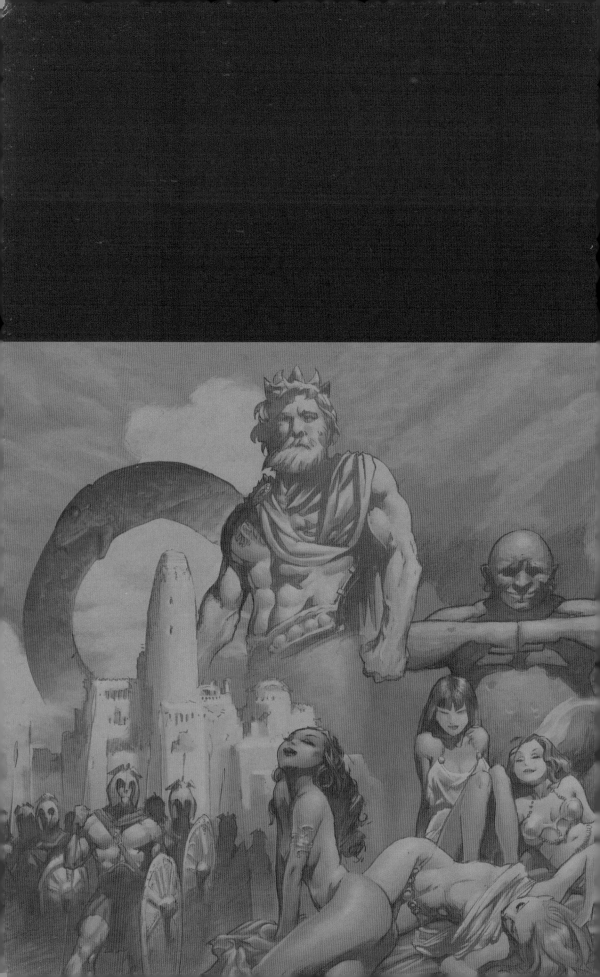

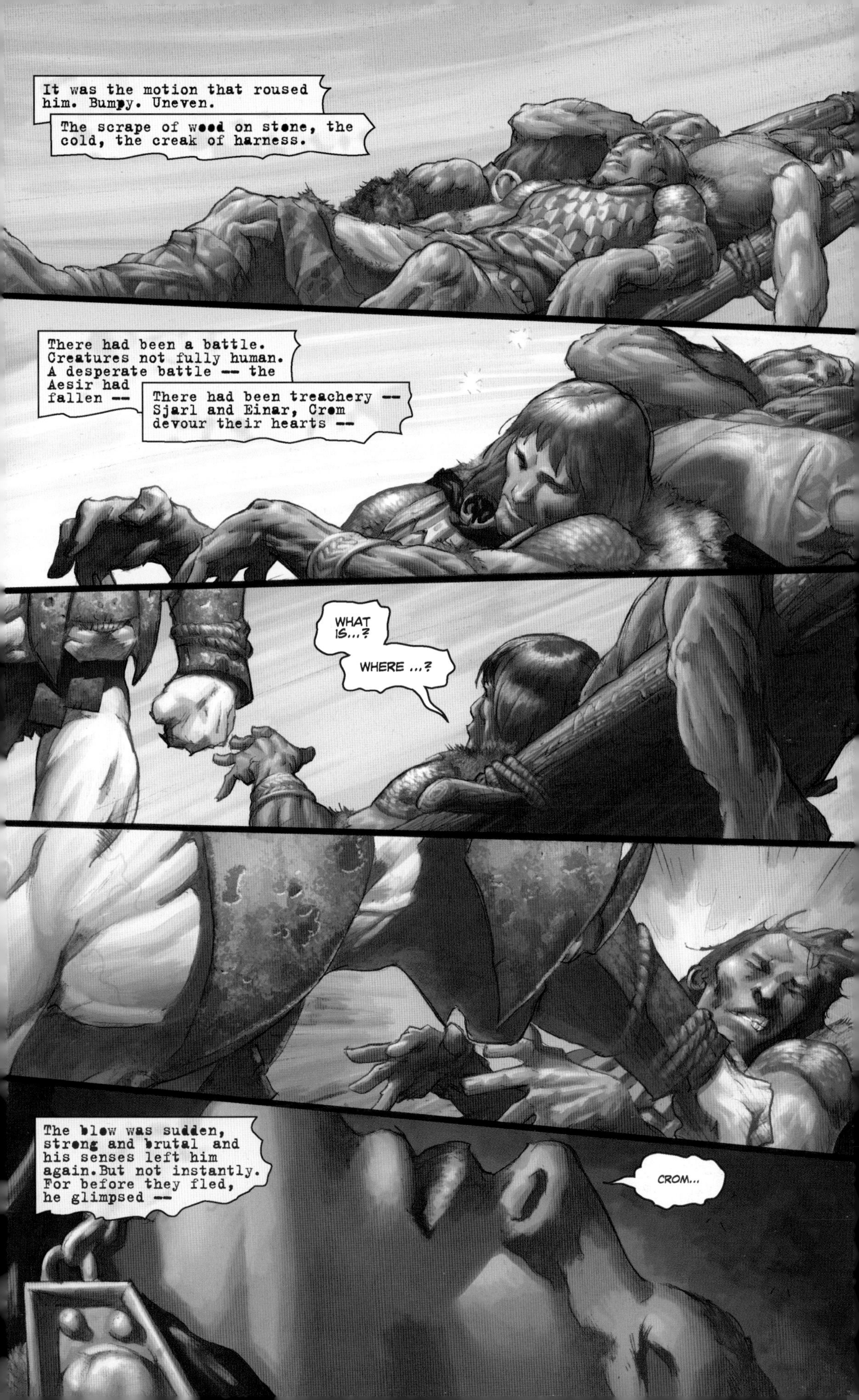
It was the motion that roused him. Bumpy. Uneven.
The scrape of wood on stone, the cold, the creak of harness.
There had been a battle. Creatures not fully human. A desperate battle -- the Aesir had fallen --
There had been treachery -- Sjarl and Einar, Crom devour their hearts --
WHAT IS...?
WHERE ...?
The blow was sudden, strong and brutal and his senses left him again. But not instantly. For before they fled, he glimpsed --
CROM...

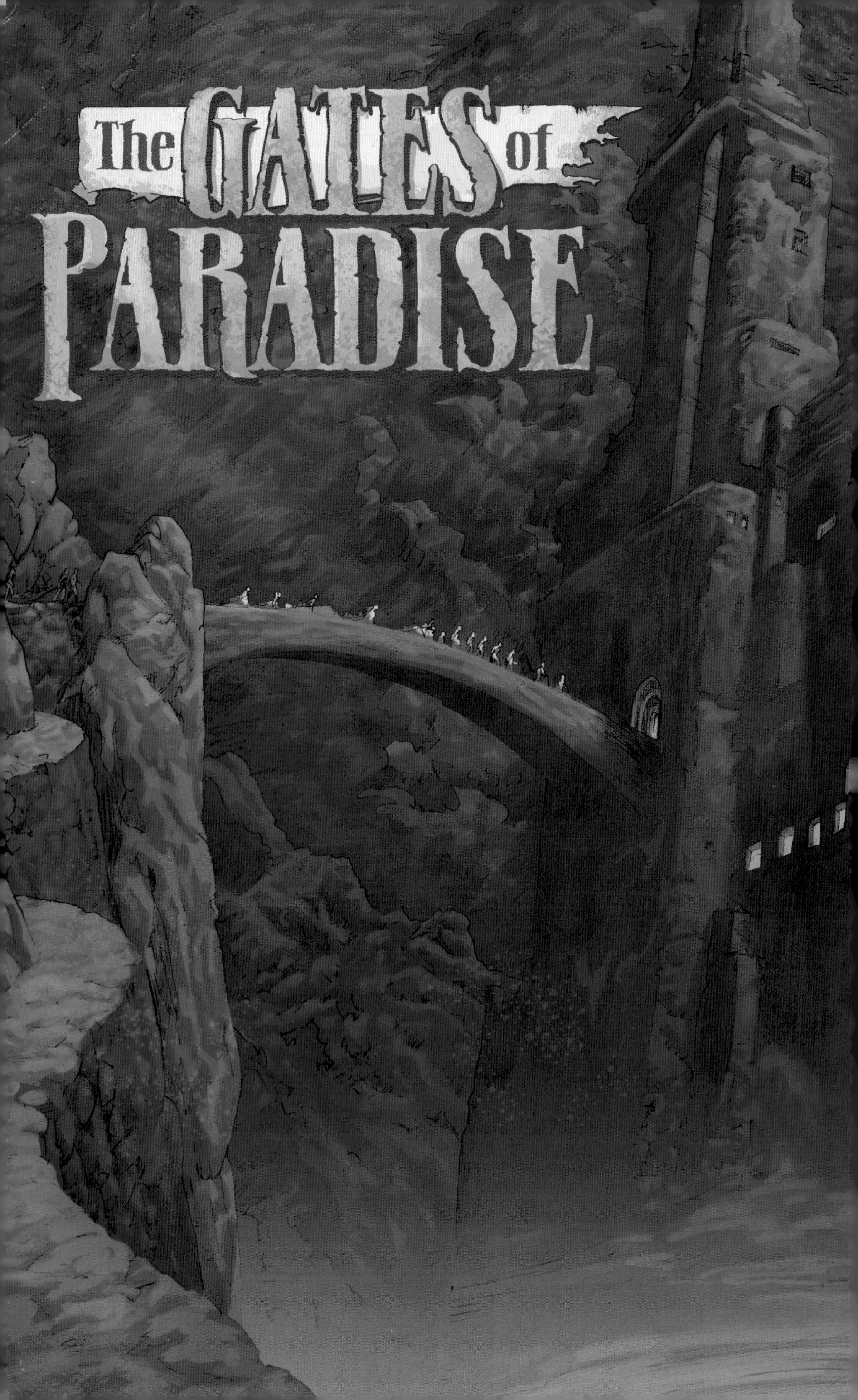
The GATES of PARADISE

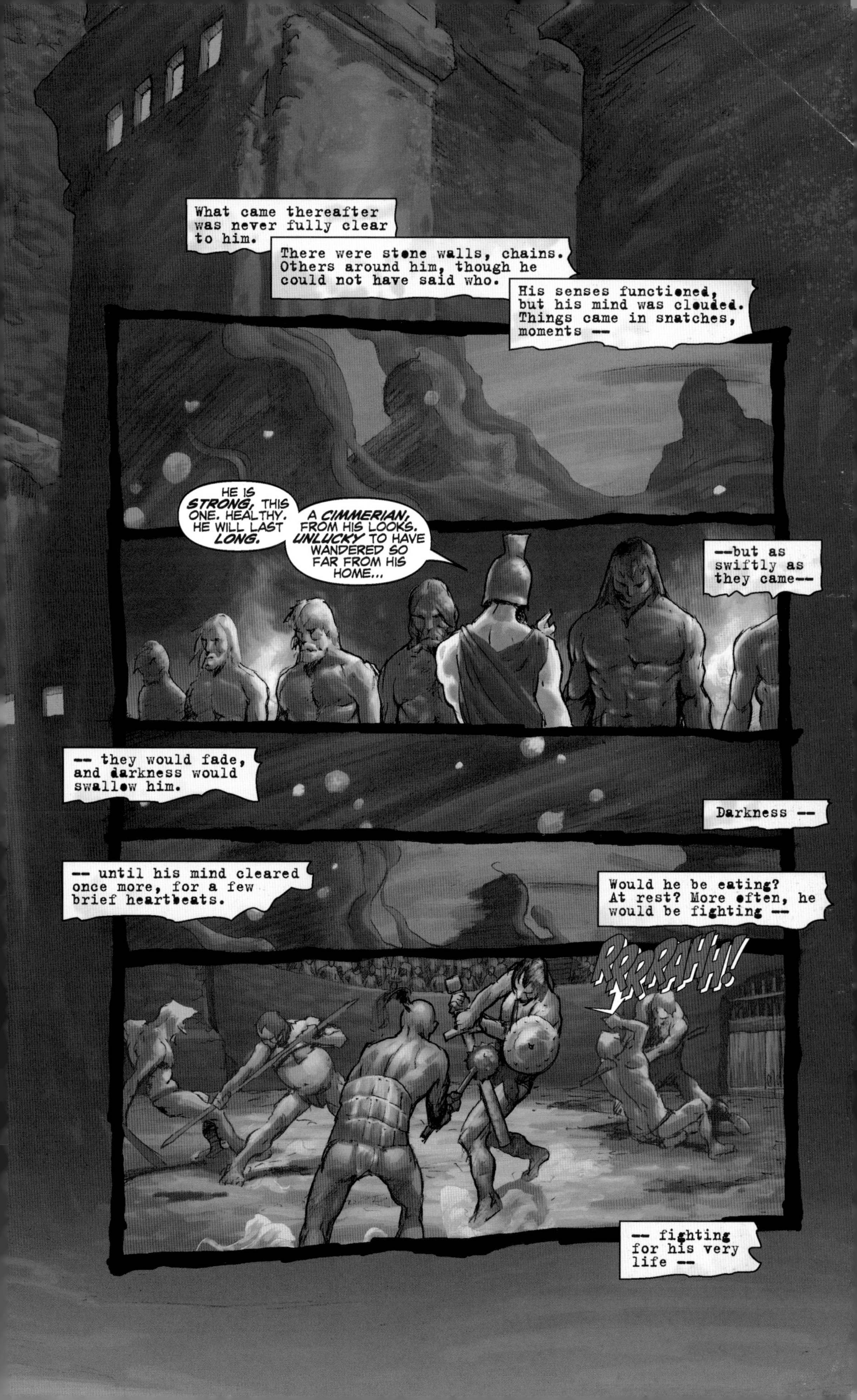
What came thereafter was never fully clear to him.
There were stone walls, chains. Others around him, though he could not have said who.
His senses functioned, but his mind was clouded. Things came in snatches, moments --
HE IS STRONG, THIS ONE. HEALTHY. HE WILL LAST LONG.
A CIMMERIAN, FROM HIS LOOKS. UNLUCKY TO HAVE WANDERED SO FAR FROM HIS HOME...
--but as swiftly as they came--
-- they would fade, and darkness would swallow him.
Darkness --
-- until his mind cleared once more, for a few brief heartbeats.
Would he be eating? At rest? More often, he would be fighting --
RRRRAHH!
-- fighting for his very life --

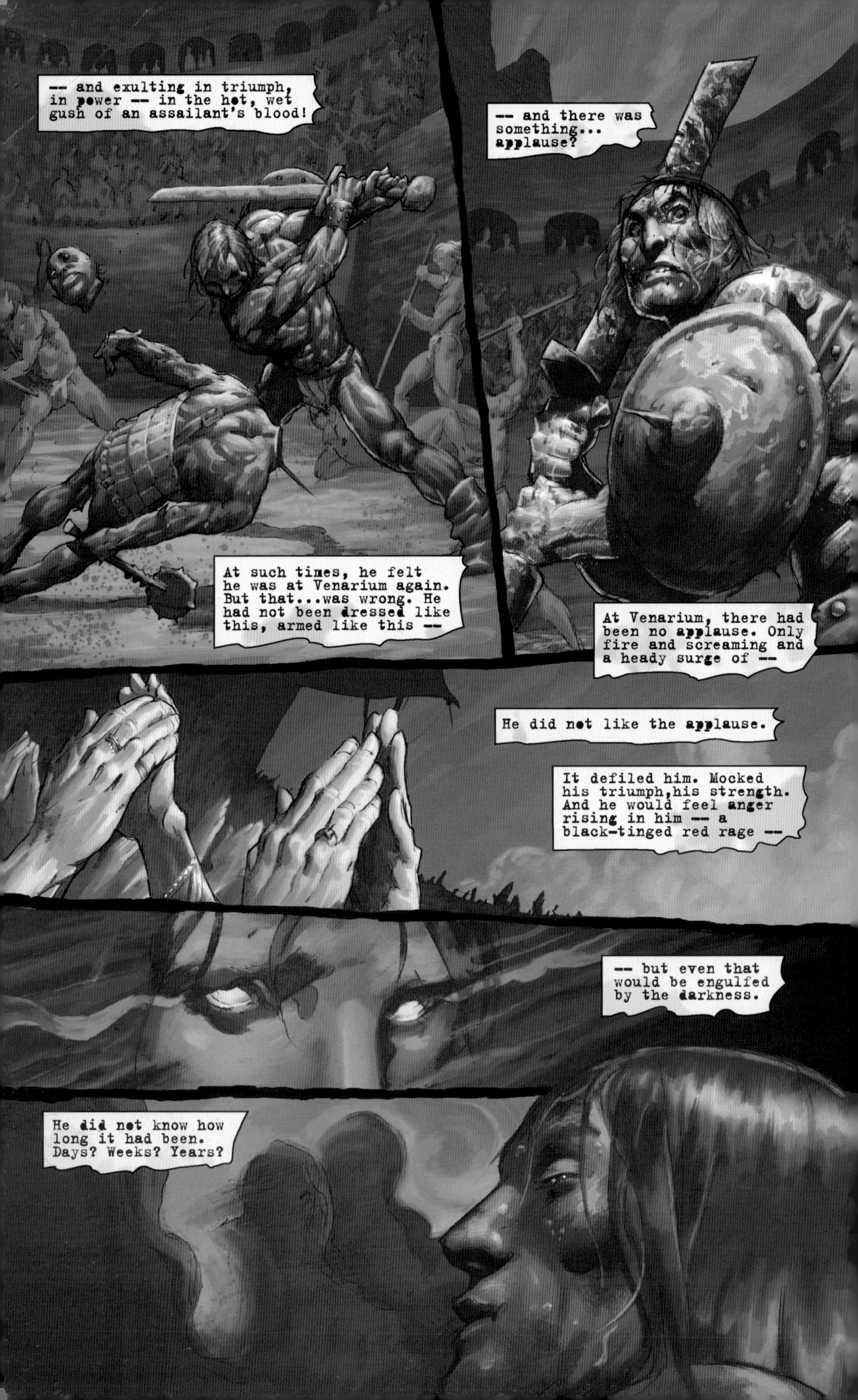
-- and exulting in triumph, in power -- in the hot, wet gush of an assailant's blood!
-- and there was something... applause?
At such times, he felt he was at Venarium again. But that...was wrong. He had not been dressed like this, armed like this --
At Venarium, there had been no applause. Only fire and screaming and a heady surge of --
He did not like the applause.
It defiled him. Mocked his triumph,his strength. And he would feel anger rising in him -- a black-tinged red rage --
-- but even that would be engulfed by the darkness.
He did not know how long it had been. Days? Weeks? Years?

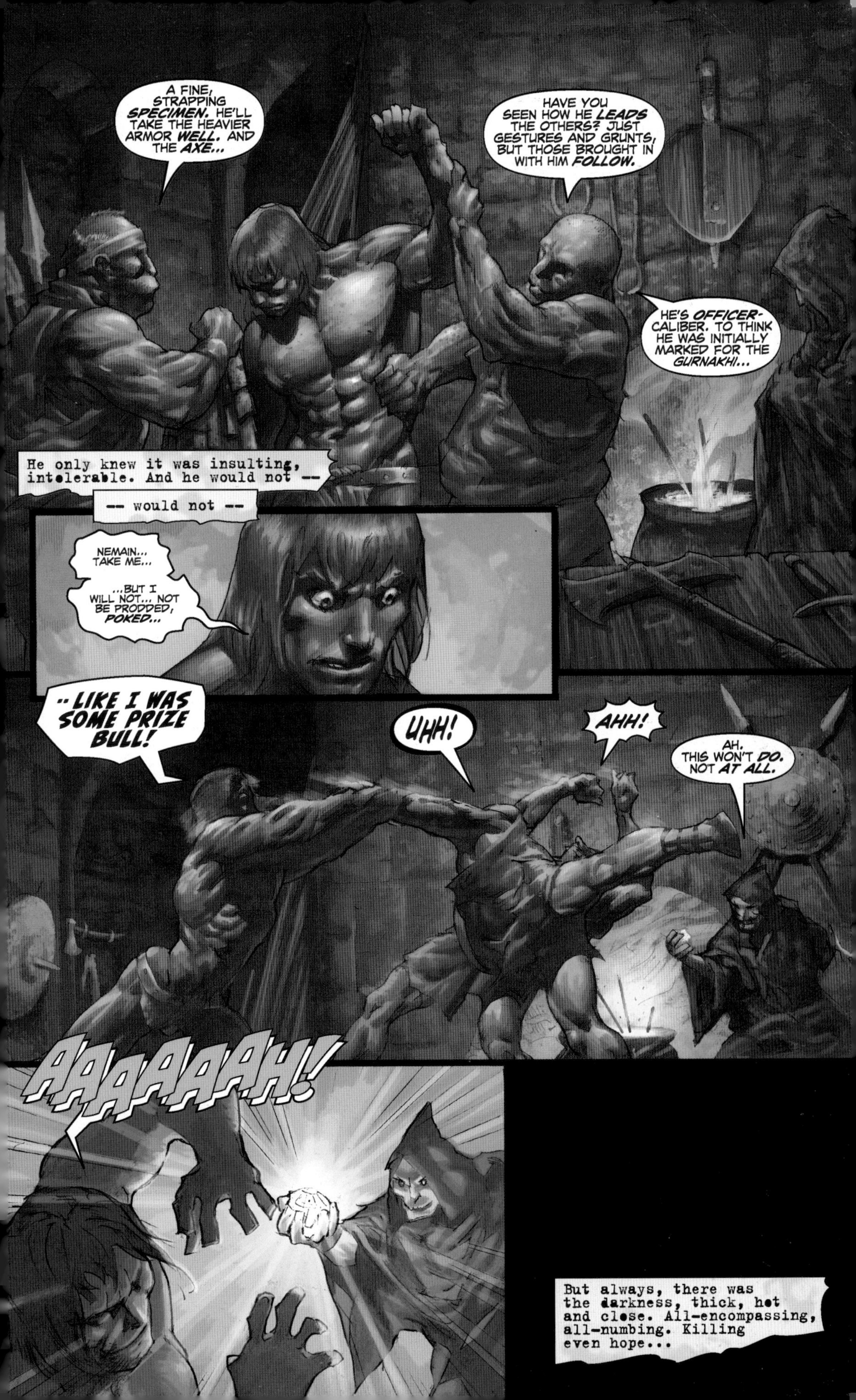
A FINE, STRAPPING SPECIMEN. HE'LL TAKE THE HEAVIER ARMOR WELL. AND THE AXE...
HAVE YOU SEEN HOW HE LEADS THE OTHERS? JUST GESTURES AND GRUNTS, BUT THOSE BROUGHT IN WITH HIM FOLLOW.
HE'S OFFICER-CALIBER. TO THINK HE WAS INITIALLY MARKED FOR THE GURNAKHI...
He only knew it was insulting, intolerable. And he would not --
-- would not --
NEMAIN... TAKE ME...
...BUT I WILL NOT... NOT BE PRODDED, POKED...
..LIKE I WAS SOME PRIZE BULL!
UHH!
AHH!
AH. THIS WON'T DO. NOT AT ALL.
AAAAAAAH!
But always, there was the darkness, thick, hot and close. All-encompassing, all-numbing. Killing even hope...

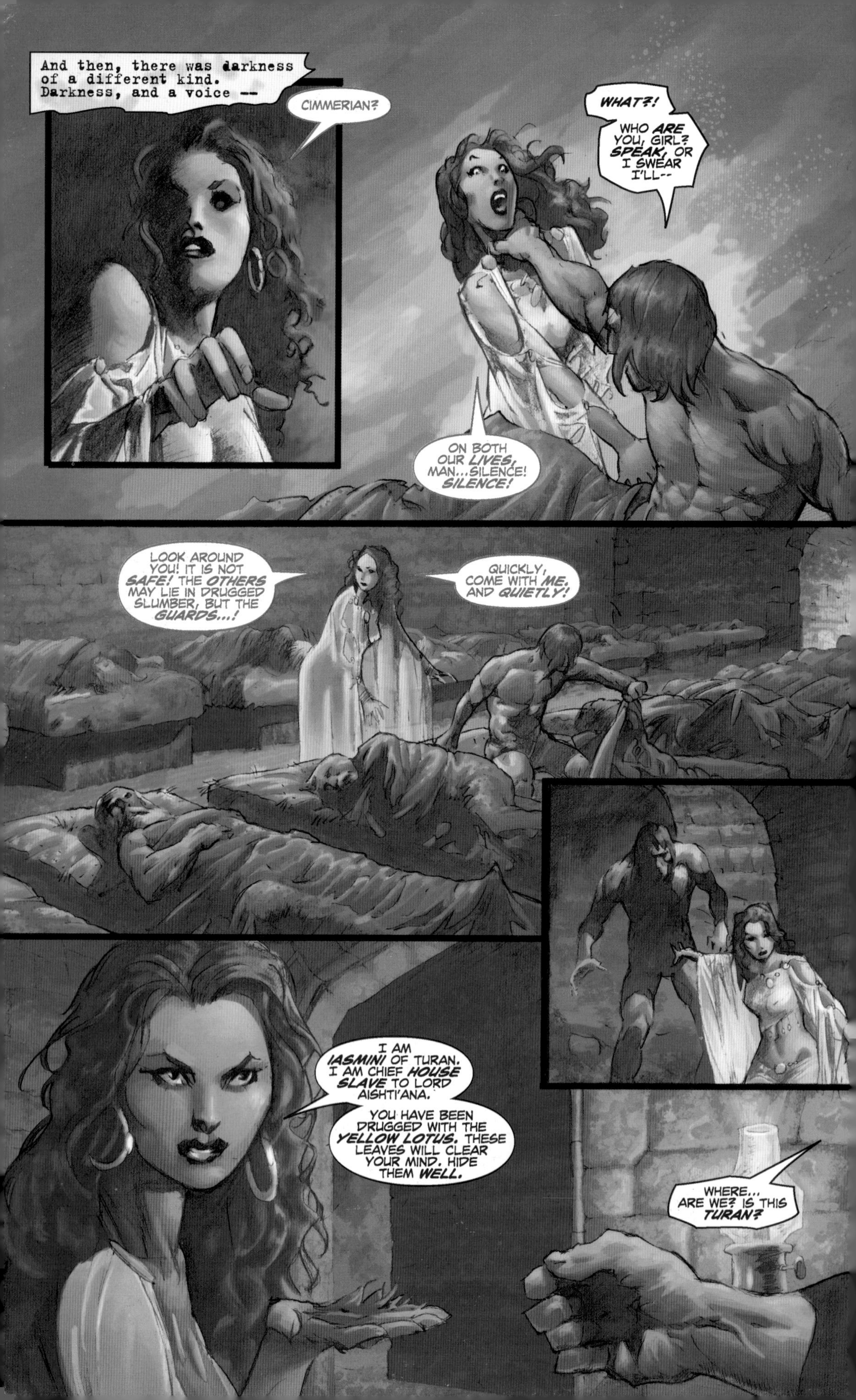
And then, there was darkness of a different kind. Darkness, and a voice --
CIMMERIAN?
WHAT?!
WHO ARE YOU, GIRL? SPEAK, OR I SWEAR I'LL--
ON BOTH OUR LIVES, MAN...SILENCE! SILENCE!
LOOK AROUND YOU! IT IS NOT SAFE! THE OTHERS MAY LIE IN DRUGGED SLUMBER, BUT THE GUARDS...!
QUICKLY, COME WITH ME. AND QUIETLY!
I AM IASMINI OF TURAN. I AM CHIEF HOUSE SLAVE TO LORD AISHTI'ANA.
YOU HAVE BEEN DRUGGED WITH THE YELLOW LOTUS. THESE LEAVES WILL CLEAR YOUR MIND. HIDE THEM WELL.
WHERE... ARE WE? IS THIS TURAN?

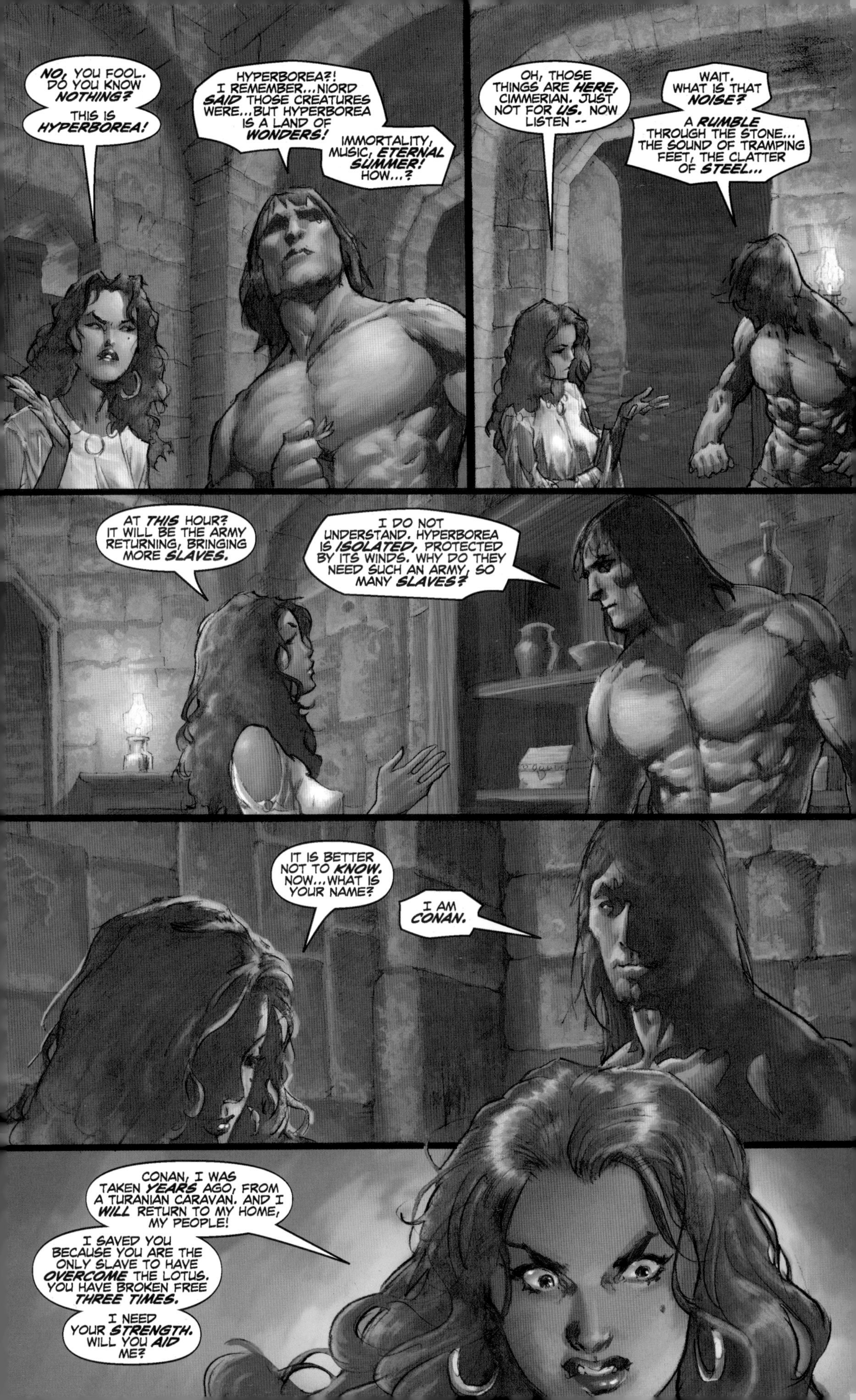
NO, YOU FOOL. DO YOU KNOW NOTHING?
THIS IS HYPERBOREA!
HYPERBOREA?! I REMEMBER...NIORD SAID THOSE CREATURES WERE...BUT HYPERBOREA IS A LAND OF WONDERS!
IMMORTALITY, MUSIC, ETERNAL SUMMER! HOW...?
OH, THOSE THINGS ARE HERE, CIMMERIAN. JUST NOT FOR US. NOW LISTEN --
WAIT. WHAT IS THAT NOISE?
A RUMBLE THROUGH THE STONE... THE SOUND OF TRAMPING FEET, THE CLATTER OF STEEL...
AT THIS HOUR? IT WILL BE THE ARMY RETURNING, BRINGING MORE SLAVES.
I DO NOT UNDERSTAND. HYPERBOREA IS ISOLATED, PROTECTED BY ITS WINDS. WHY DO THEY NEED SUCH AN ARMY, SO MANY SLAVES?
IT IS BETTER NOT TO KNOW. NOW...WHAT IS YOUR NAME?
I AM CONAN.
CONAN, I WAS TAKEN YEARS AGO, FROM A TURANIAN CARAVAN. AND I WILL RETURN TO MY HOME, MY PEOPLE!
I SAVED YOU BECAUSE YOU ARE THE ONLY SLAVE TO HAVE OVERCOME THE LOTUS. YOU HAVE BROKEN FREE THREE TIMES.
I NEED YOUR STRENGTH. WILL YOU AID ME?

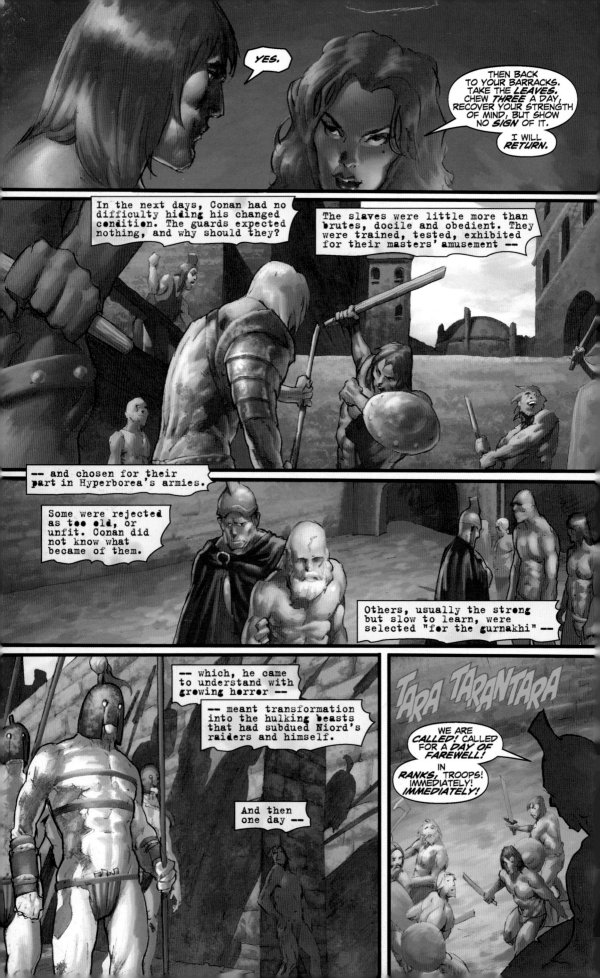

YES.

THEN BACK TO YOUR *BARRACKS.* TAKE THE *LEAVES.* CHEW *THREE* A DAY, RECOVER YOUR STRENGTH OF MIND, BUT SHOW NO *SIGN* OF IT.

I WILL *RETURN.*

In the next days, Conan had no difficulty hiding his changed condition. The guards expected nothing, and why should they?

The slaves were little more than brutes, docile and obedient. They were trained, tested, exhibited for their masters' amusement --

-- and chosen for their part in Hyperborea's armies.

Some were rejected as too old, or unfit. Conan did not know what became of them.

Others, usually the strong but slow to learn, were selected "for the gurnakhi" --

-- which, he came to understand with growing horror --

-- meant transformation into the hulking beasts that had subdued Niord's raiders and himself.

And then one day --

TARA TARANTARA

WE ARE *CALLED!* CALLED FOR A *DAY OF FAREWELL!* IN *RANKS,* TROOPS! *IMMEDIATELY! IMMEDIATELY!*

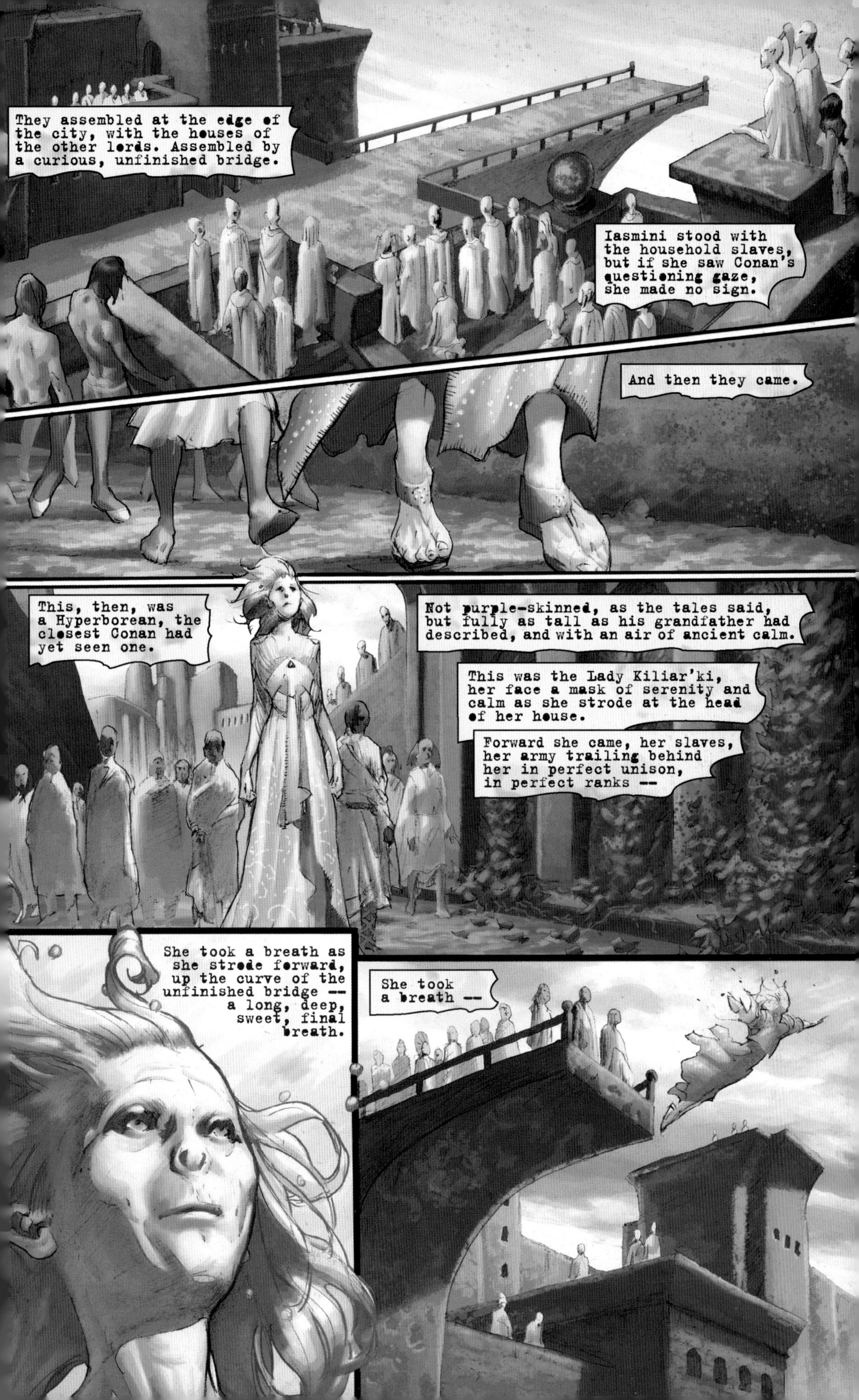
They assembled at the edge of the city, with the houses of the other lords. Assembled by a curious, unfinished bridge.
Iasmini stood with the household slaves, but if she saw Conan's questioning gaze, she made no sign.
And then they came.
This, then, was a Hyperborean, the closest Conan had yet seen one.
Not purple-skinned, as the tales said, but fully as tall as his grandfather had described, and with an air of ancient calm.
This was the Lady Kiliar'ki, her face a mask of serenity and calm as she strode at the head of her house.
Forward she came, her slaves, her army trailing behind her in perfect unison, in perfect ranks --
She took a breath as she strode forward, up the curve of the unfinished bridge -- a long, deep, sweet, final breath.
She took a breath --

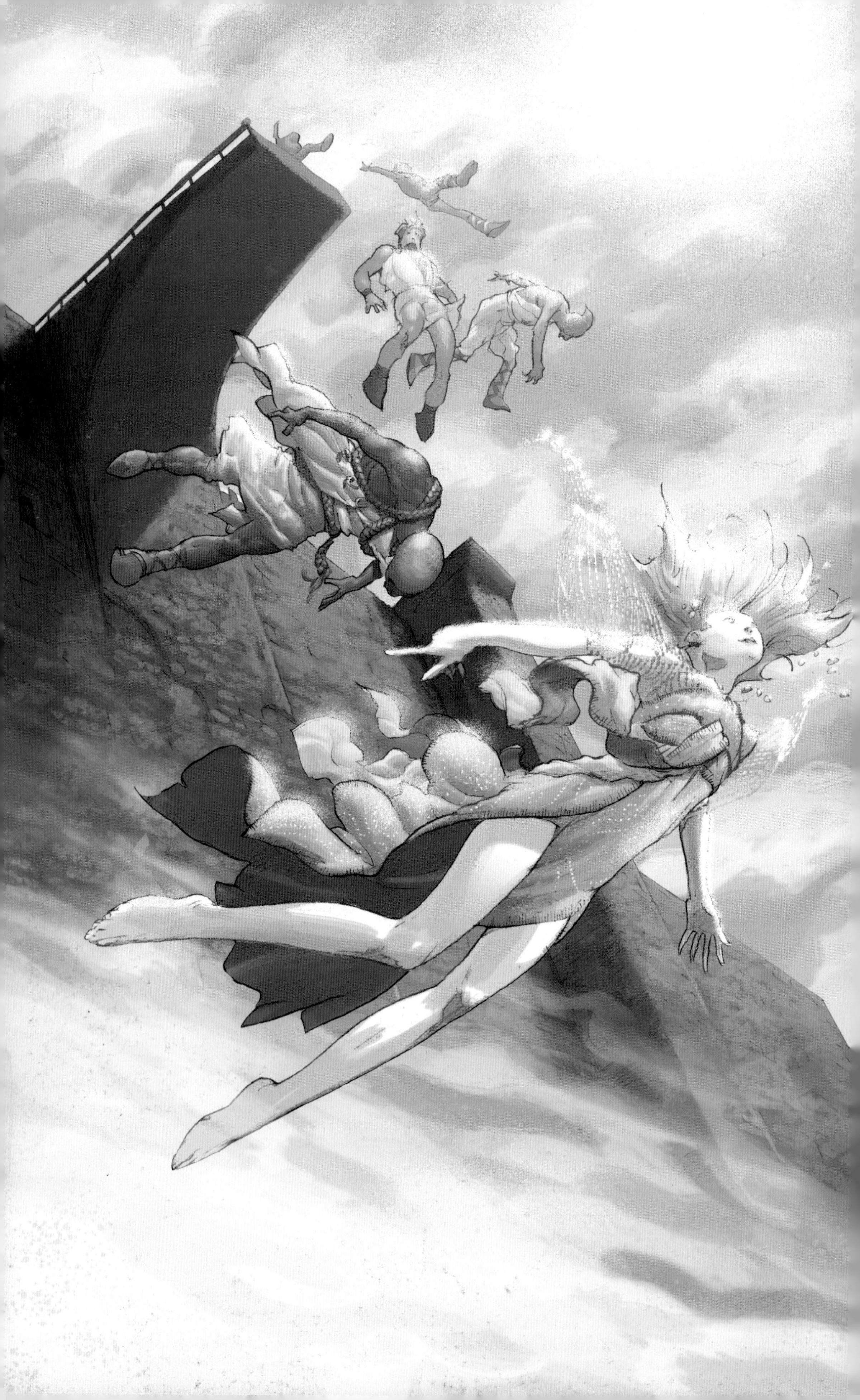

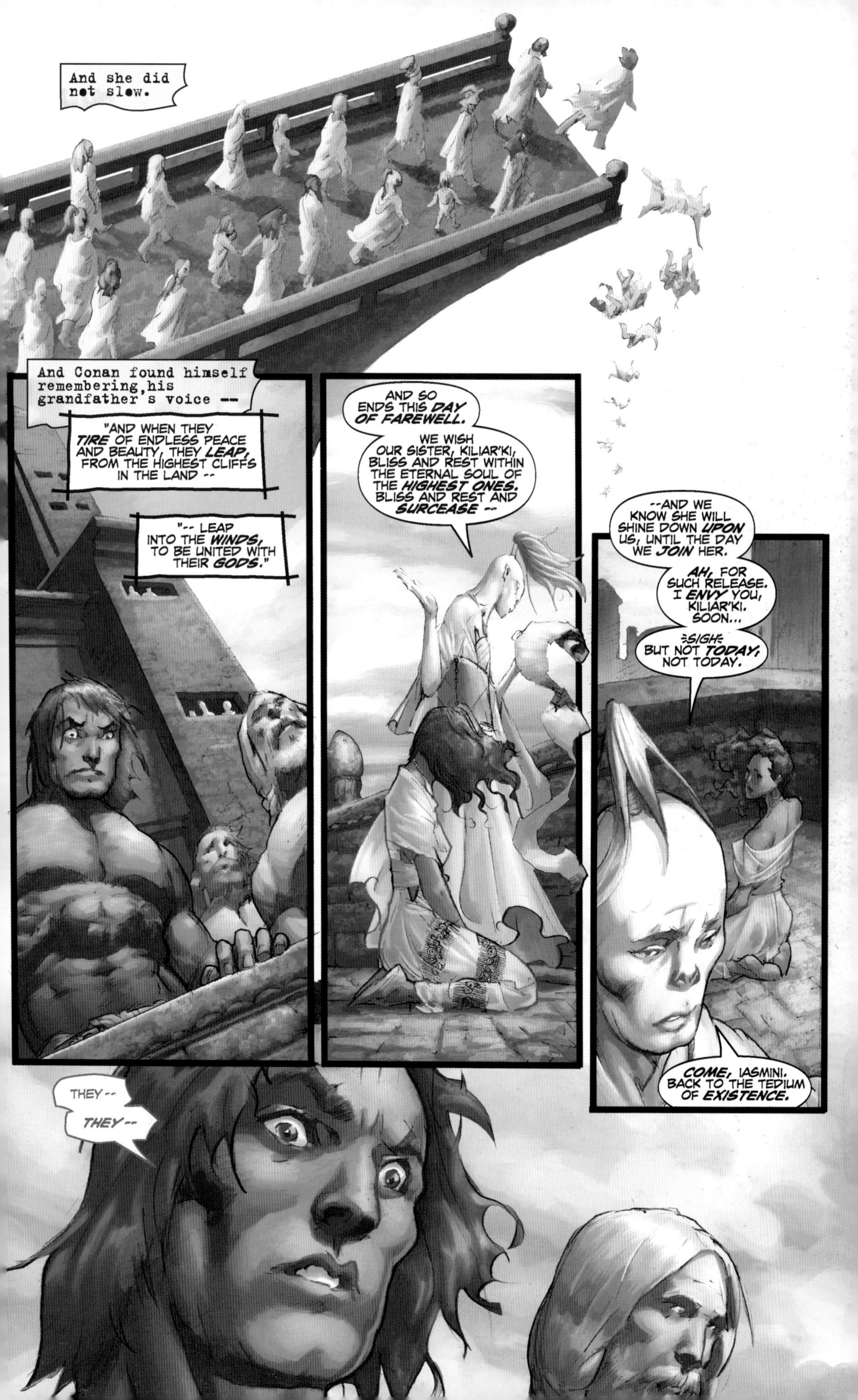
And she did not slow.
And Conan found himself remembering, his grandfather's voice --
"AND WHEN THEY TIRE OF ENDLESS PEACE AND BEAUTY, THEY LEAP, FROM THE HIGHEST CLIFFS IN THE LAND --
"-- LEAP INTO THE WINDS, TO BE UNITED WITH THEIR GODS."
AND SO ENDS THIS DAY OF FAREWELL.
WE WISH OUR SISTER, KILIAR'KI, BLISS AND REST WITHIN THE ETERNAL SOUL OF THE HIGHEST ONES. BLISS AND REST AND SURCEASE --
--AND WE KNOW SHE WILL SHINE DOWN UPON US, UNTIL THE DAY WE JOIN HER.
AH, FOR SUCH RELEASE. I ENVY YOU, KILIAR'KI. SOON...
SIGH
BUT NOT TODAY, NOT TODAY.
COME, IASMINI. BACK TO THE TEDIUM OF EXISTENCE.
THEY --
THEY --

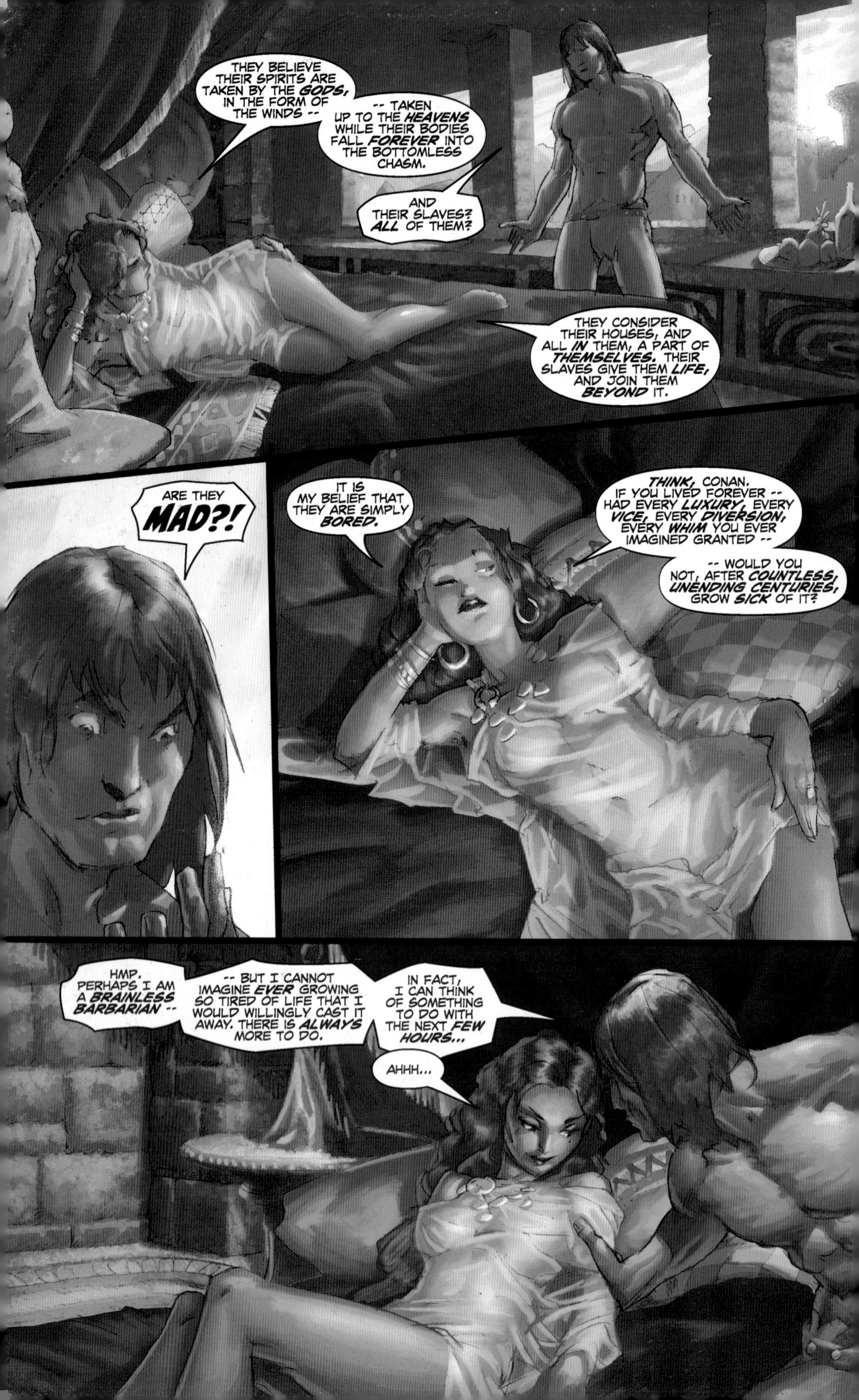
THEY BELIEVE THEIR SPIRITS ARE TAKEN BY THE GODS, IN THE FORM OF THE WINDS --
-- TAKEN UP TO THE HEAVENS WHILE THEIR BODIES FALL FOREVER INTO THE BOTTOMLESS CHASM.
AND THEIR SLAVES? ALL OF THEM?
THEY CONSIDER THEIR HOUSES, AND ALL IN THEM, A PART OF THEMSELVES. THEIR SLAVES GIVE THEM LIFE, AND JOIN THEM BEYOND IT.
ARE THEY MAD?!
IT IS MY BELIEF THAT THEY ARE SIMPLY BORED.
THINK, CONAN. IF YOU LIVED FOREVER -- HAD EVERY LUXURY, EVERY VICE, EVERY DIVERSION, EVERY WHIM YOU EVER IMAGINED GRANTED --
-- WOULD YOU NOT, AFTER COUNTLESS, UNENDING CENTURIES, GROW SICK OF IT?
HMP. PERHAPS I AM A BRAINLESS BARBARIAN --
-- BUT I CANNOT IMAGINE EVER GROWING SO TIRED OF LIFE THAT I WOULD WILLINGLY CAST IT AWAY. THERE IS ALWAYS MORE TO DO.
IN FACT, I CAN THINK OF SOMETHING TO DO WITH THE NEXT FEW HOURS...
AHHH...

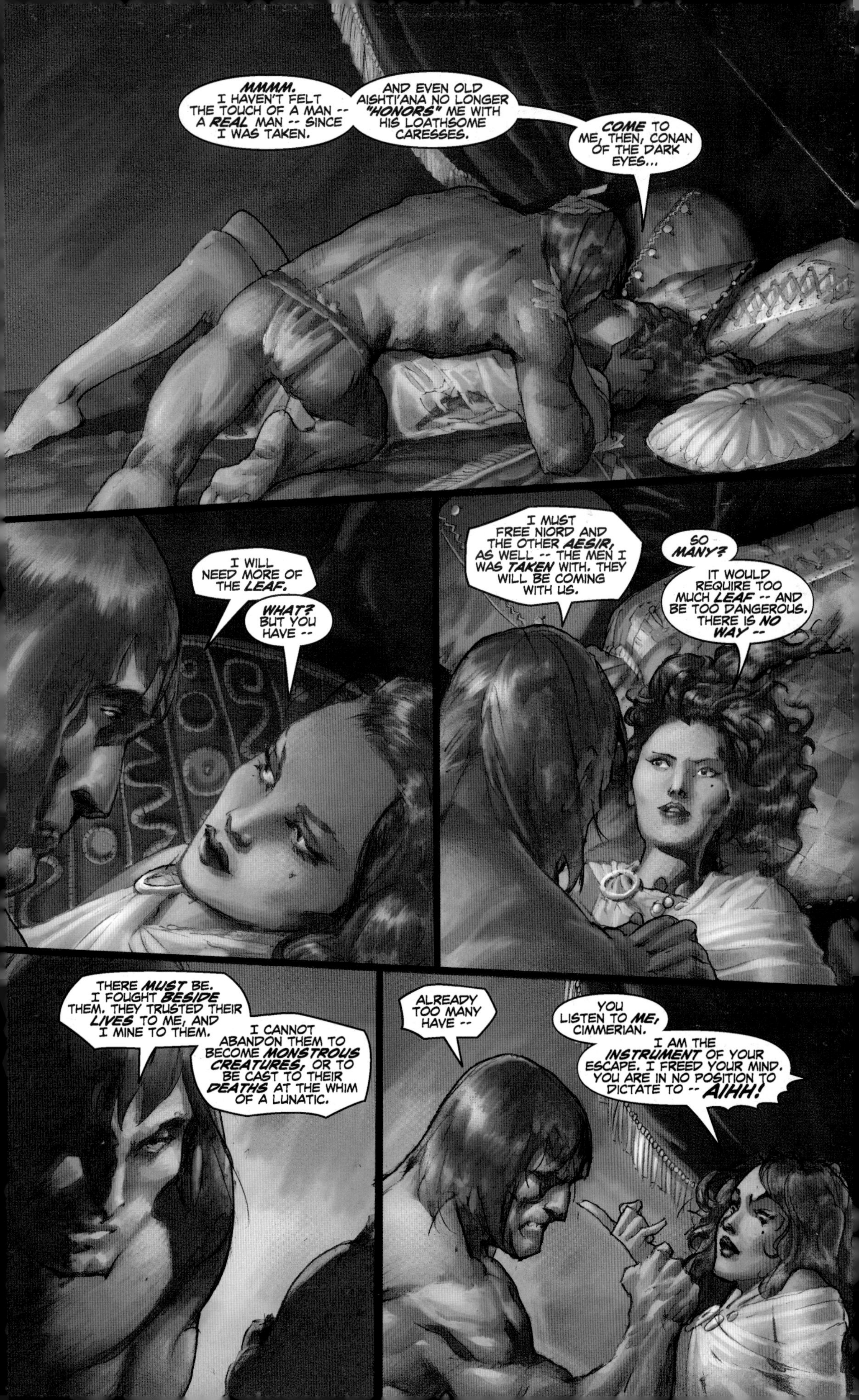
MMMM. I HAVEN'T FELT THE TOUCH OF A MAN -- A REAL MAN -- SINCE I WAS TAKEN.
AND EVEN OLD AISHTI'ANA NO LONGER "HONORS" ME WITH HIS LOATHSOME CARESSES.
COME TO ME, THEN, CONAN OF THE DARK EYES...
I WILL NEED MORE OF THE LEAF.
WHAT? BUT YOU HAVE --
I MUST FREE NIORD AND THE OTHER AESIR, AS WELL -- THE MEN I WAS TAKEN WITH. THEY WILL BE COMING WITH US.
SO MANY?
IT WOULD REQUIRE TOO MUCH LEAF -- AND BE TOO DANGEROUS. THERE IS NO WAY --
THERE MUST BE. I FOUGHT BESIDE THEM. THEY TRUSTED THEIR LIVES TO ME, AND I MINE TO THEM.
I CANNOT ABANDON THEM TO BECOME MONSTROUS CREATURES, OR TO BE CAST TO THEIR DEATHS AT THE WHIM OF A LUNATIC.
ALREADY TOO MANY HAVE --
YOU LISTEN TO ME, CIMMERIAN.
I AM THE INSTRUMENT OF YOUR ESCAPE. I FREED YOUR MIND. YOU ARE IN NO POSITION TO DICTATE TO -- AIHH!

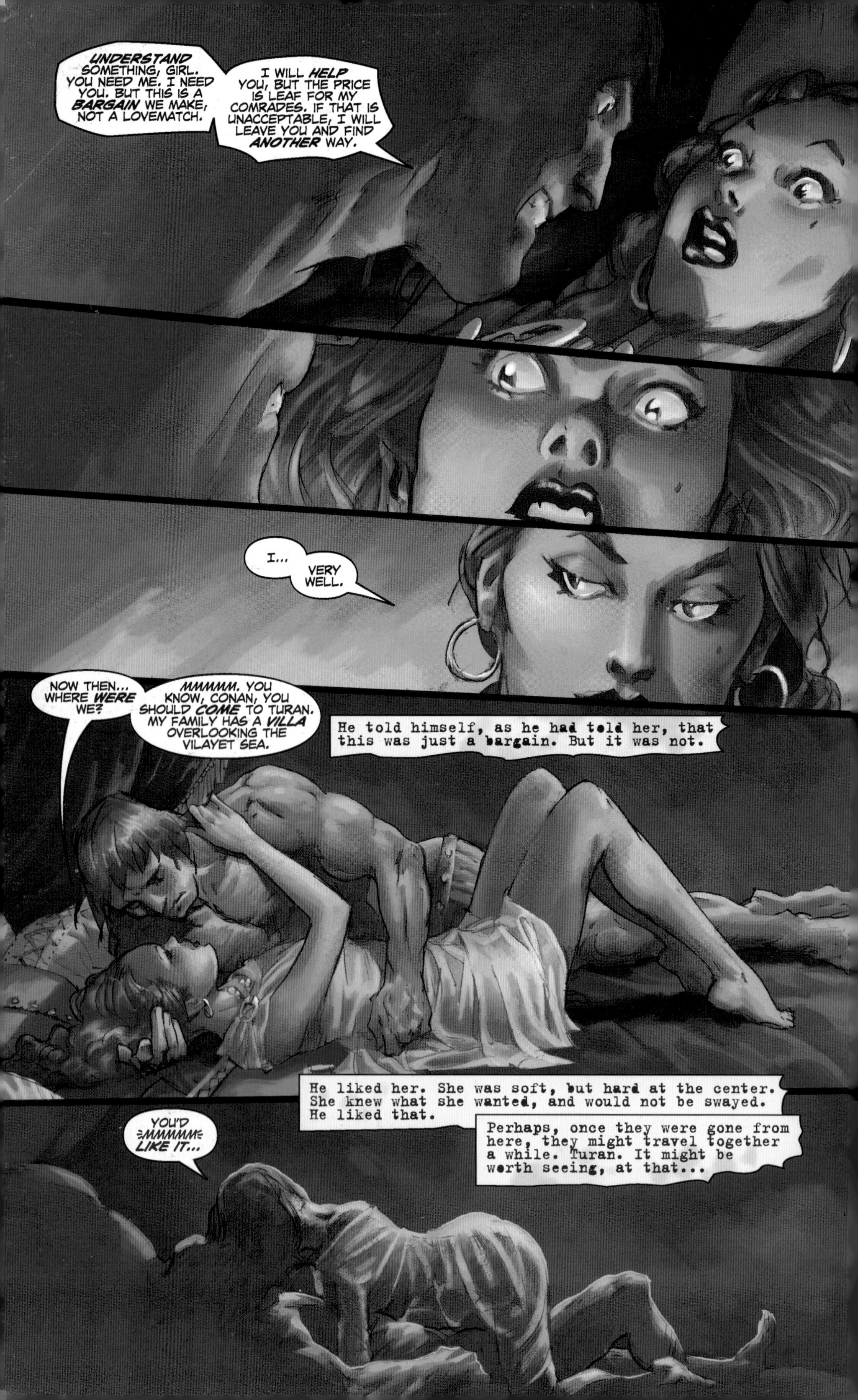
UNDERSTAND SOMETHING, GIRL. YOU NEED ME. I NEED YOU. BUT THIS IS A BARGAIN WE MAKE, NOT A LOVEMATCH.
I WILL HELP YOU, BUT THE PRICE IS LEAF FOR MY COMRADES. IF THAT IS UNACCEPTABLE, I WILL LEAVE YOU AND FIND ANOTHER WAY.
I... VERY WELL.
NOW THEN... WHERE WERE WE?
MMMMM. YOU KNOW, CONAN, YOU SHOULD COME TO TURAN. MY FAMILY HAS A VILLA OVERLOOKING THE VILAYET SEA.
He told himself, as he had told her, that this was just a bargain. But it was not.
He liked her. She was soft, but hard at the center. She knew what she wanted, and would not be swayed. He liked that.
YOU'D MMMMM LIKE IT...
Perhaps, once they were gone from here, they might travel together a while. Turan. It might be worth seeing, at that...

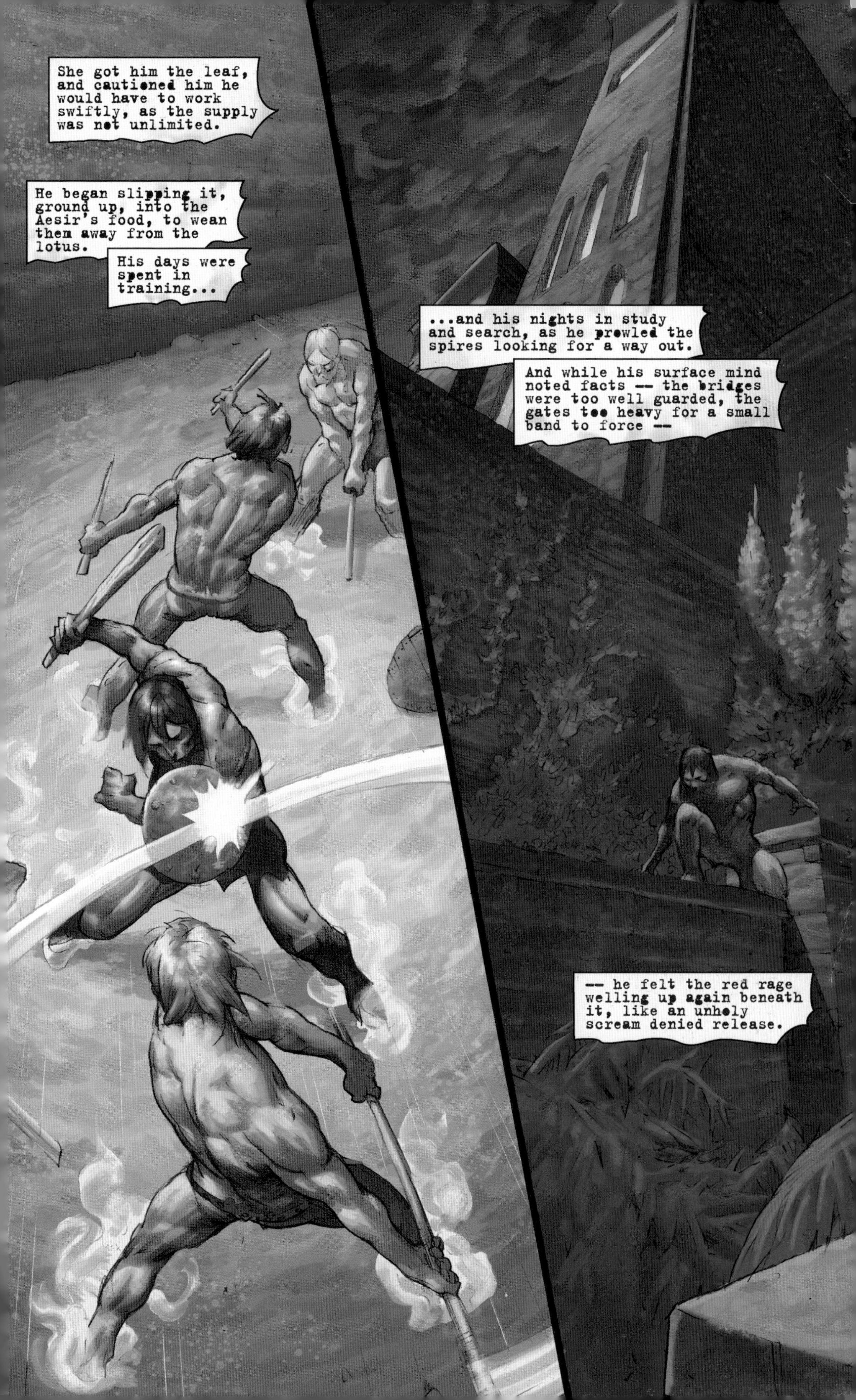
She got him the leaf, and cautioned him he would have to work swiftly, as the supply was not unlimited.
He began slipping it, ground up, into the Aesir's food, to wean them away from the lotus.
His days were spent in training...
...and his nights in study and search, as he prowled the spires looking for a way out.
And while his surface mind noted facts -- the bridges were too well guarded, the gates too heavy for a small band to force --
-- he felt the red rage welling up again beneath it, like an unholy scream denied release.

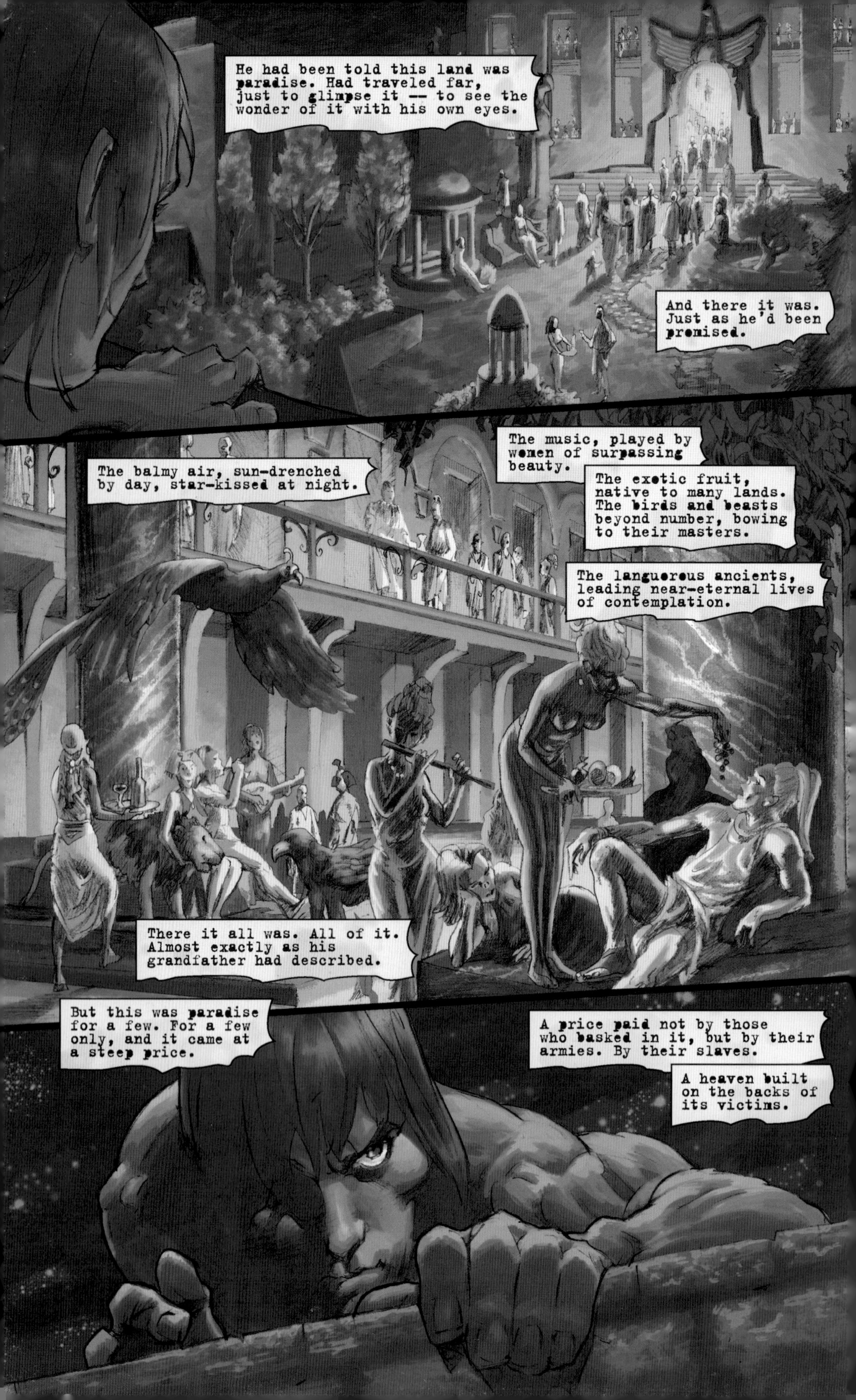

He had been told this land was paradise. Had traveled far, just to glimpse it -- to see the wonder of it with his own eyes.
And there it was. Just as he'd been promised.
The balmy air, sun-drenched by day, star-kissed at night.
The music, played by women of surpassing beauty.
The exotic fruit, native to many lands. The birds and beasts beyond number, bowing to their masters.
The languorous ancients, leading near-eternal lives of contemplation.
There it all was. All of it. Almost exactly as his grandfather had described.
But this was paradise for a few. For a few only, and it came at a steep price.
A price paid not by those who basked in it, but by their armies. By their slaves.
A heaven built on the backs of its victims.

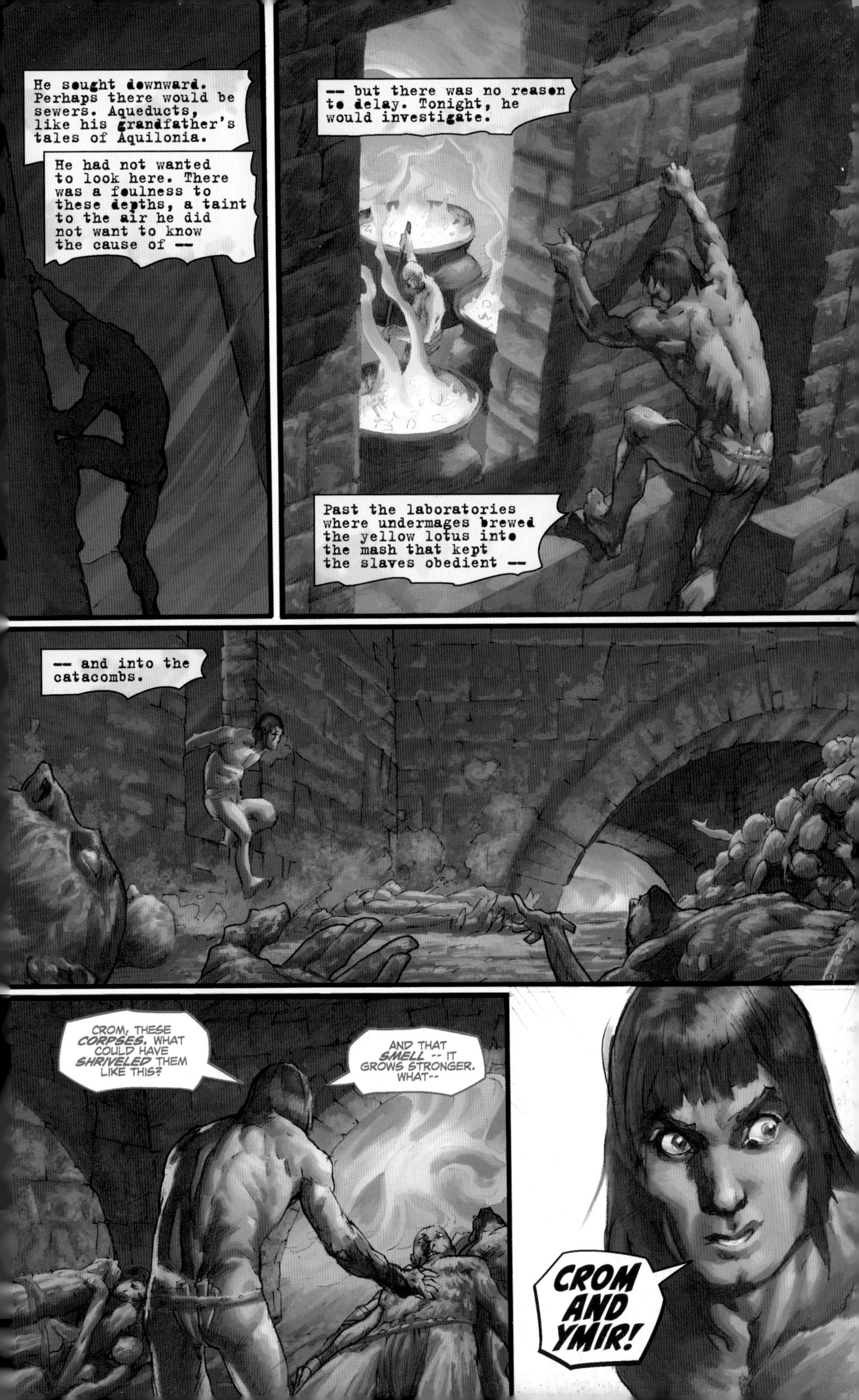
He sought downward. Perhaps there would be sewers. Aqueducts, like his grandfather's tales of Aquilonia.
He had not wanted to look here. There was a foulness to these depths, a taint to the air he did not want to know the cause of --
-- but there was no reason to delay. Tonight, he would investigate.
Past the laboratories where undermages brewed the yellow lotus into the mash that kept the slaves obedient --
-- and into the catacombs.
CROM, THESE CORPSES. WHAT COULD HAVE SHRIVELED THEM LIKE THIS?
AND THAT SMELL -- IT GROWS STRONGER. WHAT--
CROM AND YMIR!

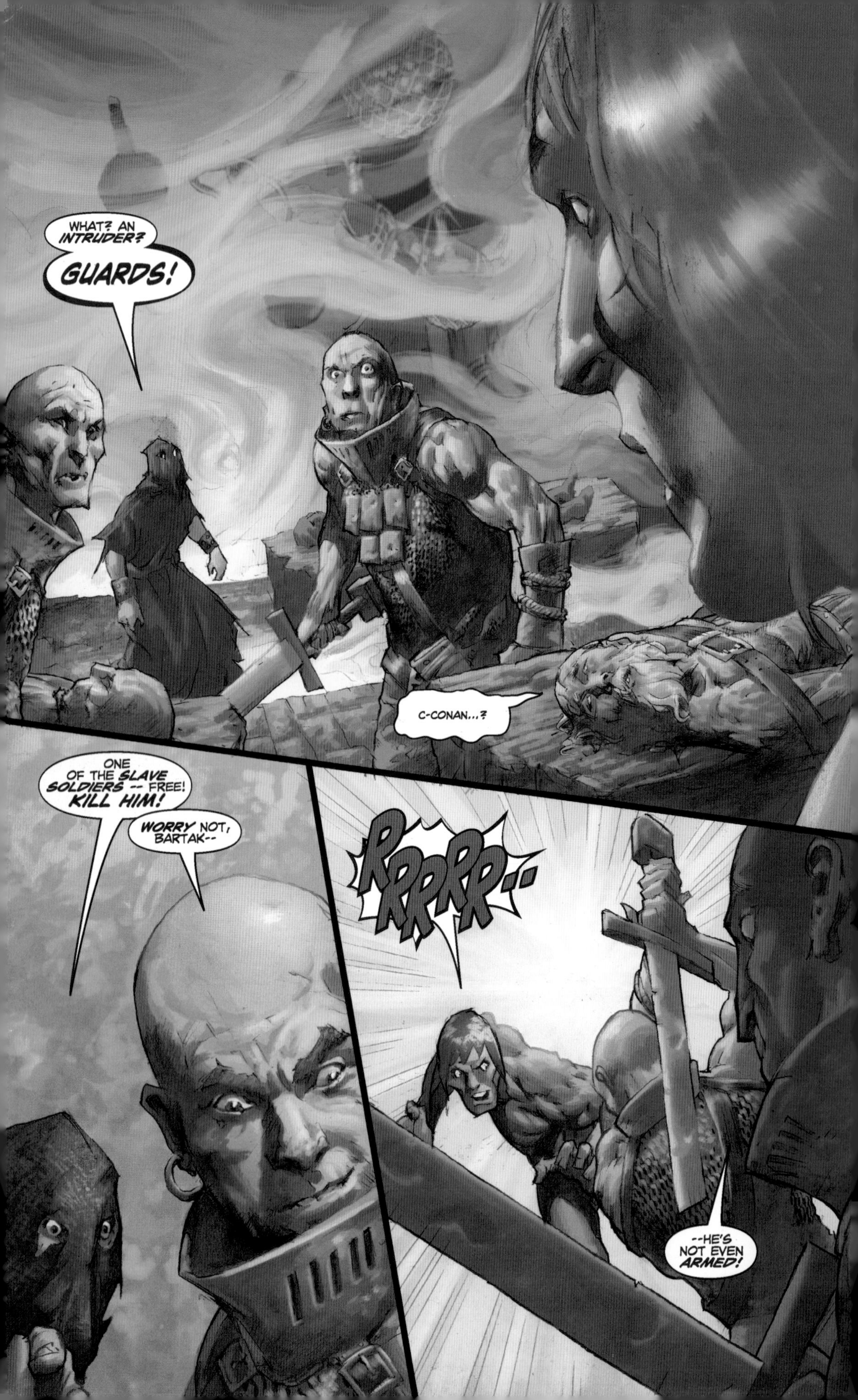
WHAT? AN INTRUDER?
GUARDS!
C-CONAN...?
ONE OF THE SLAVE SOLDIERS -- FREE! KILL HIM!
WORRY NOT, BARTAK--
RRRRR--
--HE'S NOT EVEN ARMED!

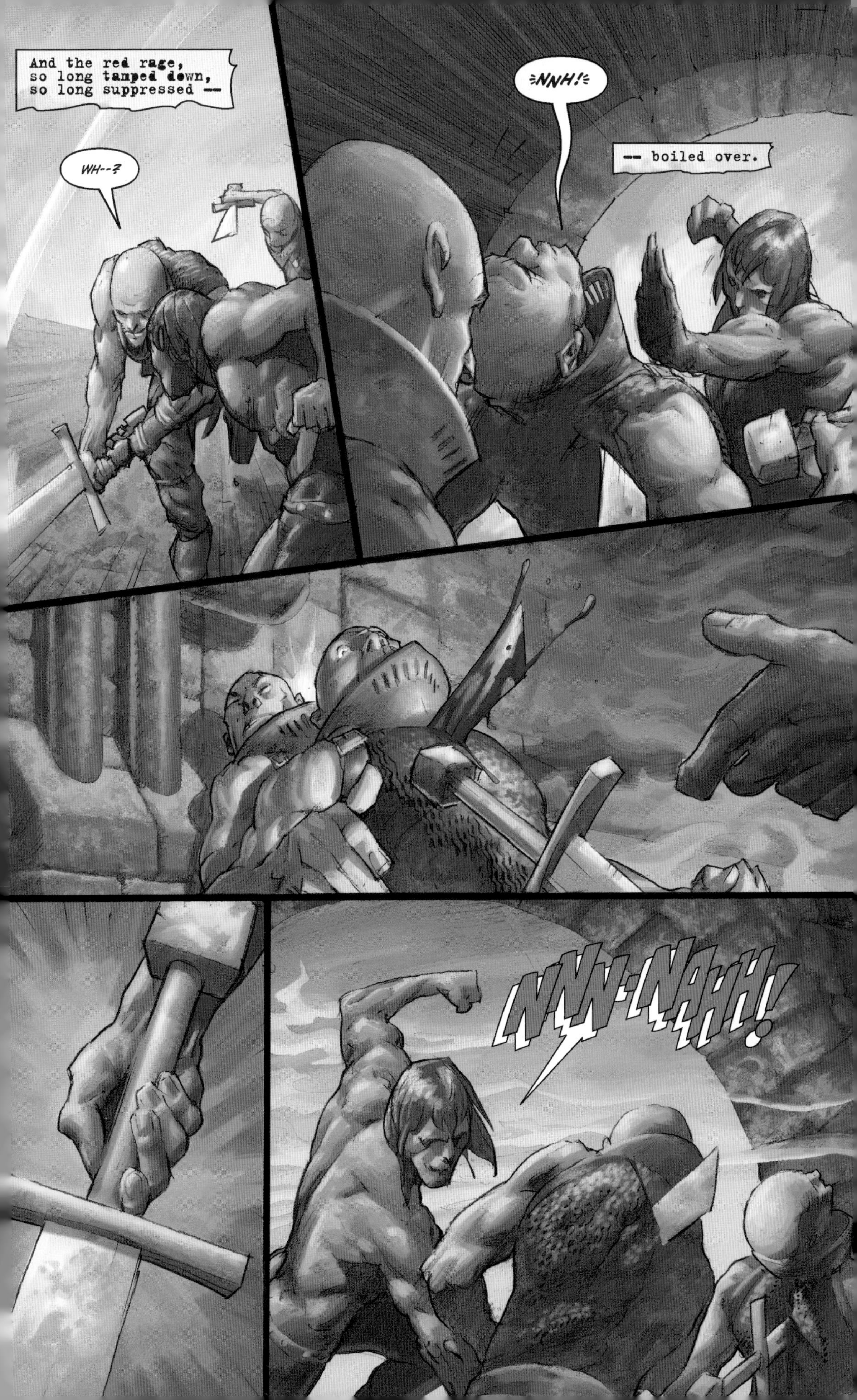
And the red rage, so long tamped down, so long suppressed --
WH--?
NNH!
-- boiled over.
NNN-NAHH!

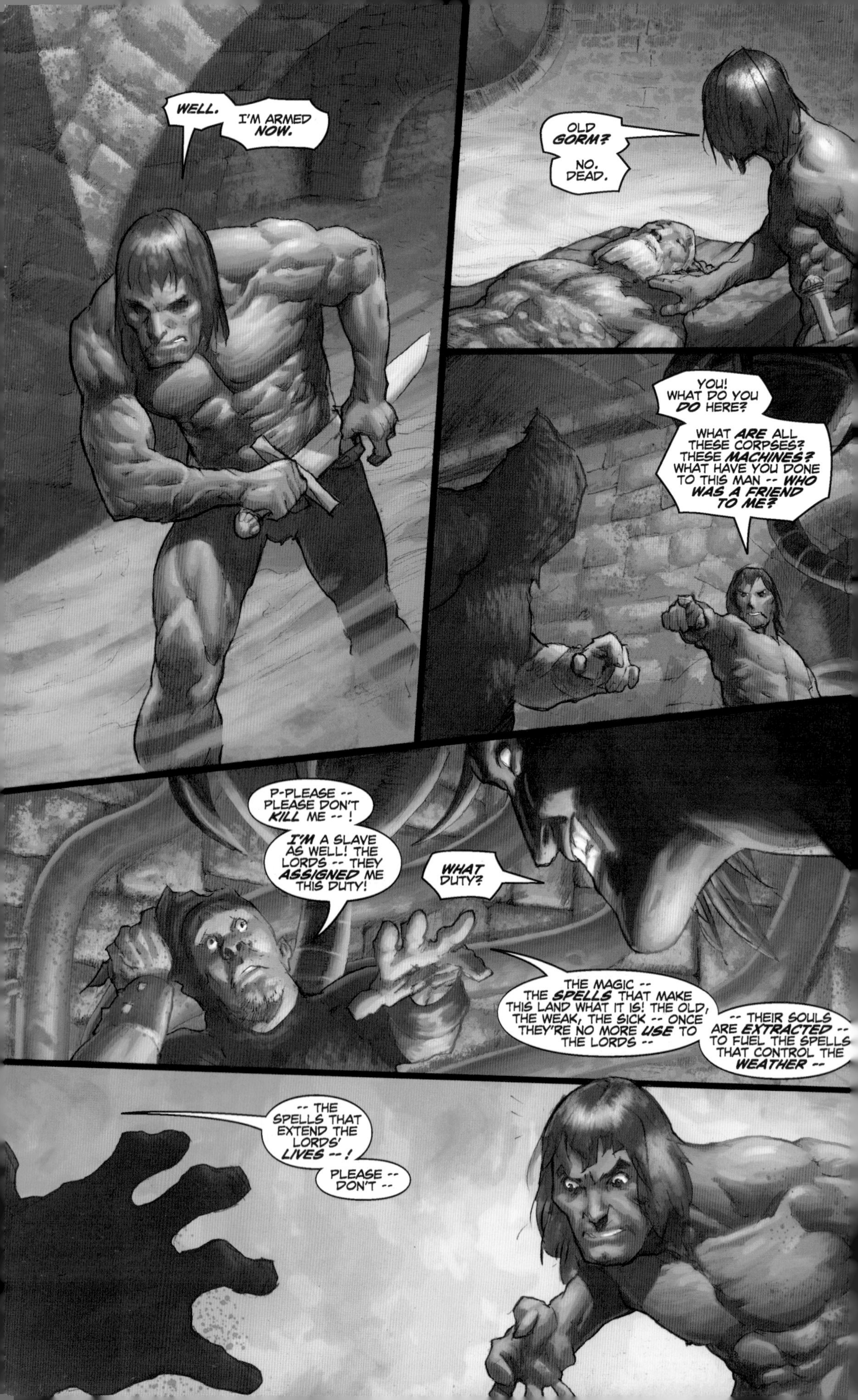
WELL.
I'M ARMED NOW.
OLD GORM?
NO. DEAD.
YOU! WHAT DO YOU DO HERE?
WHAT ARE ALL THESE CORPSES? THESE MACHINES? WHAT HAVE YOU DONE TO THIS MAN -- WHO WAS A FRIEND TO ME?
P-PLEASE -- PLEASE DON'T KILL ME -- !
I'M A SLAVE AS WELL! THE LORDS -- THEY ASSIGNED ME THIS DUTY!
WHAT DUTY?
THE MAGIC -- THE SPELLS THAT MAKE THIS LAND WHAT IT IS! THE OLD, THE WEAK, THE SICK -- ONCE THEY'RE NO MORE USE TO THE LORDS --
-- THEIR SOULS ARE EXTRACTED -- TO FUEL THE SPELLS THAT CONTROL THE WEATHER --
-- THE SPELLS THAT EXTEND THE LORDS' LIVES -- !
PLEASE -- DON'T --

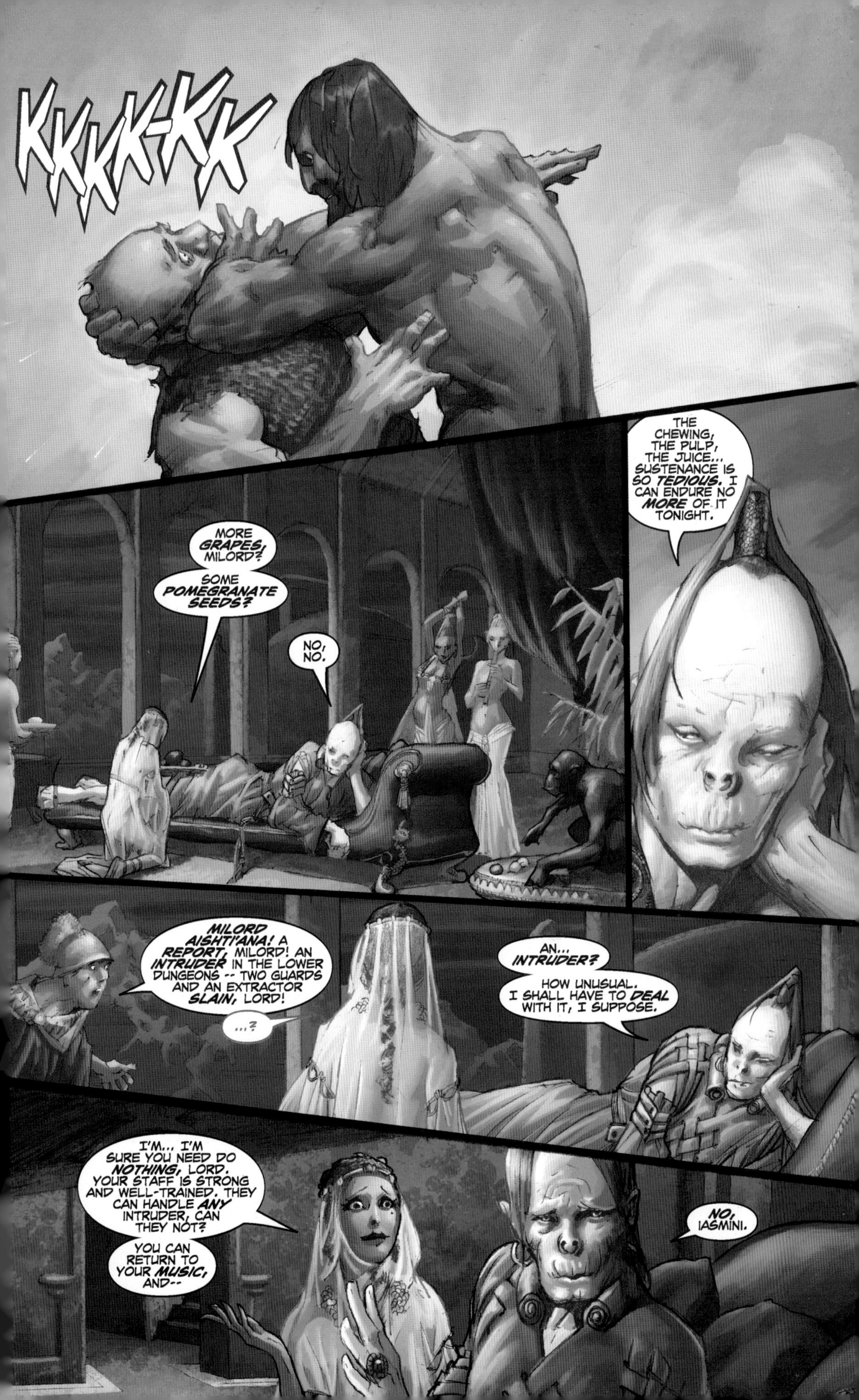
KKKK-KK
MORE GRAPES, MILORD?
SOME POMEGRANATE SEEDS?
NO, NO.
THE CHEWING, THE PULP, THE JUICE... SUSTENANCE IS SO TEDIOUS. I CAN ENDURE NO MORE OF IT TONIGHT.
MILORD AISHTI'ANA! A REPORT, MILORD! AN INTRUDER IN THE LOWER DUNGEONS -- TWO GUARDS AND AN EXTRACTOR SLAIN, LORD!
...?
AN... INTRUDER?
HOW UNUSUAL. I SHALL HAVE TO DEAL WITH IT, I SUPPOSE.
I'M... I'M SURE YOU NEED DO NOTHING, LORD. YOUR STAFF IS STRONG AND WELL-TRAINED. THEY CAN HANDLE ANY INTRUDER, CAN THEY NOT?
YOU CAN RETURN TO YOUR MUSIC, AND--
NO, IASMINI.

 IT IS *MY* HOUSE THAT IS IN DISORDER. IT IS *MY* DUTY TO CORRECT MATTERS.

 ≈SIGH≈ THERE...

 "...MY *LIONS* WILL DISPOSE OF THE INTRUDER.

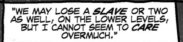 "WE MAY LOSE A *SLAVE* OR TWO AS WELL, ON THE LOWER LEVELS, BUT I CANNOT SEEM TO *CARE* OVERMUCH."

 MILORD, YOU--

SILENCE, IASMINI. MY HOUSE IS MY BODY. IF MY *BODY* IS IN *DISORDER*, IT IS BECAUSE I HAVE NOT *TENDED* TO IT PROPERLY.

AND I AM FORCED TO THE REALIZATION THAT I HAVE NOT *TENDED* IT PROPERLY BECAUSE I NO LONGER *CARE* TO.

WE WILL *DEAL* WITH THE DISARRAY. IT WOULD NOT DO TO LEAVE AN *UNTIDY* HOUSE.

LEAVE...?

YES, IASMINI. YOU MAY MAKE THE ARRANGEMENTS. I *TIRE* OF LIFE...

...AND OUR *DAY OF FAREWELL* IS UPON US.

CHAPTER FIVE

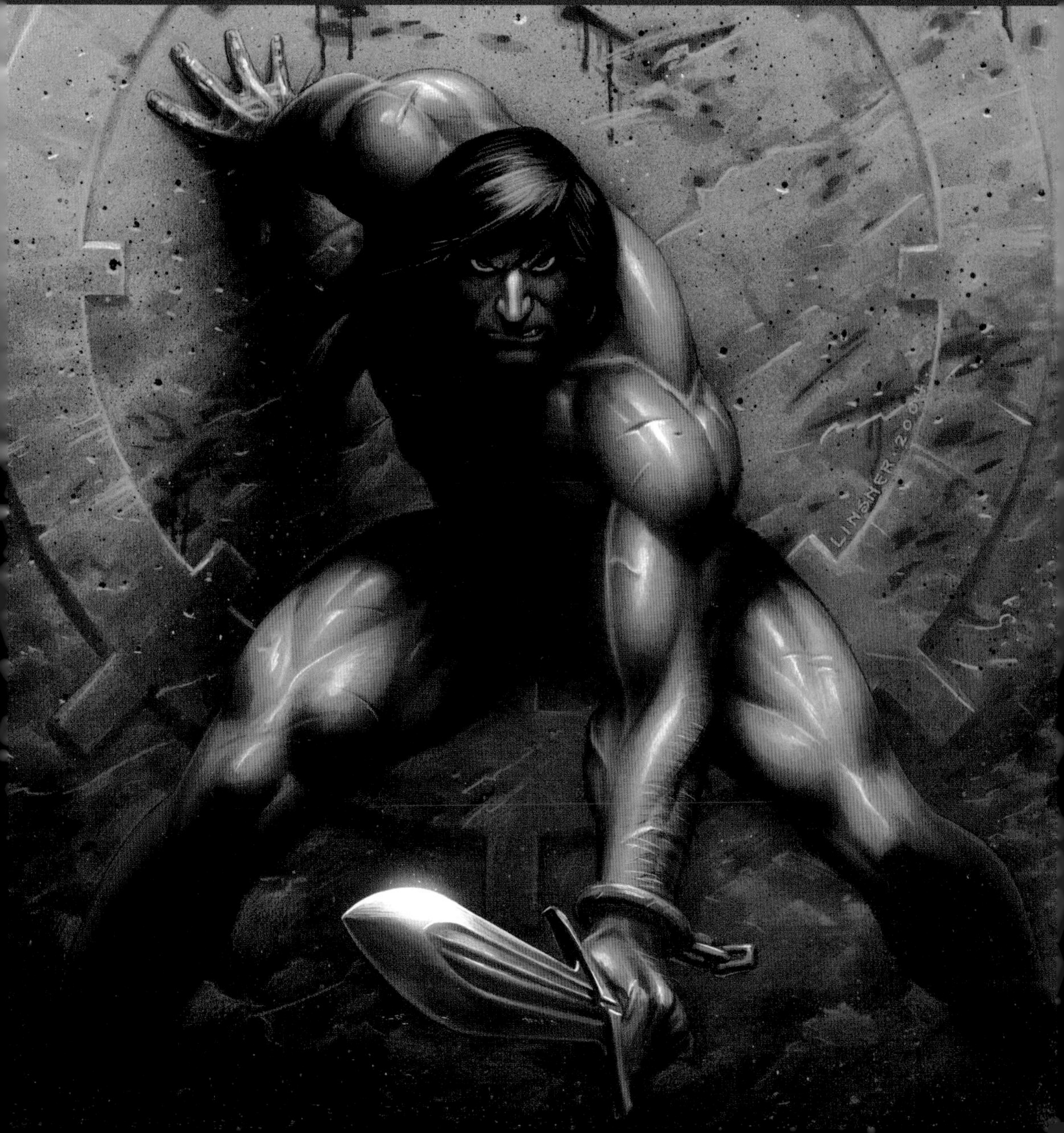

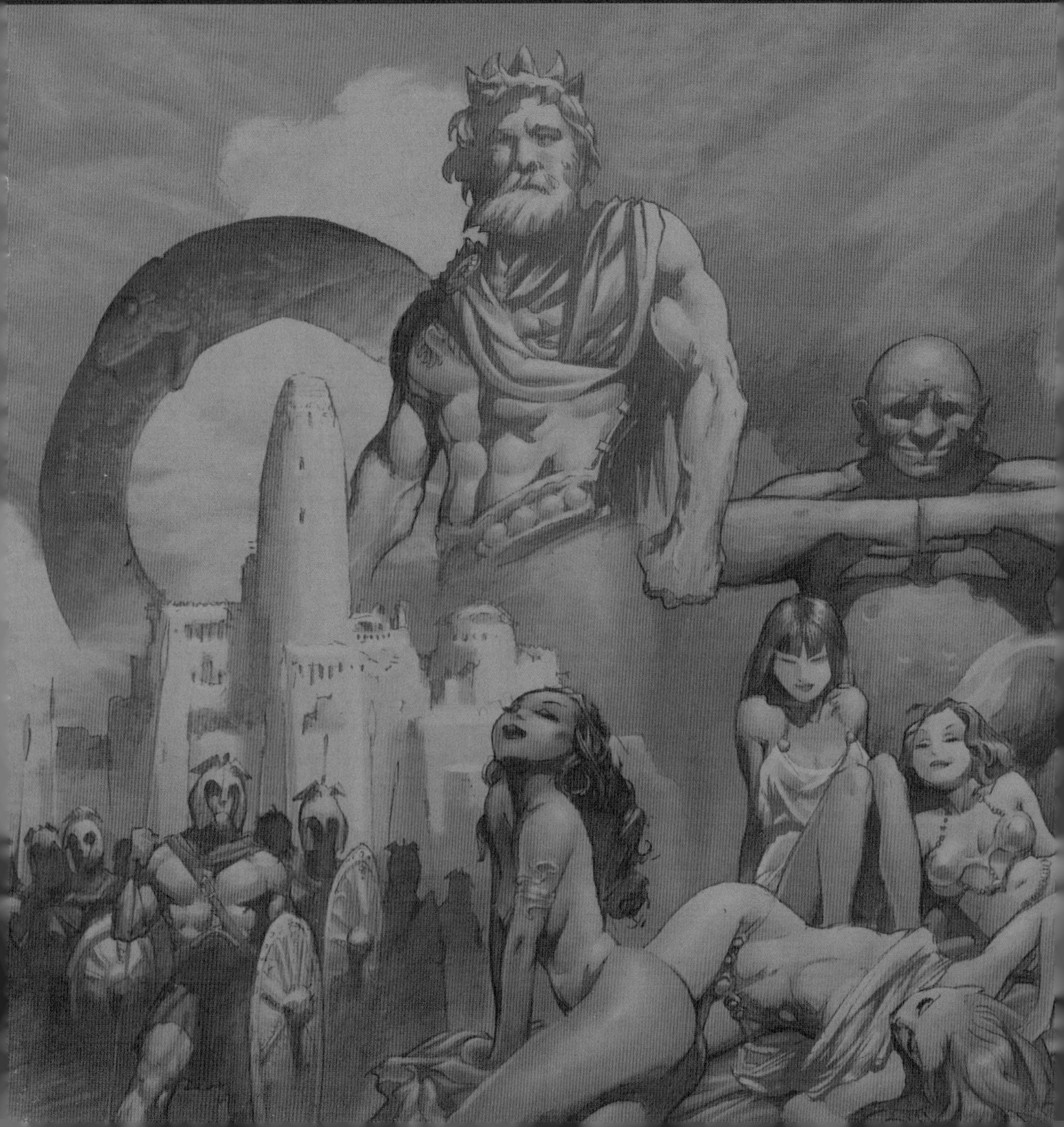

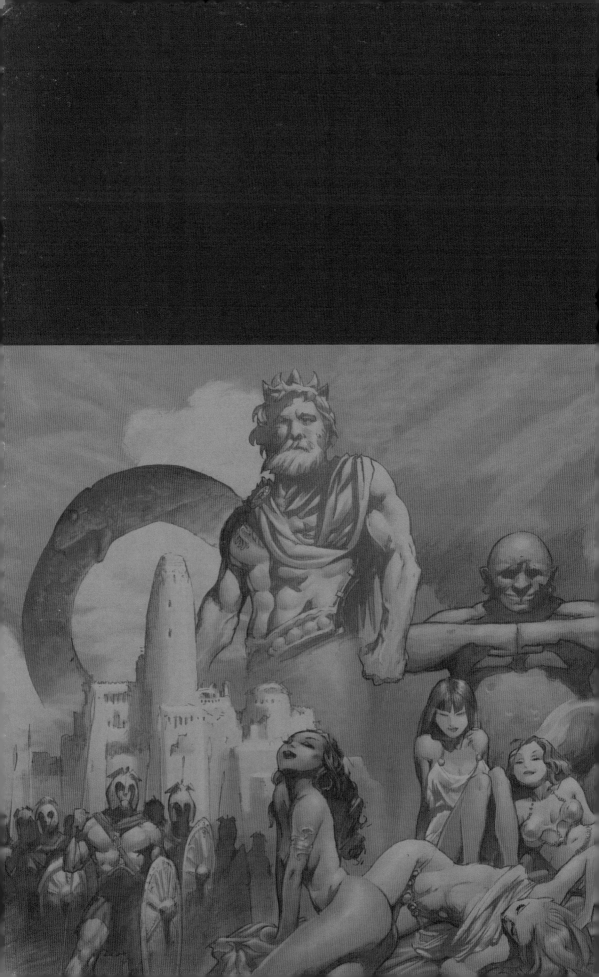

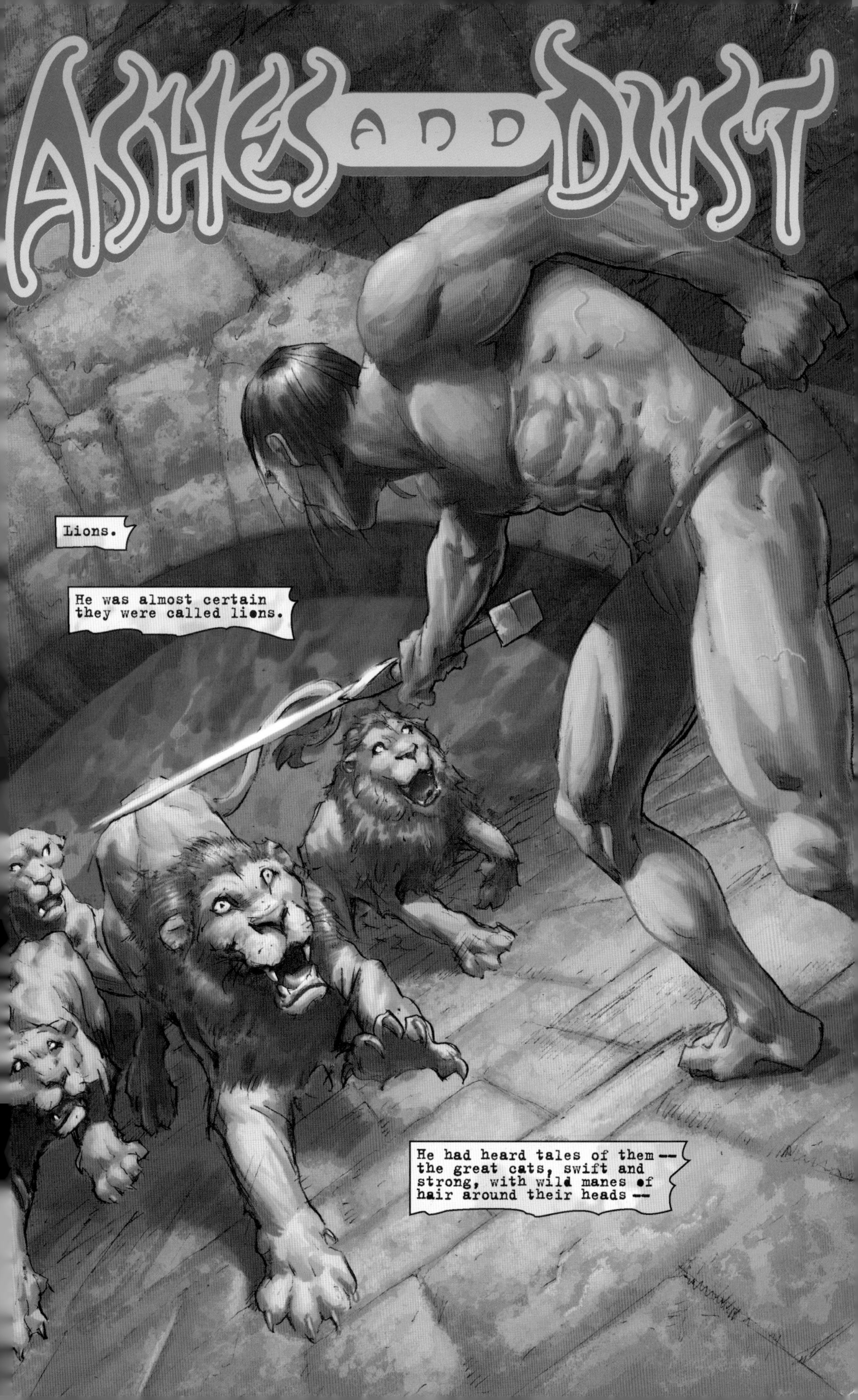
ASHES AND DUST
Lions.
He was almost certain they were called lions.
He had heard tales of them -- the great cats, swift and strong, with wild manes of hair around their heads --

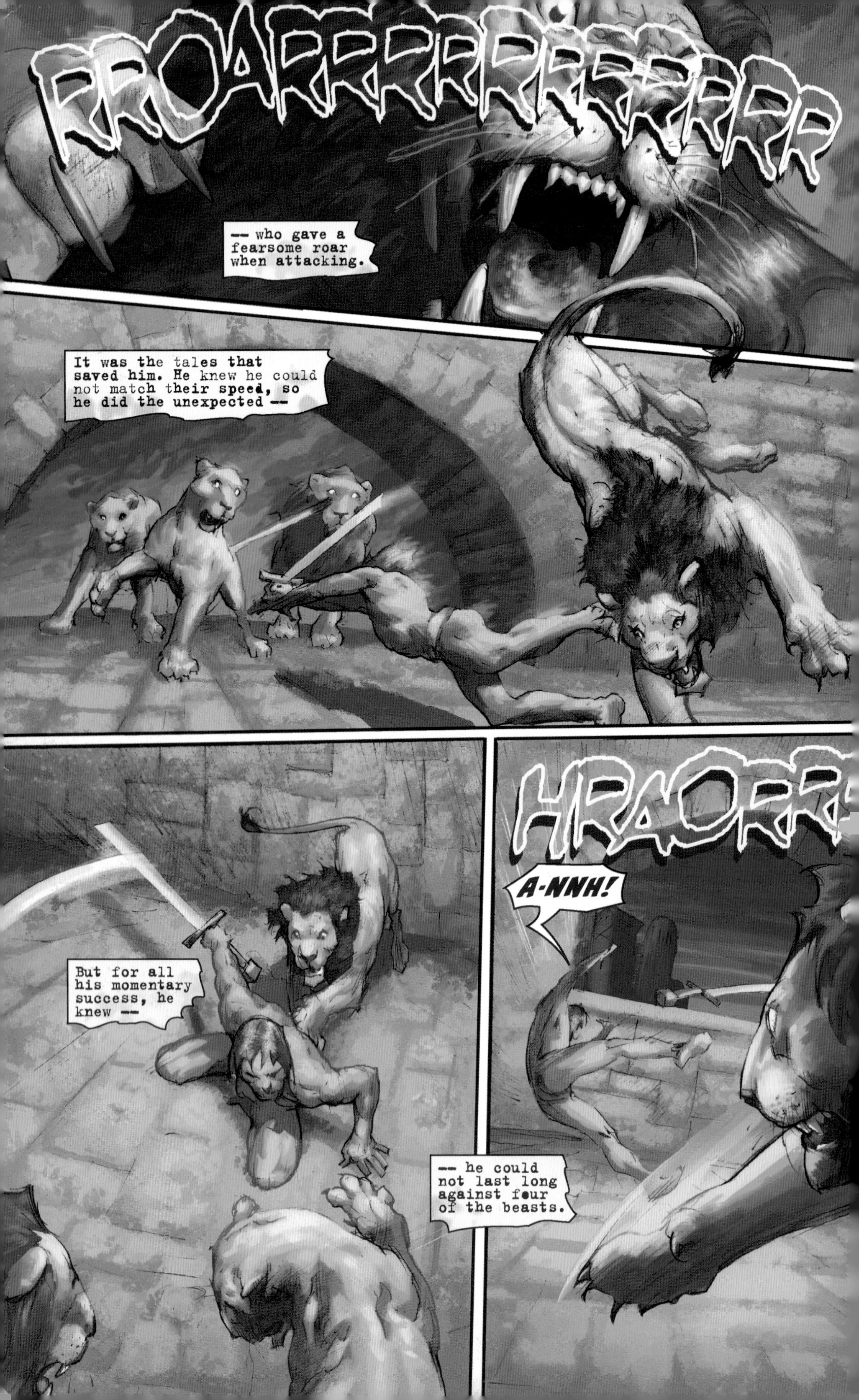
RROARRRRRRRRRRRR
-- who gave a fearsome roar when attacking.
It was the tales that saved him. He knew he could not match their speed, so he did the unexpected --
But for all his momentary success, he knew --
HRAORRR
A-NNH!
-- he could not last long against four of the beasts.

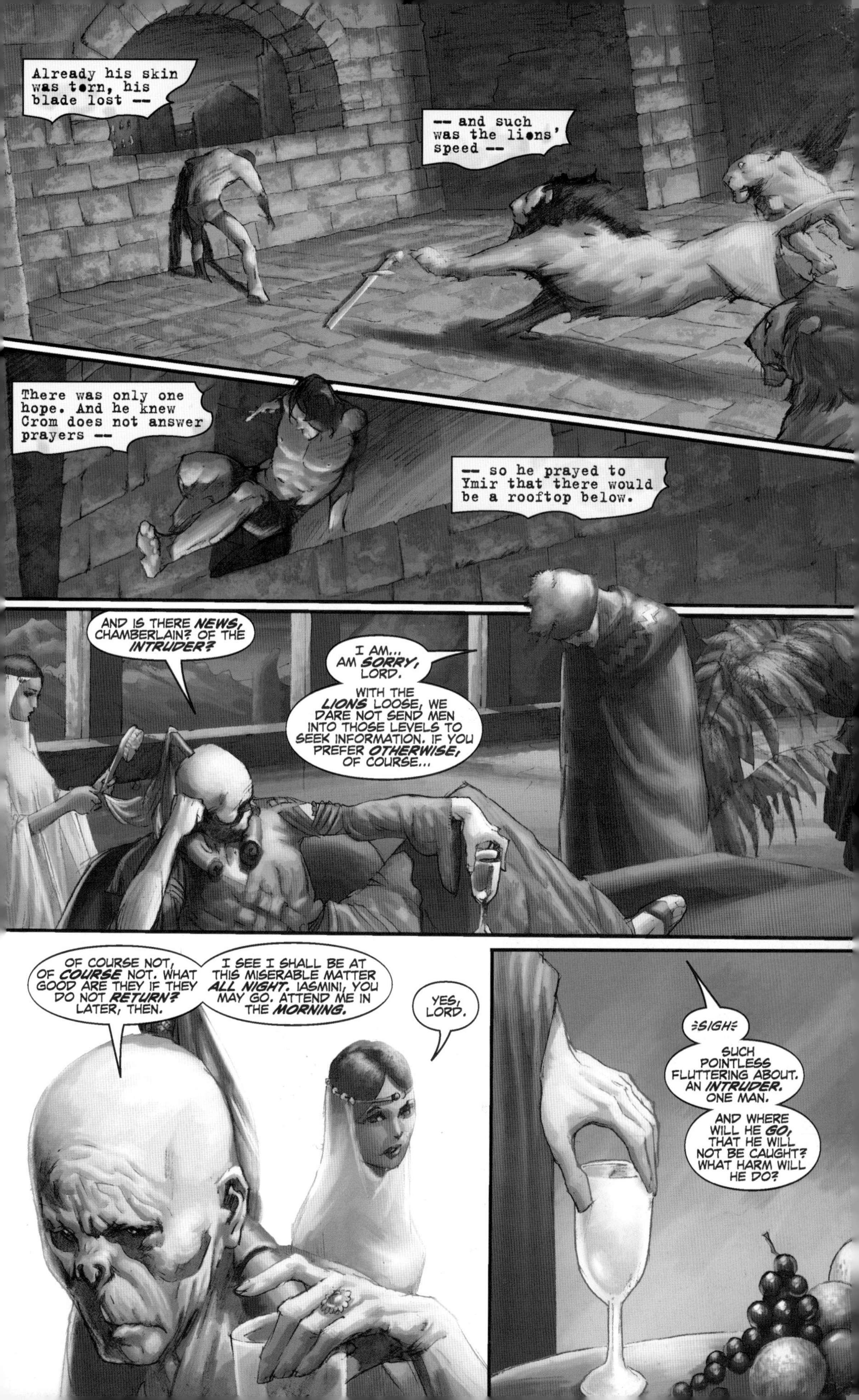

Already his skin was torn, his blade lost --
-- and such was the lions' speed --
There was only one hope. And he knew Crom does not answer prayers --
-- so he prayed to Ymir that there would be a rooftop below.
AND IS THERE NEWS, CHAMBERLAIN? OF THE INTRUDER?
I AM... AM SORRY, LORD.
WITH THE LIONS LOOSE, WE DARE NOT SEND MEN INTO THOSE LEVELS TO SEEK INFORMATION. IF YOU PREFER OTHERWISE, OF COURSE...
OF COURSE NOT, OF COURSE NOT. WHAT GOOD ARE THEY IF THEY DO NOT RETURN? LATER, THEN.
I SEE I SHALL BE AT THIS MISERABLE MATTER ALL NIGHT. IASMINI, YOU MAY GO. ATTEND ME IN THE MORNING.
YES, LORD.
SIGH
SUCH POINTLESS FLUTTERING ABOUT. AN INTRUDER. ONE MAN.
AND WHERE WILL HE GO, THAT HE WILL NOT BE CAUGHT? WHAT HARM WILL HE DO?

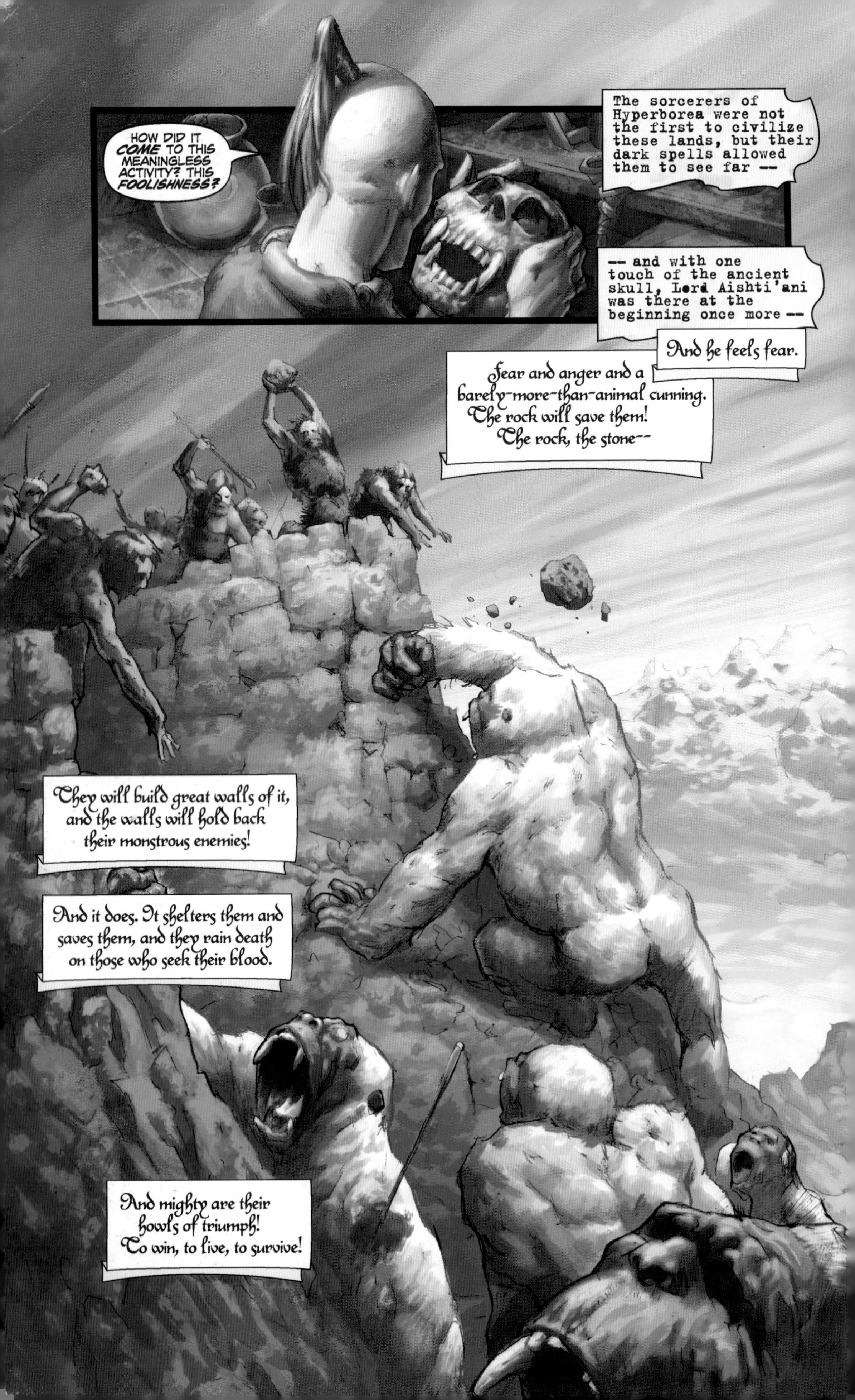
HOW DID IT COME TO THIS MEANINGLESS ACTIVITY? THIS FOOLISHNESS?
The sorcerers of Hyperborea were not the first to civilize these lands, but their dark spells allowed them to see far --
-- and with one touch of the ancient skull, Lord Aishti'ani was there at the beginning once more --
And he feels fear.
Fear and anger and a barely-more-than-animal cunning. The rock will save them! The rock, the stone--
They will build great walls of it, and the walls will hold back their monstrous enemies!
And it does. It shelters them and saves them, and they rain death on those who seek their blood.
And mighty are their howls of triumph! To win, to live, to survive!

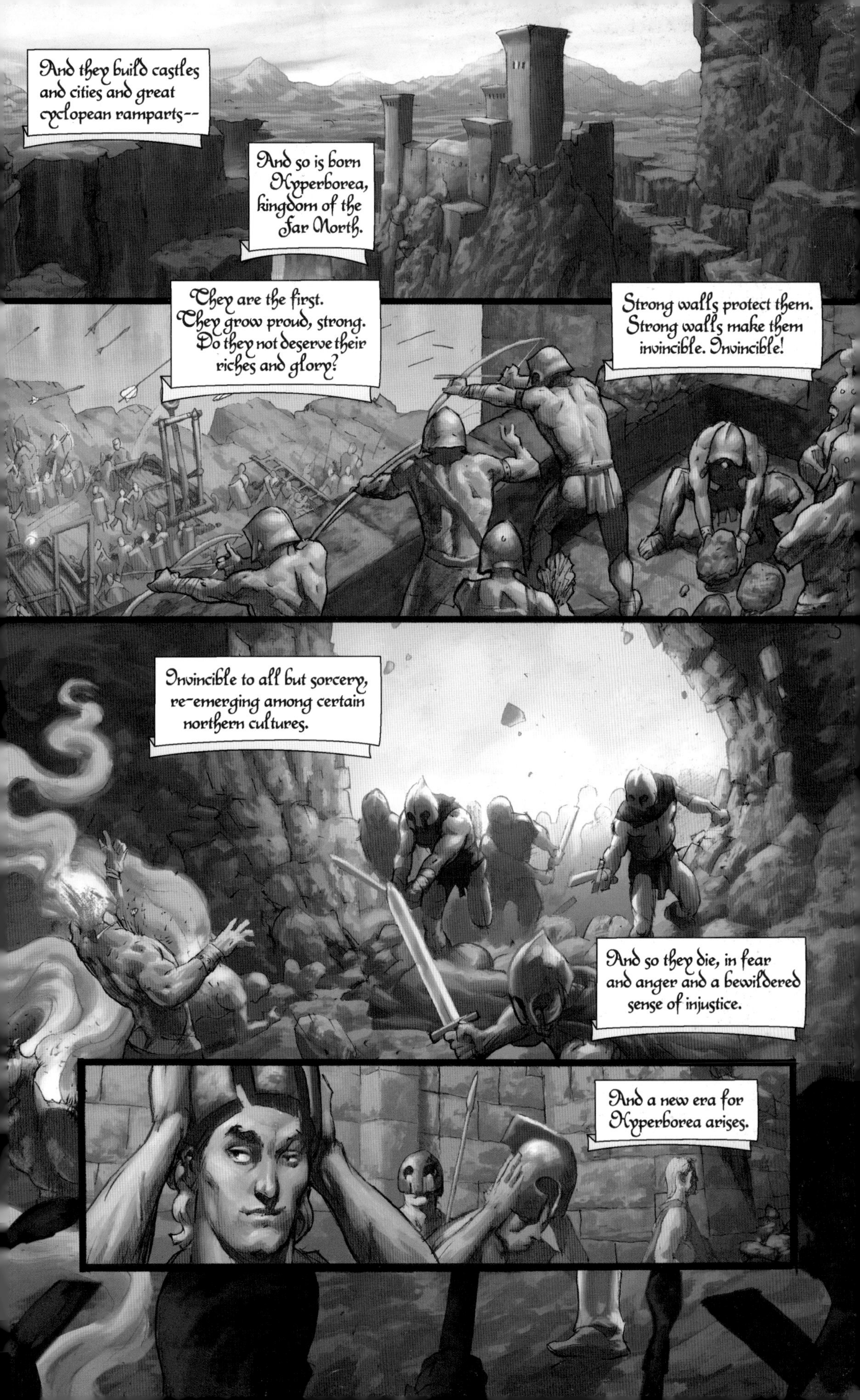
And they build castles and cities and great cyclopean ramparts--
And so is born Hyperborea, kingdom of the Far North.
They are the first. They grow proud, strong. Do they not deserve their riches and glory?
Strong walls protect them. Strong walls make them invincible. Invincible!
Invincible to all but sorcery, re-emerging among certain northern cultures.
And so they die, in fear and anger and a bewildered sense of injustice.
And a new era for Hyperborea arises.

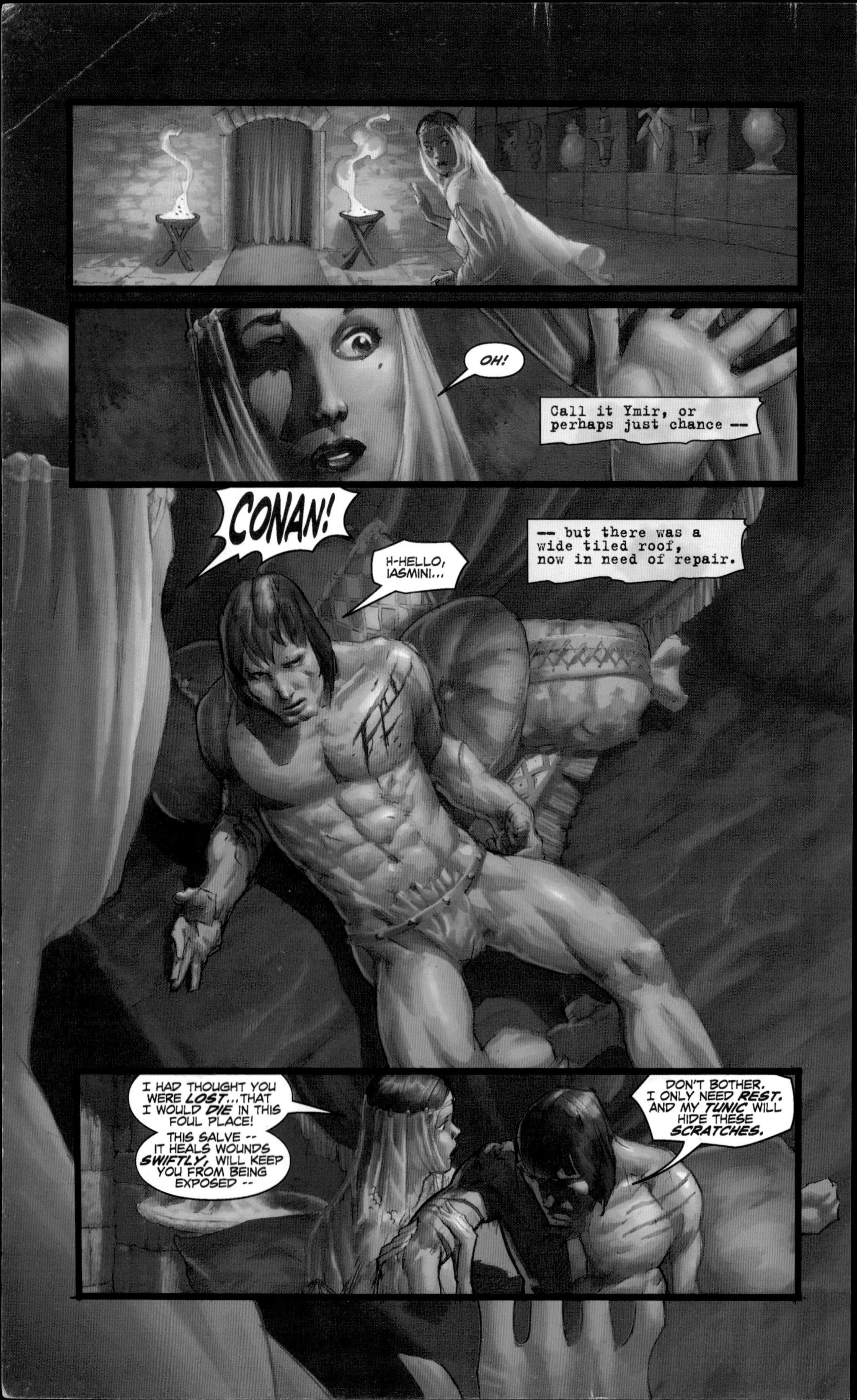
OH!
Call it Ymir, or perhaps just chance --
CONAN!
H-HELLO, IASMINI...
-- but there was a wide tiled roof, now in need of repair.
I HAD THOUGHT YOU WERE LOST... THAT I WOULD DIE IN THIS FOUL PLACE!
THIS SALVE -- IT HEALS WOUNDS SWIFTLY, WILL KEEP YOU FROM BEING EXPOSED --
DON'T BOTHER. I ONLY NEED REST. AND MY TUNIC WILL HIDE THESE SCRATCHES.

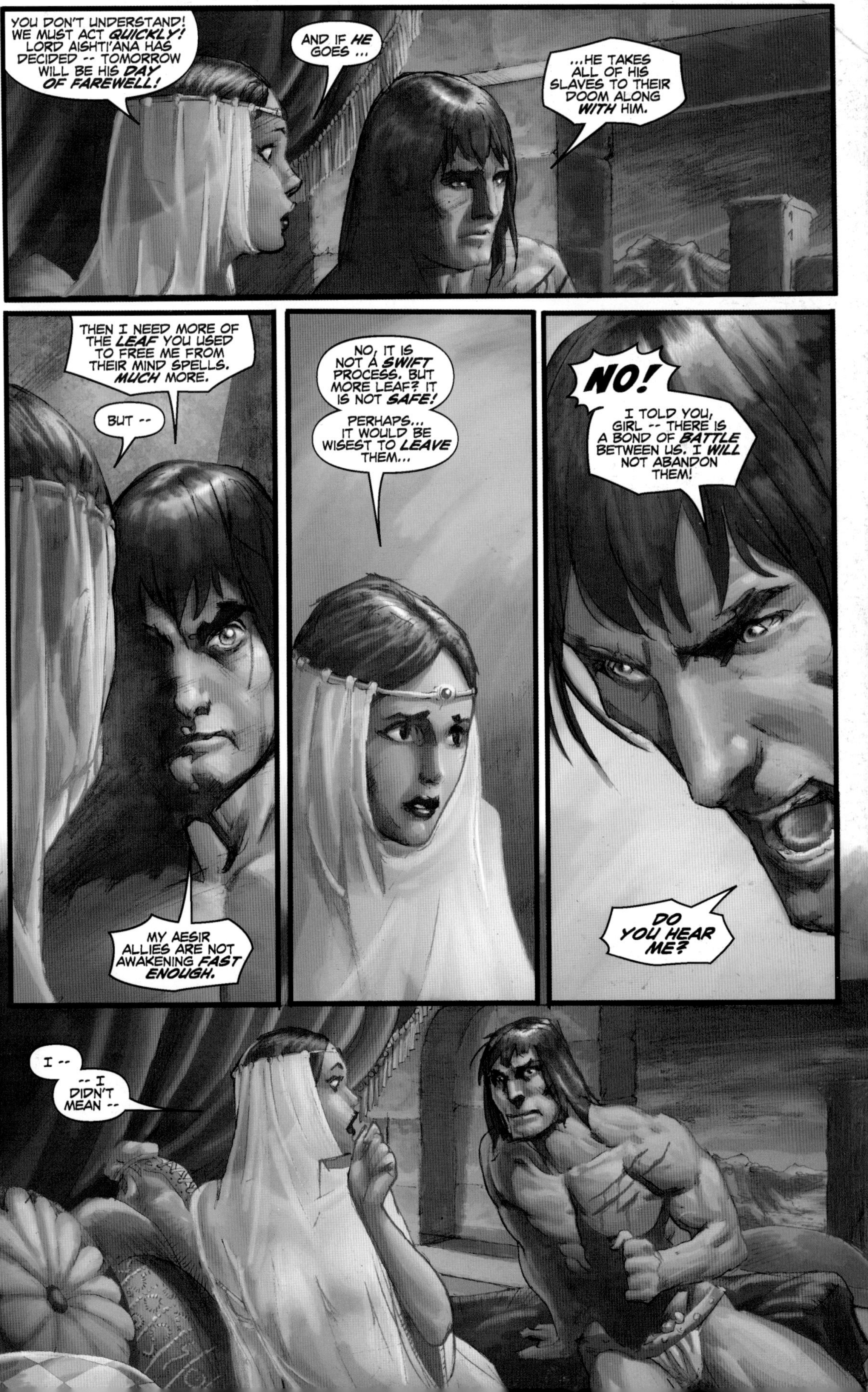
YOU DON'T UNDERSTAND! WE MUST ACT QUICKLY! LORD AISHTI'ANA HAS DECIDED -- TOMORROW WILL BE HIS DAY OF FAREWELL!
AND IF HE GOES ...
...HE TAKES ALL OF HIS SLAVES TO THEIR DOOM ALONG WITH HIM.
THEN I NEED MORE OF THE LEAF YOU USED TO FREE ME FROM THEIR MIND SPELLS. MUCH MORE.
BUT --
MY AESIR ALLIES ARE NOT AWAKENING FAST ENOUGH.
NO, IT IS NOT A SWIFT PROCESS. BUT MORE LEAF? IT IS NOT SAFE!
PERHAPS... IT WOULD BE WISEST TO LEAVE THEM...
NO!
I TOLD YOU, GIRL -- THERE IS A BOND OF BATTLE BETWEEN US. I WILL NOT ABANDON THEM!
DO YOU HEAR ME?
I --
-- I DIDN'T MEAN --

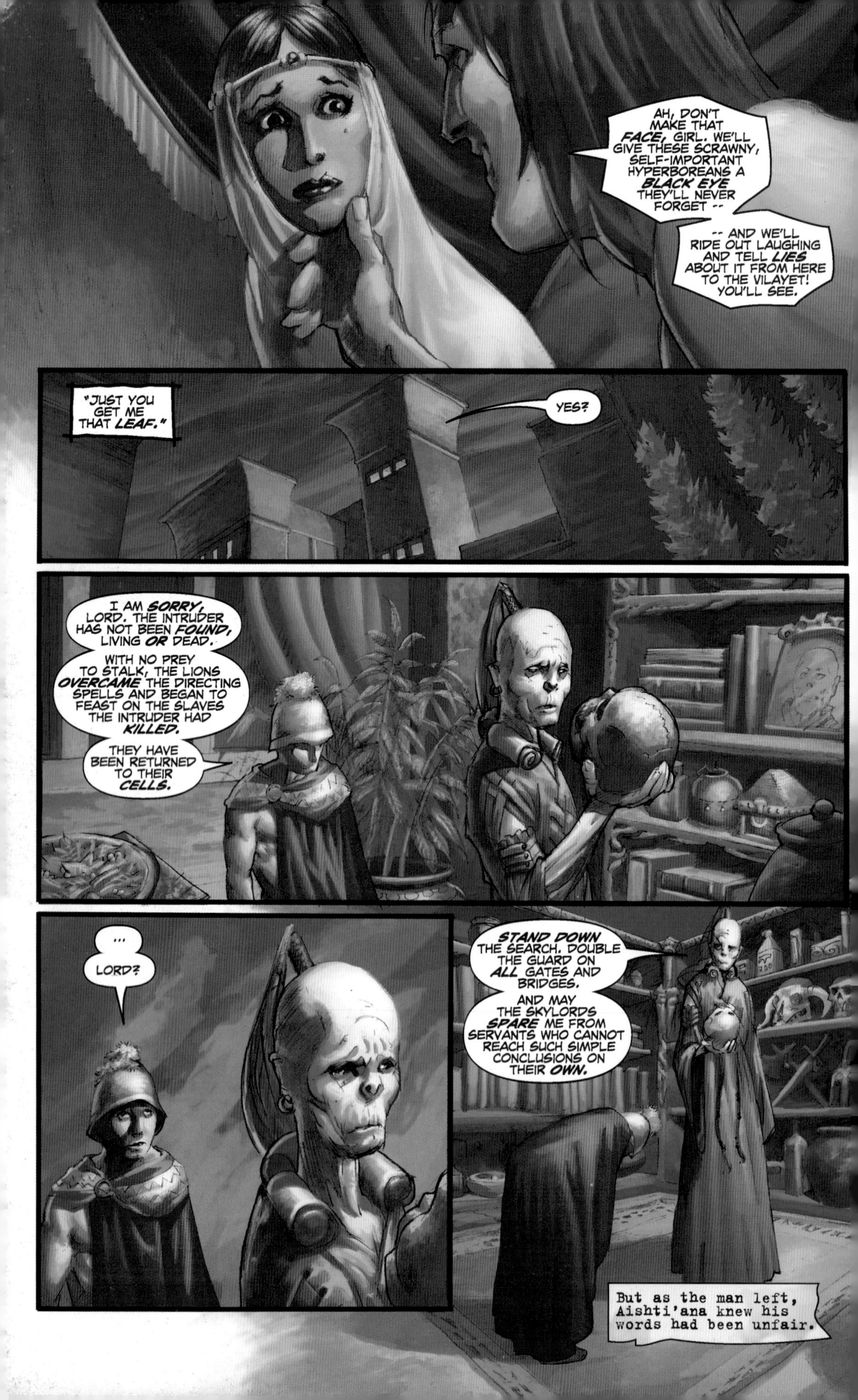
AH, DON'T MAKE THAT FACE, GIRL. WE'LL GIVE THESE SCRAWNY, SELF-IMPORTANT HYPERBOREANS A BLACK EYE THEY'LL NEVER FORGET --
-- AND WE'LL RIDE OUT LAUGHING AND TELL LIES ABOUT IT FROM HERE TO THE VILAYET! YOU'LL SEE.
"JUST YOU GET ME THAT LEAF."
YES?
I AM SORRY, LORD. THE INTRUDER HAS NOT BEEN FOUND, LIVING OR DEAD.
WITH NO PREY TO STALK, THE LIONS OVERCAME THE DIRECTING SPELLS AND BEGAN TO FEAST ON THE SLAVES THE INTRUDER HAD KILLED.
THEY HAVE BEEN RETURNED TO THEIR CELLS.
...
LORD?
STAND DOWN THE SEARCH. DOUBLE THE GUARD ON ALL GATES AND BRIDGES.
AND MAY THE SKYLORDS SPARE ME FROM SERVANTS WHO CANNOT REACH SUCH SIMPLE CONCLUSIONS ON THEIR OWN.
But as the man left, Aishti'ana knew his words had been unfair.

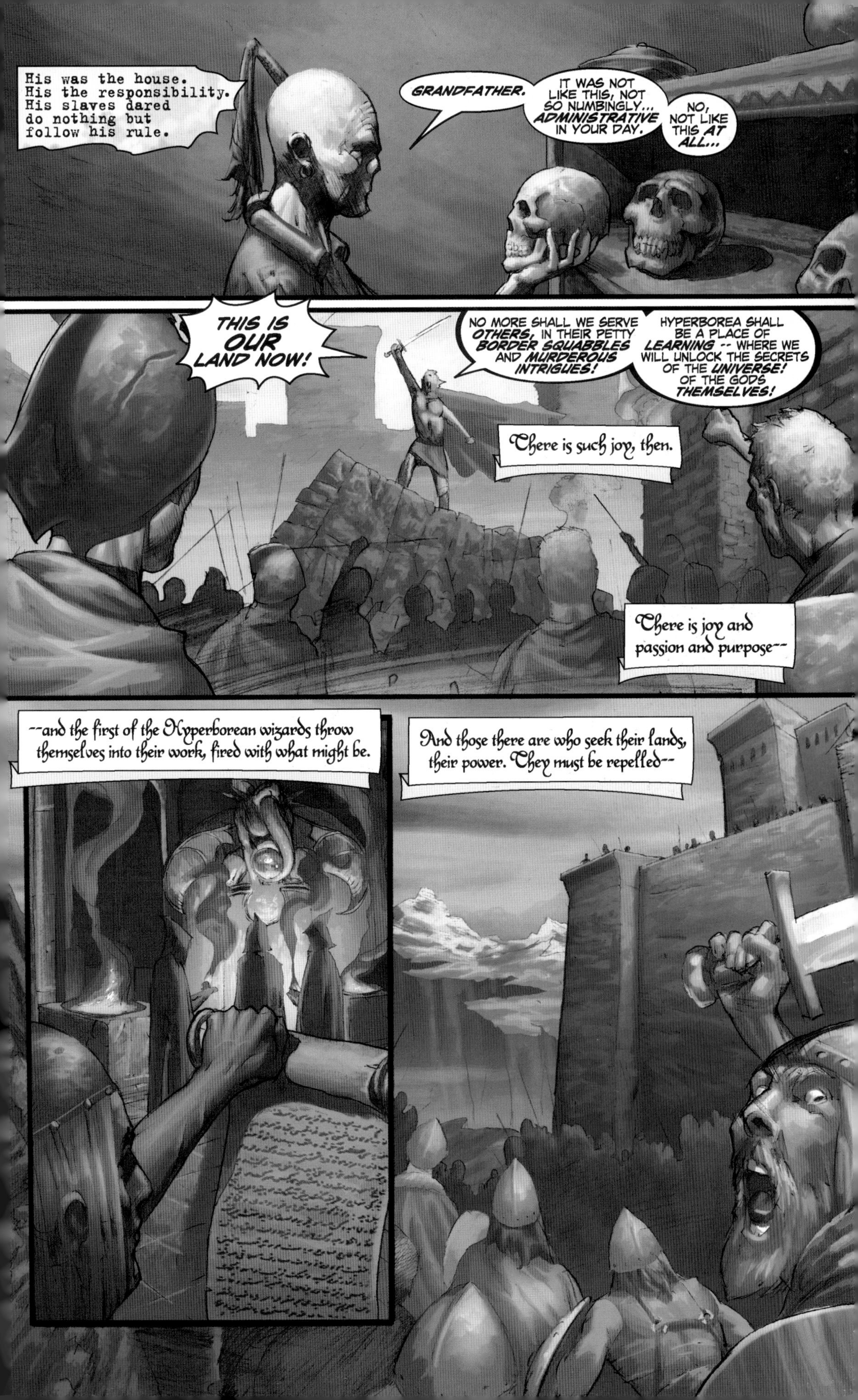

His was the house. His the responsibility. His slaves dared do nothing but follow his rule.
GRANDFATHER.
IT WAS NOT LIKE THIS, NOT SO NUMBINGLY... ADMINISTRATIVE IN YOUR DAY.
NO, NOT LIKE THIS AT ALL...
THIS IS OUR LAND NOW!
NO MORE SHALL WE SERVE OTHERS, IN THEIR PETTY BORDER SQUABBLES AND MURDEROUS INTRIGUES!
HYPERBOREA SHALL BE A PLACE OF LEARNING -- WHERE WE WILL UNLOCK THE SECRETS OF THE UNIVERSE! OF THE GODS THEMSELVES!
There is such joy, then.
There is joy and passion and purpose--
--and the first of the Hyperborean wizards throw themselves into their work, fired with what might be.
And those there are who seek their lands, their power. They must be repelled--

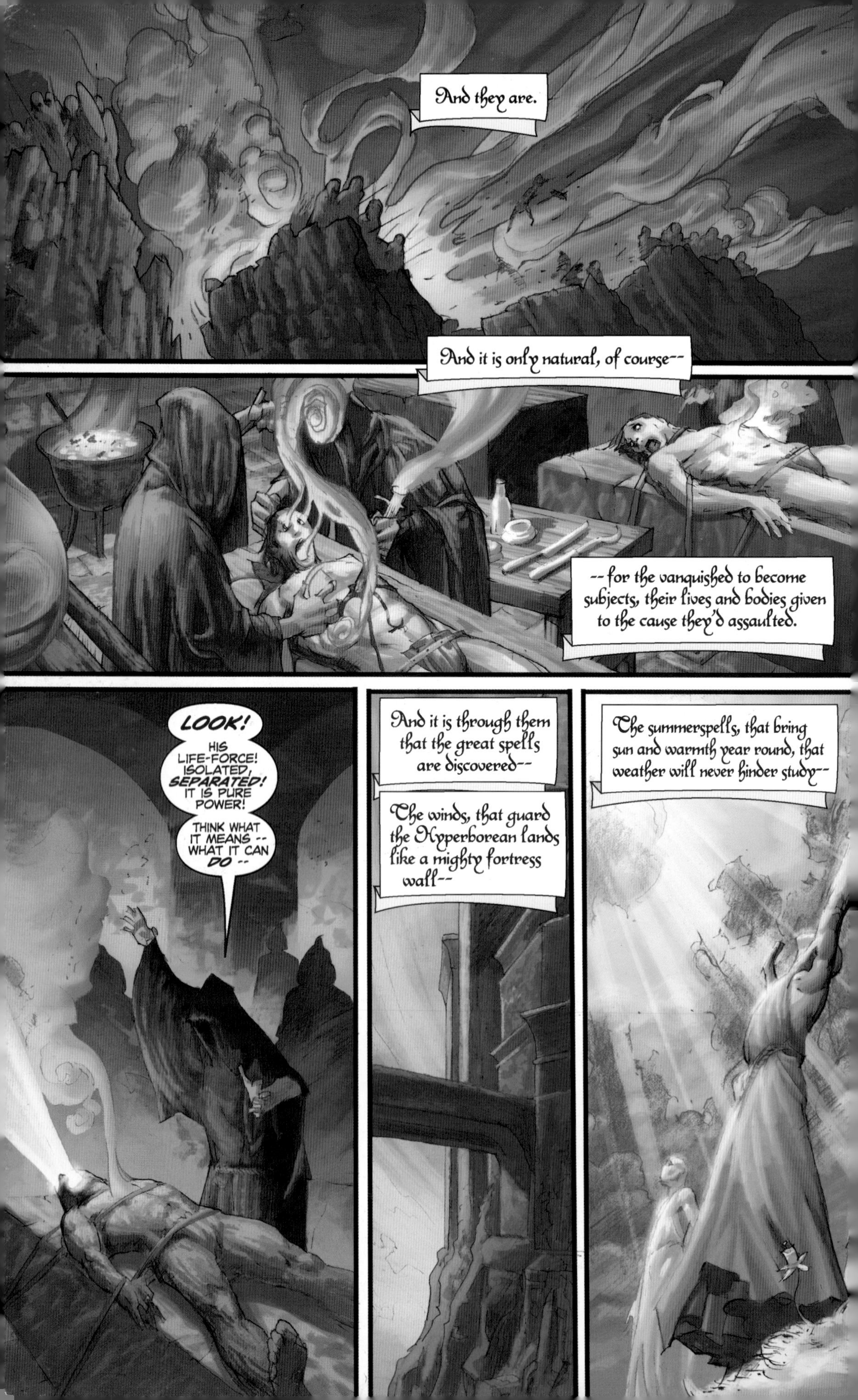
And they are.
And it is only natural, of course--
--for the vanquished to become subjects, their lives and bodies given to the cause they'd assaulted.
LOOK!
HIS LIFE-FORCE! ISOLATED, SEPARATED! IT IS PURE POWER!
THINK WHAT IT MEANS -- WHAT IT CAN DO --
And it is through them that the great spells are discovered--
The winds, that guard the Hyperborean lands like a mighty fortress wall--
The summerspells, that bring sun and warmth year round, that weather will never hinder study--

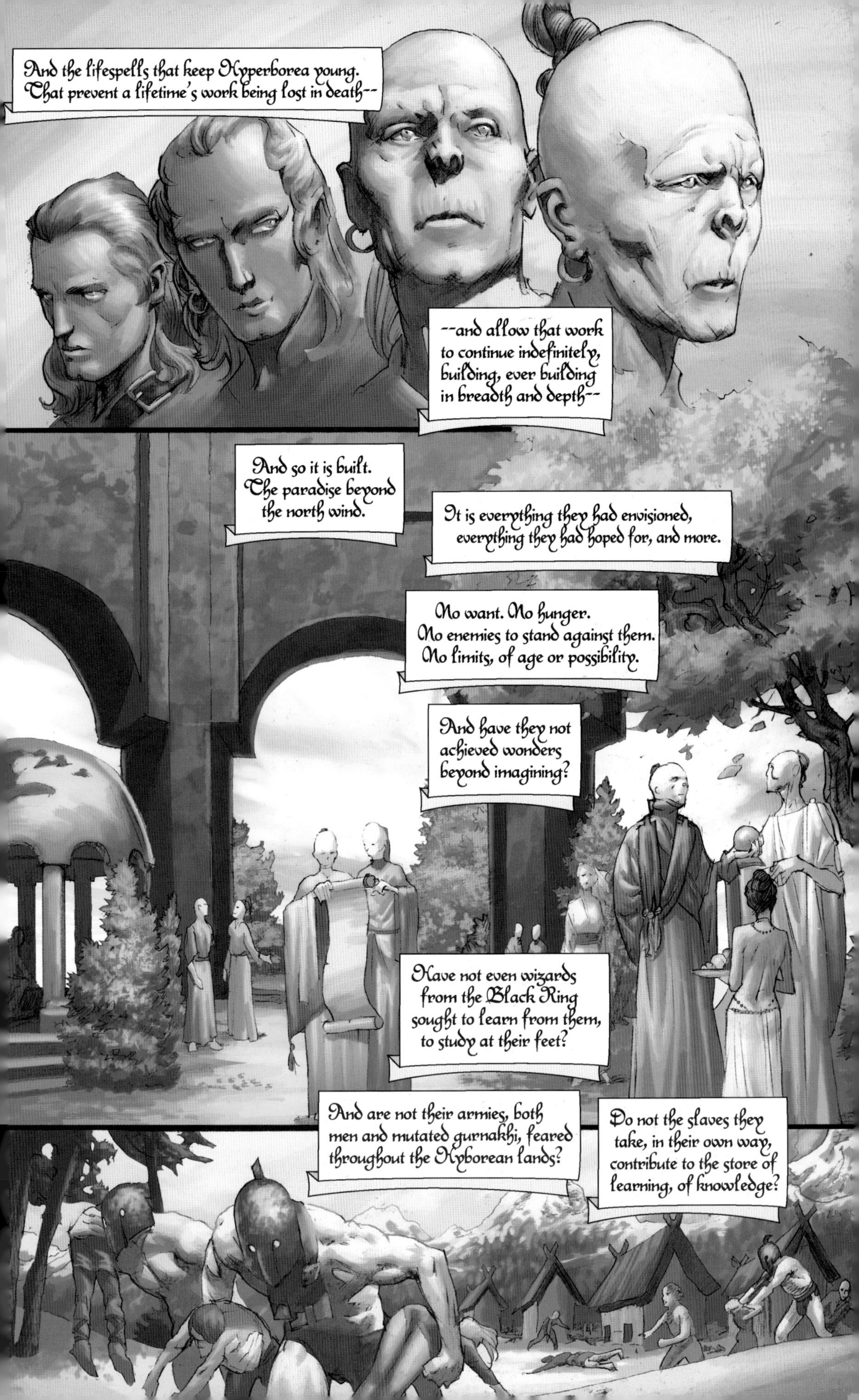
And the lifespells that keep Hyperborea young. That prevent a lifetime's work being lost in death--
--and allow that work to continue indefinitely, building, ever building in breadth and depth--
And so it is built. The paradise beyond the north wind.
It is everything they had envisioned, everything they had hoped for, and more.
No want. No hunger. No enemies to stand against them. No limits, of age or possibility.
And have they not achieved wonders beyond imagining?
Have not even wizards from the Black Ring sought to learn from them, to study at their feet?
And are not their armies, both men and mutated gurnakhi, feared throughout the Hyborean lands?
Do not the slaves they take, in their own way, contribute to the store of learning, of knowledge?

Is that not a noble purpose?

I COULD *RUN*, PACK SOME SUPPLIES -- TRY TO SLIP *PAST* THE GATE GUARDS --

THROUGH THE WINDS, THE ICE --

ERLIK *TAKE* YOU, WOMAN. YOU WOULDN'T REACH THE *GATE*, LET ALONE THE SNOWS...

CONAN WILL *SUCCEED*. CONAN AND HIS *AESIR*, AND WE'LL LAUGH AND LIE ABOUT IT...

CONAN WILL SUCCEED. HE *WILL*...

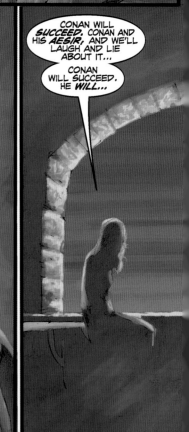

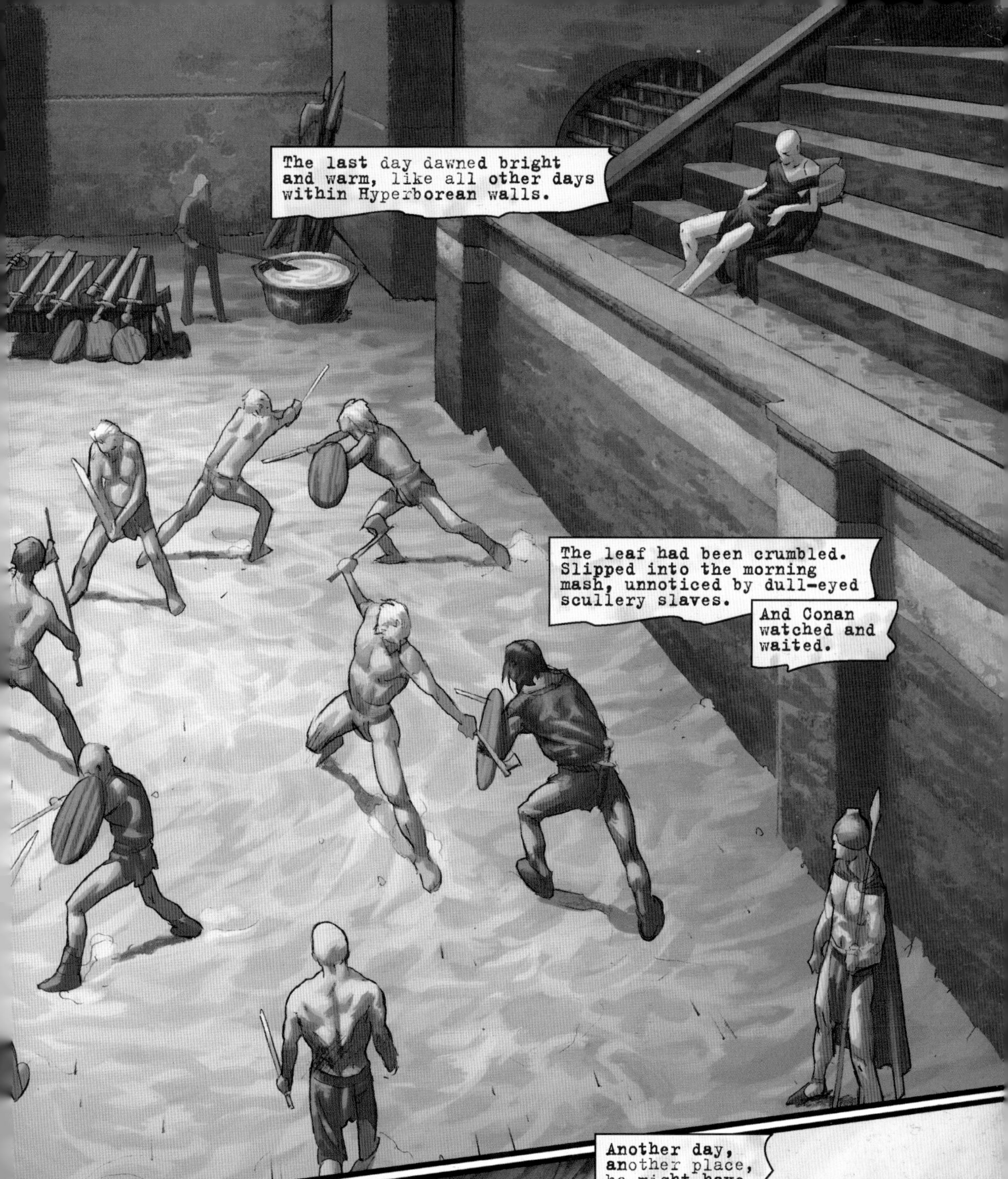
The last day dawned bright and warm, like all other days within Hyperborean walls.
The leaf had been crumbled. Slipped into the morning mash, unnoticed by dull-eyed scullery slaves.
And Conan watched and waited.

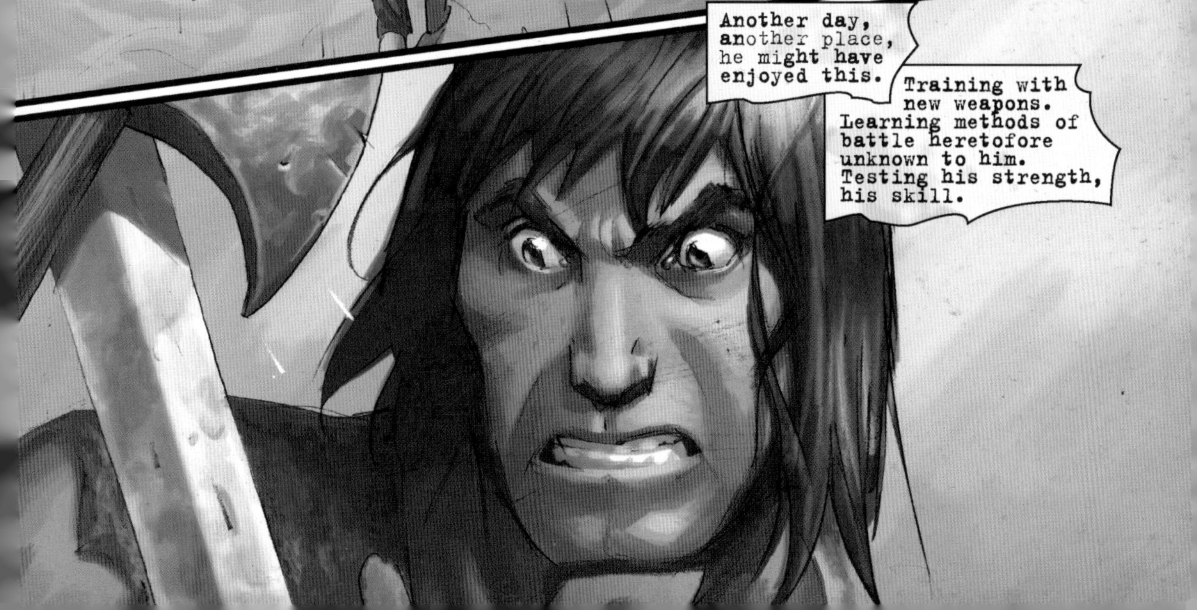
Another day, another place, he might have enjoyed this.
Training with new weapons. Learning methods of battle heretofore unknown to him. Testing his strength, his skill.

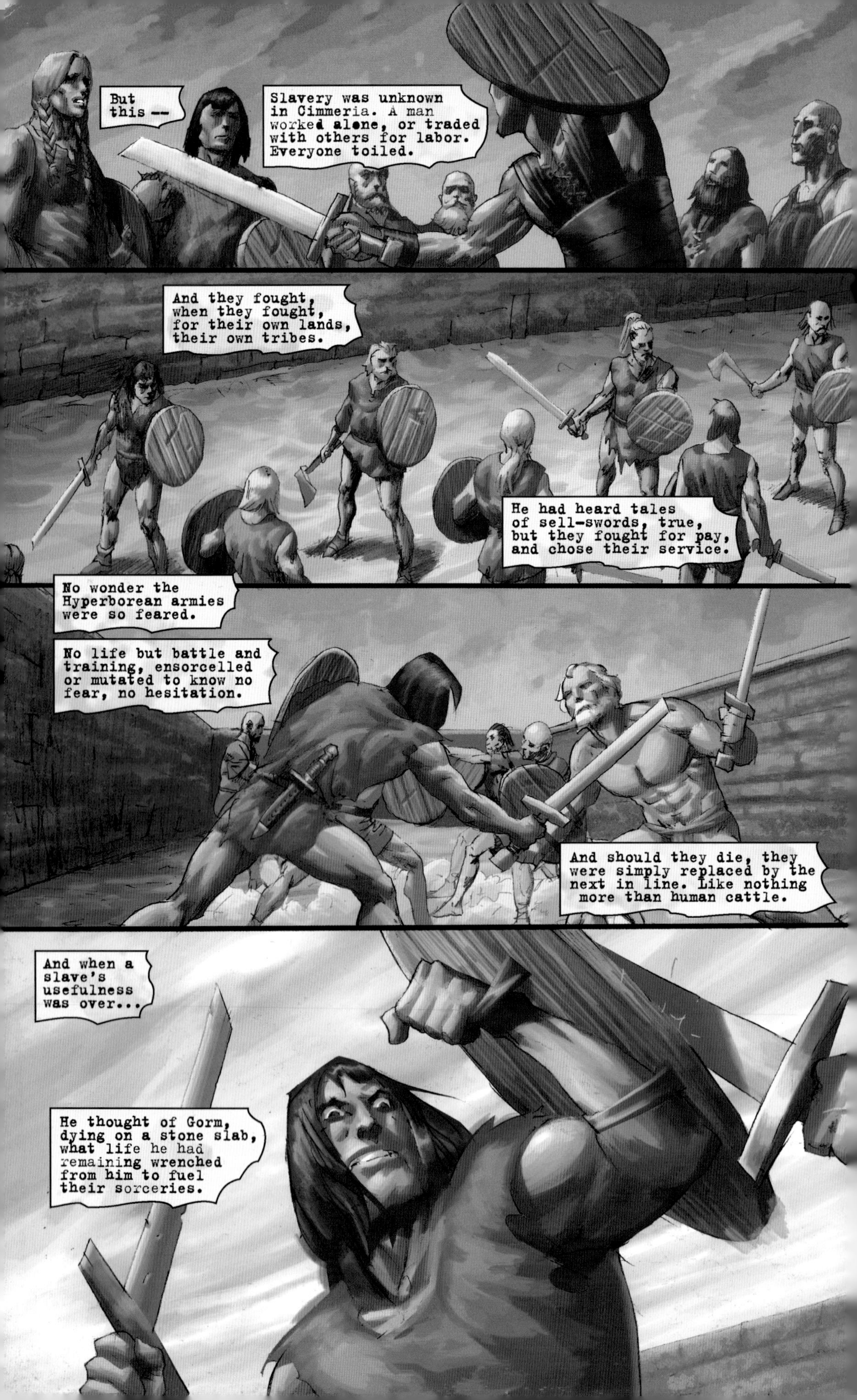
But this --
Slavery was unknown in Cimmeria. A man worked alone, or traded with others for labor. Everyone toiled.
And they fought, when they fought, for their own lands, their own tribes.
He had heard tales of sell-swords, true, but they fought for pay, and chose their service.
No wonder the Hyperborean armies were so feared.
No life but battle and training, ensorcelled or mutated to know no fear, no hesitation.
And should they die, they were simply replaced by the next in line. Like nothing more than human cattle.
And when a slave's usefulness was over...
He thought of Gorm, dying on a stone slab, what life he had remaining wrenched from him to fuel their sorceries.

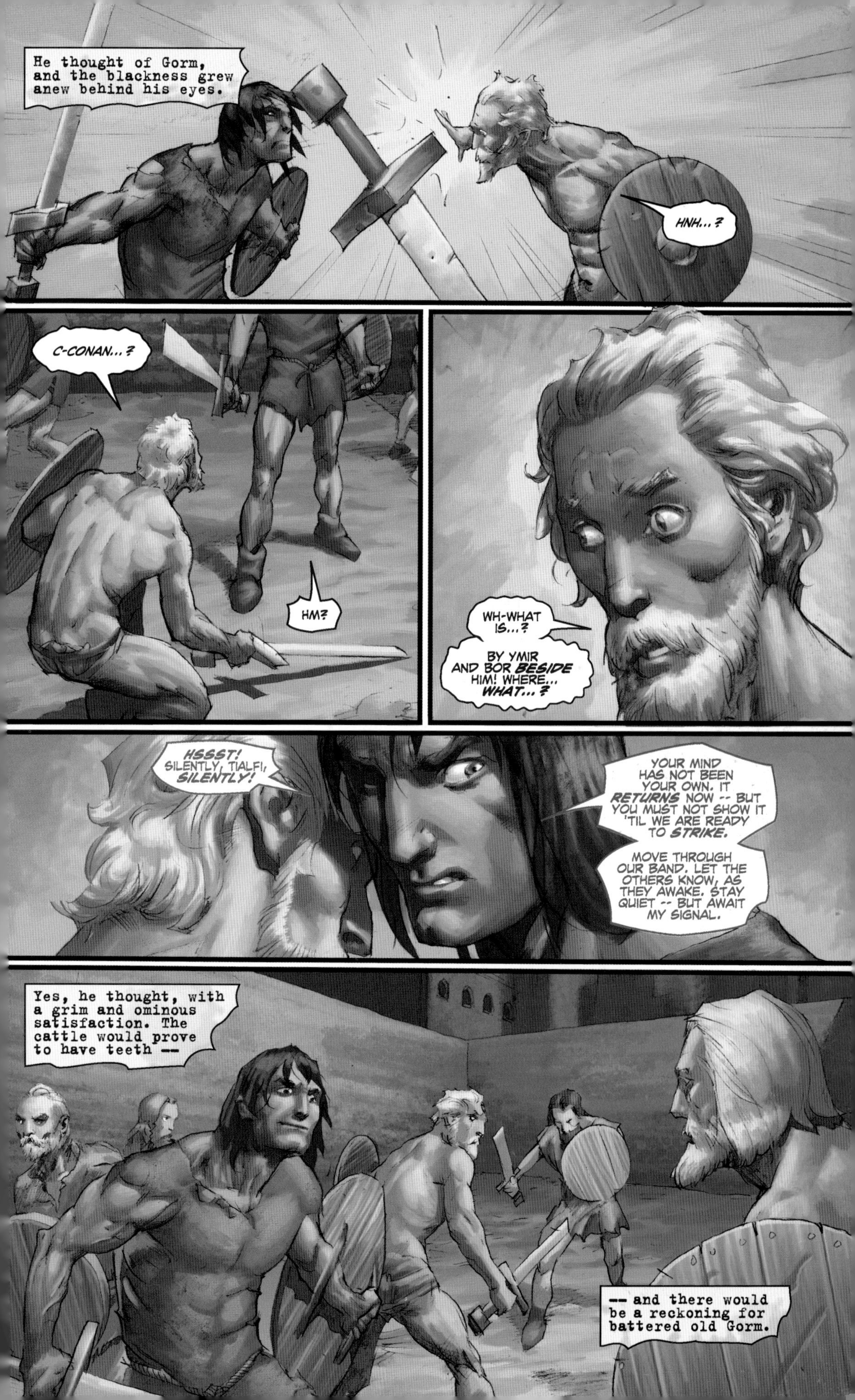
He thought of Gorm, and the blackness grew anew behind his eyes.
HNH...?
C-CONAN...?
HM?
WH-WHAT IS...?
BY YMIR AND BOR *BESIDE* HIM! WHERE... *WHAT...?*
HSSST! SILENTLY, TIALFI, *SILENTLY!*
YOUR MIND HAS NOT BEEN YOUR OWN. IT *RETURNS* NOW -- BUT YOU MUST NOT SHOW IT 'TIL WE ARE READY TO *STRIKE.*
MOVE THROUGH OUR BAND. LET THE OTHERS KNOW, AS THEY AWAKE. STAY QUIET -- BUT AWAIT MY SIGNAL.
Yes, he thought, with a grim and ominous satisfaction. The cattle would prove to have teeth --
-- and there would be a reckoning for battered old Gorm.

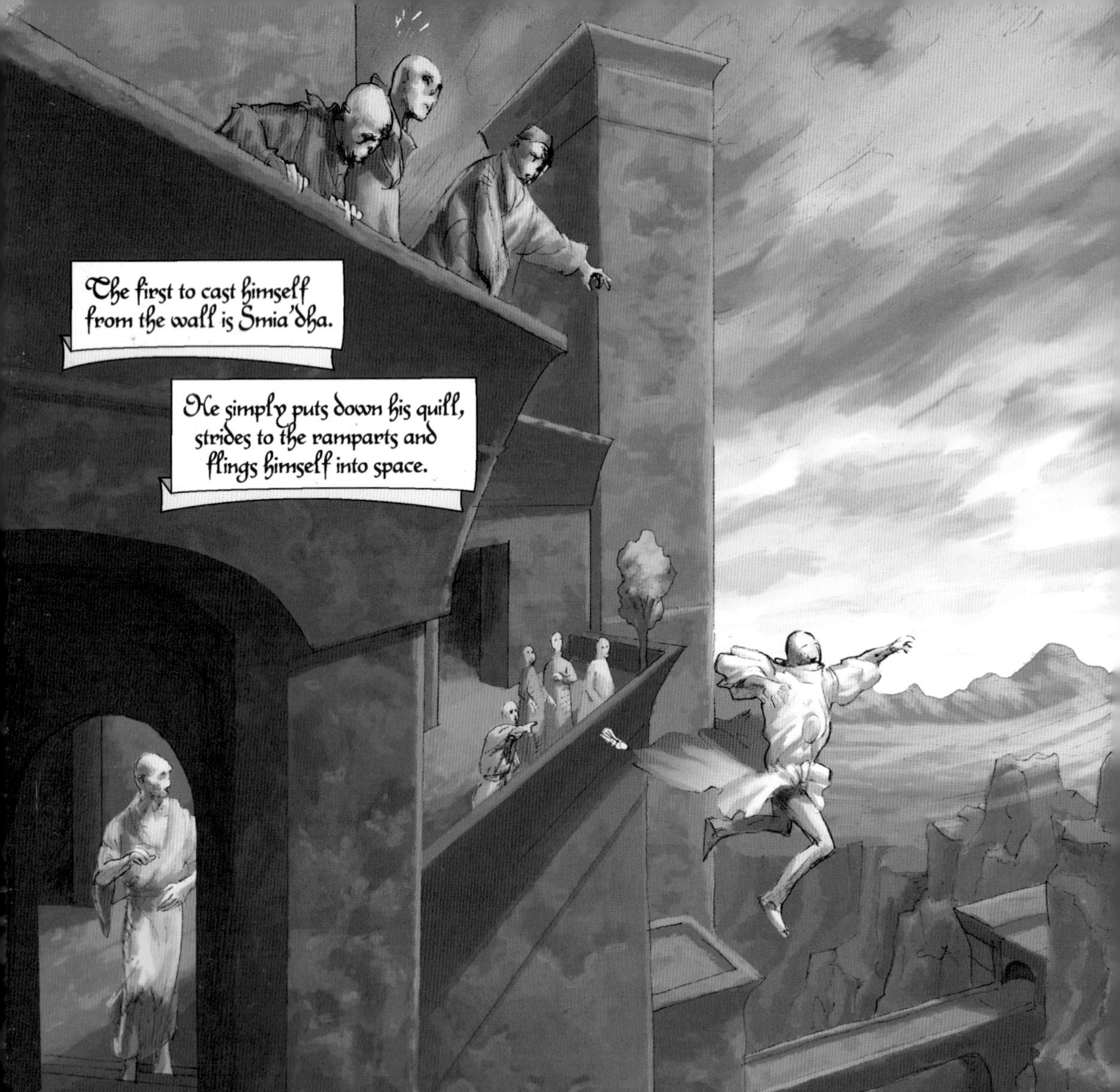
The first to cast himself from the wall is Smia'dha.
He simply puts down his quill, strides to the ramparts and flings himself into space.
It is surprising how little shock there is at the act.

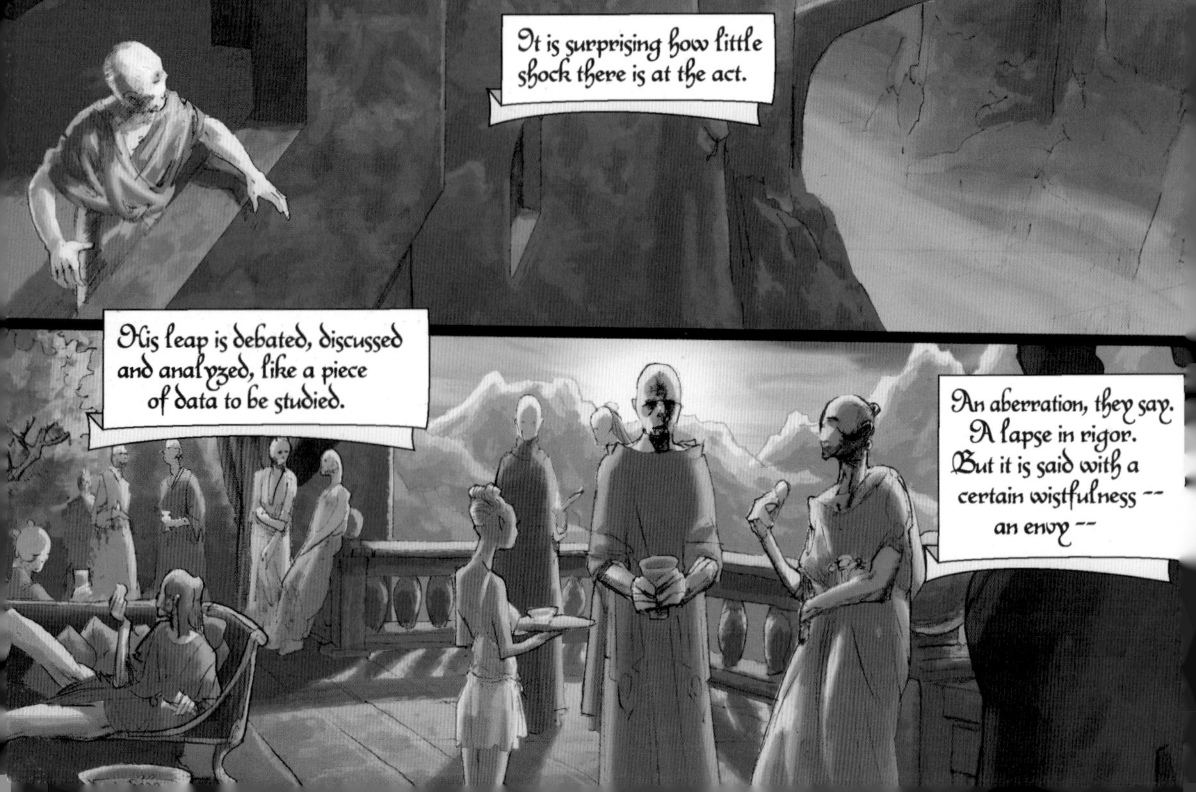
His leap is debated, discussed and analyzed, like a piece of data to be studied.
An aberration, they say. A lapse in rigor. But it is said with a certain wistfulness -- an envy --

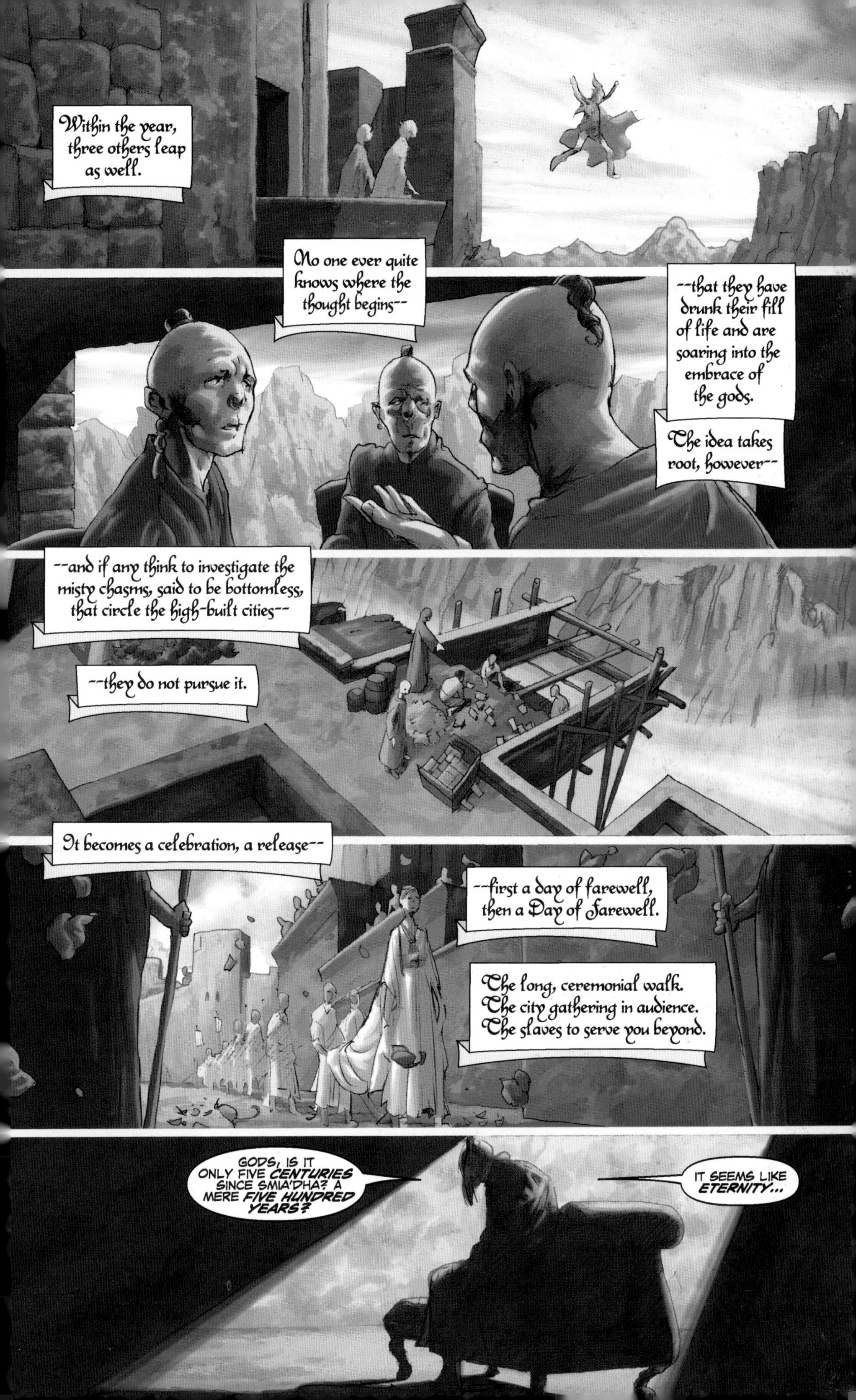
Within the year, three others leap as well.
No one ever quite knows where the thought begins--
--that they have drunk their fill of life and are soaring into the embrace of the gods.
The idea takes root, however--
--and if any think to investigate the misty chasms, said to be bottomless, that circle the high-built cities--
--they do not pursue it.
It becomes a celebration, a release--
--first a day of farewell, then a Day of Farewell.
The long, ceremonial walk. The city gathering in audience. The slaves to serve you beyond.
GODS, IS IT ONLY FIVE CENTURIES SINCE SMIA'DHA? A MERE FIVE HUNDRED YEARS?
IT SEEMS LIKE ETERNITY...

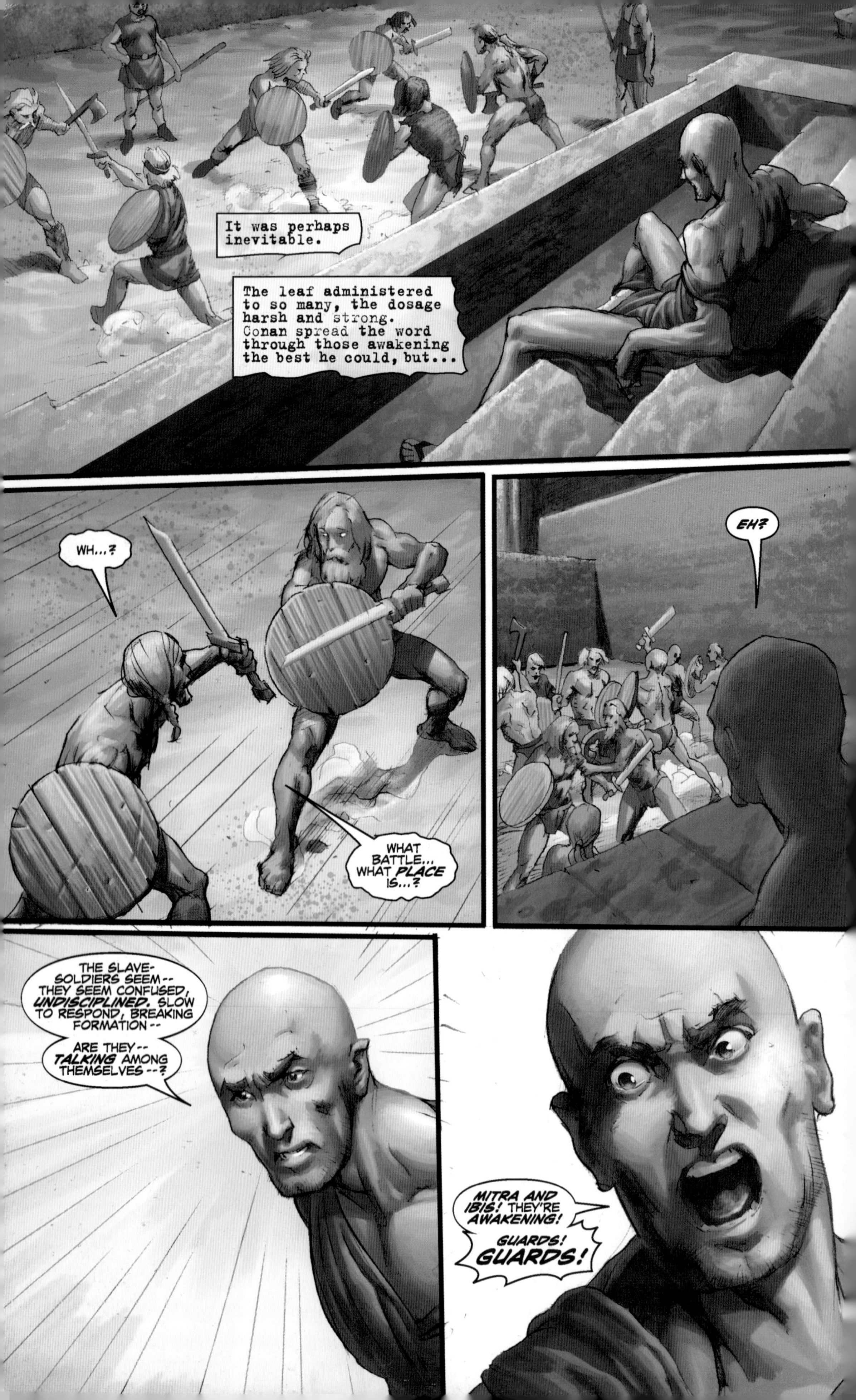
It was perhaps inevitable.
The leaf administered to so many, the dosage harsh and strong. Conan spread the word through those awakening the best he could, but...
WH...?
WHAT BATTLE... WHAT PLACE IS...?
EH?
THE SLAVE-SOLDIERS SEEM-- THEY SEEM CONFUSED, UNDISCIPLINED. SLOW TO RESPOND, BREAKING FORMATION--
ARE THEY-- TALKING AMONG THEMSELVES--?
MITRA AND IBIS! THEY'RE AWAKENING!
GUARDS! GUARDS!

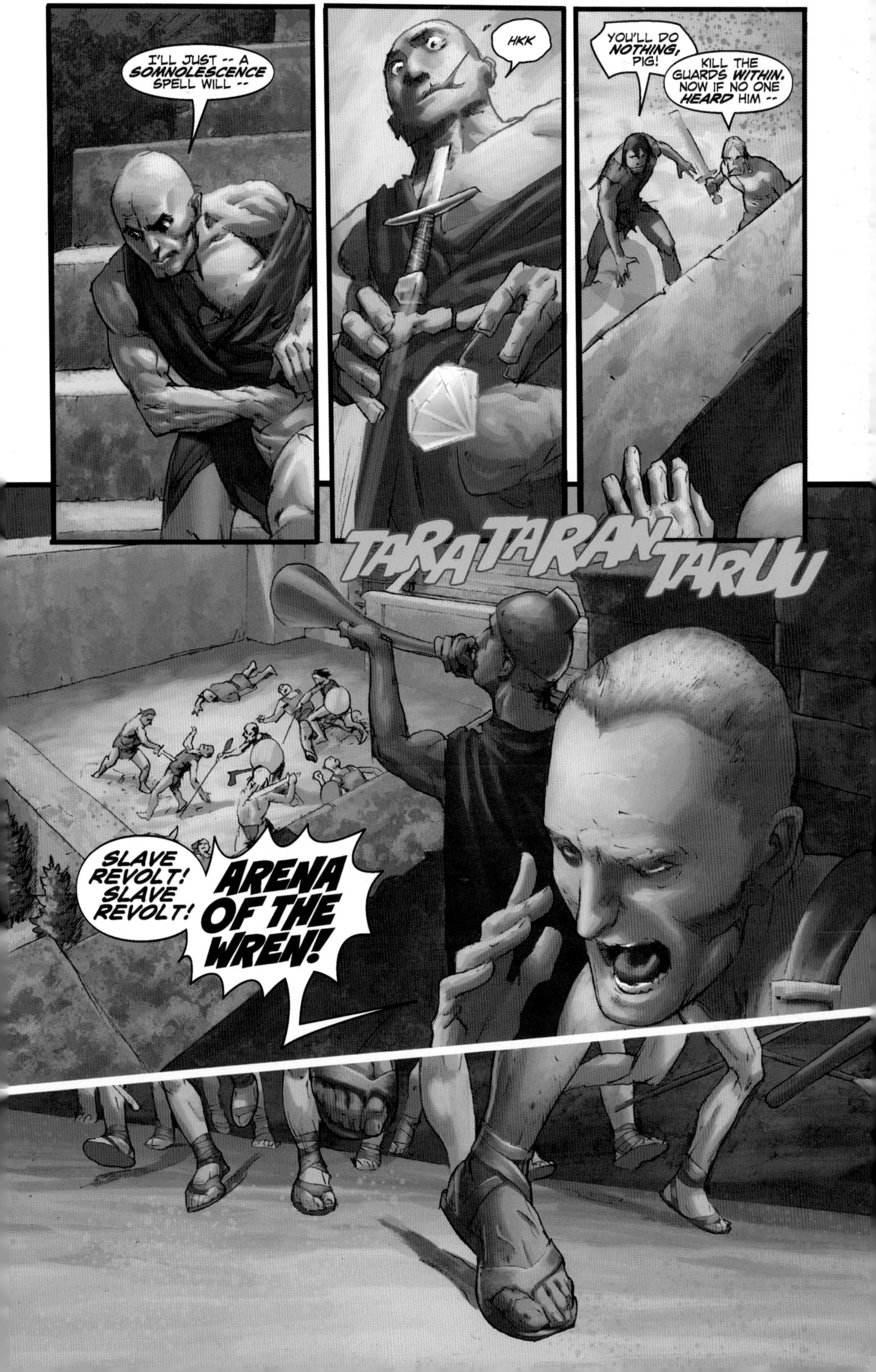
I'LL JUST -- A SOMNOLESCENCE SPELL WILL --
HKK
YOU'LL DO NOTHING, PIG!
KILL THE GUARDS WITHIN. NOW IF NO ONE HEARD HIM --
TARATARANTARUU
SLAVE REVOLT! SLAVE REVOLT!
ARENA OF THE WREN!

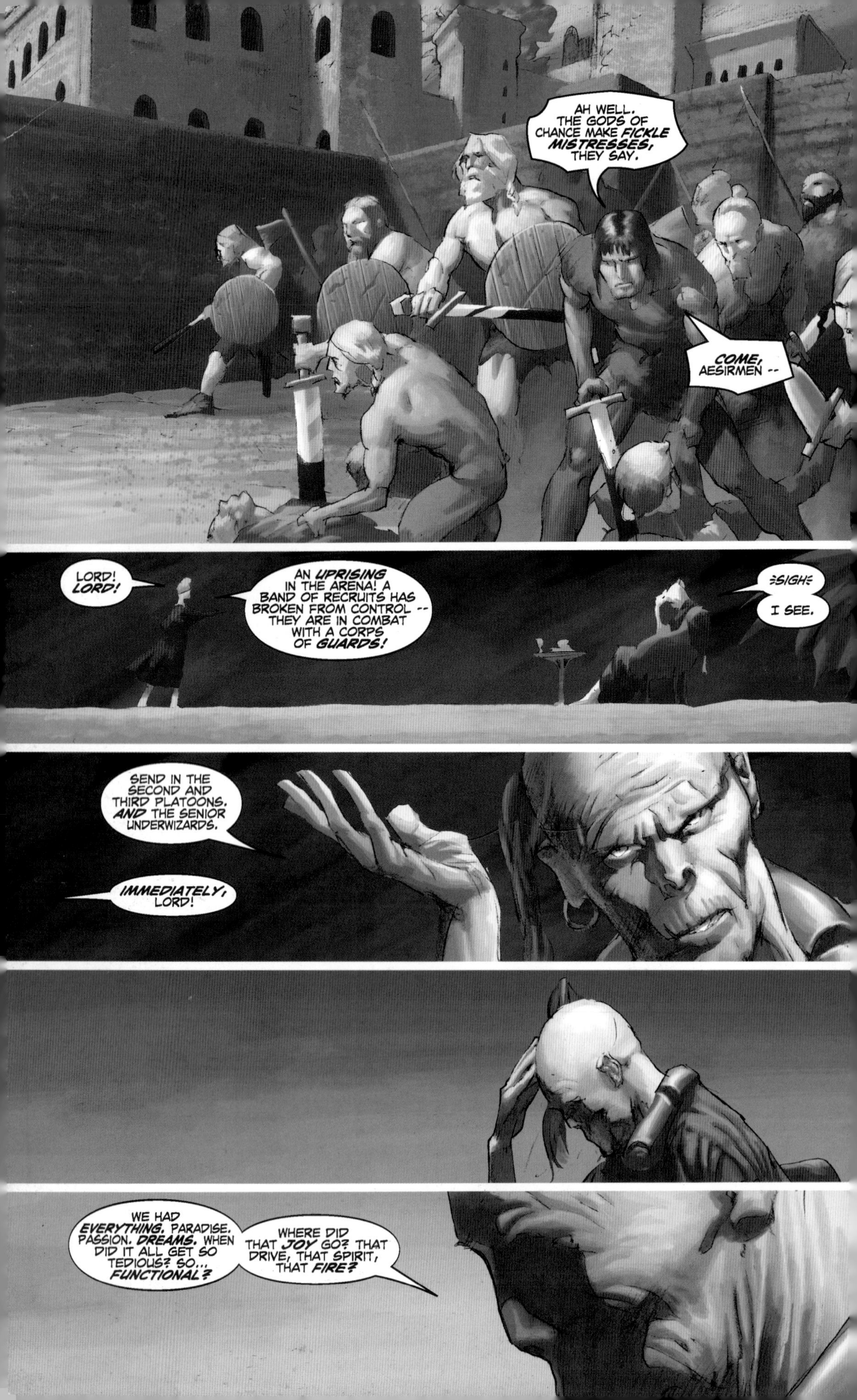
AH WELL. THE GODS OF CHANCE MAKE FICKLE MISTRESSES, THEY SAY.
COME, AESIRMEN --
LORD! LORD!
AN UPRISING IN THE ARENA! A BAND OF RECRUITS HAS BROKEN FROM CONTROL -- THEY ARE IN COMBAT WITH A CORPS OF GUARDS!
SIGH
I SEE.
SEND IN THE SECOND AND THIRD PLATOONS. AND THE SENIOR UNDERWIZARDS.
IMMEDIATELY, LORD!
WE HAD EVERYTHING. PARADISE. PASSION. DREAMS. WHEN DID IT ALL GET SO TEDIOUS? SO... FUNCTIONAL?
WHERE DID THAT JOY GO? THAT DRIVE, THAT SPIRIT, THAT FIRE?

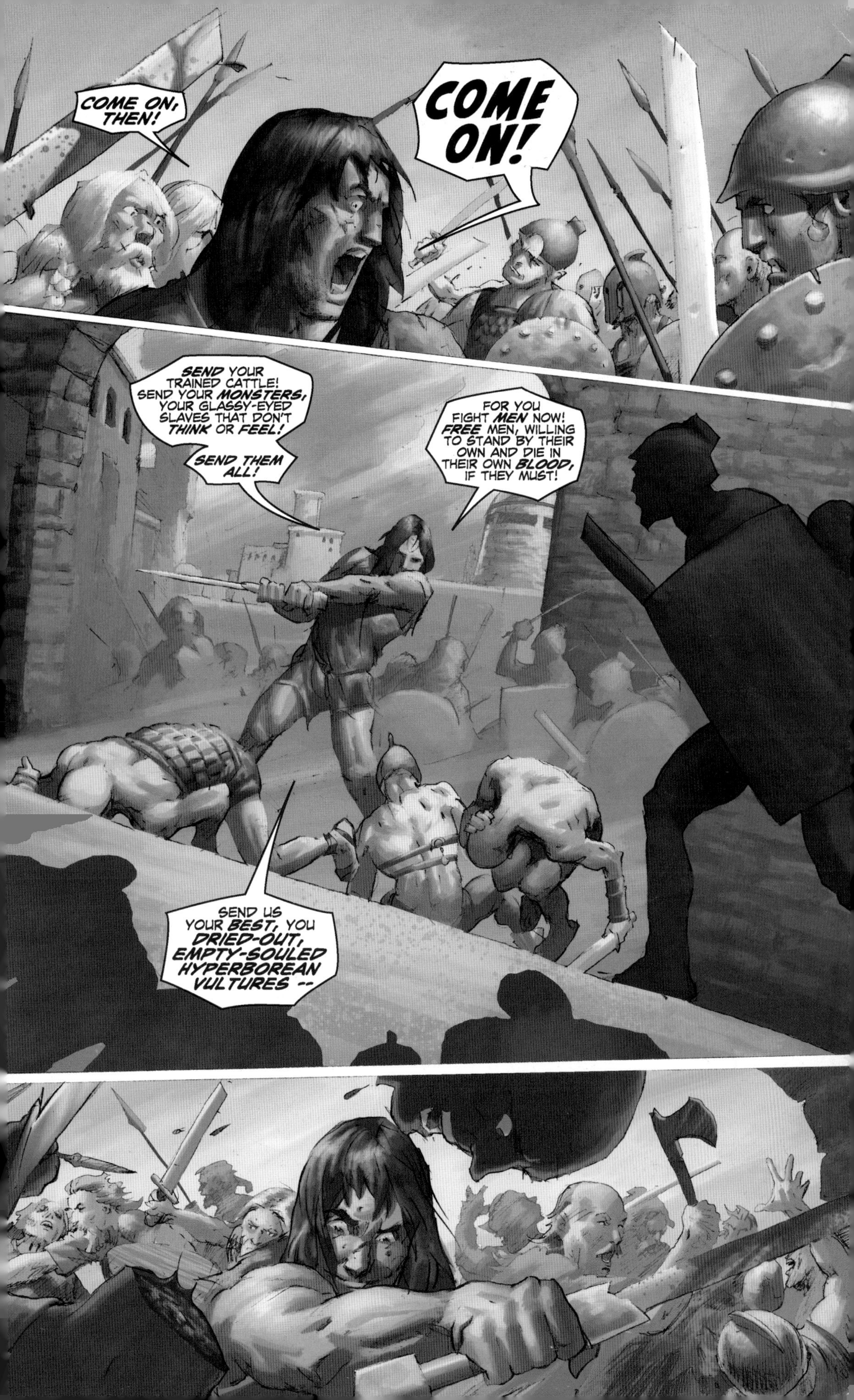
COME ON, THEN!
COME ON!
SEND YOUR TRAINED CATTLE! SEND YOUR MONSTERS, YOUR GLASSY-EYED SLAVES THAT DON'T THINK OR FEEL!
SEND THEM ALL!
FOR YOU FIGHT MEN NOW! FREE MEN, WILLING TO STAND BY THEIR OWN AND DIE IN THEIR OWN BLOOD, IF THEY MUST!
SEND US YOUR BEST, YOU DRIED-OUT, EMPTY-SOULED HYPERBOREAN VULTURES --

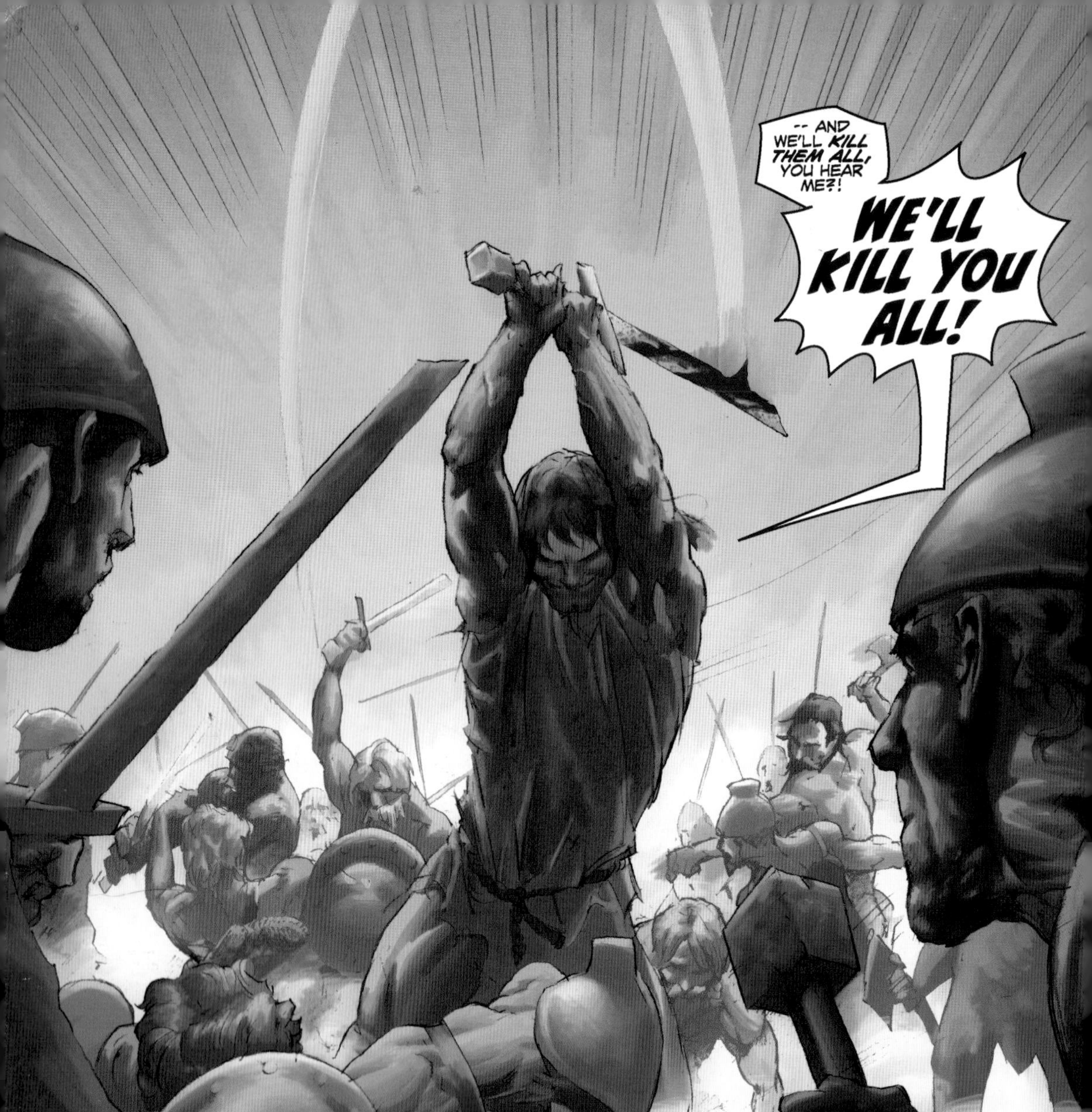
-- AND WE'LL KILL THEM ALL, YOU HEAR ME?!
WE'LL KILL YOU ALL!

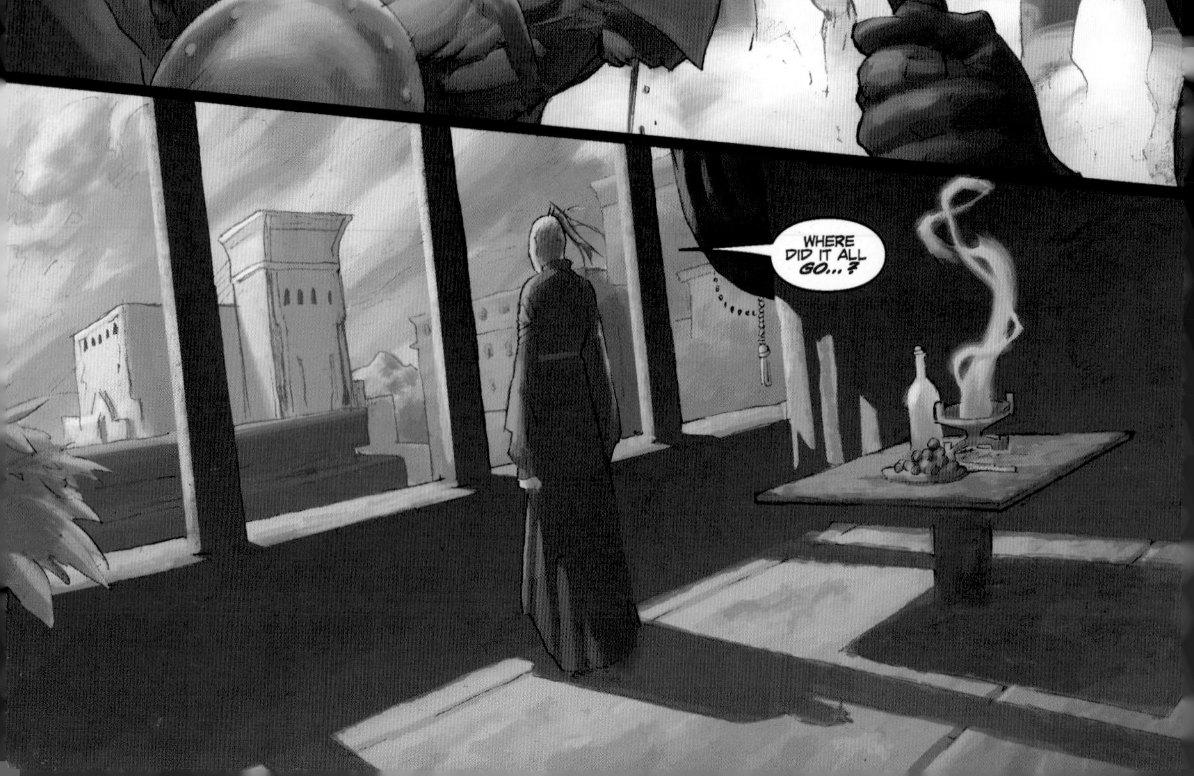
WHERE DID IT ALL GO...?

CHAPTER SIX

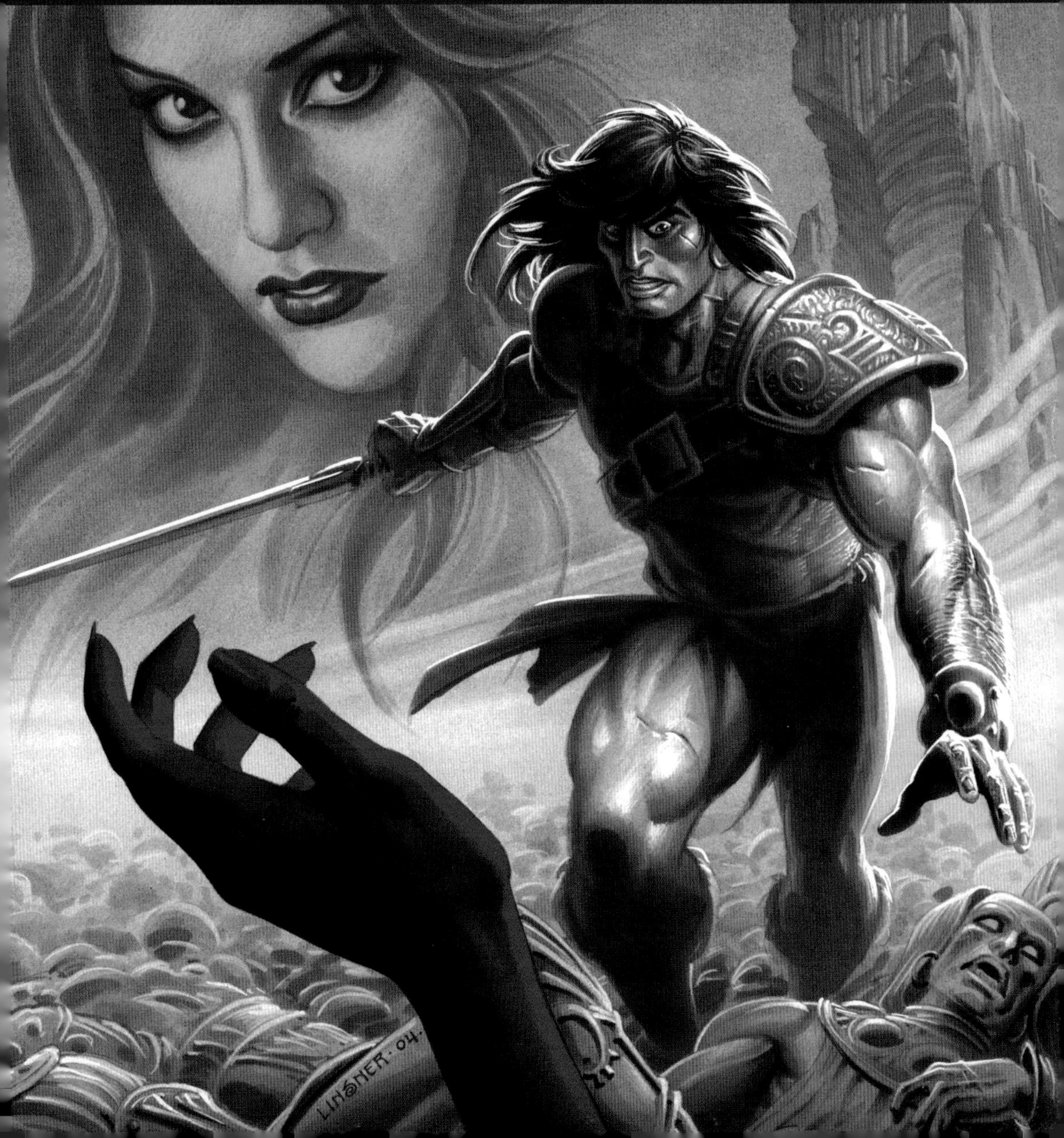
LINSNER·04.

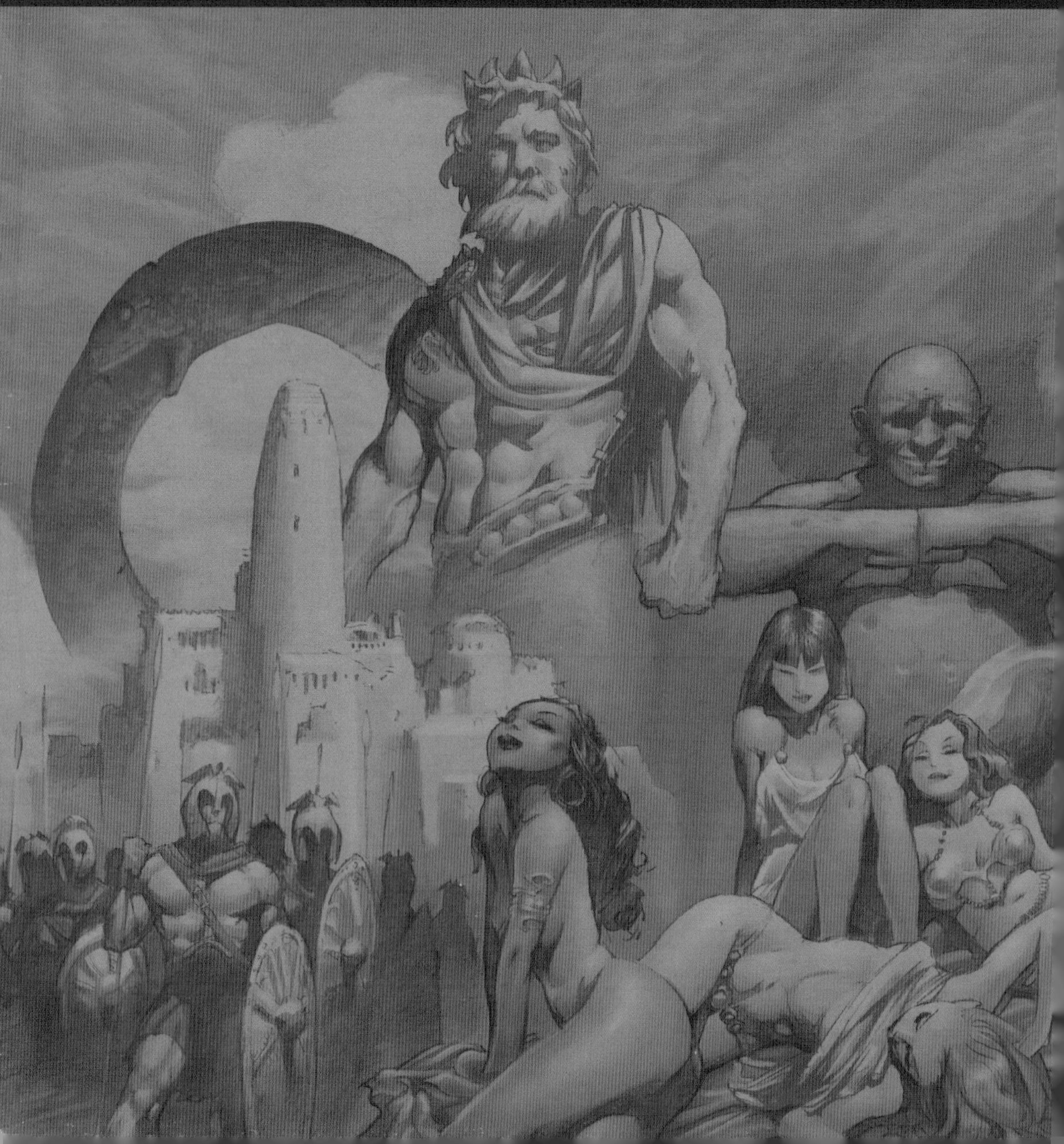

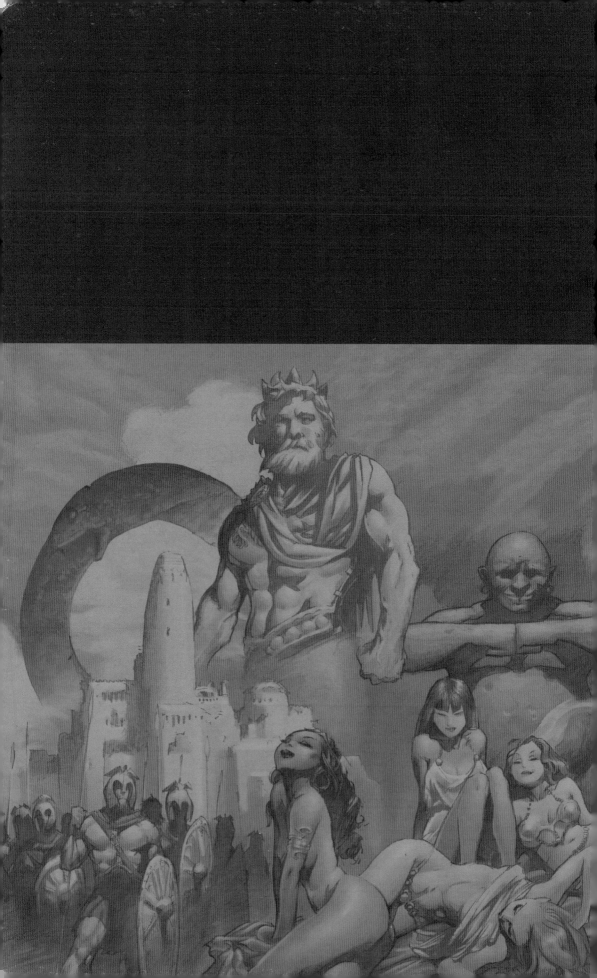

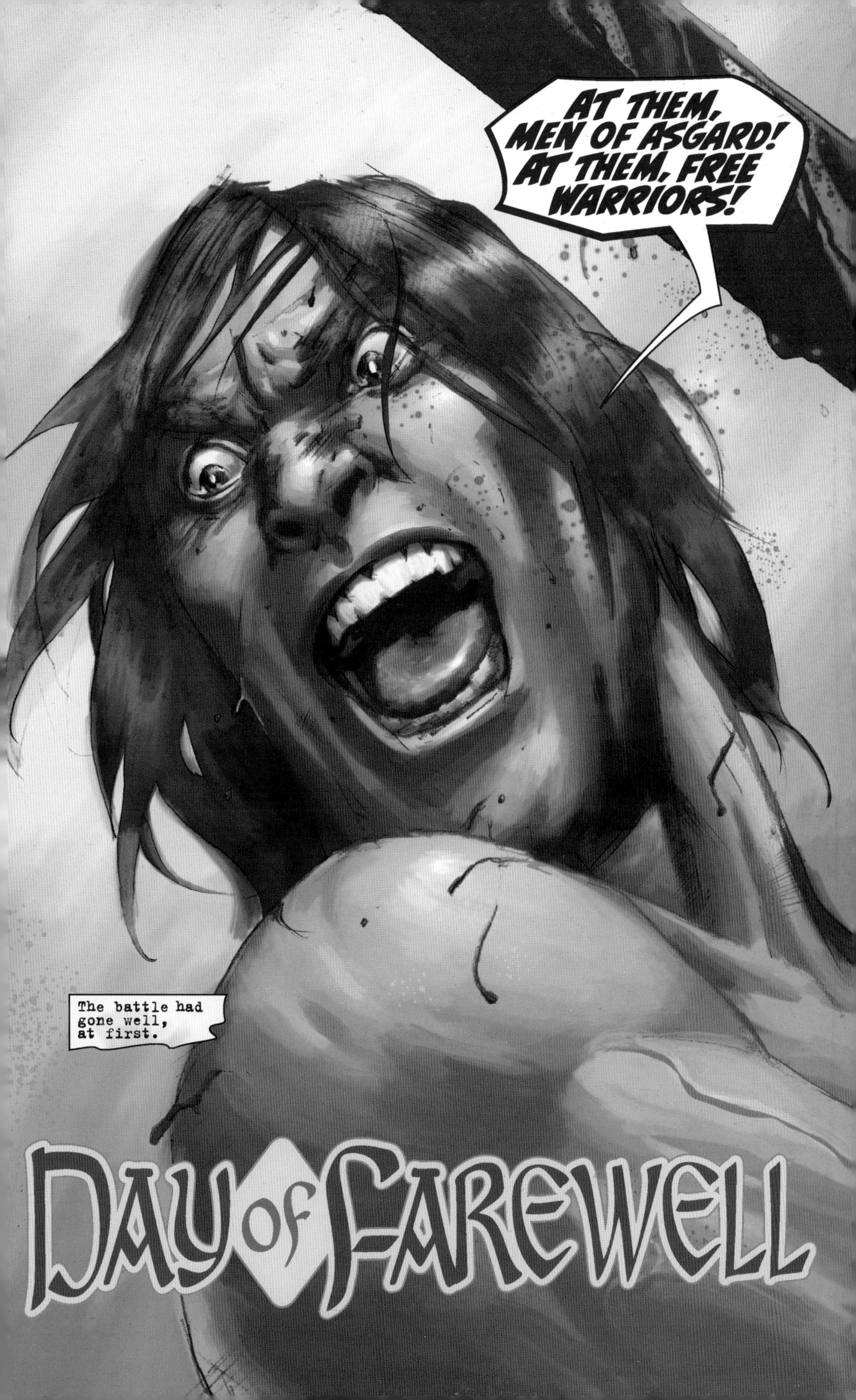
AT THEM, MEN OF ASGARD! AT THEM, FREE WARRIORS!
The battle had gone well, at first.
DAY OF FAREWELL

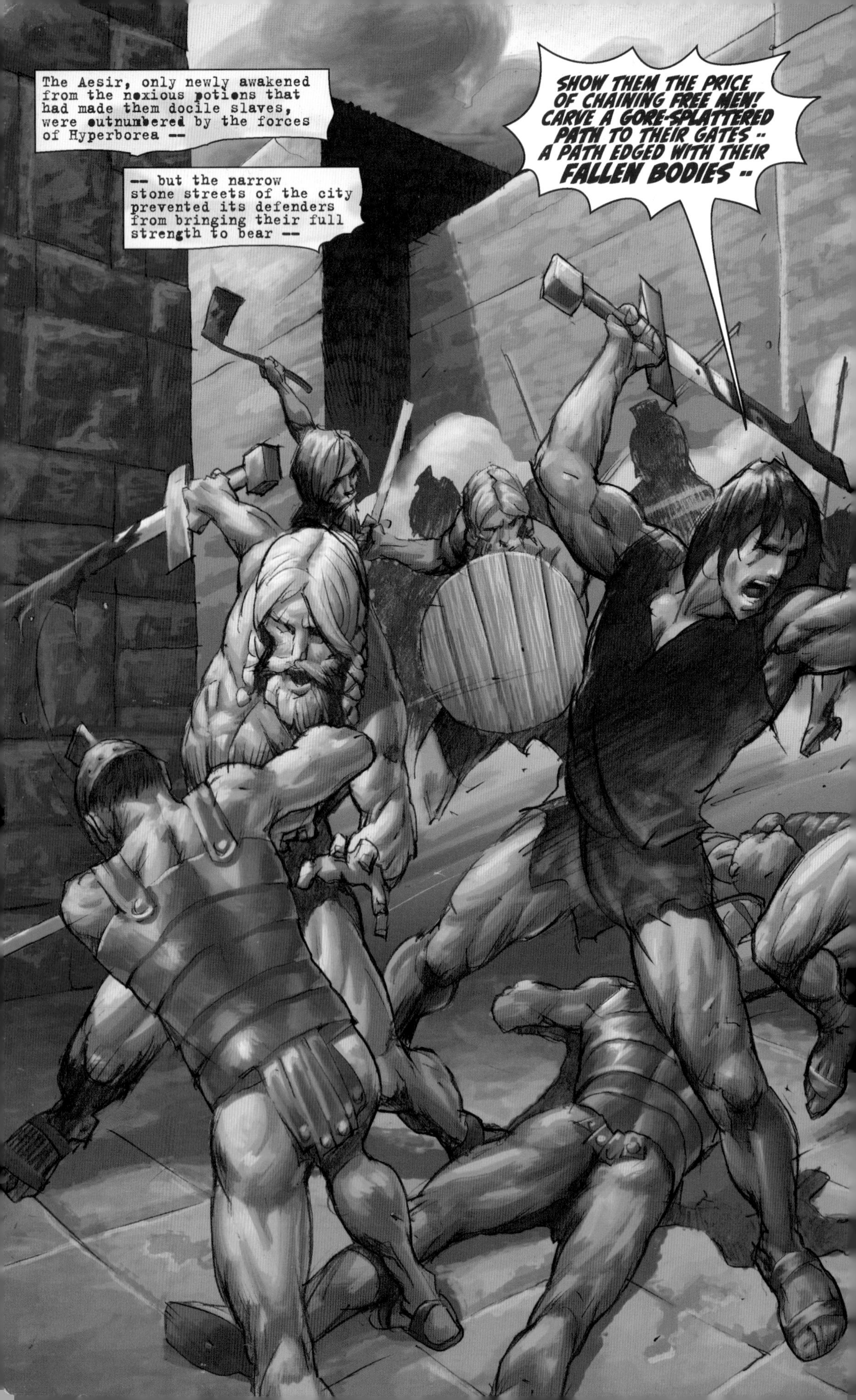
The Aesir, only newly awakened from the noxious potions that had made them docile slaves, were outnumbered by the forces of Hyperborea --
-- but the narrow stone streets of the city prevented its defenders from bringing their full strength to bear --
SHOW THEM THE PRICE OF CHAINING FREE MEN! CARVE A GORE-SPLATTERED PATH TO THEIR GATES -- A PATH EDGED WITH THEIR FALLEN BODIES --

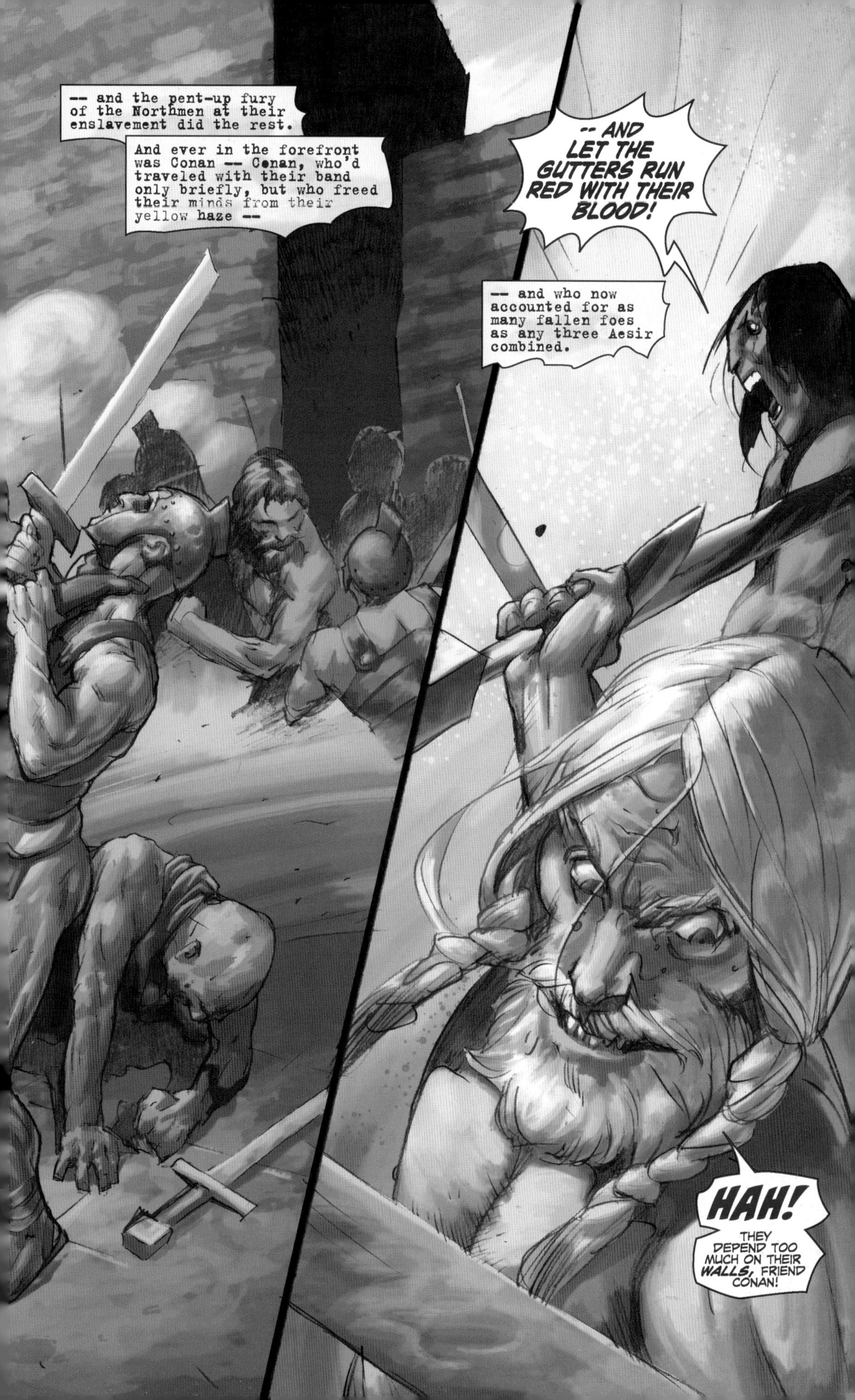
-- and the pent-up fury of the Northmen at their enslavement did the rest.
And ever in the forefront was Conan -- Conan, who'd traveled with their band only briefly, but who freed their minds from their yellow haze --
-- AND LET THE GUTTERS RUN RED WITH THEIR BLOOD!
-- and who now accounted for as many fallen foes as any three Aesir combined.
HAH! THEY DEPEND TOO MUCH ON THEIR WALLS, FRIEND CONAN!

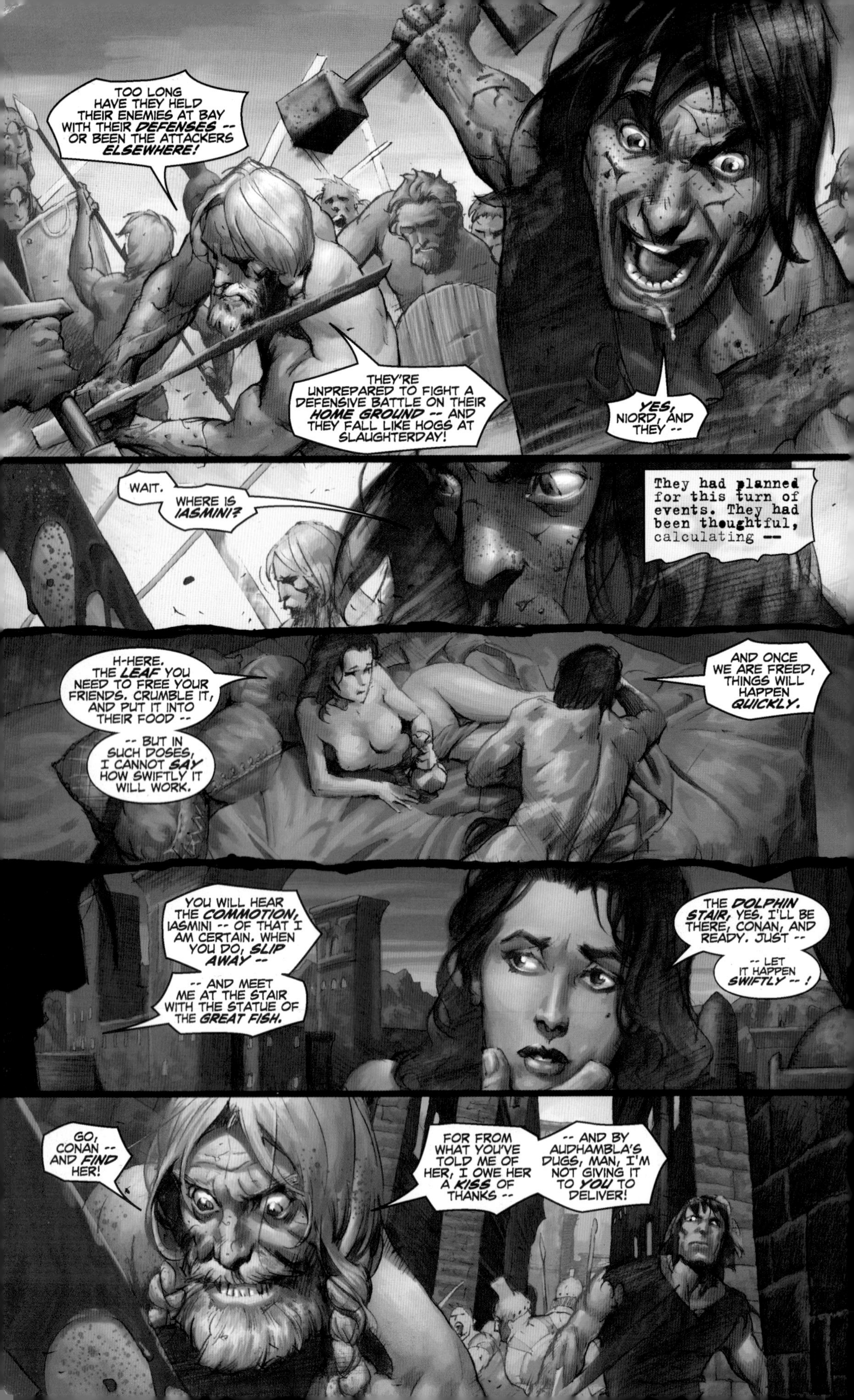
TOO LONG HAVE THEY HELD THEIR ENEMIES AT BAY WITH THEIR DEFENSES -- OR BEEN THE ATTACKERS ELSEWHERE!
THEY'RE UNPREPARED TO FIGHT A DEFENSIVE BATTLE ON THEIR HOME GROUND -- AND THEY FALL LIKE HOGS AT SLAUGHTERDAY!
YES, NIORD, AND THEY --
WAIT.
WHERE IS IASMINI?
They had planned for this turn of events. They had been thoughtful, calculating --
H-HERE. THE LEAF YOU NEED TO FREE YOUR FRIENDS. CRUMBLE IT, AND PUT IT INTO THEIR FOOD --
-- BUT IN SUCH DOSES, I CANNOT SAY HOW SWIFTLY IT WILL WORK.
AND ONCE WE ARE FREED, THINGS WILL HAPPEN QUICKLY.
YOU WILL HEAR THE COMMOTION, IASMINI -- OF THAT I AM CERTAIN. WHEN YOU DO, SLIP AWAY --
-- AND MEET ME AT THE STAIR WITH THE STATUE OF THE GREAT FISH.
THE DOLPHIN STAIR, YES. I'LL BE THERE, CONAN, AND READY. JUST --
-- LET IT HAPPEN SWIFTLY -- !
GO, CONAN -- AND FIND HER!
FOR FROM WHAT YOU'VE TOLD ME OF HER, I OWE HER A KISS OF THANKS --
-- AND BY AUDHAMBLA'S DUGS, MAN, I'M NOT GIVING IT TO YOU TO DELIVER!

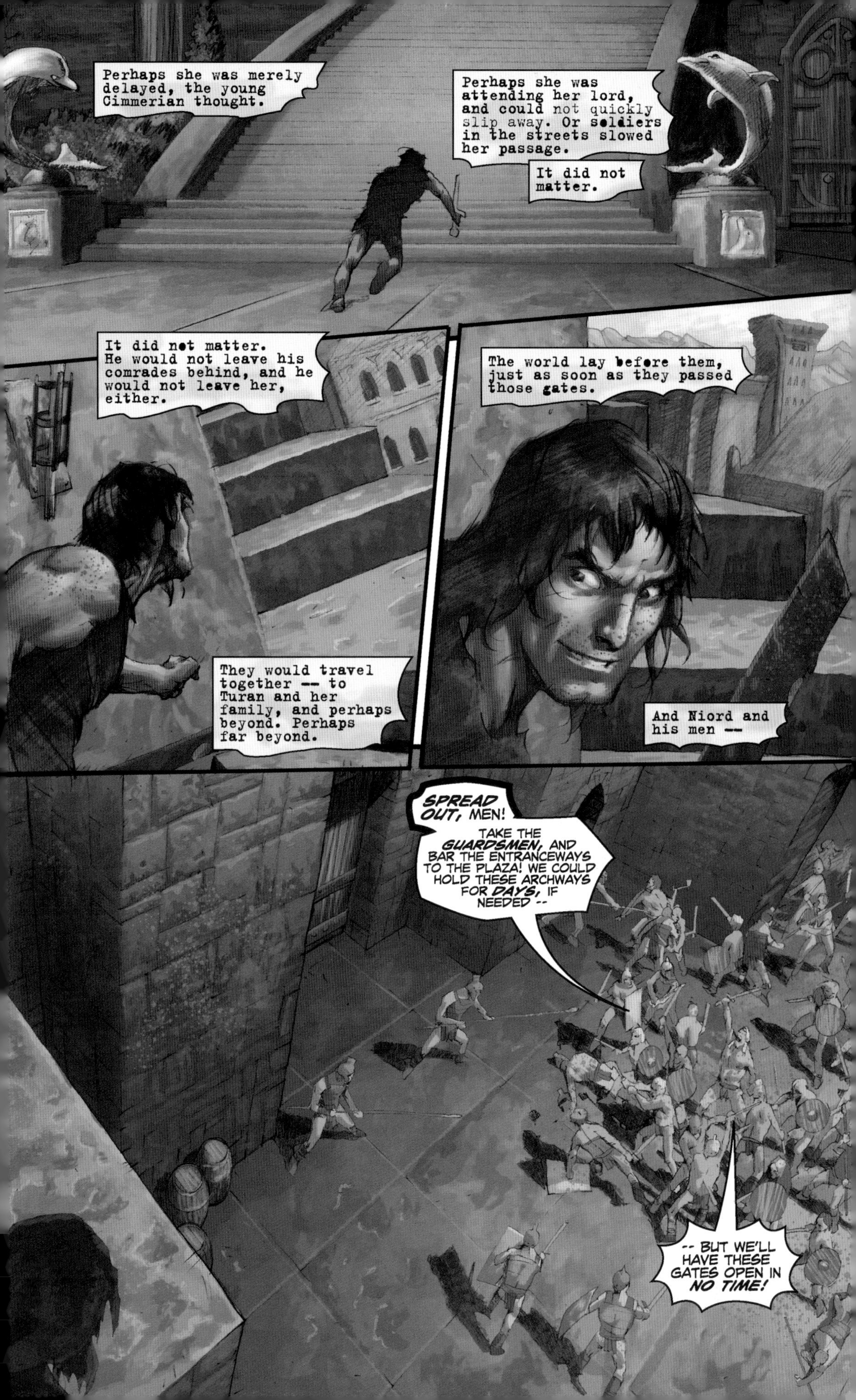
Perhaps she was merely delayed, the young Cimmerian thought.
Perhaps she was attending her lord, and could not quickly slip away. Or soldiers in the streets slowed her passage.
It did not matter.
It did not matter. He would not leave his comrades behind, and he would not leave her, either.
They would travel together -- to Turan and her family, and perhaps beyond. Perhaps far beyond.
The world lay before them, just as soon as they passed those gates.
And Niord and his men --
SPREAD OUT, MEN!
TAKE THE GUARDSMEN, AND BAR THE ENTRANCEWAYS TO THE PLAZA! WE COULD HOLD THESE ARCHWAYS FOR DAYS, IF NEEDED --
-- BUT WE'LL HAVE THESE GATES OPEN IN NO TIME!

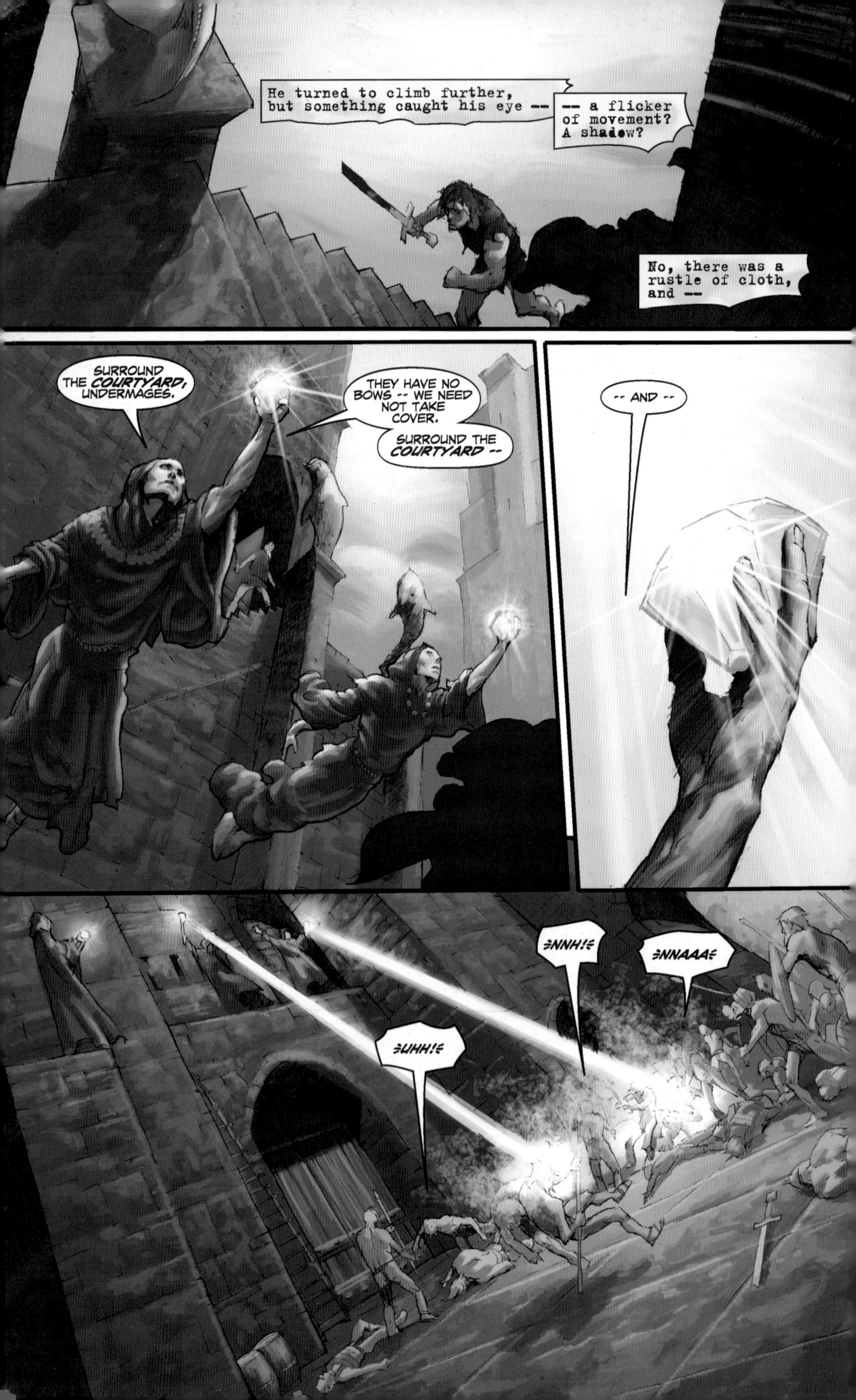
He turned to climb further, but something caught his eye --
-- a flicker of movement? A shadow?
No, there was a rustle of cloth, and --
SURROUND THE COURTYARD, UNDERMAGES.
THEY HAVE NO BOWS -- WE NEED NOT TAKE COVER.
SURROUND THE COURTYARD --
-- AND --
NNH!
NNAAA
UHH!

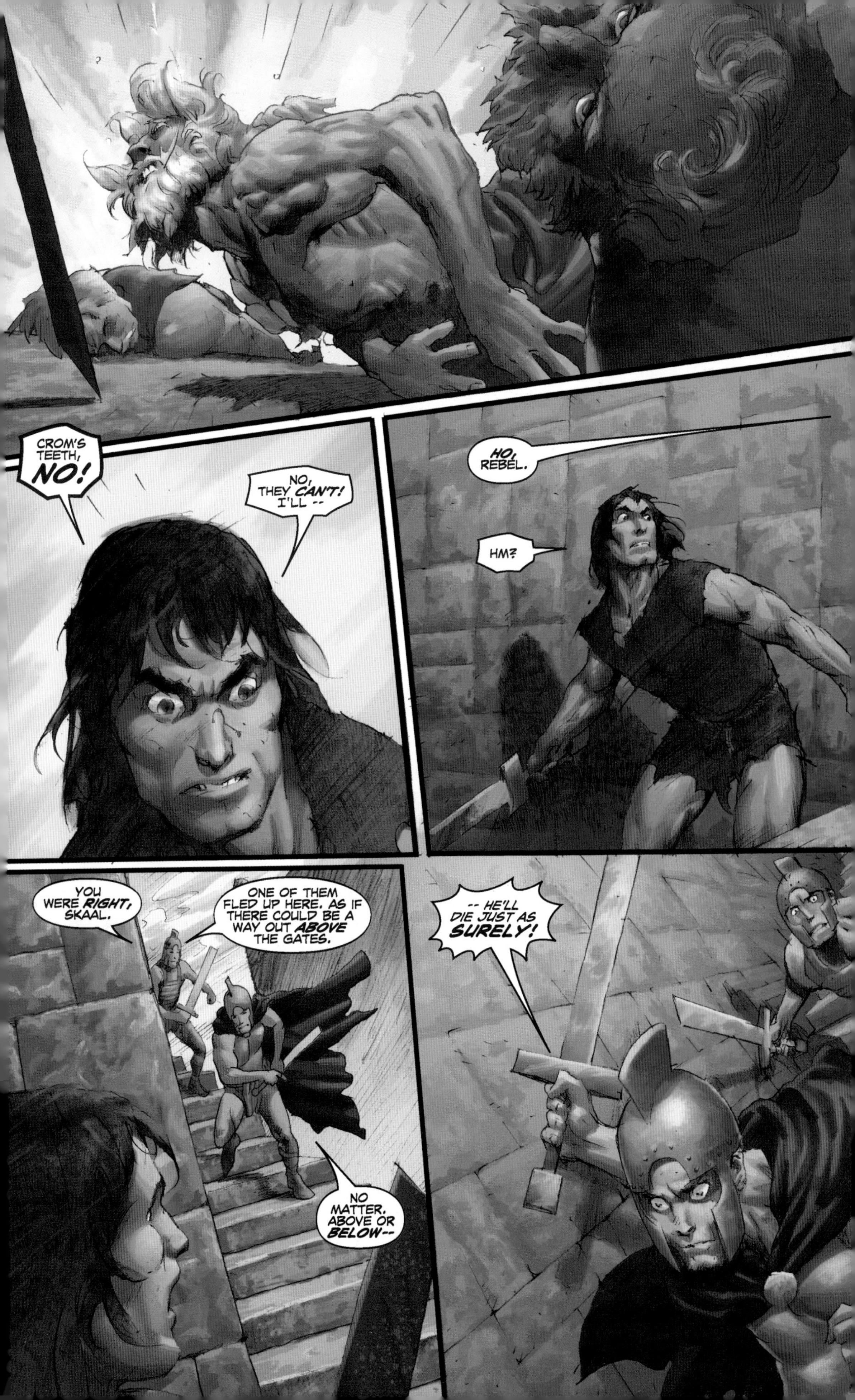
CROM'S TEETH, NO!
NO, THEY CAN'T! I'LL --
HO, REBEL.
HM?
YOU WERE RIGHT, SKAAL.
ONE OF THEM FLED UP HERE. AS IF THERE COULD BE A WAY OUT ABOVE THE GATES.
NO MATTER. ABOVE OR BELOW--
-- HE'LL DIE JUST AS SURELY!

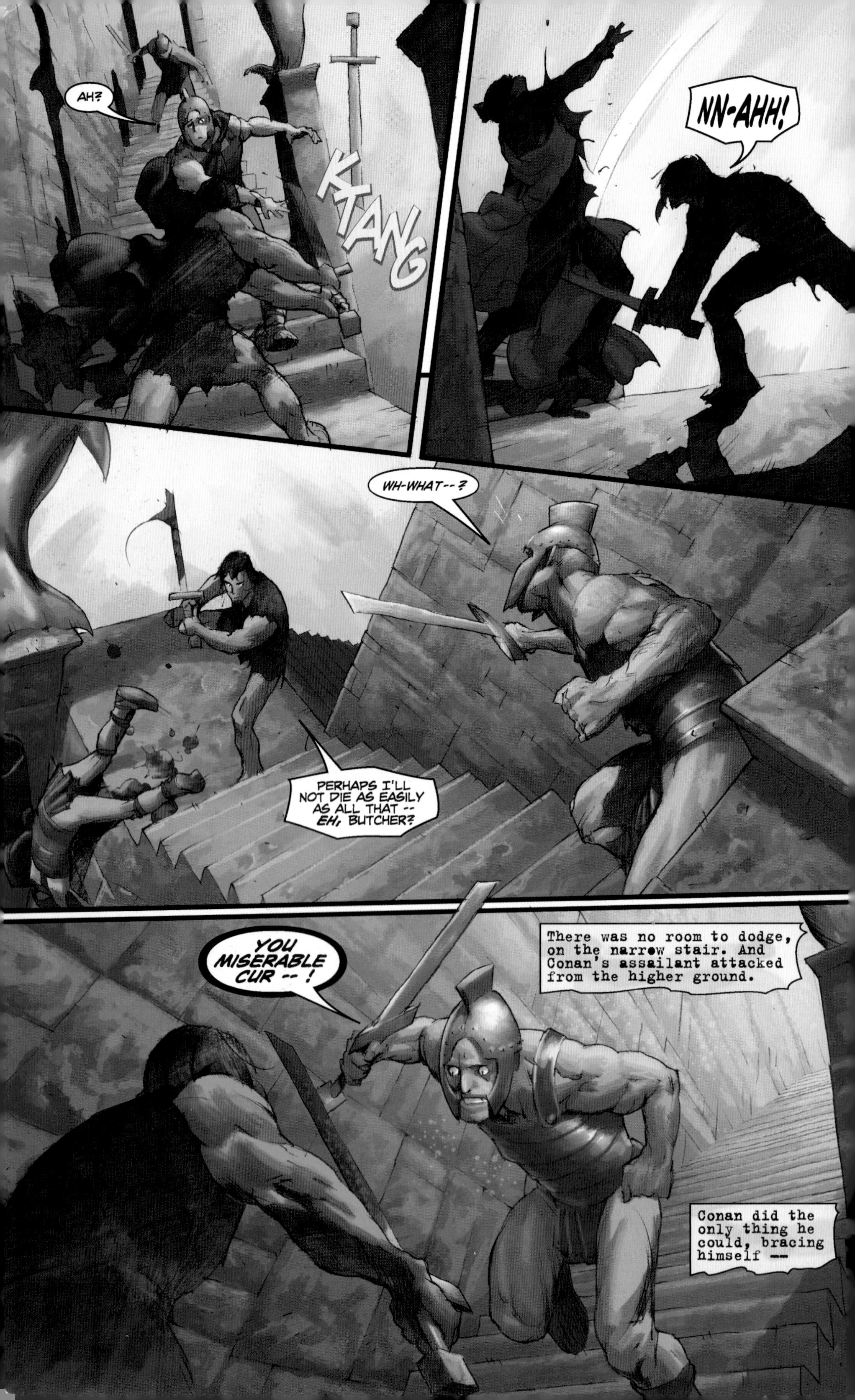

AH?
KKANG
NN-AHH!
WH-WHAT--?
PERHAPS I'LL NOT DIE AS EASILY AS ALL THAT -- EH, BUTCHER?
YOU MISERABLE CUR -- !
There was no room to dodge, on the narrow stair. And Conan's assailant attacked from the higher ground.
Conan did the only thing he could, bracing himself --

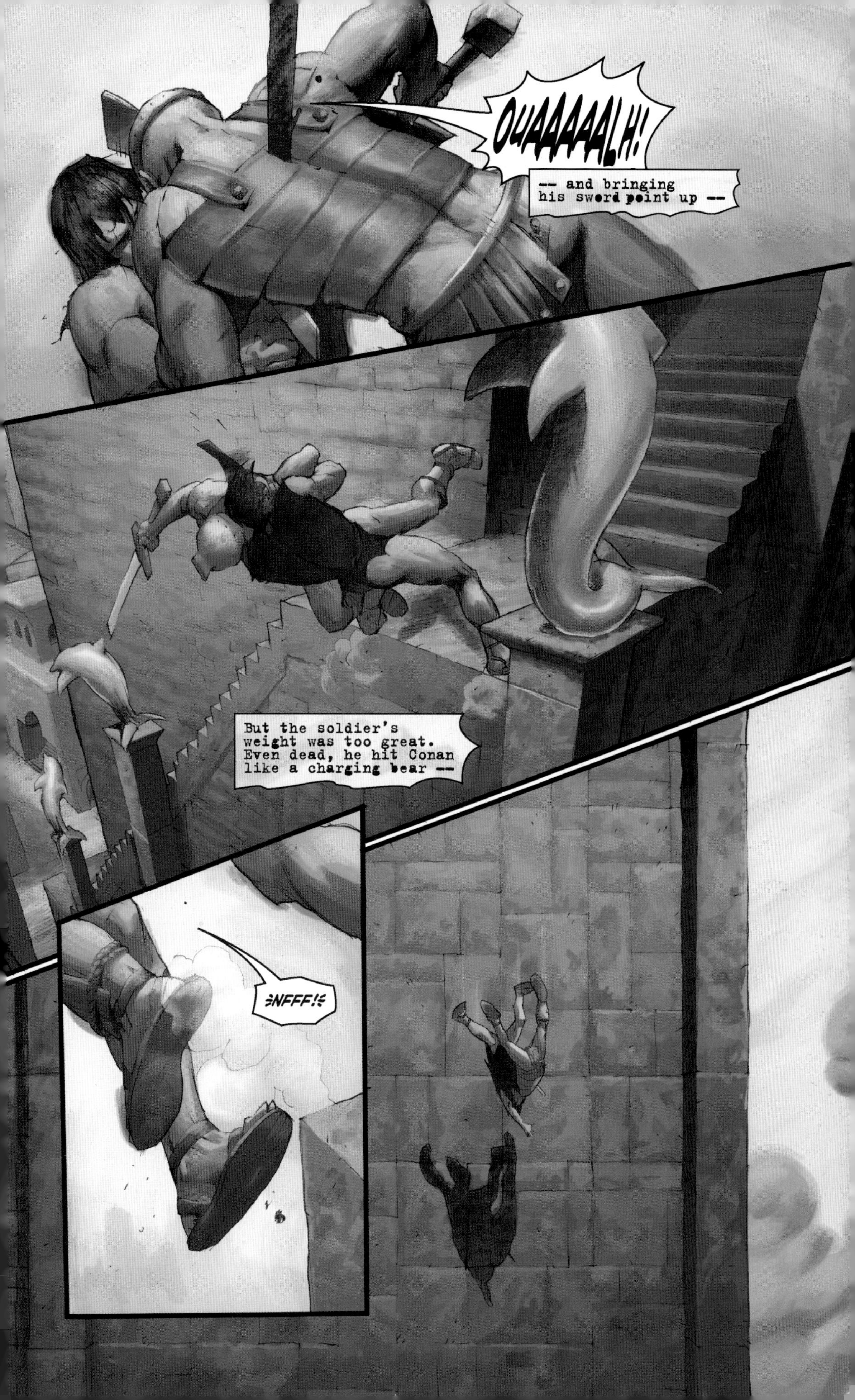
OUAAAAALH!
-- and bringing his sword point up --
But the soldier's weight was too great. Even dead, he hit Conan like a charging bear --
NFFF!

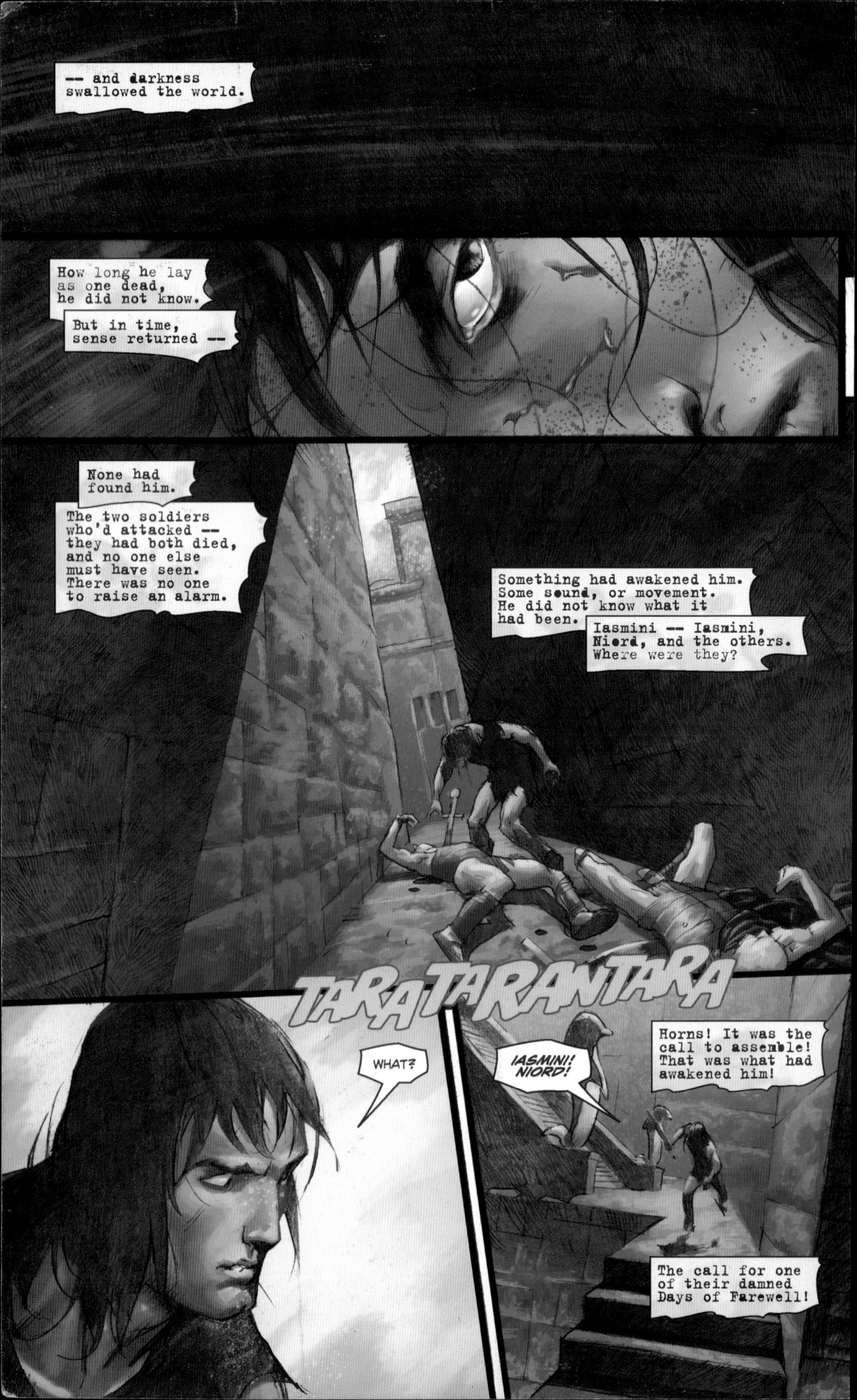
-- and darkness swallowed the world.
How long he lay as one dead, he did not know.
But in time, sense returned --
None had found him.
The two soldiers who'd attacked -- they had both died, and no one else must have seen. There was no one to raise an alarm.
Something had awakened him. Some sound, or movement. He did not know what it had been.
Iasmini -- Iasmini, Niord, and the others. Where were they?
TARA TARANTARA
WHAT?
IASMINI! NIORD!
Horns! It was the call to assemble! That was what had awakened him!
The call for one of their damned Days of Farewell!

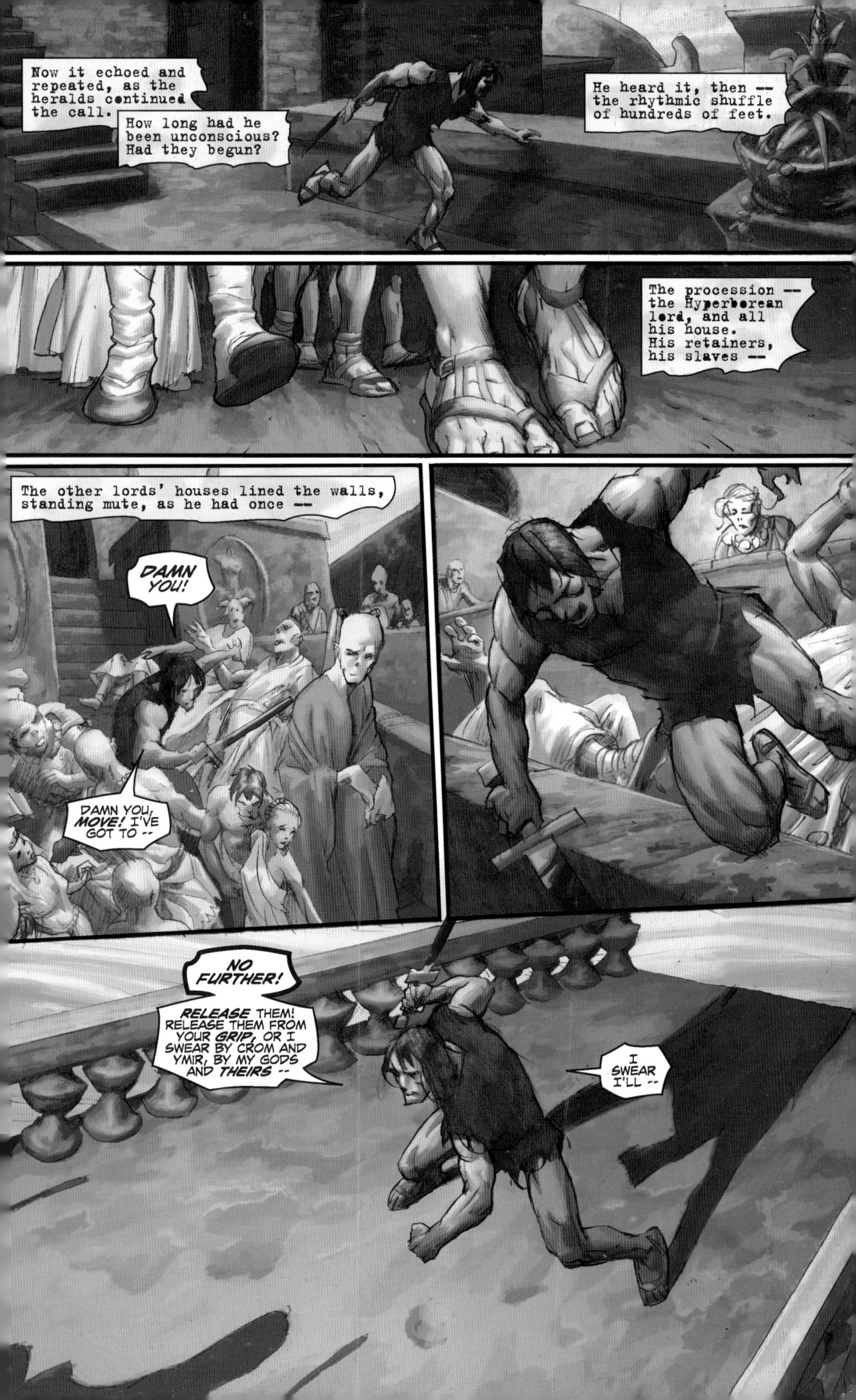

Now it echoed and repeated, as the heralds continued the call.
How long had he been unconscious? Had they begun?
He heard it, then -- the rhythmic shuffle of hundreds of feet.
The procession -- the Hyperborean lord, and all his house. His retainers, his slaves --
The other lords' houses lined the walls, standing mute, as he had once --
DAMN YOU!
DAMN YOU, MOVE! I'VE GOT TO --
NO FURTHER!
RELEASE THEM! RELEASE THEM FROM YOUR GRIP, OR I SWEAR BY CROM AND YMIR, BY MY GODS AND THEIRS --
I SWEAR I'LL --

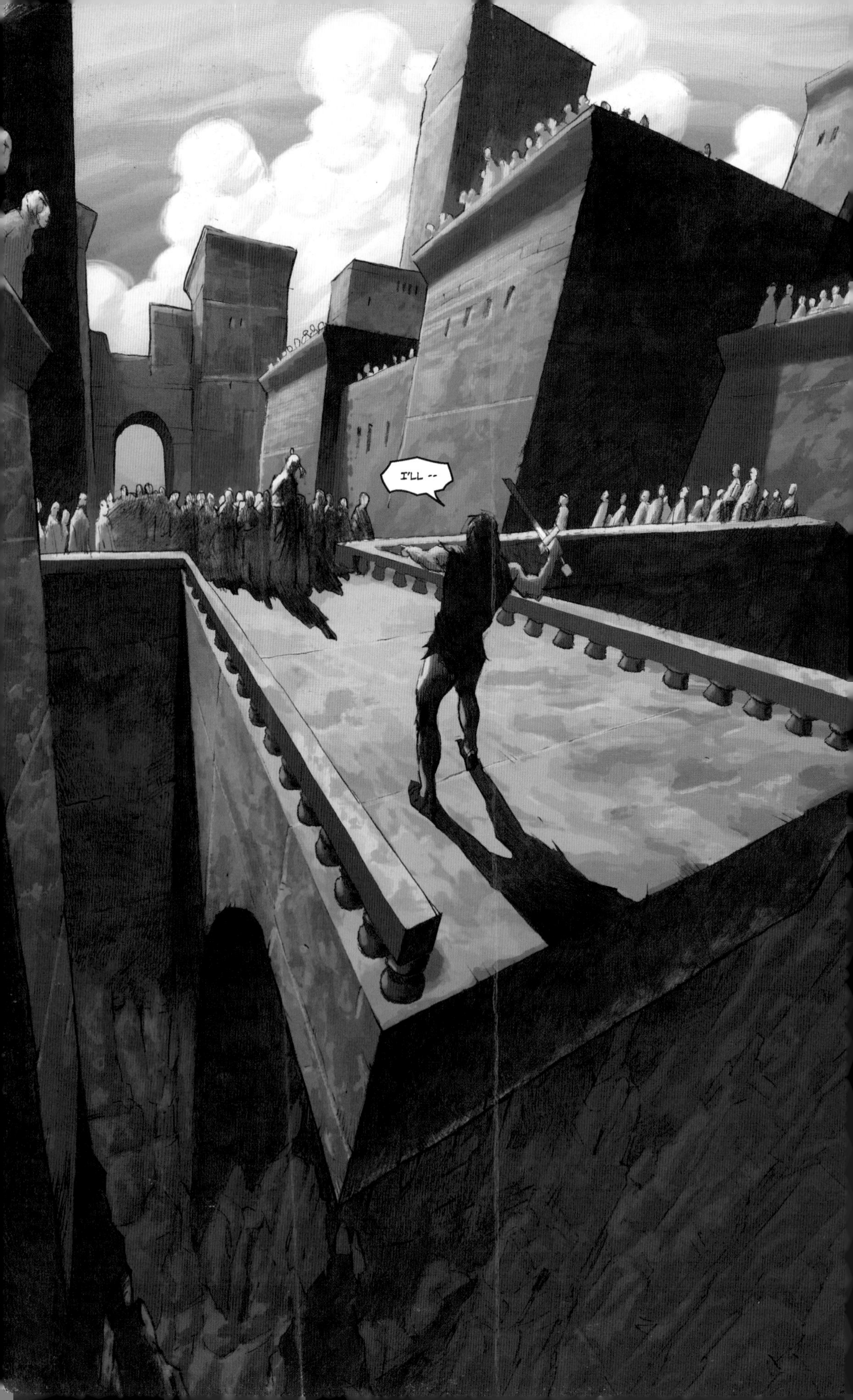
I'LL --

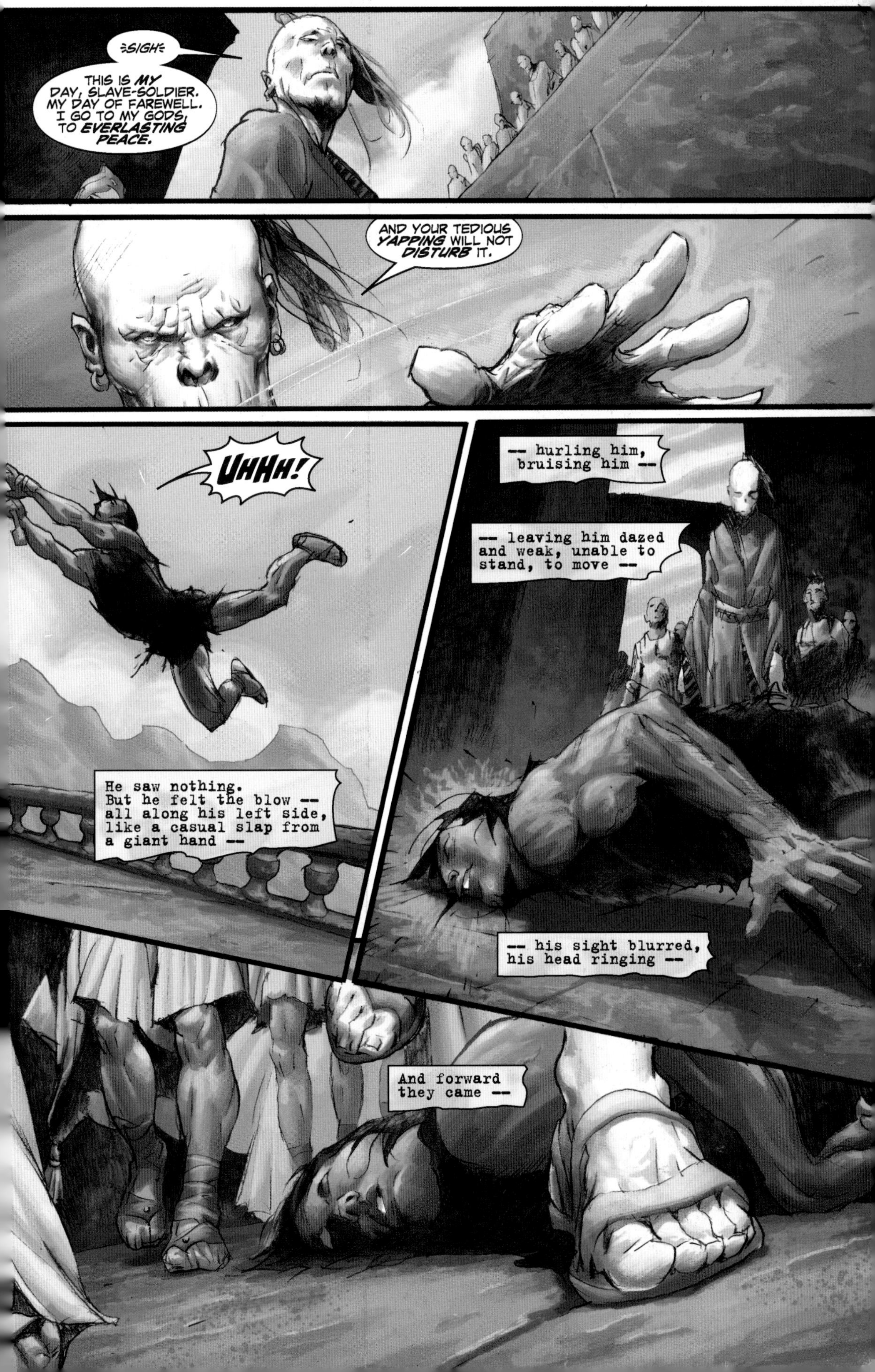

SIGH
THIS IS MY DAY, SLAVE-SOLDIER. MY DAY OF FAREWELL. I GO TO MY GODS, TO EVERLASTING PEACE.
AND YOUR TEDIOUS YAPPING WILL NOT DISTURB IT.
UHHH!
He saw nothing. But he felt the blow -- all along his left side, like a casual slap from a giant hand --
-- hurling him, bruising him --
-- leaving him dazed and weak, unable to stand, to move --
-- his sight blurred, his head ringing --
And forward they came --

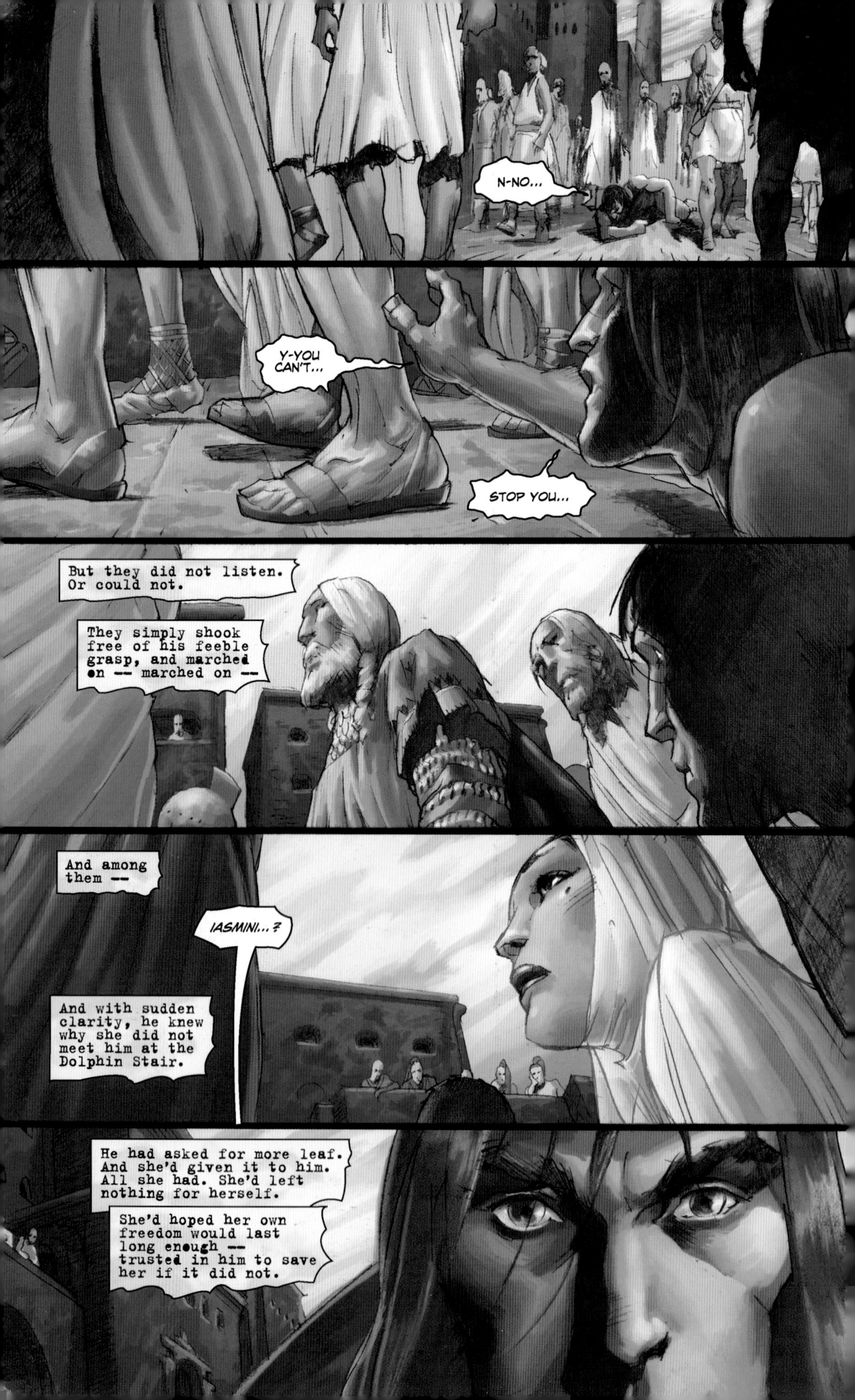
N-NO...
Y-YOU CAN'T...
STOP YOU...
But they did not listen. Or could not.
They simply shook free of his feeble grasp, and marched on -- marched on --
And among them --
IASMINI...?
And with sudden clarity, he knew why she did not meet him at the Dolphin Stair.
He had asked for more leaf. And she'd given it to him. All she had. She'd left nothing for herself.
She'd hoped her own freedom would last long enough -- trusted in him to save her if it did not.

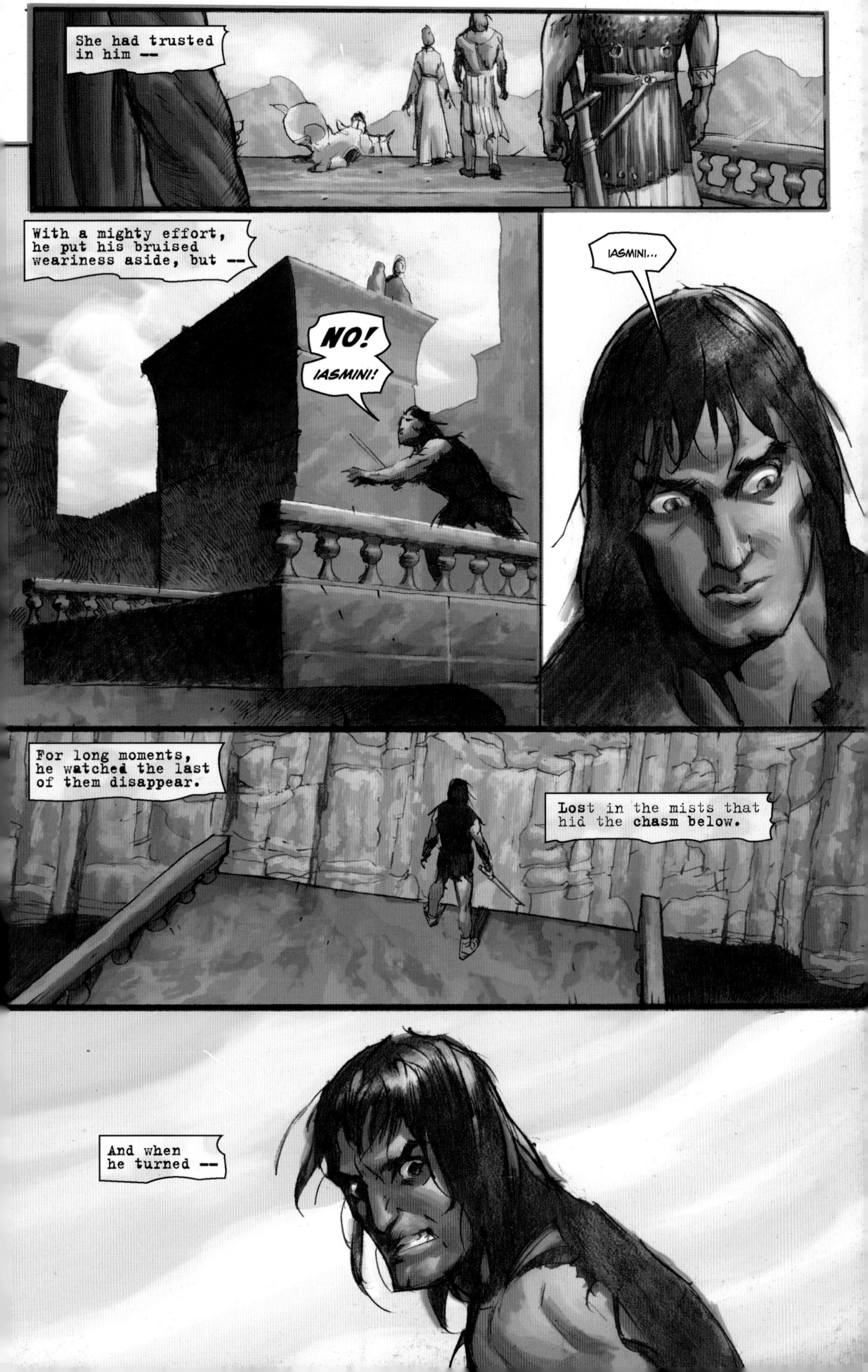
She had trusted in him --
With a mighty effort, he put his bruised weariness aside, but --
NO!
IASMINI!
IASMINI...
For long moments, he watched the last of them disappear.
Lost in the mists that hid the chasm below.
And when he turned --

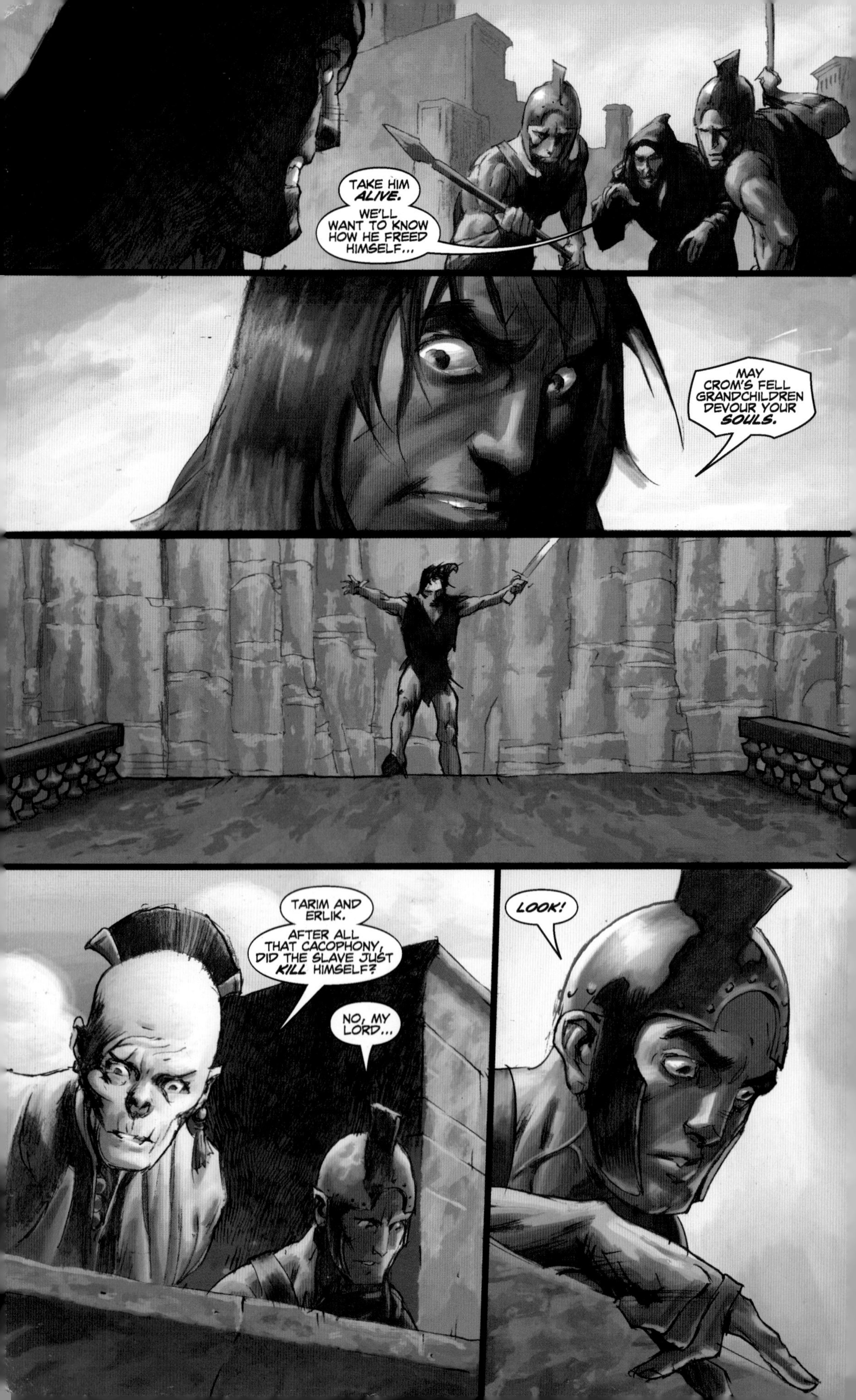
TAKE HIM ALIVE. WE'LL WANT TO KNOW HOW HE FREED HIMSELF...
MAY CROM'S FELL GRANDCHILDREN DEVOUR YOUR SOULS.
TARIM AND ERLIK. AFTER ALL THAT CACOPHONY, DID THE SLAVE JUST KILL HIMSELF?
NO, MY LORD...
LOOK!

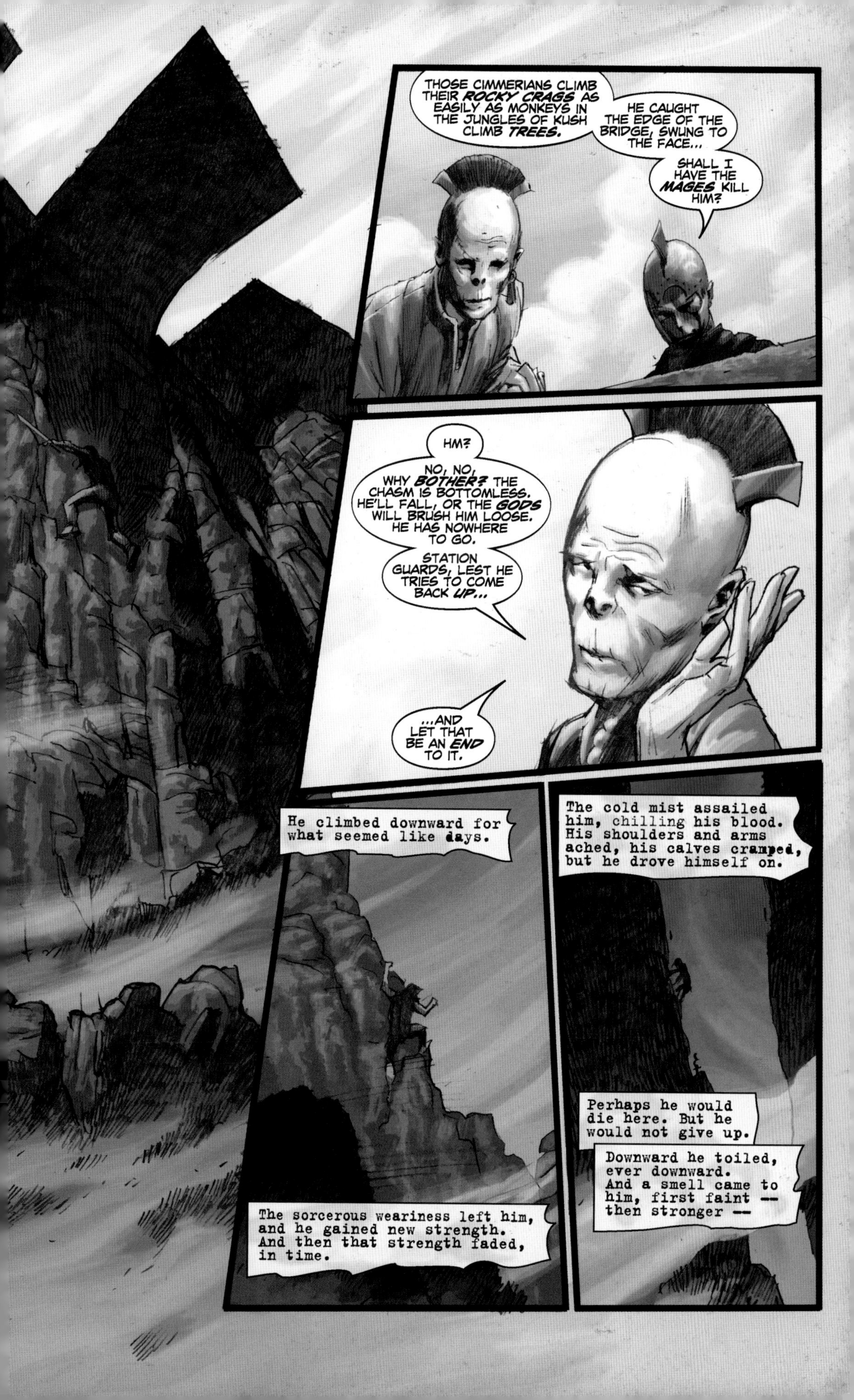
THOSE CIMMERIANS CLIMB THEIR ROCKY CRAGS AS EASILY AS MONKEYS IN THE JUNGLES OF KUSH CLIMB TREES.
HE CAUGHT THE EDGE OF THE BRIDGE, SWUNG TO THE FACE...
SHALL I HAVE THE MAGES KILL HIM?
HM?
NO, NO, WHY BOTHER? THE CHASM IS BOTTOMLESS. HE'LL FALL, OR THE GODS WILL BRUSH HIM LOOSE. HE HAS NOWHERE TO GO.
STATION GUARDS, LEST HE TRIES TO COME BACK UP...
...AND LET THAT BE AN END TO IT.
He climbed downward for what seemed like days.
The sorcerous weariness left him, and he gained new strength. And then that strength faded, in time.
The cold mist assailed him, chilling his blood. His shoulders and arms ached, his calves cramped, but he drove himself on.
Perhaps he would die here. But he would not give up.
Downward he toiled, ever downward. And a smell came to him, first faint -- then stronger --

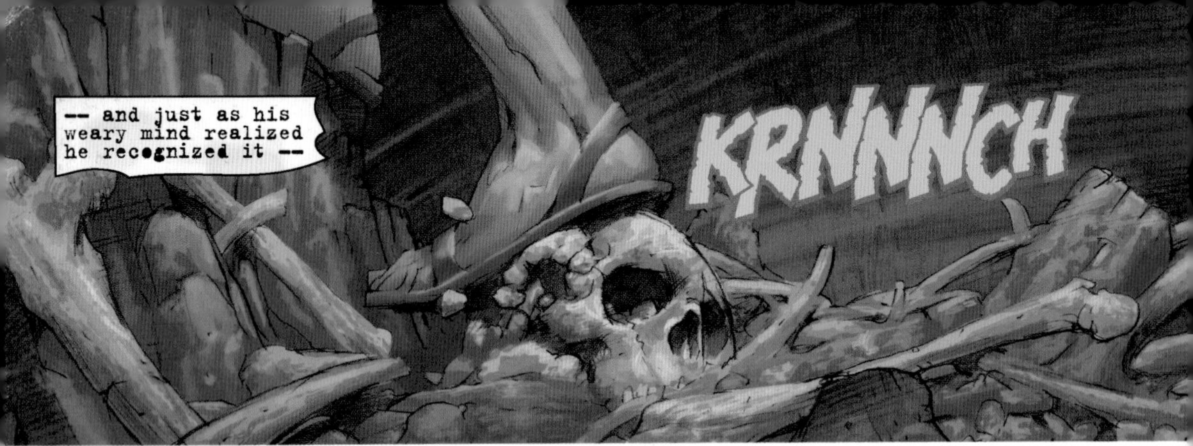
-- and just as his weary mind realized he recognized it --
KRNNNCH

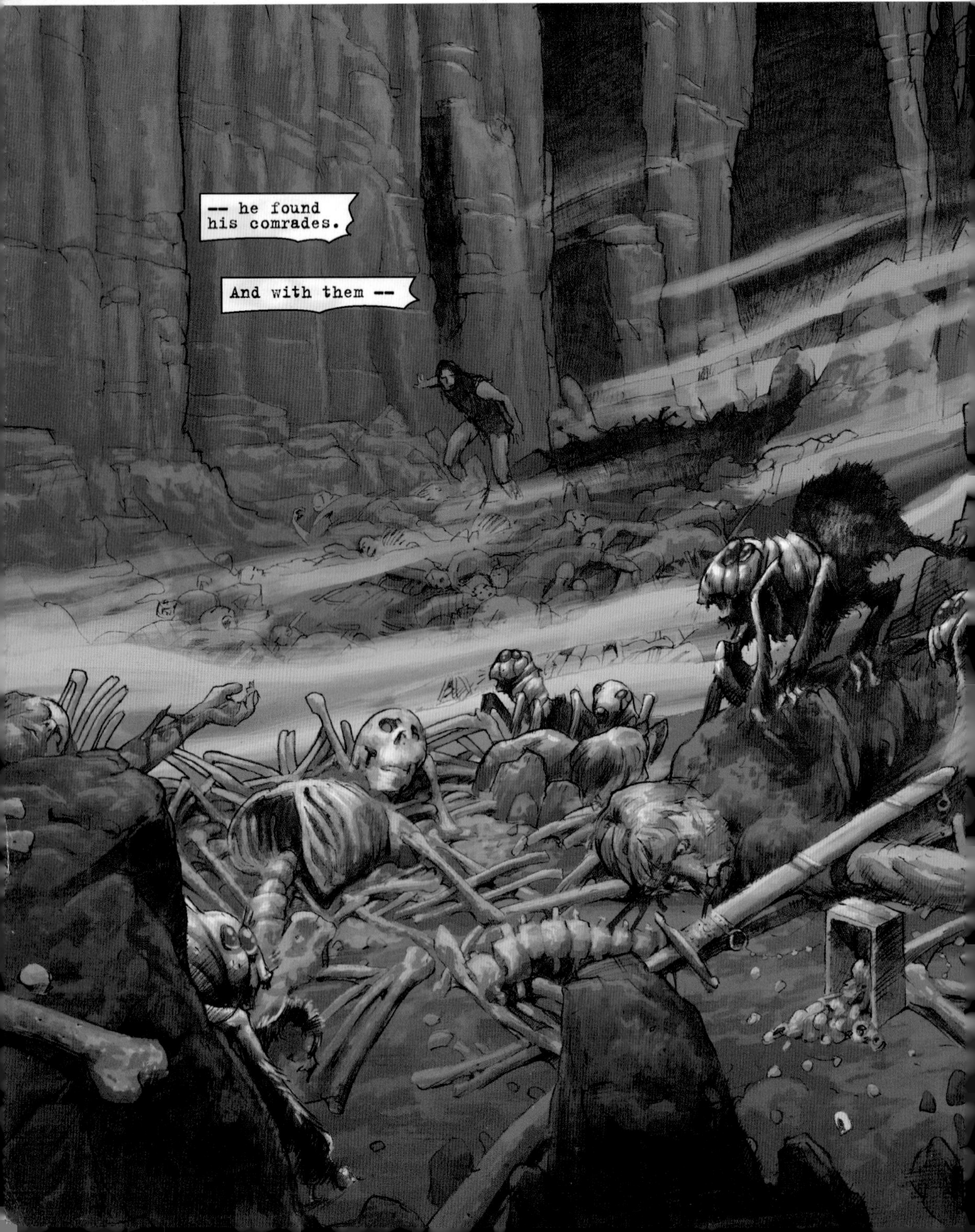
-- he found his comrades.
And with them --

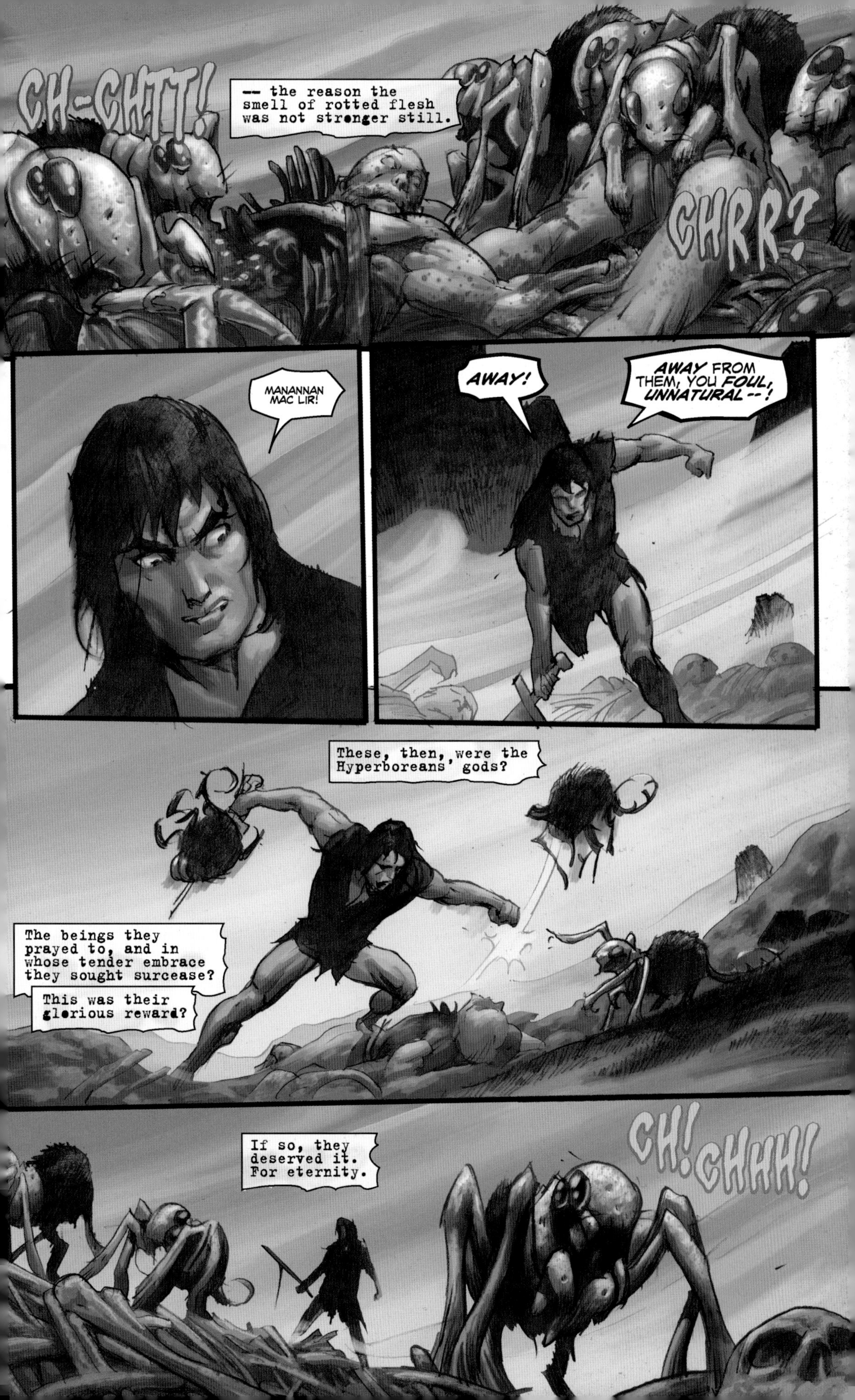
CH-CHTT!
-- the reason the smell of rotted flesh was not stronger still.
CHRR?
MANANNAN MAC LIR!
AWAY!
AWAY FROM THEM, YOU FOUL, UNNATURAL --!
These, then, were the Hyperboreans' gods?
The beings they prayed to, and in whose tender embrace they sought surcease?
This was their glorious reward?
If so, they deserved it. For eternity.
CH!CHHH!

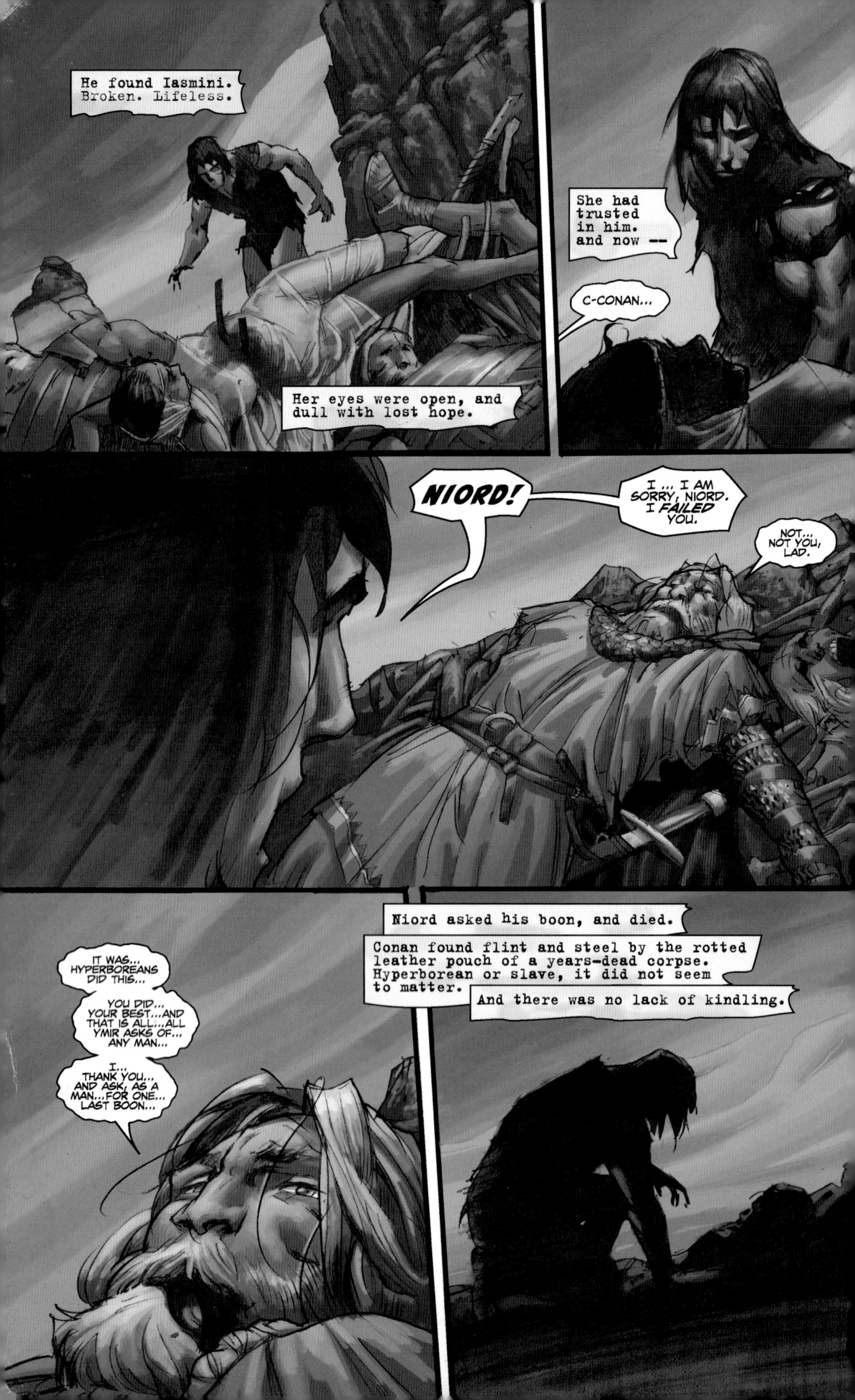
He found Iasmini.
Broken. Lifeless.
Her eyes were open, and dull with lost hope.
She had trusted in him. and now --
C-CONAN...
NIORD!
I... I AM SORRY, NIORD. I FAILED YOU.
NOT... NOT YOU, LAD.
IT WAS... HYPERBOREANS DID THIS...
YOU DID... YOUR BEST...AND THAT IS ALL...ALL YMIR ASKS OF... ANY MAN...
I... THANK YOU... AND ASK, AS A MAN...FOR ONE... LAST BOON...
Niord asked his boon, and died.
Conan found flint and steel by the rotted leather pouch of a years-dead corpse. Hyperborean or slave, it did not seem to matter.
And there was no lack of kindling.

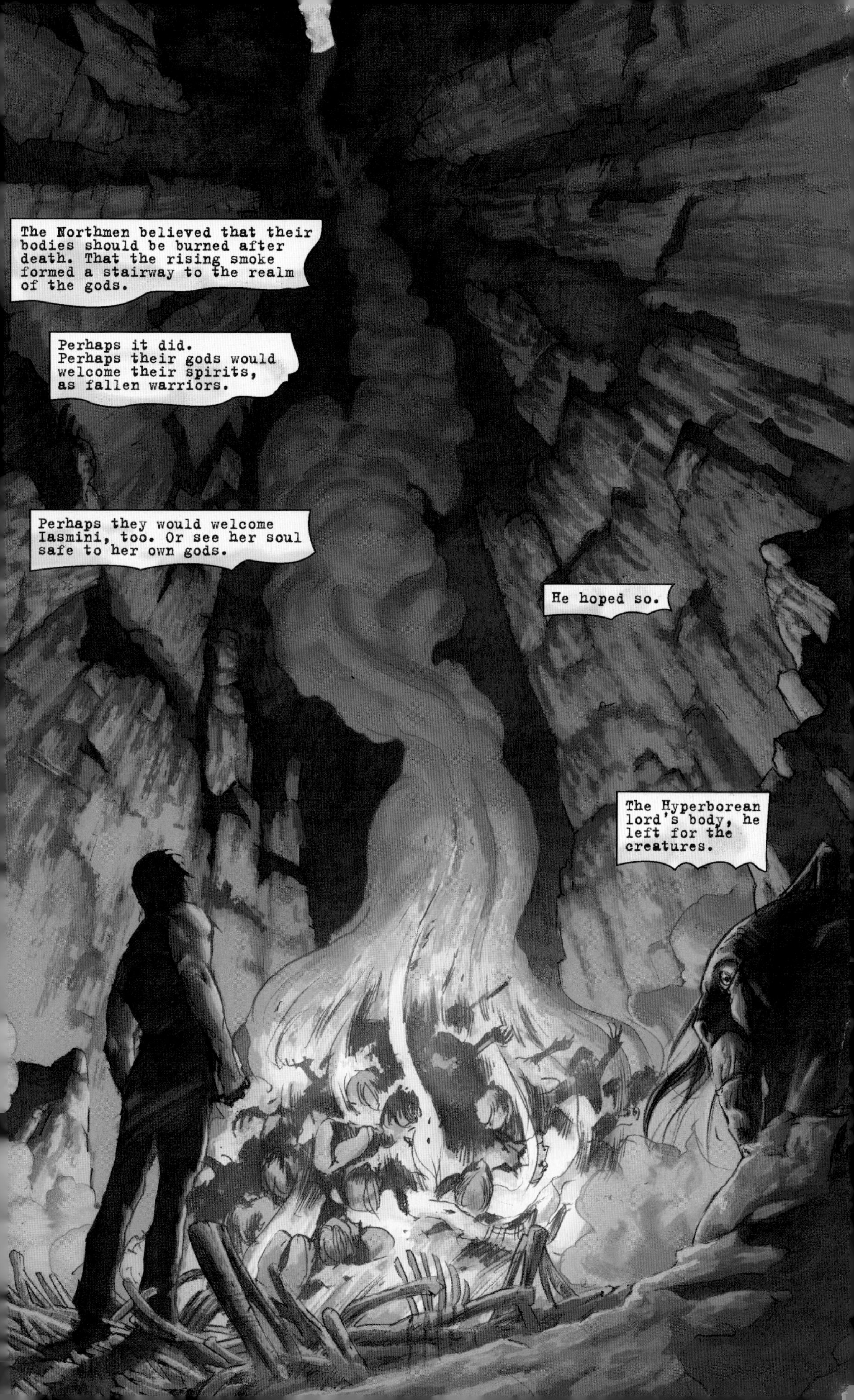
The Northmen believed that their bodies should be burned after death. That the rising smoke formed a stairway to the realm of the gods.
Perhaps it did. Perhaps their gods would welcome their spirits, as fallen warriors.
Perhaps they would welcome Iasmini, too. Or see her soul safe to her own gods.
He hoped so.
The Hyperborean lord's body, he left for the creatures.

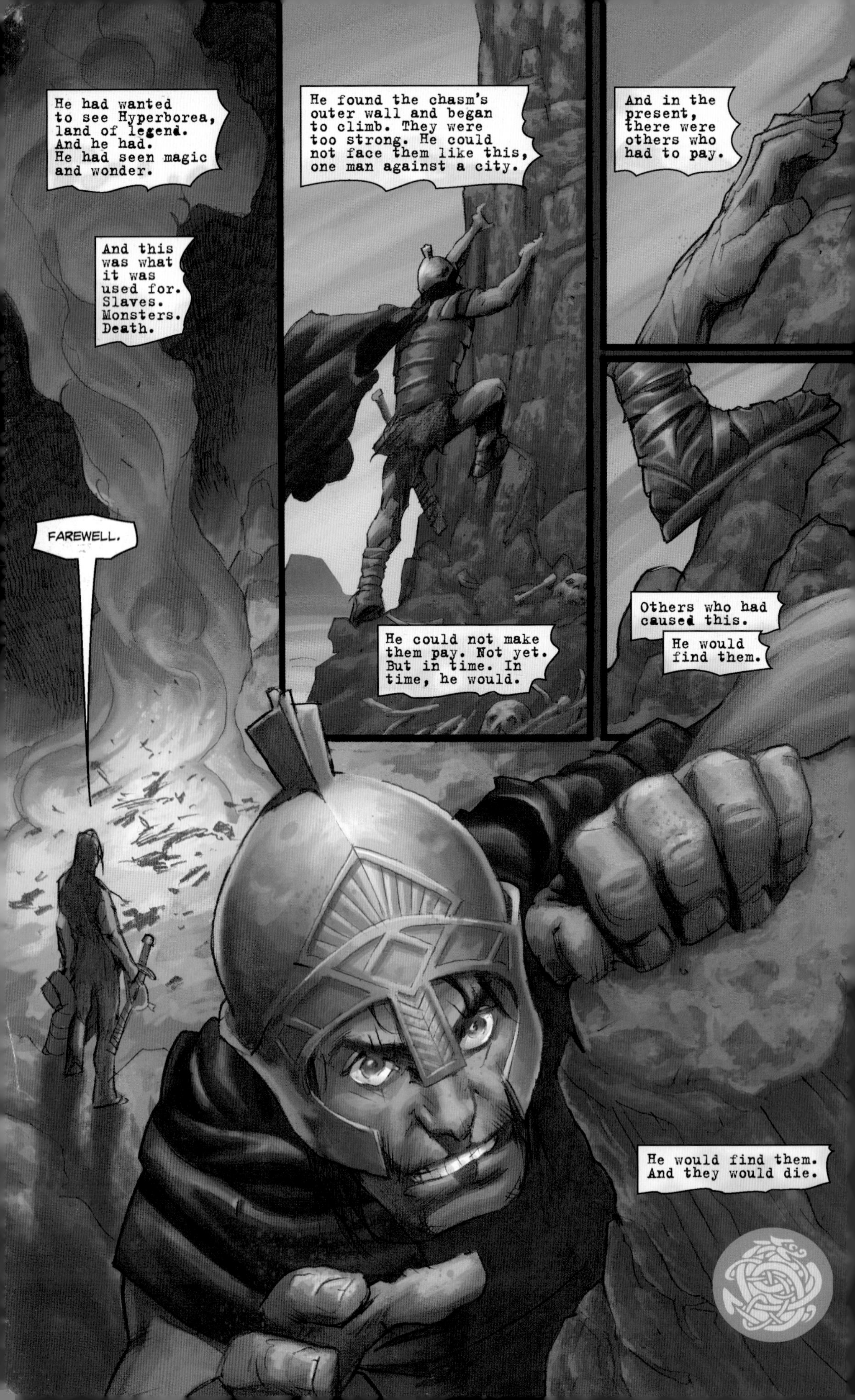
He had wanted to see Hyperborea, land of legend. And he had. He had seen magic and wonder.
And this was what it was used for. Slaves. Monsters. Death.
FAREWELL.
He found the chasm's outer wall and began to climb. They were too strong. He could not face them like this, one man against a city.
He could not make them pay. Not yet. But in time. In time, he would.
And in the present, there were others who had to pay.
Others who had caused this.
He would find them.
He would find them. And they would die.

CHAPTER SEVEN

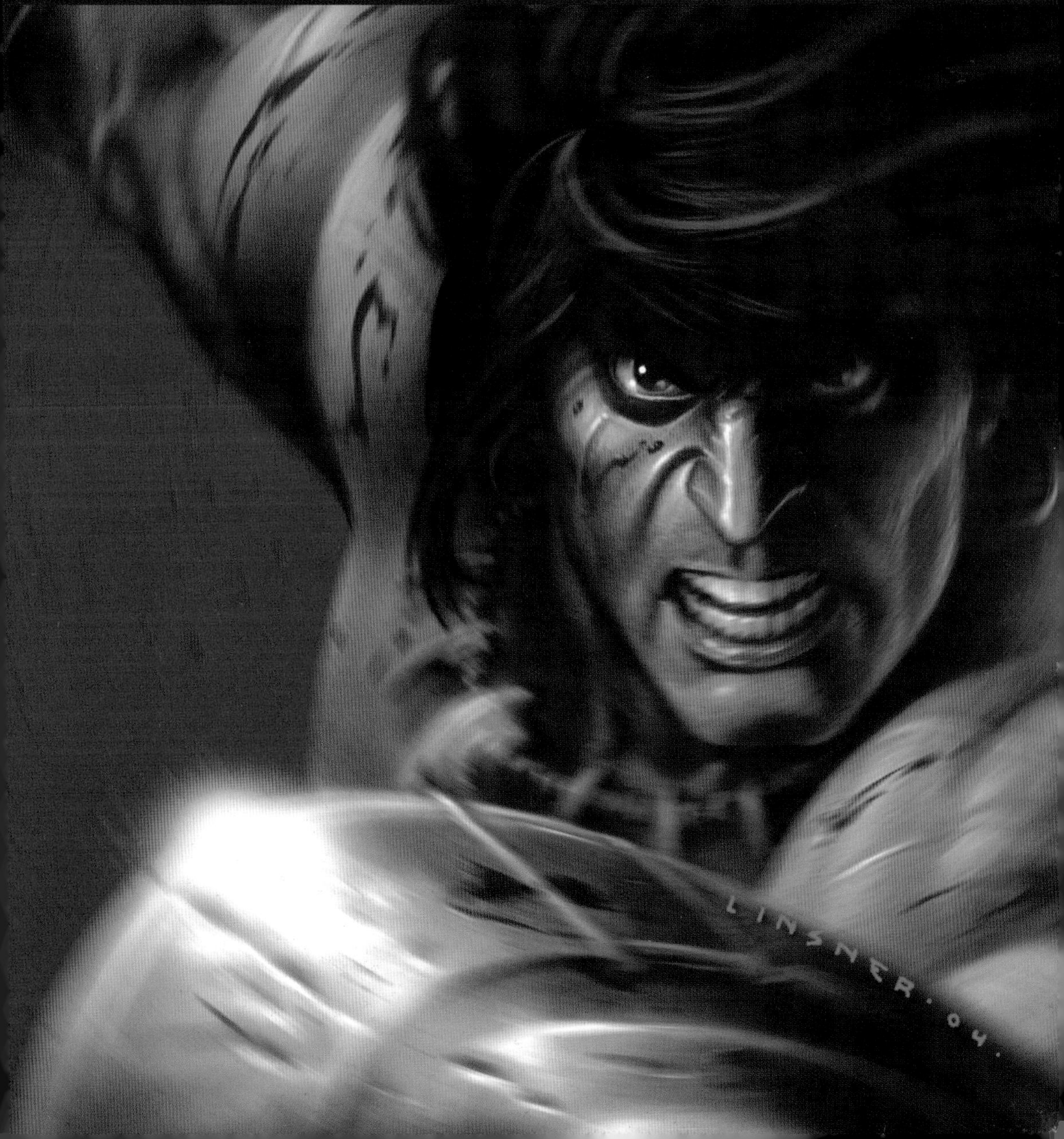
LINSNER.04.

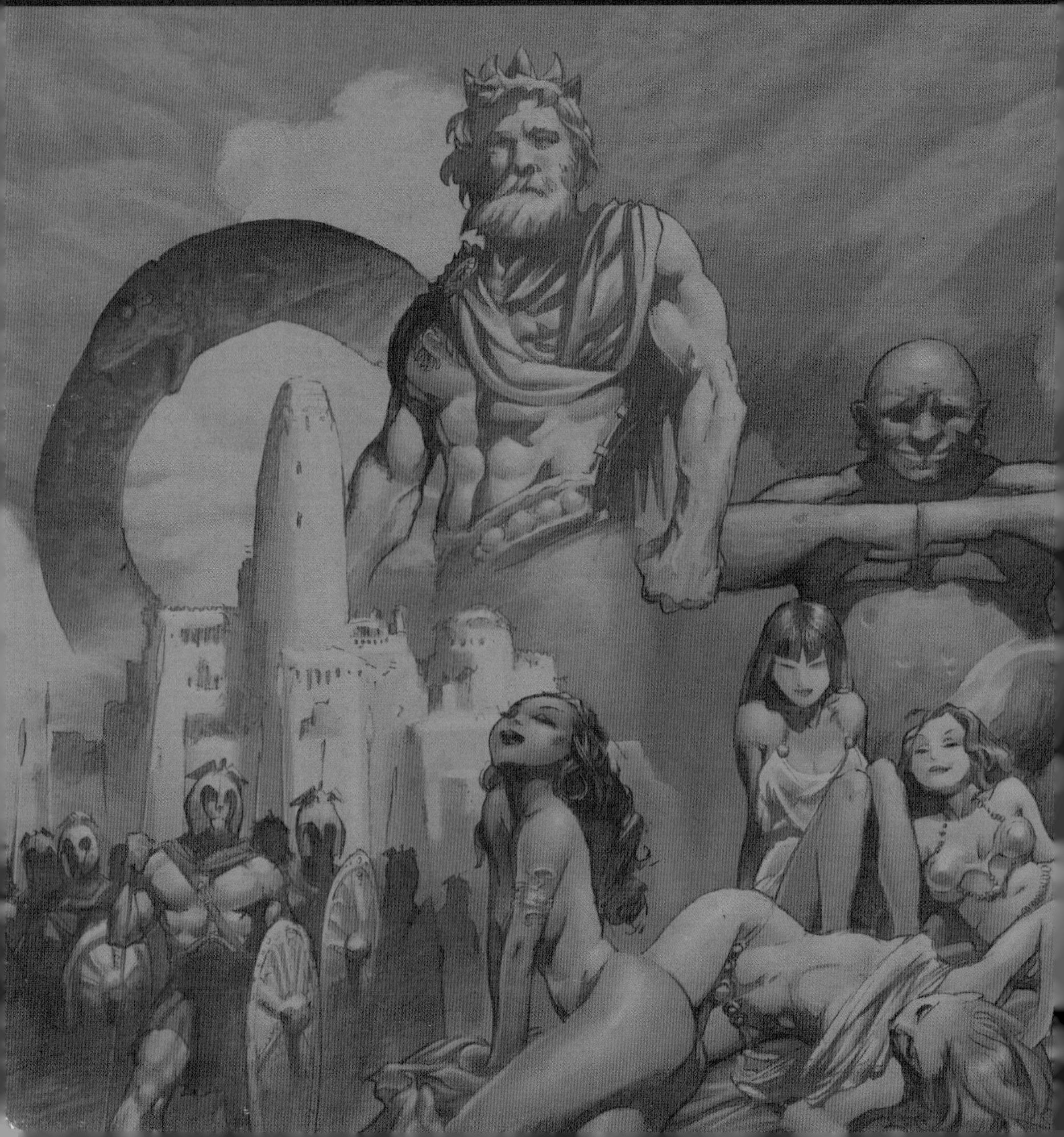

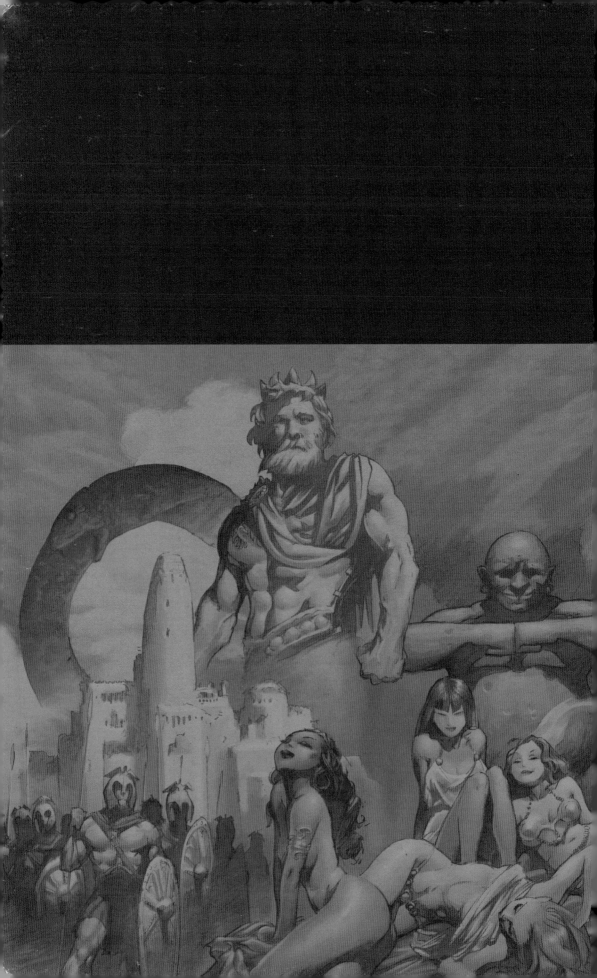

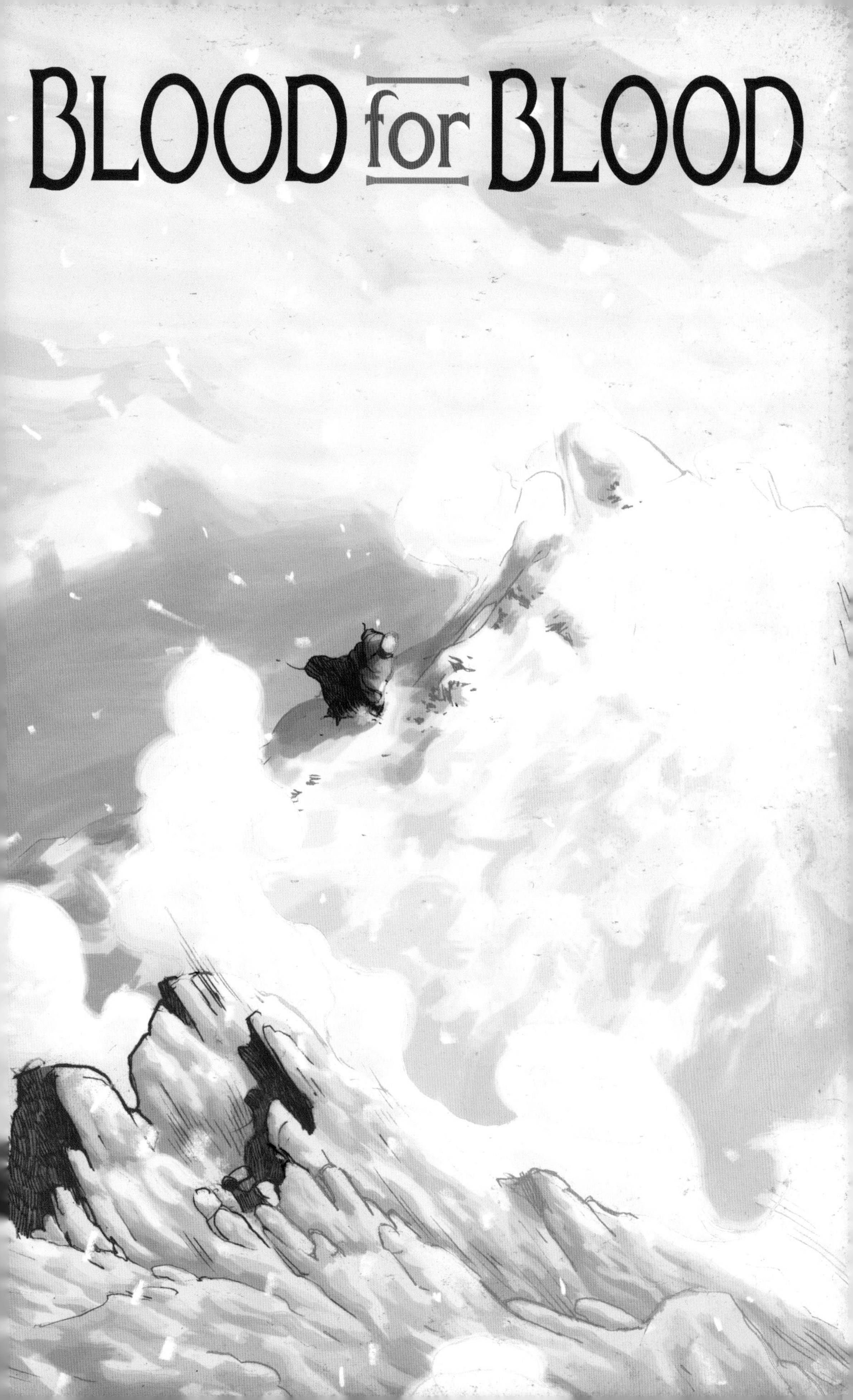
BLOOD for BLOOD

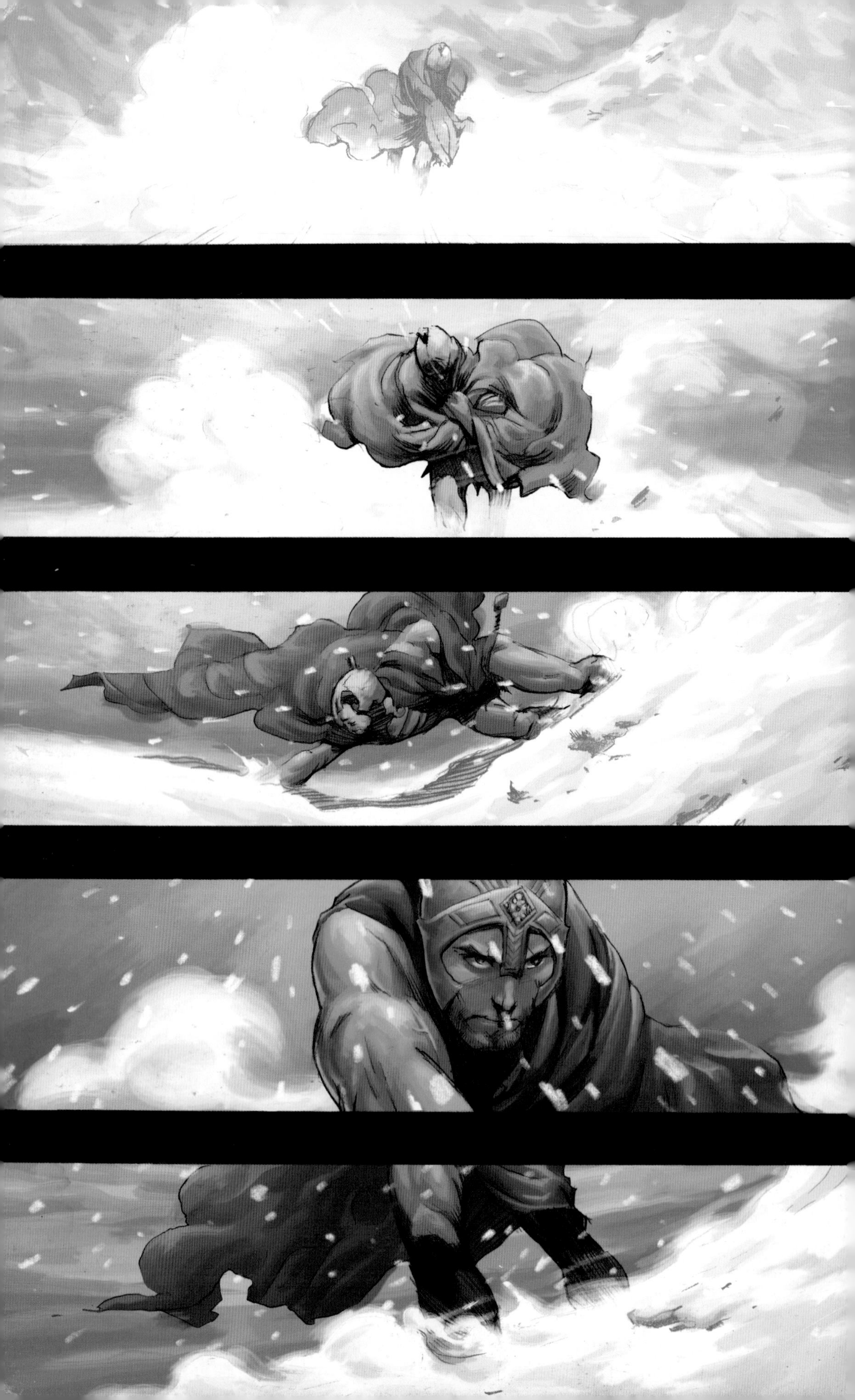

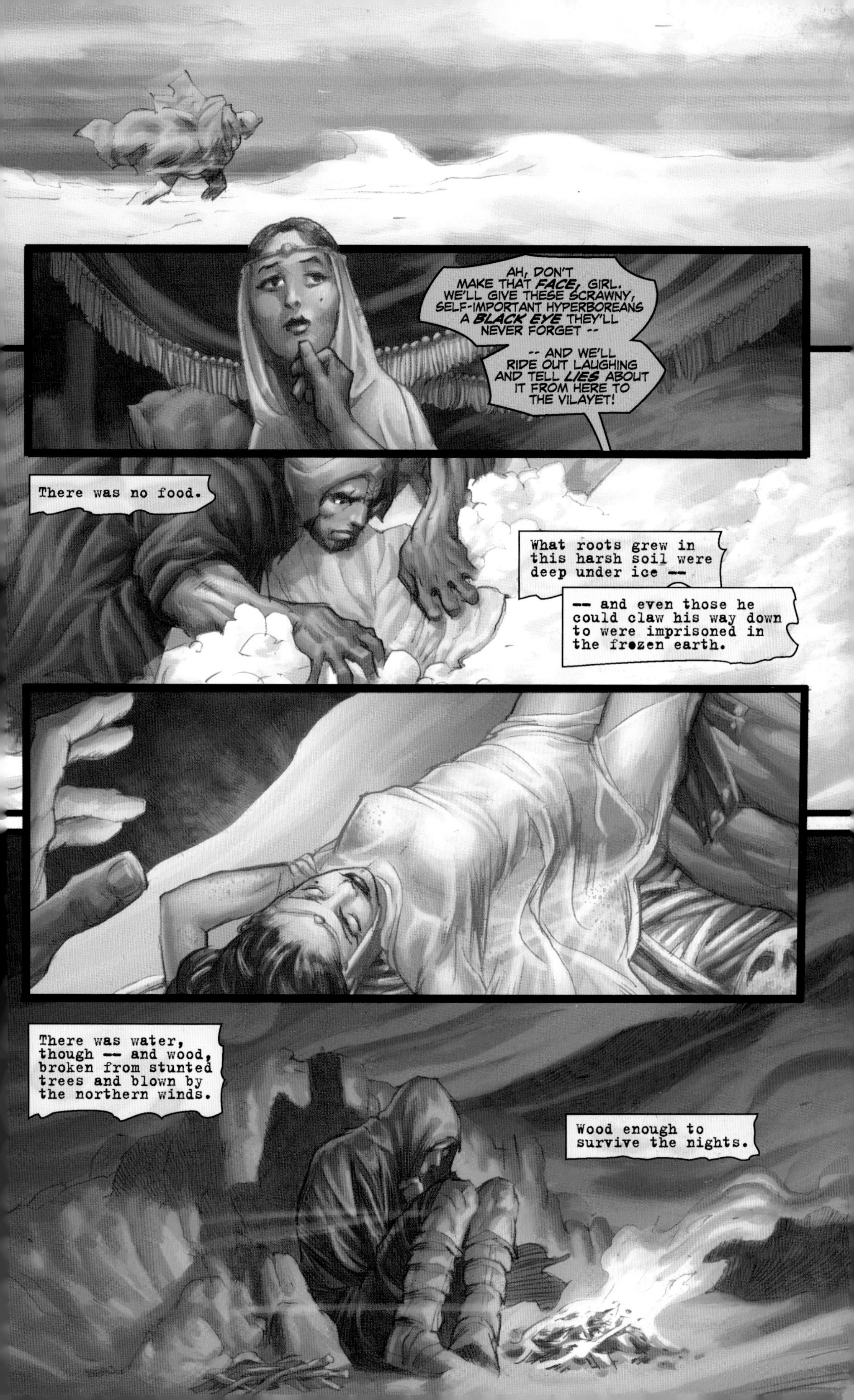
AH, DON'T MAKE THAT FACE, GIRL. WE'LL GIVE THESE SCRAWNY, SELF-IMPORTANT HYPERBOREANS A BLACK EYE THEY'LL NEVER FORGET --
-- AND WE'LL RIDE OUT LAUGHING AND TELL LIES ABOUT IT FROM HERE TO THE VILAYET!
There was no food.
What roots grew in this harsh soil were deep under ice --
-- and even those he could claw his way down to were imprisoned in the frozen earth.
There was water, though -- and wood, broken from stunted trees and blown by the northern winds.
Wood enough to survive the nights.

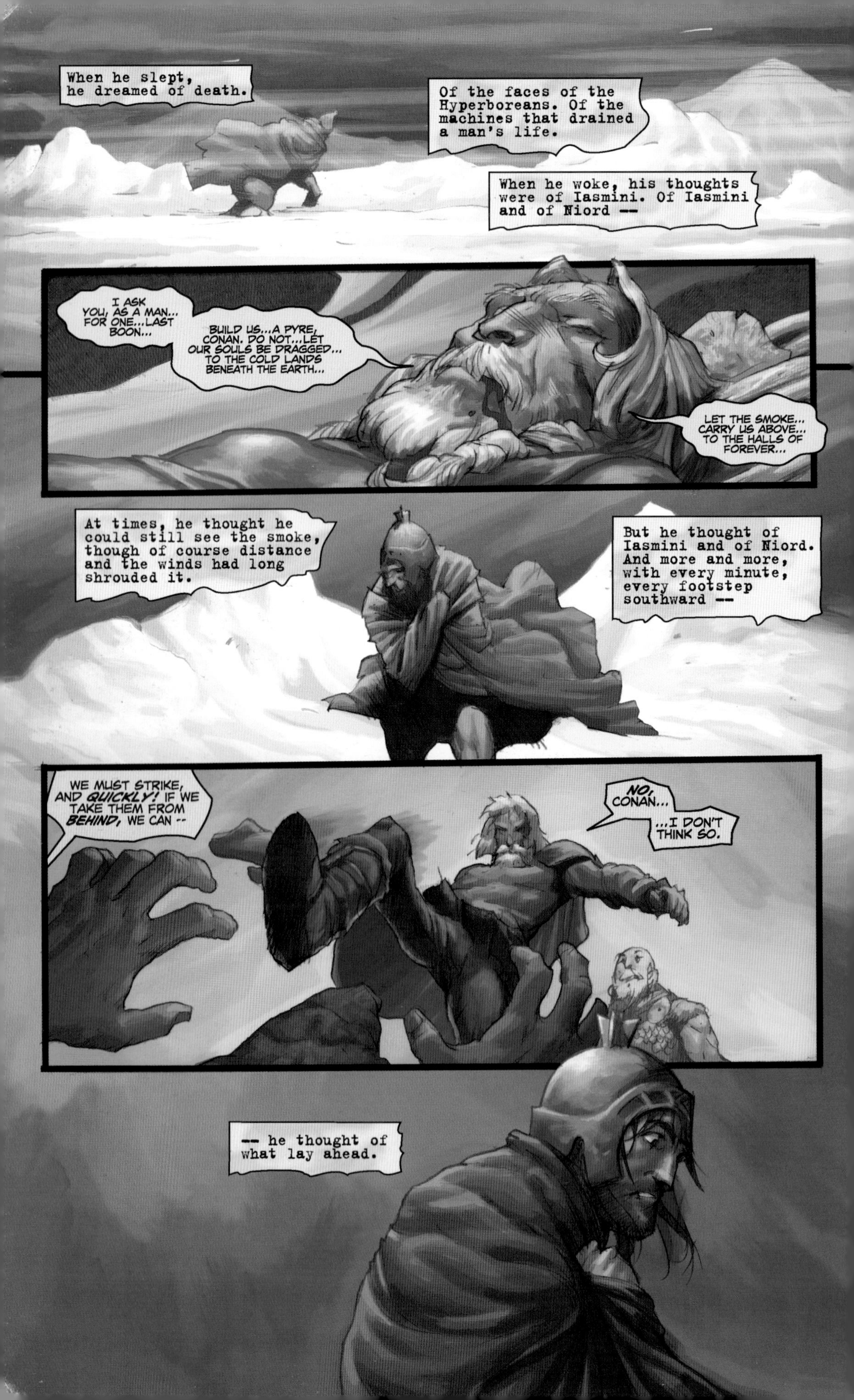
When he slept, he dreamed of death.
Of the faces of the Hyperboreans. Of the machines that drained a man's life.
When he woke, his thoughts were of Iasmini. Of Iasmini and of Niord --
I ASK YOU, AS A MAN... FOR ONE...LAST BOON...
BUILD US...A PYRE, CONAN. DO NOT...LET OUR SOULS BE DRAGGED... TO THE COLD LANDS BENEATH THE EARTH...
LET THE SMOKE... CARRY US ABOVE... TO THE HALLS OF FOREVER...
At times, he thought he could still see the smoke, though of course distance and the winds had long shrouded it.
But he thought of Iasmini and of Niord. And more and more, with every minute, every footstep southward --
WE MUST STRIKE, AND QUICKLY! IF WE TAKE THEM FROM BEHIND, WE CAN --
NO, CONAN...
...I DON'T THINK SO.
-- he thought of what lay ahead.

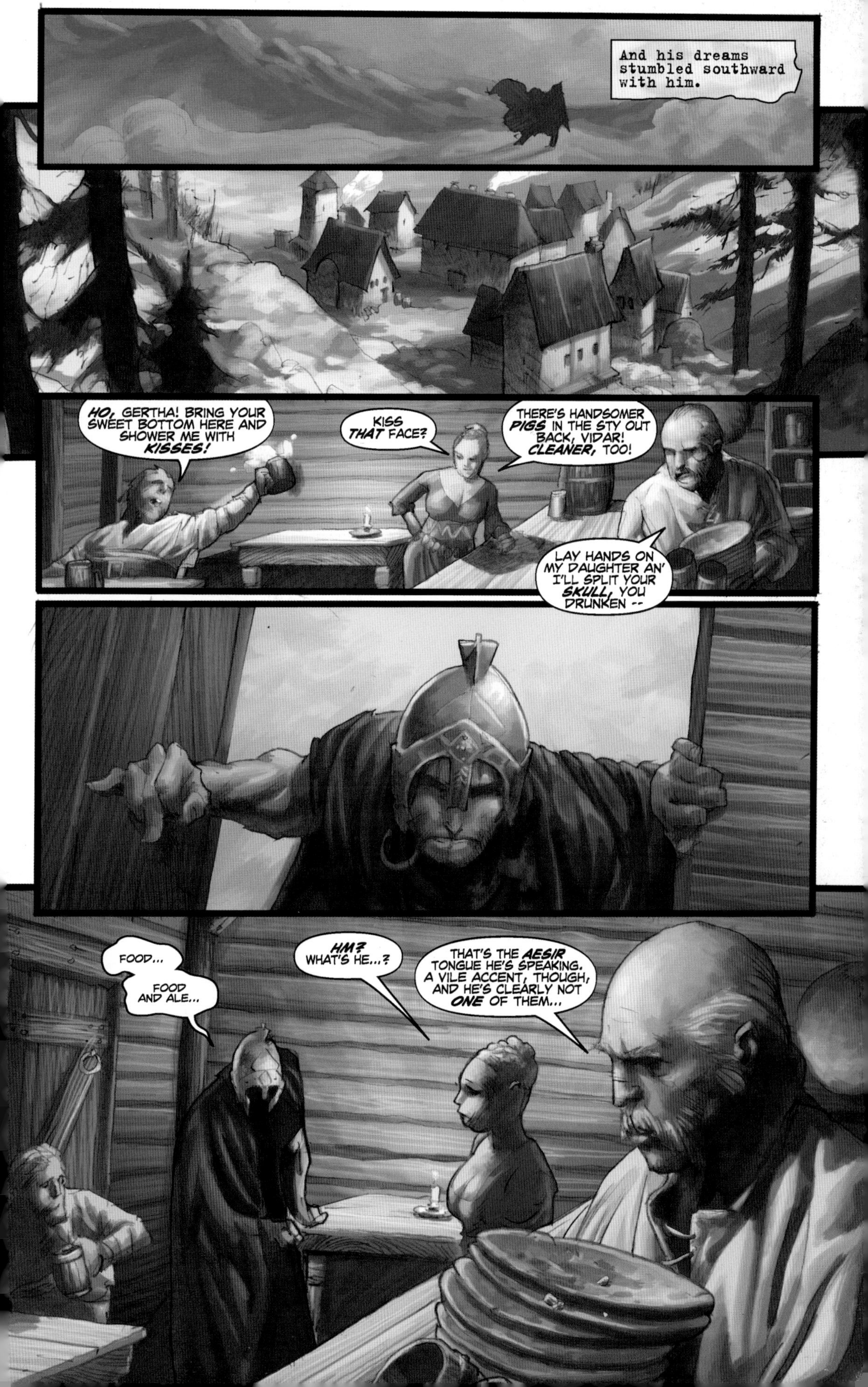
And his dreams stumbled southward with him.
HO, GERTHA! BRING YOUR SWEET BOTTOM HERE AND SHOWER ME WITH KISSES!
KISS THAT FACE?
THERE'S HANDSOMER PIGS IN THE STY OUT BACK, VIDAR! CLEANER, TOO!
LAY HANDS ON MY DAUGHTER AN' I'LL SPLIT YOUR SKULL, YOU DRUNKEN --
FOOD...
FOOD AND ALE...
HM? WHAT'S HE...?
THAT'S THE AESIR TONGUE HE'S SPEAKING. A VILE ACCENT, THOUGH, AND HE'S CLEARLY NOT ONE OF THEM...

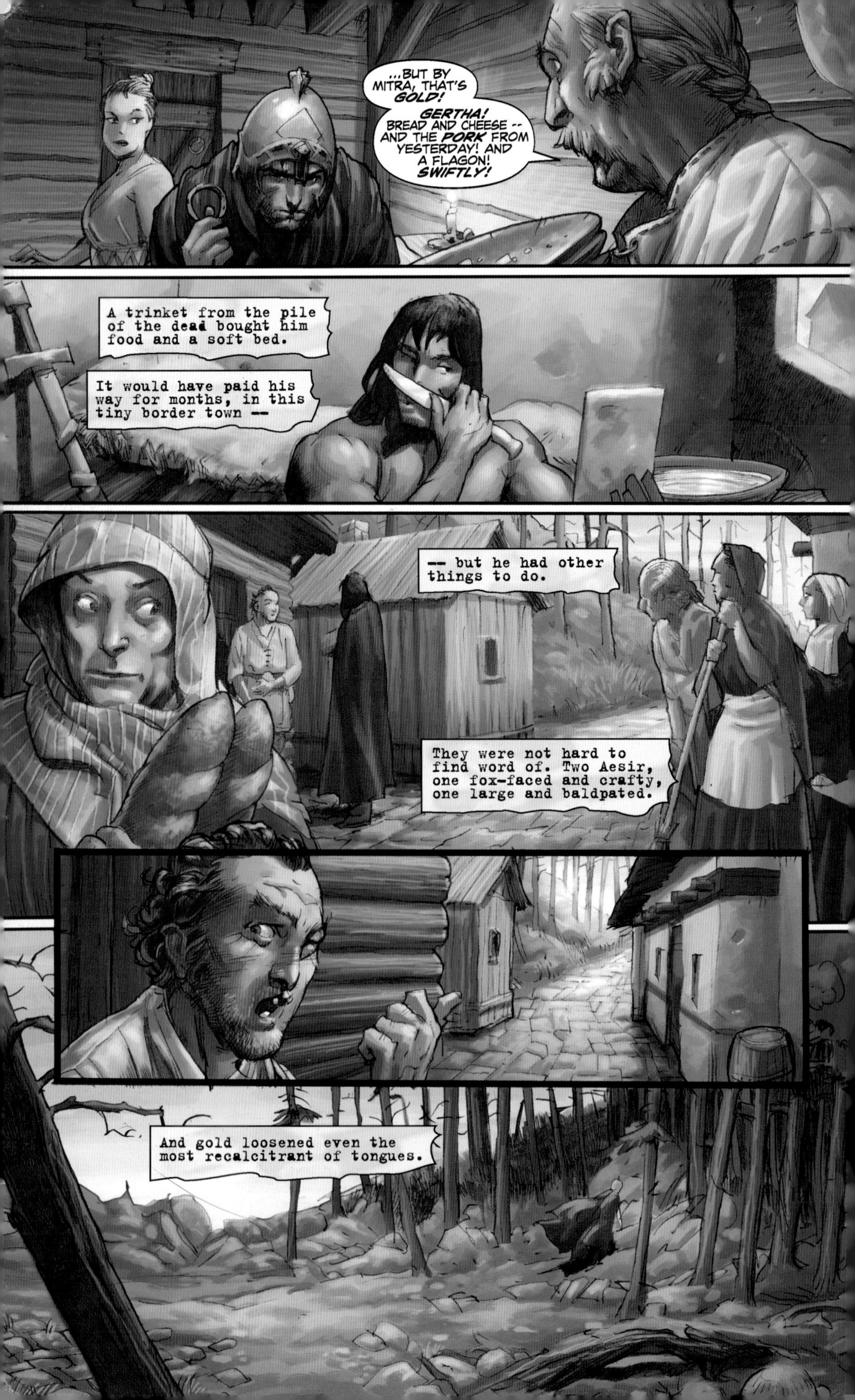
...BUT BY MITRA, THAT'S GOLD!
GERTHA! BREAD AND CHEESE -- AND THE PORK FROM YESTERDAY! AND A FLAGON! SWIFTLY!
A trinket from the pile of the dead bought him food and a soft bed.
It would have paid his way for months, in this tiny border town --
-- but he had other things to do.
They were not hard to find word of. Two Aesir, one fox-faced and crafty, one large and baldpated.
And gold loosened even the most recalcitrant of tongues.

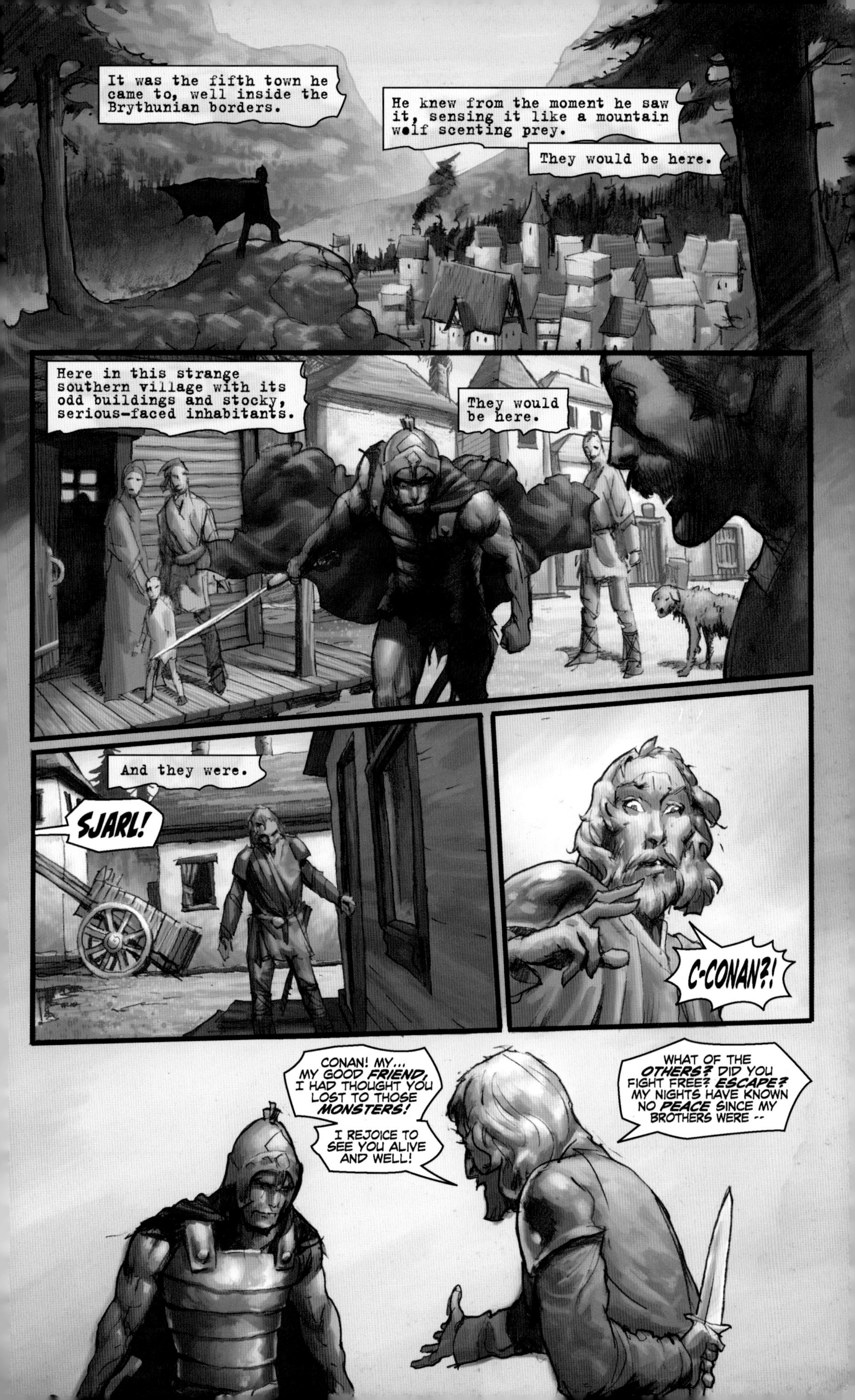
It was the fifth town he came to, well inside the Brythunian borders.
He knew from the moment he saw it, sensing it like a mountain wolf scenting prey.
They would be here.
Here in this strange southern village with its odd buildings and stocky, serious-faced inhabitants.
They would be here.
And they were.
SJARL!
C-CONAN?!
CONAN! MY... MY GOOD FRIEND, I HAD THOUGHT YOU LOST TO THOSE MONSTERS!
I REJOICE TO SEE YOU ALIVE AND WELL!
WHAT OF THE OTHERS? DID YOU FIGHT FREE? ESCAPE? MY NIGHTS HAVE KNOWN NO PEACE SINCE MY BROTHERS WERE --

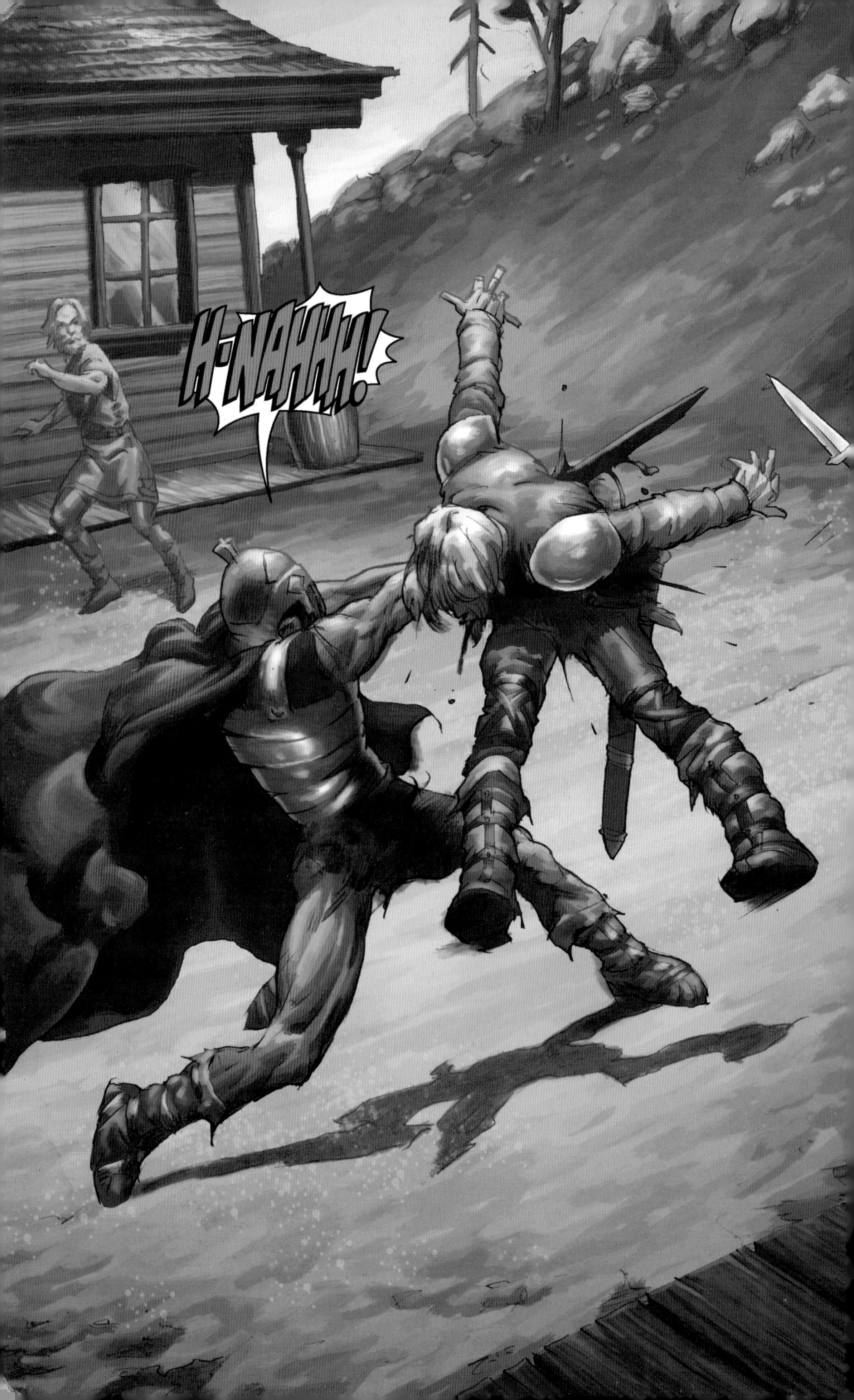
H-NAHHH!

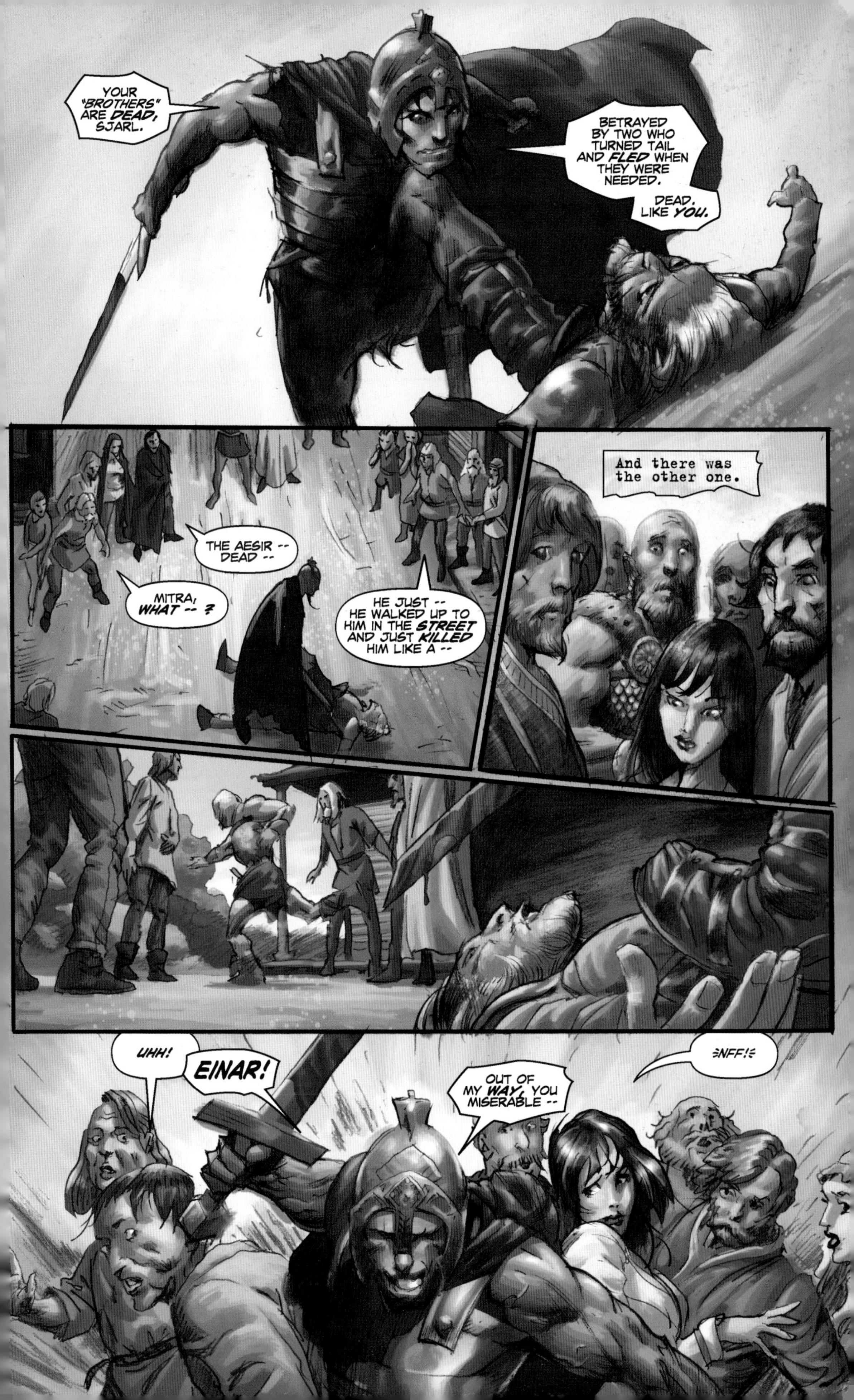
YOUR "BROTHERS" ARE DEAD, SJARL.
BETRAYED BY TWO WHO TURNED TAIL AND FLED WHEN THEY WERE NEEDED.
DEAD. LIKE YOU.
THE AESIR -- DEAD --
MITRA, WHAT -- ?
HE JUST -- HE WALKED UP TO HIM IN THE STREET AND JUST KILLED HIM LIKE A --
And there was the other one.
UHH!
EINAR!
OUT OF MY WAY, YOU MISERABLE --
=NFF!=

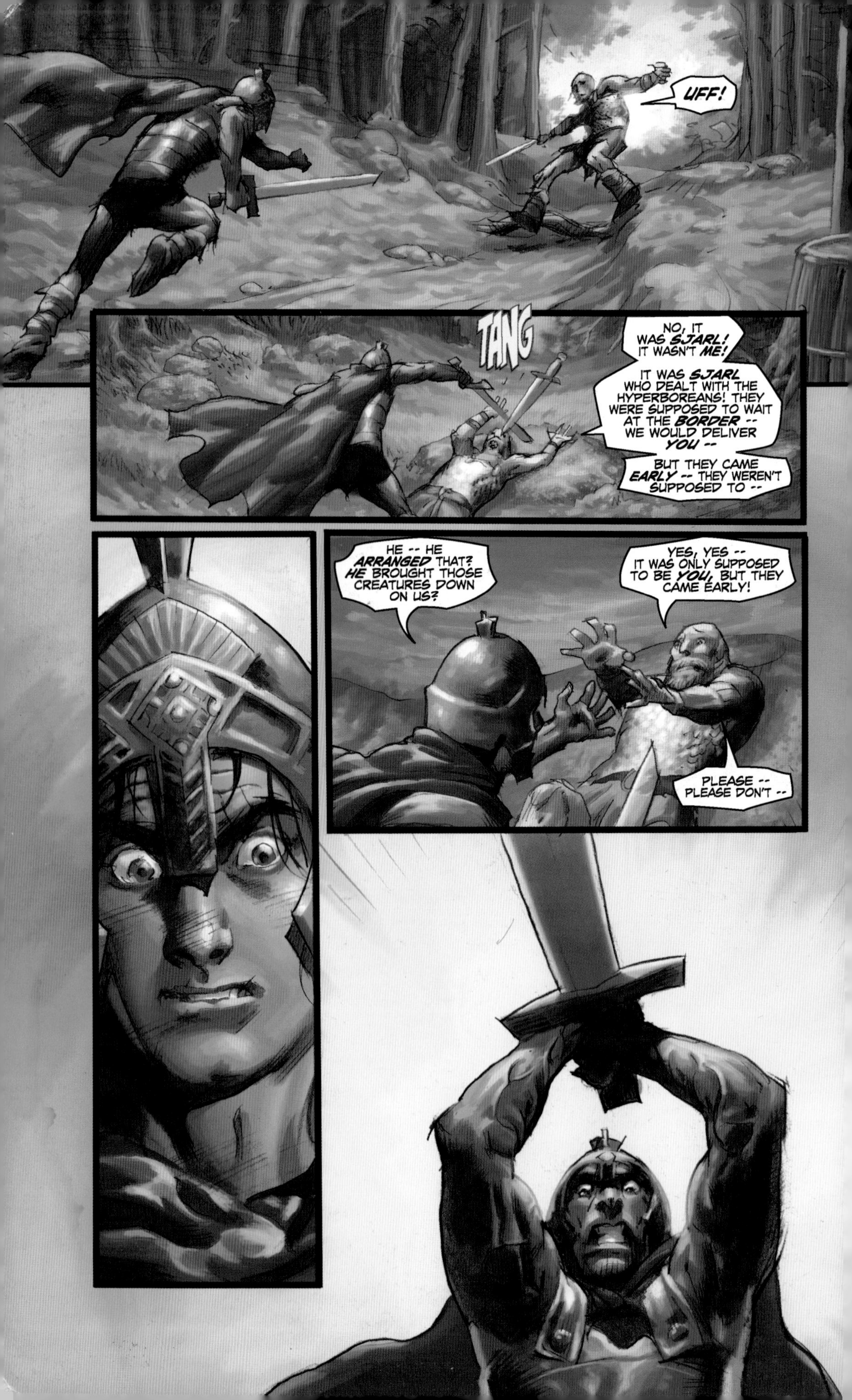
UFF!
TANG
NO, IT WAS SJARL! IT WASN'T ME!
IT WAS SJARL WHO DEALT WITH THE HYPERBOREANS! THEY WERE SUPPOSED TO WAIT AT THE BORDER -- WE WOULD DELIVER YOU --
BUT THEY CAME EARLY -- THEY WEREN'T SUPPOSED TO --
HE -- HE ARRANGED THAT? HE BROUGHT THOSE CREATURES DOWN ON US?
YES, YES -- IT WAS ONLY SUPPOSED TO BE YOU, BUT THEY CAME EARLY!
PLEASE -- PLEASE DON'T --

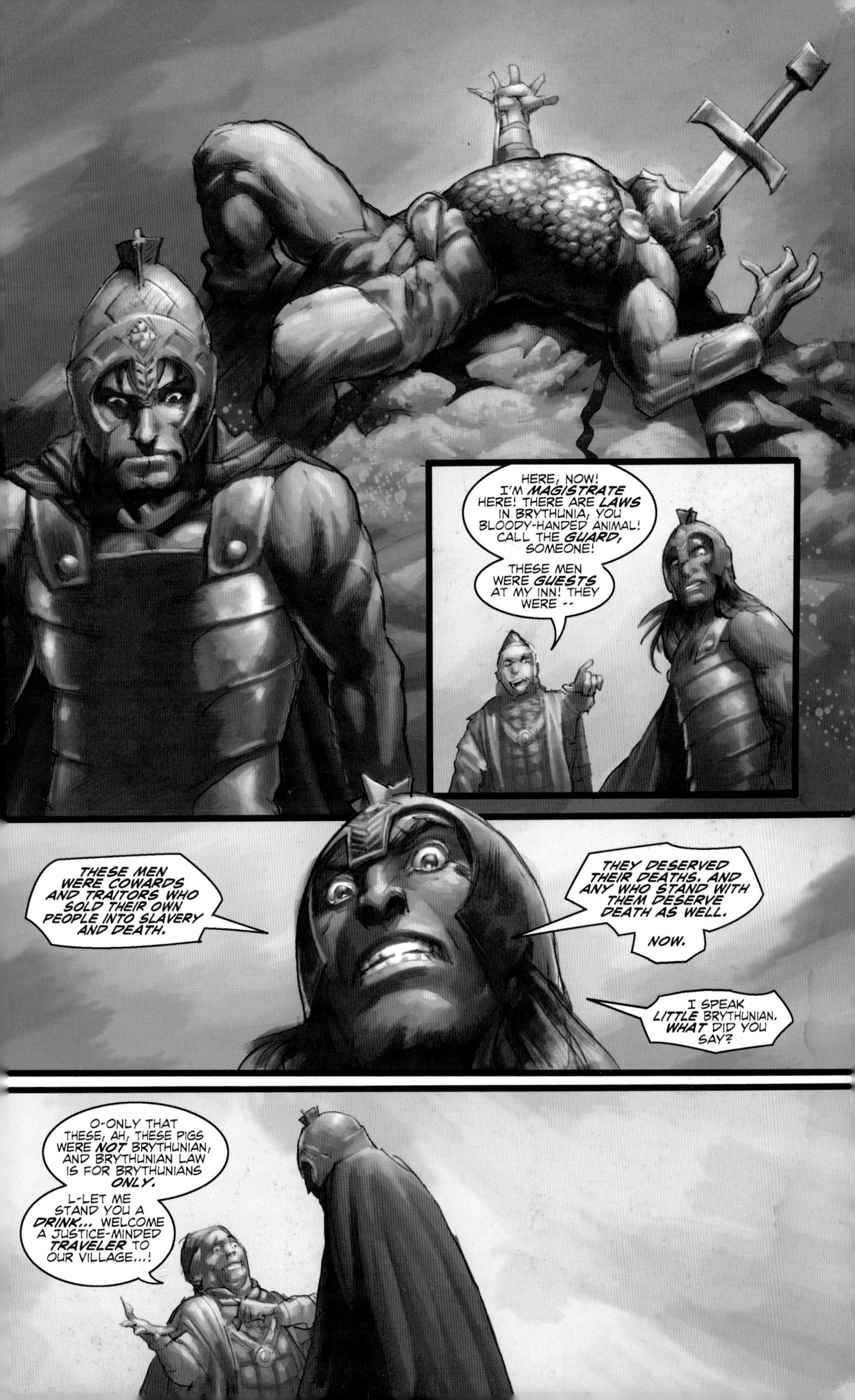
HERE, NOW! I'M MAGISTRATE HERE! THERE ARE LAWS IN BRYTHUNIA, YOU BLOODY-HANDED ANIMAL! CALL THE GUARD, SOMEONE!
THESE MEN WERE GUESTS AT MY INN! THEY WERE --
THESE MEN WERE COWARDS AND TRAITORS WHO SOLD THEIR OWN PEOPLE INTO SLAVERY AND DEATH.
THEY DESERVED THEIR DEATHS. AND ANY WHO STAND WITH THEM DESERVE DEATH AS WELL.
NOW.
I SPEAK LITTLE BRYTHUNIAN. WHAT DID YOU SAY?
O-ONLY THAT THESE, AH, THESE PIGS WERE NOT BRYTHUNIAN, AND BRYTHUNIAN LAW IS FOR BRYTHUNIANS ONLY.
L-LET ME STAND YOU A DRINK... WELCOME A JUSTICE-MINDED TRAVELER TO OUR VILLAGE...!

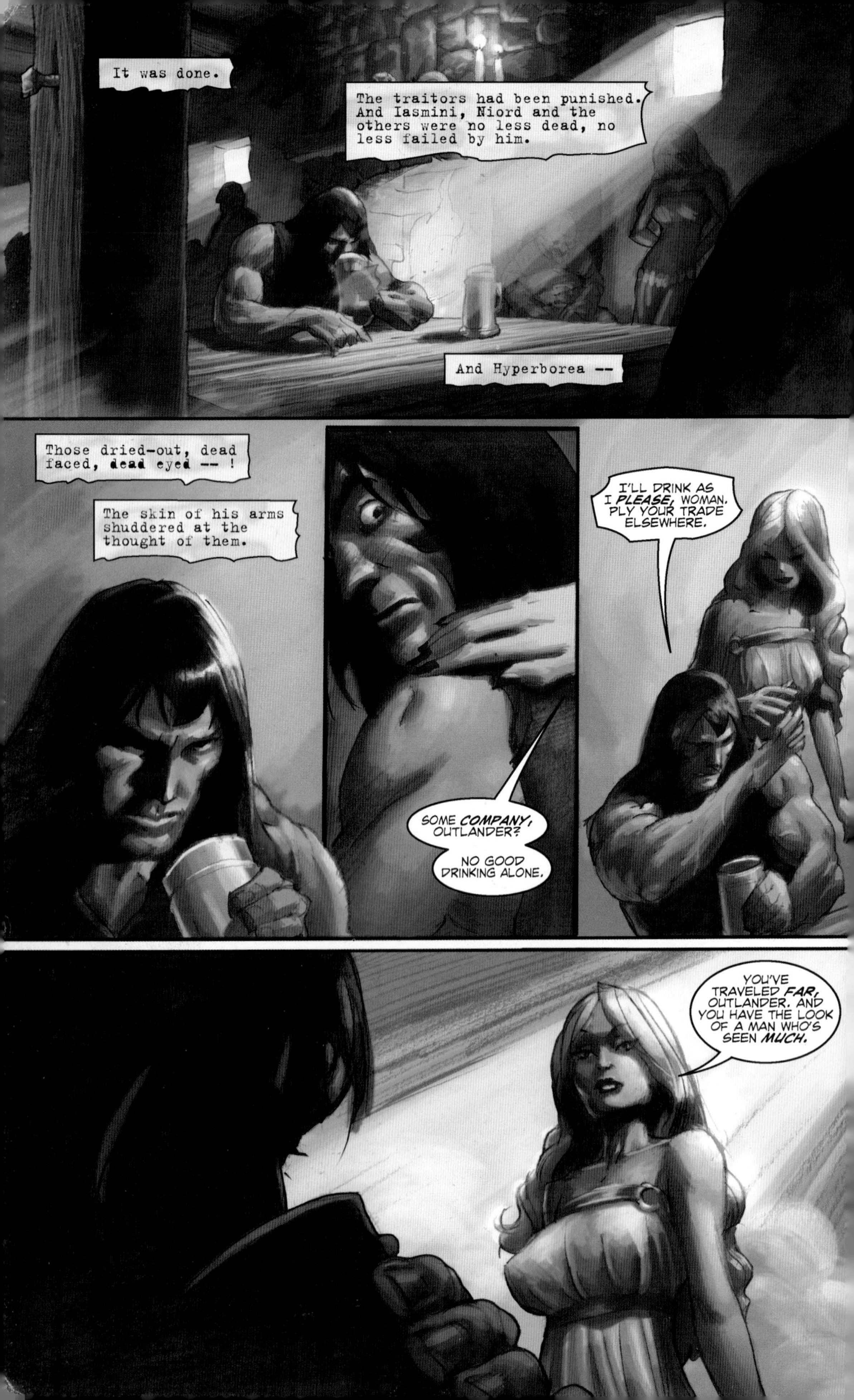
It was done.
The traitors had been punished. And Iasmini, Niord and the others were no less dead, no less failed by him.
And Hyperborea --
Those dried-out, dead faced, dead eyed -- !
The skin of his arms shuddered at the thought of them.
SOME COMPANY, OUTLANDER?
NO GOOD DRINKING ALONE.
I'LL DRINK AS I PLEASE, WOMAN. PLY YOUR TRADE ELSEWHERE.
YOU'VE TRAVELED FAR, OUTLANDER. AND YOU HAVE THE LOOK OF A MAN WHO'S SEEN MUCH.

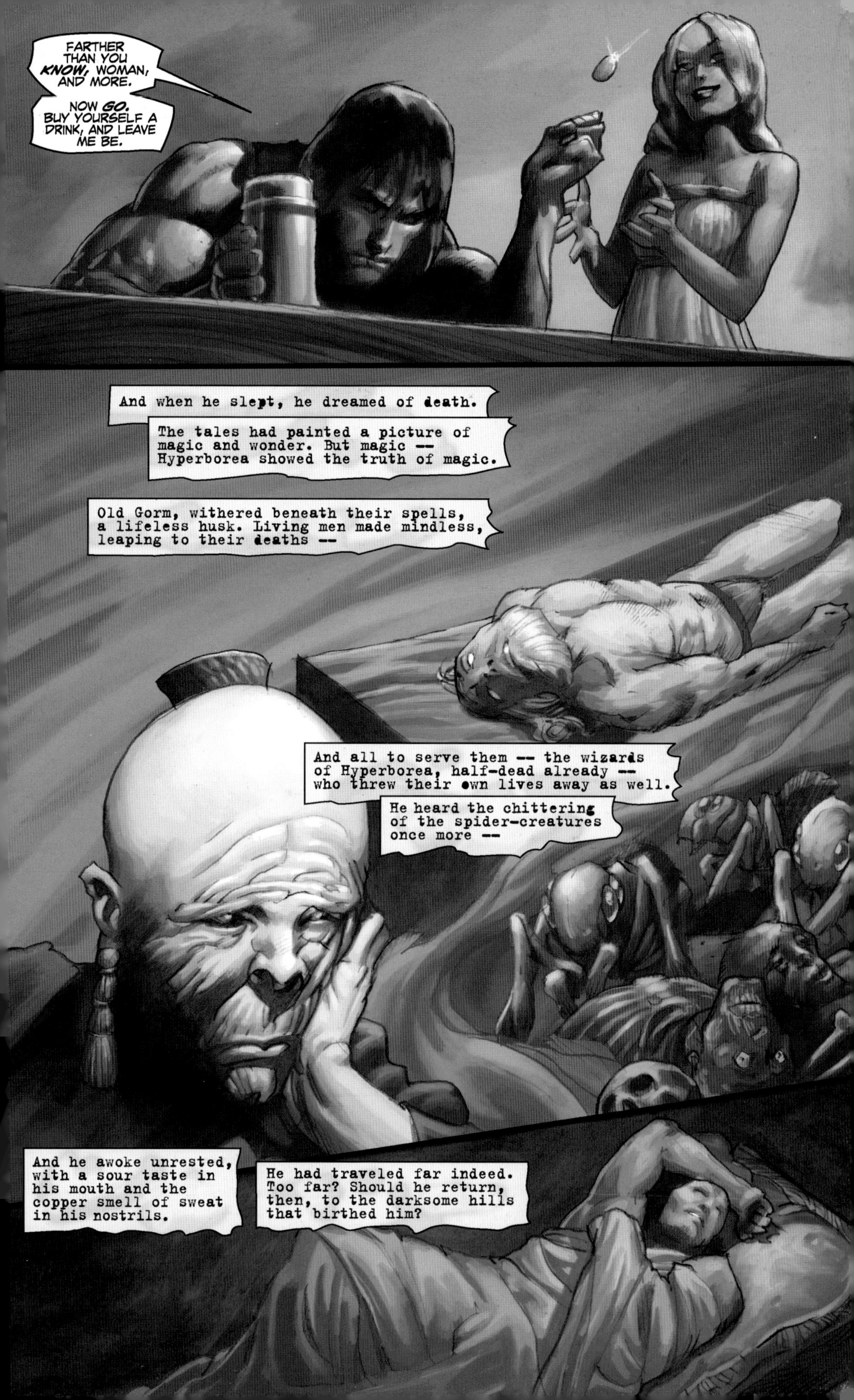
FARTHER THAN YOU KNOW, WOMAN, AND MORE.
NOW GO. BUY YOURSELF A DRINK, AND LEAVE ME BE.
And when he slept, he dreamed of death.
The tales had painted a picture of magic and wonder. But magic -- Hyperborea showed the truth of magic.
Old Gorm, withered beneath their spells, a lifeless husk. Living men made mindless, leaping to their deaths --
And all to serve them -- the wizards of Hyperborea, half-dead already -- who threw their own lives away as well.
He heard the chittering of the spider-creatures once more --
And he awoke unrested, with a sour taste in his mouth and the copper smell of sweat in his nostrils.
He had traveled far indeed. Too far? Should he return, then, to the darksome hills that birthed him?

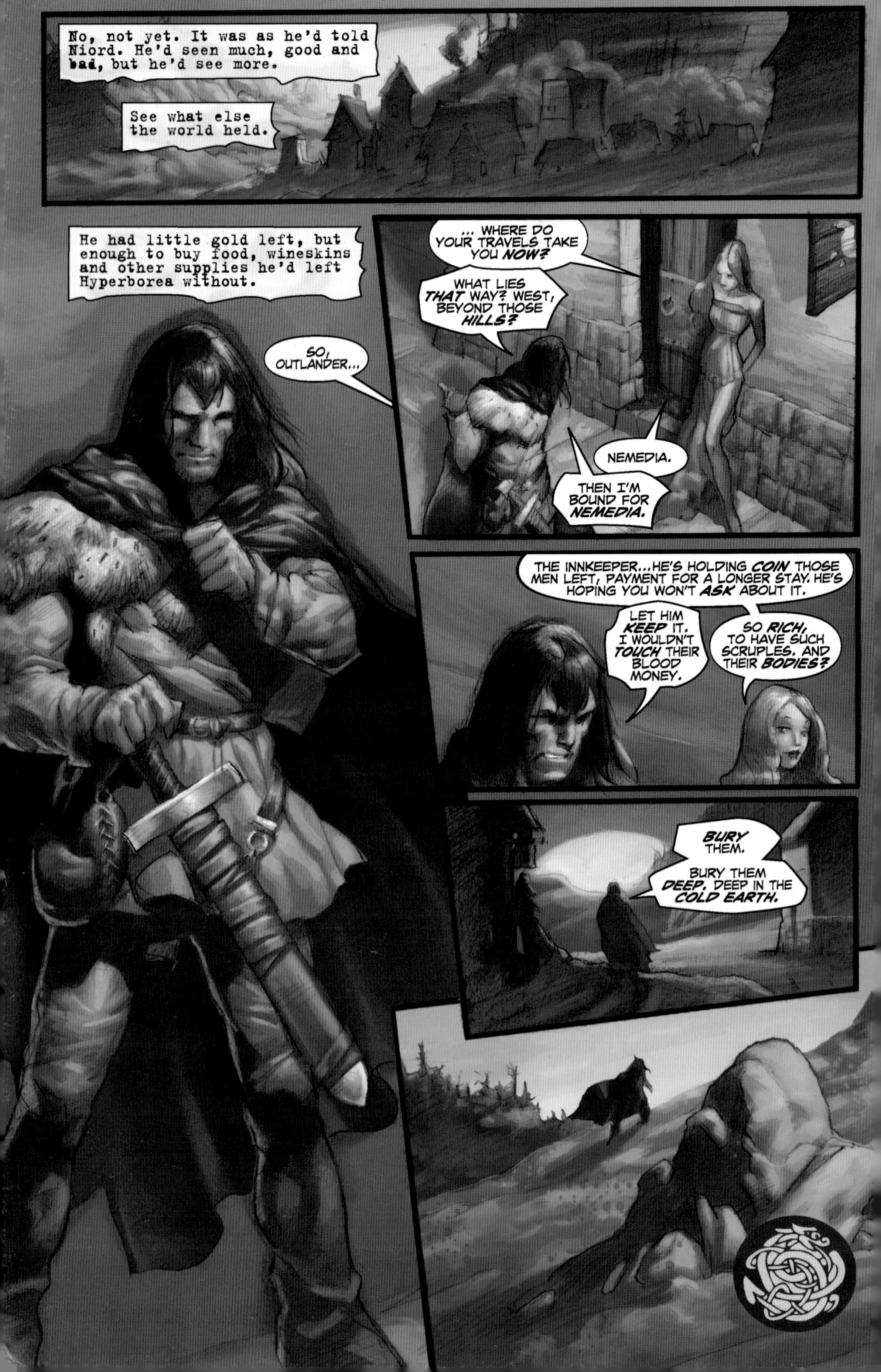
No, not yet. It was as he'd told Niord. He'd seen much, good and bad, but he'd see more.
See what else the world held.
He had little gold left, but enough to buy food, wineskins and other supplies he'd left Hyperborea without.
SO, OUTLANDER...
... WHERE DO YOUR TRAVELS TAKE YOU NOW?
WHAT LIES THAT WAY? WEST, BEYOND THOSE HILLS?
NEMEDIA.
THEN I'M BOUND FOR NEMEDIA.
THE INNKEEPER... HE'S HOLDING COIN THOSE MEN LEFT, PAYMENT FOR A LONGER STAY. HE'S HOPING YOU WON'T ASK ABOUT IT.
LET HIM KEEP IT. I WOULDN'T TOUCH THEIR BLOOD MONEY.
SO RICH, TO HAVE SUCH SCRUPLES. AND THEIR BODIES?
BURY THEM.
BURY THEM DEEP. DEEP IN THE COLD EARTH.

ROBERT E. HOWARD:
LONE STAR FANTASIST

by Mark Finn with illustrations from the sketchbook of Cary Nord

I was the first to light a torch of literature in this part of the country, however small, frail, and easily extinguished that flame may be.

Robert E. Howard
to H. P. Lovecraft, June 1933

It is impossible to calculate the impact of Robert E. Howard's work in pop culture. He has influenced as many people as Tolkien, if not more, and did so from a small house in Cross Plains, Texas. In a professional career that spanned only twelve years, Robert E. Howard generated a lifetime's worth of fiction and single-handedly created the genre of heroic fantasy. His fiction has crisscrossed the world, been translated into a dozen languages, and continues to inspire and move new generations of writers and fans some seventy years after his death. Known chiefly as the creator of the world-famous Conan the Cimmerian, Howard's literary barbarian and his world were less the culmination of his writing career, but another notch on a literary belt so varied that it defies categorization.

Robert Ervin Howard was born January 22, 1906, in Peaster, Texas. His father, Isaac M. Howard, was a country doctor, tending to farmers and their families. Dr. Howard moved his wife, Hester Jane Ervin, and their young son all over Texas, hopping from small community to small community. Robert E. Howard leaned heavily on his mother for companionship, and she encouraged his reading and studies. He was an imaginative boy, able to absorb and retain oral stories as well as written fiction, reading everything he could get his hands on.

By 1919, the family settled in Cross Plains, just slightly ahead of the oil booms of the twenties, which brought huge numbers of people into the area, causing local businesses to thrive. Thousands of people thronged to the small town looking for legitimate work in the fields, but with this crowd came the con men, gamblers, drifters, saloon girls, and of course, the fast-talking businessmen and speculators looking to make a quick buck before the oil wells dried up.

These images of sudden civilization, indolent cruelty, thievery, and boomtown decadence indelibly colored Howard's perceptions of the world, and these views of civilization in decay would turn up again and again in Howard's fiction. In a 1931 letter to *Weird Tales* editor Farnsworth Wright, Howard wrote: "I'll say one thing about an oil boom; it will teach a kid that Life's a pretty rotten thing as quick as anything I can think of."

Cross Plains was the largest community that the Howard family had lived in at that time, and, coupled with the influx of people chasing black gold, offered plenty of amusement for young boys. Howard's vivid imagination and knack for making up stories gave him an outlet for acceptance with the local kids, and his love of boxing helped him fit in with the boys.

In high school, Howard was an average student, but his skill at writing singled him out amongst his fellow classmates. At the age of fifteen, he had decided to make his living as a writer when he submitted a story to *Adventure*, one of his favorite pulp magazines. It was promptly rejected. By the time he was sixteen, Howard was winning prizes for stories and essays in the school newspaper. Howard continued to write stories, working through his reading sources and influences, looking for his voice.

Shortly after Howard graduated high school, he made his first professional sale, a caveman story called "Spear and Fang," to *Weird Tales*. He had accumulated a number of rejection slips, too, but that sale rekindled his ambition. During the early 1920s, Howard sent out and sold a number of stories to *Weird Tales* and other pulp magazines while he worked at a variety of jobs in Cross Plains, everything from stenographer to soda jerk, from errand boy to oil-field reporter. Howard was also an accomplished poet and wrote reams of verse with historical subject matter, much of which wouldn't be seen until decades after his death, though he did sell several poems to *Weird Tales*. However, *Weird Tales* paid on publication, not acceptance, and as a result, Howard was forced to find work. His father added to the pressure by wanting Howard to follow in his footsteps, or, failing that, go to college and find a vocation. Howard hated all of these menial jobs. He hated punching a clock, and he didn't like being told what to do by others.

In a letter to H.P. Lovecraft, Howard wrote: "It is no light thing to enter into a profession absolutely foreign and alien to the people among which one's lot is cast; a profession which seems as dim and faraway and unreal as the shores of Europe." The Howard family enjoyed some prestige in the community, as Dr. Howard was well-liked and took good care of the citizens of Cross Plains. Robert was expected to fit in by either taking up his father's mantle or at the very least contributing to the town in such a way that the family's prestige wasn't diminished. Some folks thought he was sponging off his parents. Others thought that he was just a little strange (an opinion not helped by his bookish side), because he didn't have the same opinions and desires as those around him.

NJORD?

HORSA?

Howard had a circle of friends that he hung out and corresponded with, but he was essentially alone in his aspirations. These pressures weighed heavily on the young man, and his writing was sometimes sporadic. He blew off steam whenever he could, most notably at the local icehouse, where he boxed with other roughnecks. Bodybuilding and exercise had turned Howard into a heroically proportioned man with a punishing punch. His wins at the icehouse allowed Howard a measure of self-respect, but his job situation and nagging at home persisted.

Robert struck a deal with his father: he would take a bookkeeping course at nearby Howard Payne university. Afterwards, he would be given one year to find success as a writer. If that failed, he would take up the profession of bookkeeping.

The die was cast. He received his diploma for the bookkeeping course in 1927, and set to work immediately thereafter, determined never to rely on it. Howard needed to produce saleable stories. Motivated by the mundane world around him and a fervent desire to make his own way, he dipped into childhood fantasies, European history, and his own rough surroundings to create a host of memorable characters.

While taking his bookkeeping course, Howard came up with a character and a story that would be very influential in his later career. He went back to the manuscript, polished it up, and sent it to *Weird Tales*. Howard was overjoyed when it was accepted for publication. "The Shadow Kingdom" was the first sword-and-sorcery story ever written, a combination of horror and heroic fantasy starring King Kull. Himself an Atlantean barbarian, Kull ascends to the throne of Valusia and is beset on all sides by conspiracy, weird menace, and diplomatic intrigue.

It was Howard's biggest sale to date, and thereafter he began to sell steadily to *Weird Tales*. Another Kull story, "The Mirrors of Tuzun Thune," was accepted and published, along with a different character Howard resuscitated from his adolescence—Solomon Kane, the dour and puritanical swordsman who fought pirates and cannibals along the coast of England and darkest Africa. Seven stories were ultimately published in *Weird Tales*, contributing greatly to Howard's income and prestige within the readership of the magazine.

Howard's second big break came in 1928 when he sold "The Pit of the Serpent" to *Fight Stories* magazine. This sale was the beginning of Howard's most personal and most overlooked character, Steve Costigan. An able-bodied sailor, Costigan roamed the Asiatic Seas with his white bulldog, Mike, in these picaresque boxing tales. Sailor Steve was gorilla-ugly, but he had a heart of gold, fists of steel, and a head full of rocks. Costigan was a bare-knuckled fighter and Howard's flair for writing vivid action served these stories well. Conflicts often revolved around a boxing match, but just as frequently took place in back alleys or other unorthodox environments. These were the first humorous stories that Howard would make a living writing, and they were extremely popular in the pages of *Fight Stories* and *Action Stories* and later, *Jack Dempsey's Fight Magazine*. The publishing company, Fiction House, paid on acceptance, as well, and by the end of 1928, all discussion about Howard taking a bookkeeping course was summarily dropped.

While the Costigan series provided steady income, Howard gave voice to another pair of childhood characters, Bran Mak Morn, King of the Picts, who clashed with the Roman armies in Britannia, and Francis Gordon, a.k.a. El Borak, the swashbuckling gunslinger who traveled the Orient. These, in addition to various horror, action, and historical stories, appeared mostly in *Weird Tales* and its companion magazine, *Oriental Tales.*

Howard wrote in most every genre, and was able to write well, quickly, and with an economy that the editors liked, since most of them paid by the word. That's not to say that Howard just knocked them out, either. He wrote multiple drafts of most of his stories, often incorporating suggestions from his editors. Howard wrote intuitively, trusting his instincts, and was able to work at a manic rate, writing stories and casting them aside, then picking them up, rewriting them, submitting them, rewriting them again when they came back, and submitting them to different editors and markets. For all of his effort, Howard had yet to create his most famous character, the one that would far outlive him and doom him at the same time.

It was in 1932 that Howard created and sold his most famous character. "The Phoenix on the Sword" was the first Conan story to appear in *Weird Tales*, and it was an immediate hit. In the story, Conan has already ascended to the throne of Aquilonia and now wears the crown of rule on an uneasy head. His right-hand man is lured away by a point of diplomacy, leaving Conan vulnerable to an assassination plot (which is helped along by the wizard, Thoth-amon). Conan, tipped off by a ghost, makes ready to welcome his would-be slayers. The conspirators, loyal to the old king, are unprepared for a half-armored Conan and he mops the floor with them in a characteristically fierce battle:

"Phoenix on the Sword" has all the primal ingredients of Howard's Conan stories: magic, adventure, swordplay, politics, and most importantly, a little of Howard's own philosophy: barbarism must ultimately triumph. In many of the stories, we see the barbaric Conan behaving with more honor and dignity than the cultivated aristocrats around him. It was a recurring theme in Howard's work, one he first explored in his earlier Kull stories.

Other stories followed, each one detailing a different phase of Conan's varied career: pirate, mercenary, thief, wanderer, and even king. In the pages of *Weird Tales*, Conan was an unqualified hit. Howard was mentioned frequently in the letters page, drawing praise from fans and fellow writers.

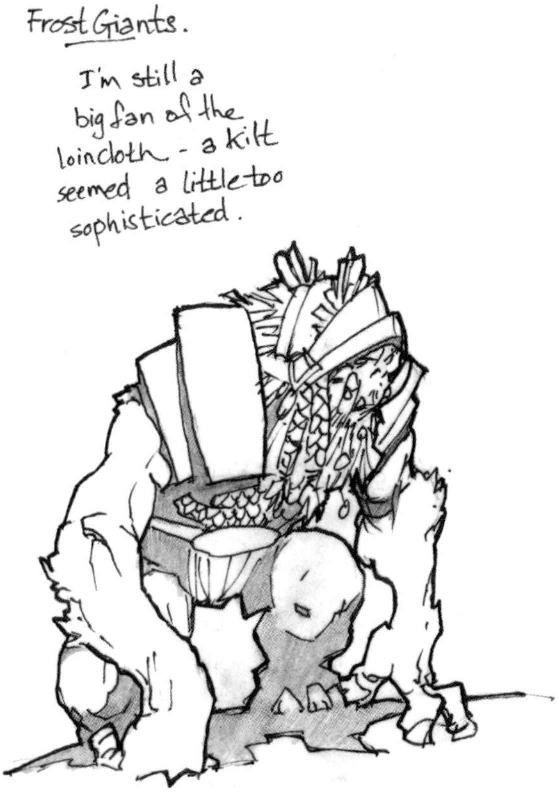
Frost Giants.
I'm still a big fan of the loincloth - a kilt seemed a little too sophisticated.

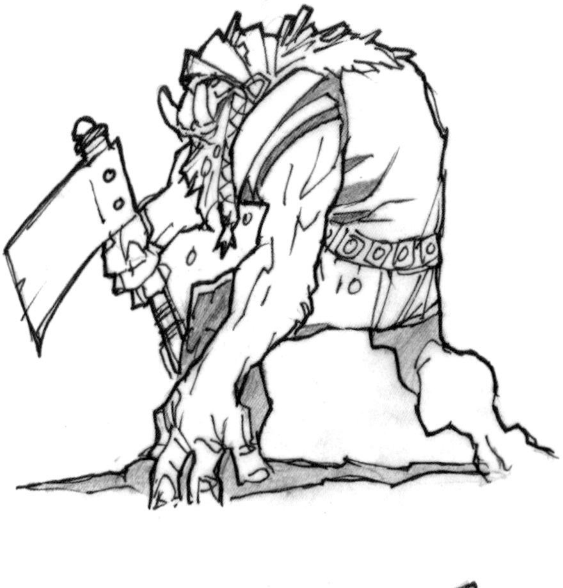

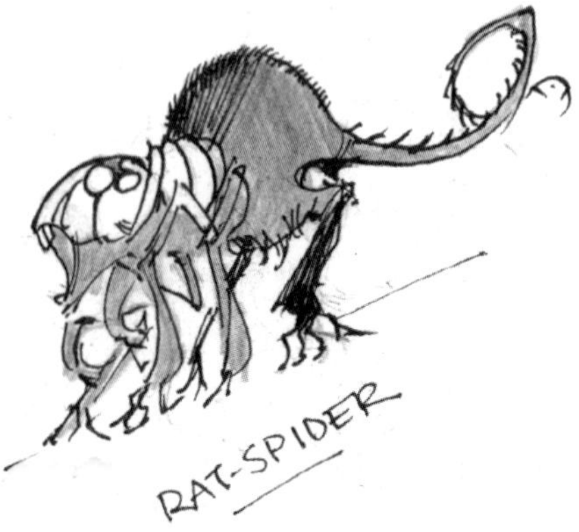
RAT-SPIDER

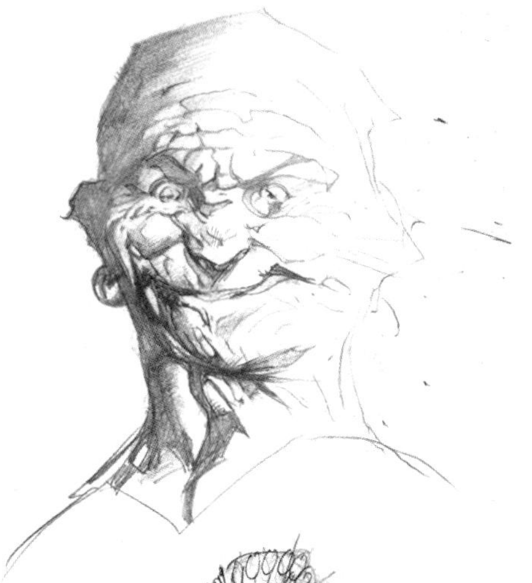

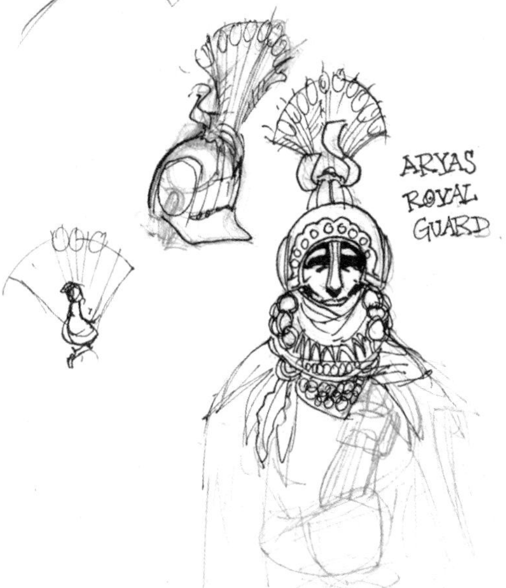
ARYAS
ROYAL
GUARD

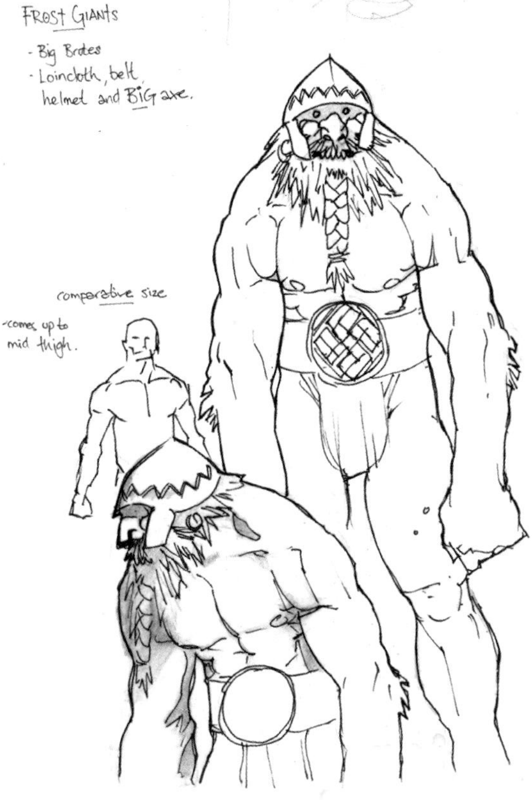
FROST GIANTS
- Big Brutes
- Loincloth, belt, helmet and BIG axe.
comparative size
-comes up to mid thigh.

Even now, Howard is referred to as one of the "three Musketeers" of *Weird Tales*, along with H. P. Lovecraft and Clark Ashton Smith. These three writers set the bar for quality and originality.

No one had done anything like Conan before. As both a character and a genre, the work was utterly unique. Howard's inspiration was a varied and fickle thing. He told Clark Ashton Smith that: "[Conan] is simply a combination of a number of men I have known ... some mechanism in my subconscious took the dominant characteristics of various prizefighters, gunmen, bootleggers, oil field bullies, gamblers and honest workmen I have come in contact with, and combining them all, produced the amalgamation I call Conan the Cimmerian."

That Howard was able to vividly conjure up a historical world that never existed and a character that was the American "everyman"—an orphaned immigrant who pulls himself up by his bootstraps to become a king—all from a small town in Texas, is an astonishing thing. But it was Howard's determination to succeed as a writer without moving to one of the major publishing centers, Los Angeles, Chicago, or New York, that is truly remarkable. Howard was merciless in his onslaught to various markets. When one story came back, rejected, he would turn it right around and send it to another market. Farnsworth Wright, the editor of *Weird Tales*, was most directly responsible for Howard's income, although Howard continued to sell stories elsewhere for the rest of his life.

In 1934, Howard turned to his surroundings to construct new stories. He started another popular series in *Action Stories* in the style of his earlier burlesque boxing sailor stories, this time about a mountain man named Breckenridge Elkins and his various goings-on. A refined mix of action and comedy, they continued to run in the magazine until two years after Howard's death. Howard wrote modern westerns, serious westerns, as well as weird westerns with ghostly or supernatural trappings in them. Again he returned to the theme of civilization being an inherently corrupting influence, and these played very well within the western mythos. His correspondence with fellow Lovecraft Circle writer August Derleth shows Howard's love of folklore, Texas history, and tall tales in the same tradition, as both men regaled each other with information about their respective states. In particular, both men were sympathetic to the plight of the Native American people, and discussed local tribes in some detail. Howard's letters with H. P. Lovecraft also show him defending the concept of the noble savage.

In spite of great success making a living as a writer in a small Texas town in the middle of the Great Depression, Howard's home life was less than satisfactory. With his father gone for extended periods of time, Howard was left alone to care for his mother, who suffered from tuberculosis. He was prone to fits of depression, what he referred to as his "black moods." He had many friends and acquaintances, and kept a regular correspondence with many fellow writers, but had very few people close to him that he could open up to.

When his mother went into a coma in June 1936, Howard wrote a final couplet:

All fled, all done, so lift me on the pyre.
The feast is over, and the lamps expire.

He committed suicide on June 11, 1936. He left behind a large stack of completed, unpublished stories, as well as his poetry. He was thirty years old.

Only at the end of the twentieth century has Robert E. Howard and his work been seriously studied by academics. Thematically, he has much in common with writers like Ernest Hemingway and Jack London. His economy of prose has been compared to fellow pulp scribe Raymond Chandler. His world, the Hyborian Age, is every bit as detailed as Tolkien's Middle Earth or other places of fantasy. Most importantly, Howard's brand of heroic fantasy (also called sword and sorcery) was unlike anything previously published: a combination of historical setting with magical or "weird" elements thrown in. His stories spawned a slew of imitators, with very few coming close to his level of craftsmanship, and as a result, Howard was critically lumped together with a number of lesser writers, and his work was not taken seriously.

What draws authors, scholars, and collectors to Howard is his intensity as a writer and his unique way of telling a story. Howard liked to revisit certain themes, such as man vs. man (usually a lone specialist against vast, innumerable hordes), or the birth and decay of civilization and the decadence that comes from said civilizations. Howard was fascinated with primitive cultures and featured them heavily in his work. He was also able to create a sense of place, in both scope and scale that was very real and immediate. His stories read naturally and ring with authenticity. His love of poetry served him well and allowed him to paint vivid, immediate pictures with very few words. But Howard's most notable skill was his portrayal of action. Few authors are able to come close to the edge-of-the-seat, nail-biting action sequences that Howard was famous for. Whether he was orchestrating a swordfight on the beach between two pirates, or a grand sweeping battle with thousands of participants, his poetical skill for violence, coupled with a flair for conversational storytelling, mark him as one of the greatest adventure writers of the twentieth century.

Barbarism is the natural state of mankind. Civilization is unnatural. It is a whim of circumstance. And barbarism must ultimately triumph.

from "Beyond the Black River"
Robert E. Howard

vp1
head
vp2
online portfolio 10 pieces
crit of the month - forum.
credits/bio/checklist.
archive

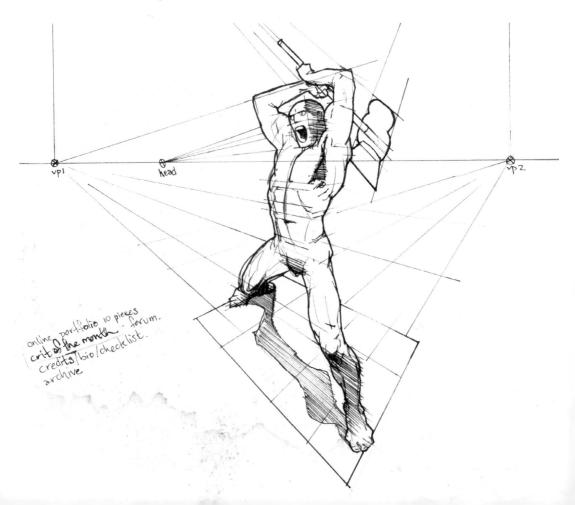

When this project began, Kurt Busiek wrote a script that we would use to audition over twenty pencillers. Rather than telling a great story, the goal was to get the artist to show us everything it takes to draw Conan, in just three pages. The following pages got Cary Nord the job, and inspired Dave Stewart to suggest coloring the book without inks.

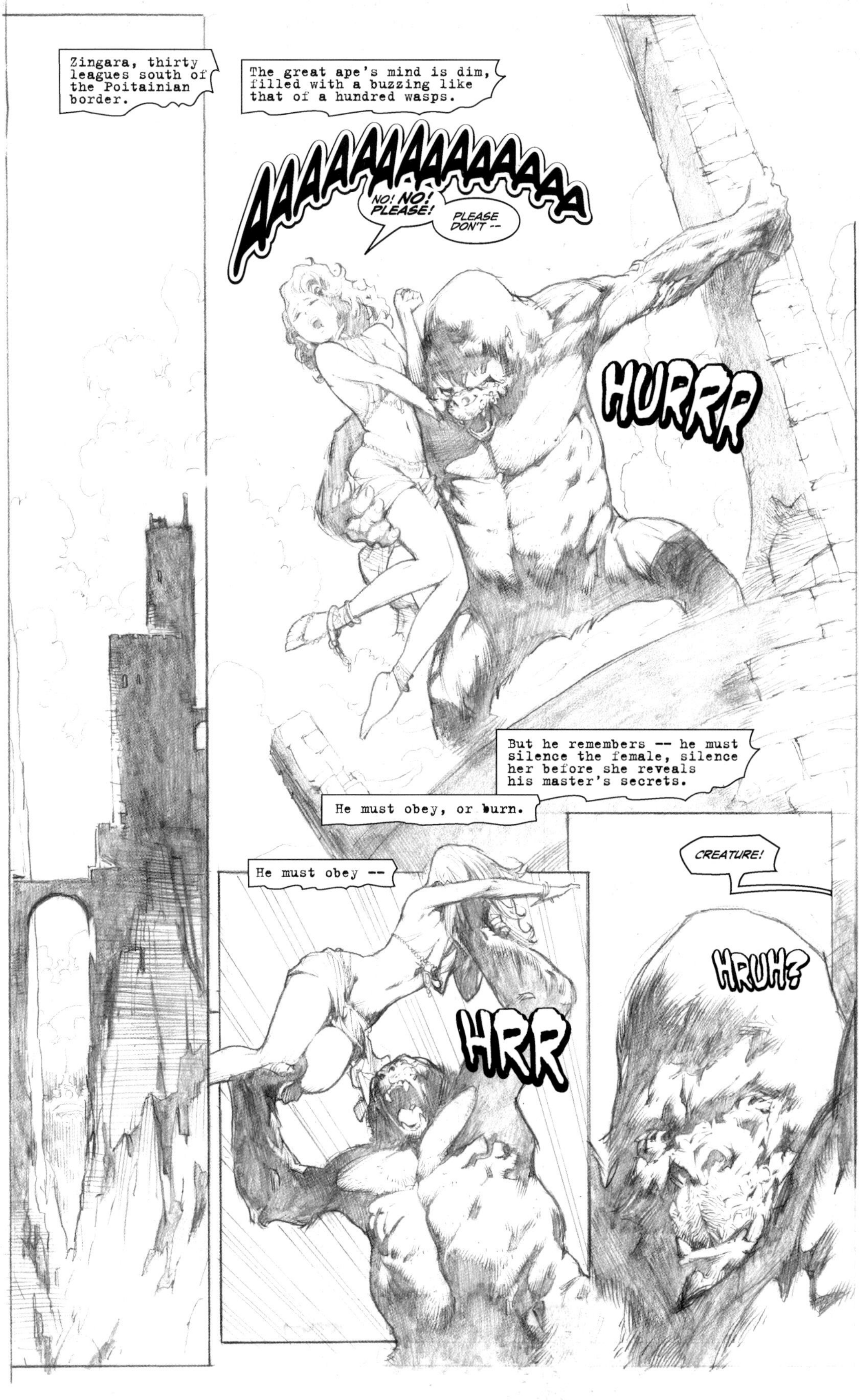

Zingara, thirty leagues south of the Poitainian border.
The great ape's mind is dim, filled with a buzzing like that of a hundred wasps.
AAAAAAAAAAAAAA
NO! NO! PLEASE!
PLEASE DON'T --
HURRR
But he remembers -- he must silence the female, silence her before she reveals his master's secrets.
He must obey, or burn.
He must obey --
HRR
CREATURE!
HRUH?

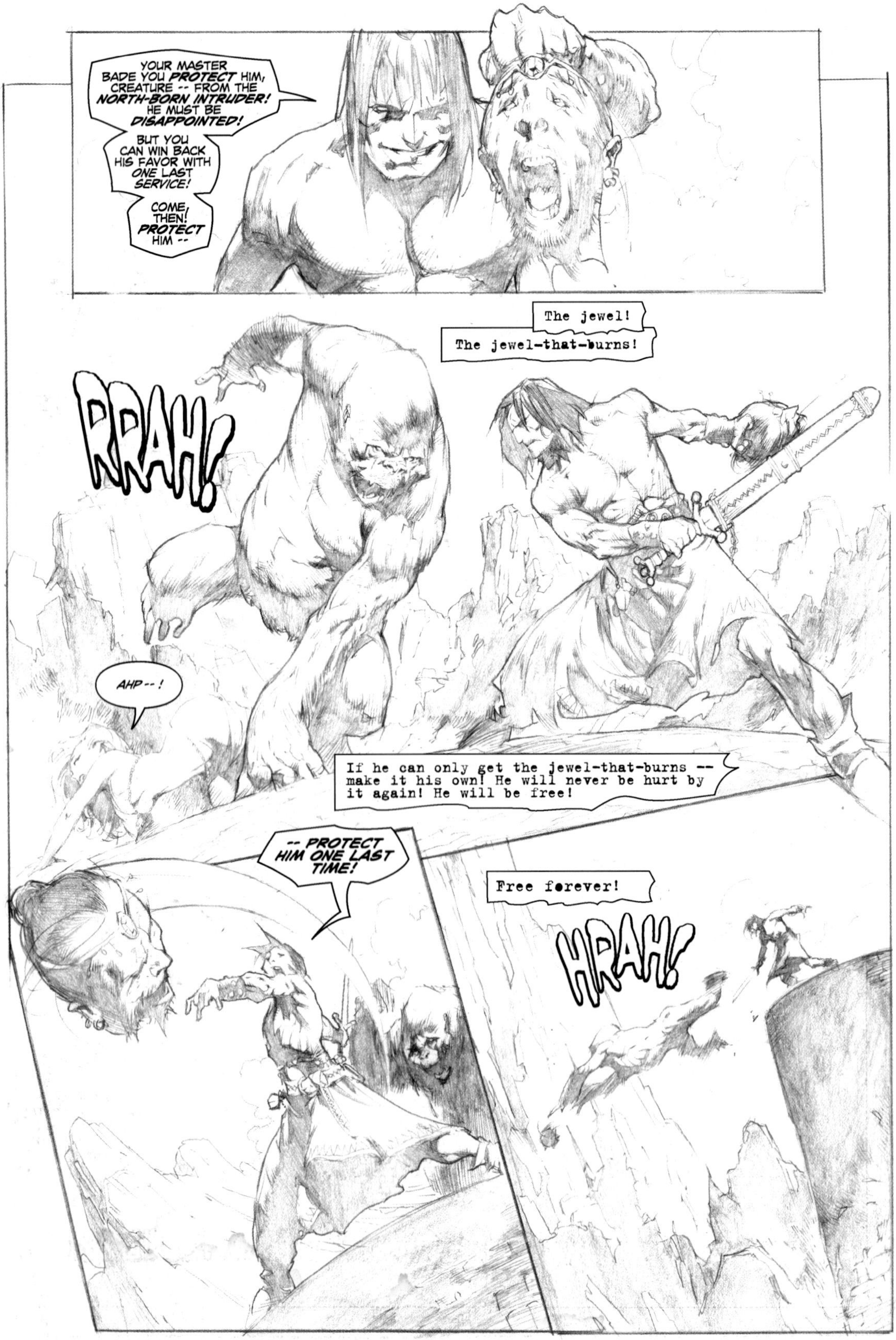
YOUR MASTER BADE YOU PROTECT HIM, CREATURE -- FROM THE NORTH-BORN INTRUDER! HE MUST BE DISAPPOINTED!
BUT YOU CAN WIN BACK HIS FAVOR WITH ONE LAST SERVICE!
COME, THEN! PROTECT HIM --
The jewel!
The jewel-that-burns!
RRAH!
AHP -- !
If he can only get the jewel-that-burns -- make it his own! He will never be hurt by it again! He will be free!
-- PROTECT HIM ONE LAST TIME!
Free forever!
HRAH!

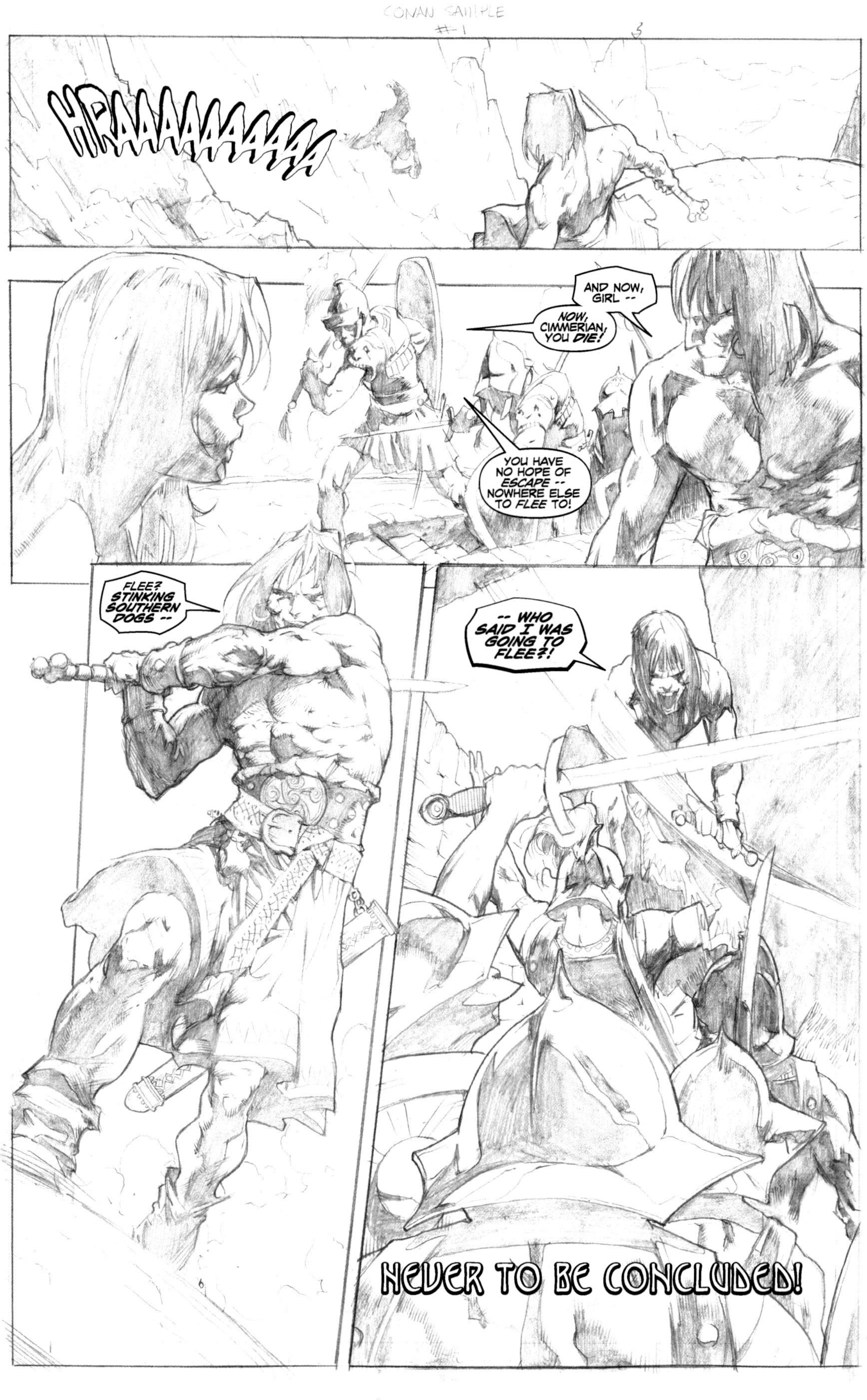
CONAN SAMPLE
#1
HRAAAAAAAAAAA
AND NOW, GIRL --
NOW, CIMMERIAN, YOU DIE!
YOU HAVE NO HOPE OF ESCAPE -- NOWHERE ELSE TO FLEE TO!
FLEE? STINKING SOUTHERN DOGS --
-- WHO SAID I WAS GOING TO FLEE?!
NEVER TO BE CONCLUDED!

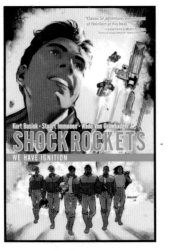